The Analysis of International Politics

THE ANALYSIS OF

International Politics

ESSAYS IN HONOR OF

Harold and Margaret Sprout

EDITED BY

James N. Rosenau, Vincent Davis, Maurice A. East

THE FREE PRESS · New York
Collier-Macmillan Limited · London

CONTENTS

PART TWO

CONCEPTUAL FOCI

PART THREE

EMPIRICAL CONCERNS

PREFACE

As indicated in the Introduction, this volume was produced to honor two distinguished students of international relations. The idea originated in a casual conversation among the editors, who realized that, as representatives of three generations of Harold Sprout's graduate students, they were ideally situated to mobilize the intellectual community of scholars in the international relations field who are indebted to the Sprouts for their many stimulating monographs and articles.

Of course, we quickly realized that it was not possible to invite essays from all those who have associated with or otherwise benefited from the Sprouts. Such a community of scholars would produce a volume much too large for a publisher to accept. We therefore decided on a basis for inviting contributors, knowing that no set of criteria could yield a list that would be entirely satisfactory to all concerned. In the end our criteria proved to be simple: we would invite those who at one time or another have worked intimately with the Sprouts in the field of international relations and/or those who are presently on the forefront of research in the field. In this way we felt we could achieve a volume that makes a substantive contribution even as it is filled with personal meaning for the Sprouts. Several of those whom we invited were not able to meet our deadline and thus regretfully had to decline the opportunity to honor Harold and Margaret in this way. But we feel that we have nevertheless realized our goal of a distinguished set of essays, many of which will, like the gentle people they honor, long be landmarks in the field.

JAMES N. ROSENAU
VINCENT DAVIS
MAURICE A. EAST

CONTRIBUTORS

Chadwick F. Alger, born in Chambersburg, Pennsylvania, 1924, is Professor of Political Science at Ohio State University, having previously been associated with Northwestern University. He is coauthor of *Simulation in International Relations: Developments for Research and Teaching* and a contributor to *International Behavior; Human Conflict and Social Science; International Politics and Foreign Policy: A Reader in Research and Theory;* and *Quantitative International Politics: Insights and Evidence;* and of articles in *Administrative Science Quarterly, American Political Science Review, Journal of Conflict Resolution, Public Opinion Quarterly,* and *World Politics.*

Cyril E. Black, born in Bryson City, North Carolina, 1915, is Duke Professor of Russian History and Director of the Center of International Studies at Princeton University. He is an editor of *World Politics,* a quarterly journal of international relations sponsored by the Center of International Studies, and has served as visiting professor at Columbia, Hokkaido, Stanford, and Yale Universities, and at the National War College. Among his publications are *The Dynamics of Modernization: A Study in Comparative History* (author); *Neutralization and World Politics* coauthor); and *The Future of the International Legal Order,* Vol. I, *Trends and Patterns* (coeditor and coauthor).

Vincent Davis, born in Chattanooga, 1930, formerly taught at Princeton, Dartmouth, Denver, and the Naval War College. In 1971 he joined the faculty of the University of Kentucky as the Director of its Patterson School of Diplomacy and International Commerce. For the 1969–70 school year he was a Research Associate at the Center of International Studies, Princeton University. From 1964 to 1970 he served as the first Executive

Director of the International Studies Association. He is the author of *Postwar Defense Policy and the U.S. Navy, The Admirals Lobby,* and *The Politics of Innovation,* among other works.

Maurice A. East, born in Trinidad, Colorado, 1941, is Assistant Professor of International Politics at the Graduate School of International Studies, University of Denver. He is also Director of the Center for Teaching International Relations and has taught at The Colorado College. Currently he is engaged in research in the areas of international systems theory and comparative foreign policy. He is the author of an article appearing in the *International Studies Quarterly*.

Richard A. Falk, born in New York City in 1930, is the Albert G. Milbank Professor of International Law and Practice at Princeton University. He has been serving as the Research Director of the North American Team in the World Order Models Project and Chairman of the Civil War Panel of the American Society of International Law. His books include *The Role of Domestic Courts in the International Legal Order, Legal Order in a Violent World,* and *The Status of Law in International Society*.

Robert Gilpin, born in Burlington, Vermont, in 1930, is Associate Professor of Politics and Public Affairs, Princeton University. He is also Faculty Associate at Princeton University's Center of International Studies and has taught at Columbia University and the London School of Economics. He is the author of *France in the Age of the Scientific State; American Scientists and Nuclear Weapons Policy;* and coauthor and coeditor of *Scientists and National Policy-Making*.

Charles F. Hermann, born in Monmouth, Illinois, 1938, is an Associate Professor of Political Science as well as Associate Director of the Mershon Center at Ohio State University. He is the author of *Crises in Foreign Policy: A Simulation Analysis* and editor of the forthcoming *Contemporary Research on International Crises*. The present chapter was written while he was on leave serving on the National Security Council Staff as an International Fellow of the Council on Foreign Relations.

Michael Haas, born in Debroit, 1938, is Associate Professor of Political Science at the University of Hawaii and has had visiting appointments at Northwestern, Purdue, and the University of California (Riverside). He is also Research Associate at the Social Science Research Institute and Dimensionality of Nations Project, both at the University of Hawaii. He is author of *Approaches to the Study of Political Science, International Organization,* and two forthcoming volumes, *Statistics and International Conflict*.

Morton A. Kaplan, born in Philadelphia, 1921, is Professor of Political Science at the University of Chicago. His most recent book is *Macro-*

politics: Selected Essays in the Philosophy and Science of Politics. His earlier works include *System and Process in International Politics.*

Klaus Knorr, Professor of International Affairs at the Woodrow Wilson School of Princeton University, is a faculty associate of the Center of International Studies at Princeton. He is an editor of *World Politics,* a quarterly journal of international relations sponsored by the Center of International Studies. He is the author of *British Colonial Theories, The War Potential of Nations, On the Uses of Military Power in the Nuclear Age,* and coauthor and editor of *The International System: Theoretical Essays.*

Charles A. McClelland, born in Oakley, Idaho, 1917, is Professor of International Relations at the University of Southern California. He edited *Background; Journal of the International Studies Association* for four years. His *Theory and the International System* appeared in 1966. He is engaged presently in a series of quantitative studies of the structure and processes of the international system.

James N. Rosenau, born in Philadelphia, 1924, is Professor of Political Science at Ohio State University. He has taught at Rutgers, Columbia and New York University. He is author of *Public Opinion and Foreign Policy* and *National Leadership and Foreign Policy;* coauthor and editor of *International Aspects of Civil Strife, Domestic Sources of Foreign Policy,* and *Linkage Politics;* and editor of *International Politics and Foreign Policy.*

Bruce M. Russett, born in North Adams, Massachusetts, 1935, is Professor of Political Science at Yale University and Director of the World Data Analysis Program there. He has also taught at M.I.T., Columbia University, and the Universite Libre de Bruxelles. He has written *Community and Contention: Britain in the Twentieth Century, World Handbook of Political and Social Indicators* (with others), *Trends in World Politics, World Politics in the General Assembly* (with H. Alker), *International Regions and the International System,* and *Economic Theories of International Politics* (edited).

Burton M. Sapin was born in New York City in 1926. He is Dean of the School of Public and International Affairs, and Professor of Political Science and International Affairs, at George Washington University. He previously taught at the University of Minnesota, Vanderbilt University, and M.I.T. and served in the Department of State from 1961 to 1965. He is author of *The Making of United States Foreign Policy,* author-editor of *Contemporary American Foreign and Military Policy,* and coauthor of *The Role of the Military in American Foreign Policy* and *Foreign Policy Decision Making.*

J. David Singer, born in New York City, 1925, is Professor of Political Science at the University of Michigan and is associated with the Mental Health Research Institute and Center for Research on Conflict Resolution there. Among his books are *Human Behavior and International Politics;* *Quantitative International Politics;* and *International War, 1815–1966: A Statistical Handbook.*

Raymond Tanter, born in Chicago, 1938, is Associate Professor of Political Science at the University of Michigan, Ann Arbor. He has taught. at Northwestern and Stanford Universities, and served as Deputy Director, Behavioral Sciences, Advanced Research Projects Agency, Department of Defense. He has received grants from the National Science, Ford, and Carnegie Foundations, and has written articles in the fields of international relations and political development.

Oran R. Young is Associate Professor of Politics and Faculty Associate of the Center of International Studies at Princeton University. He is author of *The Intermediaries: Third Parties in International Crises; Systems of Political Science,* and *The Politics of Force: Bargaining During International Crises,* and coauthor of *Neutralization and World Politics.* He is also a senior editor of *World Politics.*

Dina Zinnes, born in Germany, 1935, is Associate Professor of Political Science at Indiana University. She has contributed articles to *World Politics, Journal of Conflict Resolution,* and *Journal of Peace Research* and is a contributor to *Quantitative International Politics* and *Crises in International Politics.*

The Analysis of International Politics

Introduction

*A*n oft-told story in the professional literature of international studies during the 1950s and 1960s was the intellectual history of this scholarly enterprise. In almost all of these accounts, one item of major emphasis was the shift from the "idealism" perspective of the pre-World War II period to the "realism" perspective of the postwar period. It was a change from an essentially normative approach with few pretensions concerning method, theory, and empirical evidence systematically gathered, to an essentially nonnormative approach with great ambitions concerning method, theory, and the systematic accumulation of evidence. The pre-World War II works were often little more than hortatory descriptions of the world as one would have liked it to be, whereas the later works aspired to examine the effects and consequences of the first nuclear internationale and to report the findings in the manner of science.

The Sprouts as Scholars

In actuality, the calendar is seldom so obliging as scholars would like it to be in dividing history into neat segments. Those developments in the scholarly work on international studies, which often were assigned to the post-World War II period, in fact had significant precursors in the prewar period. Indeed, if one insisted on saying that the shift from normative exhortations to nonnormative behavioral science constituted an intellectual revolution in international studies, then several of the earliest and most important of the revolutionaries began their work in the decade before the war: Harold Lasswell, whose imaginative competence in the discipline of psychology was a forerunner of much of the interdisciplinary work of the 1950s and 1960s; Nicholas John Spykman, whose death at an early age deprived the profession of one of its most promising scholars; and Quincy Wright, who may be said to have been the primary precursor of the systematic study of international relations.

Among these distinguished scholarly specialists in international studies who began to revolutionize this field of inquiry in the 1930s must be listed Harold and Margaret Sprout. A young couple who met as undergraduates at Oberlin, the Sprouts did not enter the international field immediately. They married after Harold's graduation from Oberlin in 1924 and then went to the University of Wisconsin, where Harold studied law and Margaret completed her A.B. After one year in Madison they transferred to the Law School of Western Reserve University, expecting to practice law in Painsville, Ohio, in partnership with Margaret's father. One more year of legal study, however, led to the conclusion that the practice of law was not for them, and after a year of substitute teaching at Miami University they returned to Madison in the fall of 1927. Harold obtained his Ph.D in 1929, while Margaret settled for an A.M. in political science and geography. After a brief teaching assignment at Stanford that ended in 1931 when the University nearly went bankrupt, they moved to Princeton, where Harold taught until his retirement in 1969.

Not least among the important innovative departures which the Sprouts brought to the study of international relations in the 1930s was an emphasis upon the interconnections between national and international politics— "linkage politics" as it came to be called some thirty years later. This intimate relationship between a nation's internal politics and its foreign policies had been commented upon by Plato in his writings around 400 B.C. and Clausewitz in his writings in the early nineteenth century, among others. But international studies scholars during the first four decades of the twentieth century often ignored relationships between parts and wholes, until the Sprouts and a few others began to underscore these ties in their writings in the late 1930s. Unfortunately, the emphasis was again lost during much of the next two decades, and it did not reappear with significant force until the late 1960s.

The Sprouts initially pursued this linkage perspective in the publication of their first major book in 1939: *The Rise of American Naval Power: 1776–1918* (Princeton University Press). This monograph also contained several other major themes which were to pervade much of their remaining work. In many cases, these themes foreshadowed important developments in the professional literature of the field as a whole. For example, their conceptualization of the "styles of statecraft" of national actors in the international arena was an operationally researchable and behaviorally tenable version of the older and somewhat discredited notion of "national character" and its effects on foreign policy. And from another perspective, this attempt by the Sprouts to differentiate among states on the basis of foreign policy behavior antedates what was becoming quite fashionably known some three decades later as "comparative foreign policy studies." Their work on the Navy introduced them to Alfred Thayer Mahan's earlier writings, and Mahan's work in turn whetted their lifelong interest in the interplay between geographic factors and new developments in science and technology. In a very real sense, *The Rise of American Naval Power* can be said to represent one of the early attempts to assess the impact of science and technology on international politics. In a 1963 article in *World Politics,* ("Geopolitical Hypotheses in Technological Perspective"), Harold carried this effort further with a brilliant article relating advances in science and technology to some of the predominant geopolitically oriented theories of international politics. Mahan's work also served to stimulate the Sprouts' interest first in the British Navy in particular and then in the British social, political, and economic system more generally. Finally, and related to all of the other emerging interests noted here, the Sprouts' first book on the Navy generated their continuing concern with the relationships between man and his geophysical environment.

All of these interests were brought more sharply into focus in the context of an examination of a specific major instance of international negotiations, in the Sprouts' second book—a sequel to the first—which dealt primarily with the Washington Conference on the Limitation of Naval Armaments of 1921–22. This was the Sprouts' *Toward a New Order of Sea Power: American Naval Policy and the World Scene, 1918–1922* (Princeton University Press, 1940). Although essentially a case study, it merged the focus on national actors into the context of an international system. Moreover, it contained early hints of a recognition of systemic actors in addition to nation-states—actors in categories that later came to be called IGO's (intergovernmental organizations) and NGO's (nongovernmental organizations). In this sense, too, the Sprouts' early work foreshadowed major themes emerging much later in the professional literature of the field.

The next major milestone in the Sprouts' scholarship was the publication in 1945 of their basic textbook, *Foundations of National Power* (Princeton University Press). It was compiled during World War II at the request of Secretary of the Navy James V. Forrestal, who felt that American naval officers were inadequately educated in a fundamental subject indicated by the book's subtitle: *Readings on World Politics and American Security.* Used for many years in the training of naval officer candidates in many different Navy schools and programs, the book was put into commercial circulation by D. Van Nostrand in 1946 and a revised edition was published in 1951. Notwithstanding its origins as part of the Navy's ROTC curriculum, the book was a remarkable intellectual achievement in that it avoided being a reflection of the tumultuous but essentially transient political passions of the wartime period. Thus, rather than reflecting a narrowly parochial American perspective, it was a major effort to devise analytical categories and concepts for studying the behavior of any nation-state within the context of a complex global system composed not only of national actors, but of other kinds of actors as well, all operating within a conditioning environment made up of human as well as nonhuman elements. It endeavored to discuss the newly fashionable concept of power not in hortatory, normative, or mystical terms, but in terms of capabilities measured against possible goals within analyzable restraints and constraints. The book included readings not only from political science, but from geography, psychology, sociology, and even from the physical and natural sciences. In this sense it clearly foreshadowed the growing conviction among specialists in international studies following World War II that this was a research field requiring significant and substantial contributions from many disciplines and areas of knowledge.

Out of the older normative "idealism" and the newer nonnormative "realism" of the 1930s emerged two perspectives on power. One of these was the empassioned "power as norm" perspective, a school of thought expressing great frustration concerning and perhaps a cynical revulsion against hopeful and rosy efforts to construct a peaceful world order essentially by means of extending the principles of representative democracy to the world scene. This school, represented by Frederick Schuman, Frank Simonds and Brooks Emeny, and E.H. Carr among others, tended to suggest that the iron law of the international arena was a war of all against all in an anarchic struggle for "power," first for survival but ultimately for its own sake. This was a struggle that certain international regulatory devices could occasionally mediate, modify, or soften, but it was a struggle that took place continually and fundamentally nevertheless. "Power" was the key new term, and it appeared in the titles and/or subtitles and liberally within the texts of almost all of the books written by the authors named here. The other perspective emerging in the 1930s, the one that proved to be more enduring in terms of foreshadowing major themes in the professional literature of the first two decades after World War II, also utilized the term "power" but in the more truly nonnormative sense of capability analyses within a much more complex and open-ended conceptualization of the international system.

These two perspectives were combined in Hans J. Morgenthau's book, *Politics Among Nations,* published originally in 1948. For this reason Morgenthau's book is often cited as being the transitional turning point between "idealism" and "realism." Although the two perspectives were superficially similar and compatible in several respects—for example, in making heavy use of the term "power" and in positing an international system—in more profound respects the two were essentially incompatible. One perspective was very time-bound in being a reflection of current upheavals, heavily normative in at least a latent sense, and largely sterile in pointing the way to further research. The other was much less a reflection of current events, more genuinely serious about establishing nonnormative analytical modes of continuing utility and therefore much more fruitful in providing directions for future work. Morgenthau's work was accurately characterized as more representative of the first of these new perspectives of the 1930s, whereas the Sprouts' work was clearly more representative of the second. It therefore appears fitting, in retrospect, that the first major review of Morgenthau's *Politics Among Nations* (subtitle: *The Struggle for Power and Peace*) appeared in the April 1949 issue of *World Politics*, and it was written by Harold Sprout. Although too modest to make the distinctions that are suggested here, and saying nothing whatever concerning his own contributions, Sprout's review suggested many of the contrasting perspectives emphasized in this chapter and pointed the way to much of what has become subsequent history in the development of the scholarly field of international studies. It is a revealing review article that bears rereading.

The early 1950s were chacterized for the Sprouts by fertile and fruitful interactions with a number of their colleagues at Princeton. Although the Sprouts' early work on the Navy had utilized a focus on the nation-states as the primary actor in international politics, it was also exceedingly clear that they viewed the term "nation-state" as a collective noun referring to politically organized groups of human beings in social systems. Always carefully avoiding the anthropomorphic and teleological fallacies, they insisted from the outset of their scholarly careers that nations were basically composed of people, that the decisions of nations are at root the decisions of people who represent or speak for other people, and that one critically important way to study the behavior of nations is to study the actions and behavior and perceptions of national decisionmaking leaders. It is hard to escape the conclusion that the landmark monographic essay by Richard C. Snyder, Henry Bruck, and Burton Sapin, *Decision-making as an Approach to the Study of International Politics* (Princeton, 1954), was at least in part a product of the interaction between the Sprouts and these authors who were younger colleagues in the Department of Politics. The Snyder monograph sharply focused and systematized insights and perspectives clearly evident in the earlier work of the Sprouts.

In the middle 1950s the Sprouts returned to one of the basic themes first evident in their work on the Navy. This theme could have been summarized under the rubric of "geographic factors," but the Sprouts were unhappy with the way in which these factors were conventionally treated. In the first place, they were dissatisfied with a tendency to view geographic factors as permanent and immutable. They saw the significance of these factors to be a function of social choices concerning the allocation of resources as well as a function of the level of technology at any given time. In the second place, they were displeased with the deterministic rhetoric which so often pervaded the literature pertaining to geographic factors. Social choices appeared to be foreclosed in such literature, and this in turn obviated the need for conceptualizing any operational linkages between human behavior and the geographic factors. The Sprouts refused to accept this kind of reasoning because they refused to abandon the conviction that man is the fundamental actor in all social systems including nation-states—an actor with thought processes and decisional options. In short, they persisted in avoiding a common tendency to endow social systems with anthropomorphic and teleological qualities, and the reverse tendency to endow neither man nor his social systems with discretionary options in an ironclad natural order. At the same time, the Sprouts were not prepared to argue that geographic factors were absolutely inconsequential in human and social affairs. They therefore arrived at a conceptualization of man and his social systems as units within a comprehensive surrounding element embracing "the total aggregate of factors in space and time, to which an individual's behavior may be oriented or otherwise related (excepting only the environed individual's own hereditary structures and characteristics)." The Sprouts did not like the terms "geographic" or "environmental" to refer to this total aggregate of factors, because these older terms had too many restrictive and narrow denotations and connotations in earlier literature. They thus borrowed the French word *milieu,* and they spelled out their conceptualization of the environed unit in its possible relationships to its environment in their pathbreaking monographic essay, *Man-Milieu Relationship Hypotheses in the Context of International Politics* (Princeton, 1956). A year later they elaborated other aspects of the argument in a paper entitled "Environmental Factors in International Politics," read by Harold Sprout at the annual meeting of the American Political Science Association in September 1957. Eventually, they refined and sharpened their thinking on this subject in a book-length statement, *The Ecological Perspective on Human Affairs: With Special Reference to International Politics* (Princeton University Press, 1965).

In an even more recent work in this general area, *An Ecological Paradigm for the Study of International Politics* (Princeton, 1968), the Sprouts pointed out quite clearly the implications of an ecological approach to the study of world politics. Among the more important ramifications were the following: a greater emphasis on lower levels of abstractions, with the human actor as central to international political analysis; an increasing awareness of the interdependence of human efforts to control the environment; and the realization that coping "with the diverse, cumulatively enormous, and still proliferating human capabilities to alter the conditions of existence, even survival, upon this planet constitutes the ultimate problem of international politics." The concern with this "ultimate problem" also pervades a review article that the Sprouts published in the July 1968, issue of *World Politics,* an article that they viewed in the summer of 1969 as "the most important single piece of work that we have yet published." Such a characterization, however, may be premature, as the same concern is a basic organizing idea of their newest work, *Toward a Politics of the Planet Earth* published in 1971 (Van Nostrand Reinhold).

Many of these same conceptualizations and perspectives were also summarized in the Sprouts' textbook, *Foundations of International Politics* (D. Van Nostrand, 1962), but this textbook was much more than a restatement of the man-milieu and ecological framework. The first 69 pages constituted one of the most succinct and readable expressions of the basic logic and intellectual processes applicable to international studies that is currently extant in the literature. Indeed, it was such a valuable statement of this basic logic for the benefit of students that a number of scholars argued in favor of publishing those 69 pages as a separate handbook. The next three chapters, something over 100 pages, constituted an equally valuable delineation of the elements of the international system, encompassing not only newer insights and perspectives emerging in the professional literature of the 1950s and 1960s but also incorporating up-to-date and operationally tenable versions of older terms such as "power," "political potential," and "capabilities." The remainder of the book was in some respects an updating of the material in *Foundations of National Power,* but the very change in title suggested the extent to which older substances and terminology had been reconceptualized into a broader, more global perspective. It was no mere exercise in pouring old wine into new bottles; on the contrary, it was the culmination of a career's work in carefully defining and refining basic human and physical factors into a paradigmatic synthesis of greater analytic utility in research on international politics.

In a lifework as full of innovative departures of enduring value for the profession as the Sprouts have exhibited, it would be inappropriate to hold them accountable for a major book that they were ideally equipped to write but did not write. Yet it seemed an oddity that their enormous research on Britain, British society, British politics and British economics—providing them with much of the case study material from which their fruitful hypotheses were generated—had not resulted in a book explicitly addressing the British experience. They did in fact write a gem-like short paper of some 20 pages which was entitled, "Britain's Defense Program," but which was published in a by-now out-of-print conference report from Princeton University in 1959. The essay gave rise, however, to a carefully delineated ecological model of the competitive demands on the resources of modern nation-states. It is now a great pleasure to report that the Sprouts are incorporating this model into a full-scale analysis of the British experience. In short, the book not yet written by the Sprouts is now indeed being written.

The ability to conclude a commemorative commentary on the lifelong work of a pair of distinguished scholars with the promise that there is still more exciting work to come from their imaginative and rigorous minds is perhaps the most important over-all commentary that one can make. Most scholars are fortunate if they experience one brief burst of impressive creativity in their lives, surrounded by less creative periods that are dominated by explications of earlier ideas, occasional book reviews, perhaps edited books of readings, and other useful but routine chores. The work of the Sprouts, however, represents an extraordinary whole from the outset, opening up many fruitful avenues of inquiry. Never experiencing the intellectual arrest that is the fate of most of us, they did pursue and still do continue to pursue these avenues that they pioneered. Always in the forefront and sometimes well in advance of the frontiers of research in a number of important directions, it is notable that basic themes evident in their very earliest work—themes such as the linkage of national and international politics, the initial approaches to the idea of an international system, the emphasis on the importance of science and technology for such a system, a focus on comparative foreign policy studies, and a basic emphasis on ecological factors deriving from an initial concern for geographic factors—still appear fresh and vital as long as thirty years following the Sprouts' first explorations of these intellectual territories. They always worked at their own pace and followed their own star, never seeking to accommodate varying and transient intellectual fads merely for the sake of being fashionable, but also never missing an opportunity to build on the best work of contemporaries, young and old, in their own work.

The Sprouts as Teachers

The measure of a person, even in academic life, is by no means to be assessed solely in terms of the impact and enduring value of his published scholarship. It is a rare person who combines distinguished thought and research with the human qualities of the superior teacher. Yet the Sprouts fall into this category, and their students as much as their publications constitute their monument. They belonged to that earlier generation which believed that the best place for an academic man to do his work was at home within the academy. Following World War II they did stay home to work while younger generations experimented with newer career-building techniques characterized by frequent travel on the conference and convention circuit as well as by a variety of consulting assignments for governmental agencies. The Sprouts never confused motion with progress, nor publicity with stature, and they achieved both progress and stature in remarkable degree by sticking to what they did best: thinking, researching, and teaching.

Their distinguished students included not only a number of men who wrote their doctoral dissertations under the supervision of the Sprouts, but also many who merely took an occasional seminar under their direction only to discover later that even a single seminar was sufficient to have produced a lasting influence. Their "students" also included younger departmental colleagues and associates at Princeton and other colleges and universities who gained from counsel and correspondence with them. This is not to suggest that their impact was limited to men who later attained distinguished records of their own in academic life, because their students also included many who achieved positions of prominence and responsibility in public affairs. Not the least of these are a number of senior military officers, including one four-star general very near the top of the U.S. Army as of 1971.

The Sprouts as Persons

Aside from the human qualities of the superior teacher, the Sprouts exhibited other qualities which endeared them to all who came in contact with them. The warmth and openness and willingness to help of these two people was immediately evident to incoming students and colleagues alike. Margaret's involvement in affairs of the Princeton community made her an excellent source of information and guidance for the newcomer. Harold's years spent in the University gave him the wisdom to be able to get things done. During his tenure as graduate student advisor for the Department of Politics, his true concern for helping others was quite evident; many a student can thank Harold for a favor granted, a door opened, or a crisis eased. It was in his role as graduate student advisor that Harold initiated and strongly supported the admission of women into the graduate program of the Department of Politics.

This openness and enthusiasm displayed by the Sprouts was contagious in many respects. Harold was constantly becoming enthusiastically involved in the work of other people; in so doing he was a source of inspiration and encouragement to others. Whether it was the work of one of his colleagues at Princeton, or a book or an article written by a scholar at some other institution, or the research project or dissertation of a graduate student, Harold's enthusiasm and interest would often become quite intense. Perhaps it was this same personality trait—this ability to become involved and enthusiastic—which kept them so up-to-date in the field of international studies. Their course syllabi and writings always reflected the most current standards of scholarship, and references were frequently made to works by others which are on the frontiers of the field.

In summary, it can well be said that Harold and Margaret Sprout have, through their writings, their teaching, and their human kindness, influenced the lives of generations of students and scholars. The examples they have set in many areas of endeavor will serve as lasting mementoes for all those who know of them and their work.

Examples of the Sprouts' Influence

One of the most outstanding characteristics of the Sprouts' career was the wide scope and range of their intellectual interests and pursuits. Therefore, it is not in the least surprising to find a similarly wide range of interests and concerns represented among the contributors to this volume. Without trying to force this diversity into a superficial unifying framework, an attempt has been made to group the articles into three broad categories. The first group focuses on broad epistemological questions and theoretical problems in the discipline of international relations. The second group includes articles generally concerned with the conceptual foci of the field, whereas the third group includes those articles which provide new empirical materials and interpretations relative to substantive problems of the field.

Turning to the contributions in Part One, the "Theoretical Problems," *McClelland's* essay traces in a creative way some developments in the history of the study of international relations; it is a direct reflection of the Sprouts' concern for mapping the trends in the discipline and examining their impact upon men's conceptions of the world. All of the Sprouts' students at Princeton will recall the intense excitement and enthusiasm generated when those in the seminar heard the Sprouts' views on the histori- cal roots of the discipline and the developments that followed. *Tanter's* contribution, discussing the distinctions between explanation, prediction, and forecasting as applied to international politics, can be related to the previously noted concern of the Sprouts in Chapter 1 of their text, where these very terms are discussed. *Hermann's* creative preoccupation with the problem of clarifying and explaining foreign policy phenomena also ex- plicitly reflects the Sprouts' interest in the epistemological problems of the field. *Singer's* discussion and ultimate rejection of the theorist-empiricist distinction again can be related to the Sprouts. By their own example they have demonstrated how the more traditionally trained scholar can build upon, as well as comment on and criticize, the work of the more "scientifical- ly" oriented researcher. *Kaplan's* essay on the concept of freedom and its relevance to international politics is in many ways another aspect of the examination of this very same concept carried out by the Sprouts when they explored, in *The Ecological Perspective on Human Affairs*, environmental determinism and its implications for freedom in the realm of international politics.

In Part Two, the "Conceptual Foci," *Russett's* major point is that the environment of politics has been too much neglected. The role of environ- mental factors in affecting what Russett refers to as the "menu of political choice" is an issue which coincides perfectly with the Sprouts' lifelong work along similar lines. *Young's* piece, describing the degree to which inter- national politics theorizing has been dominated by the nation-state-as-actor perspective and asserting the rise of the mixed-actor system of world poli- tics, parallels the much earlier discussion by the Sprouts of the role of actors other than nation-states in the events leading up to and comprising the Washington Conference for the Limitation of Armaments. *Rosenau's* article is an explicit attempt to build upon the Sprouts' analysis of environ- mental factors by bringing these factors into foreign policy studies in a more systematic manner. *Gilpin's* essay assesses the impact of modern technology on international politics; this reflects directly the aforementioned early concern of the Sprouts about such matters. *Knorr* explicitly directs his attention to the concept of capability as it recurs throughout the Sprouts' work, particularly in their monograph, *An Ecological Paradigm*. Finally, *Falk* has contributed a stimulating essay examining the geopolitically inspired concept of "zone." This attempt to identify and discuss patterns of superordinate-subordinate relationships and their distribution around the globe is also reflective of a recurrent theme in the Sprouts' writings.

Part Three, consisting of the articles with "Empirical Concerns," starts with *Zinnes'* attempt to determine the degree to which the Sprouts' basic model relating environment, perception, and behavior is supported by the findings of some of the more recent quantitative studies of international politics. *Haas'* contribution is also a review of the more recent literature, with the purpose of identifying the major sources of internation conflict at three levels: the interpersonal, the societal, and the systemic. In a very real sense, the Sprouts' early text was an attempt at this same kind of assessment. They were concerned with what was then called the security problem, and they proceeded to analyze this problem from several perspectives: the nation-state and its capabilities, the multistate system and its structure, the perceptions and demands of individual decision-makers, and the systemic effects of geopolitical factors. *Alger's* piece is a provocative example of the use of the multiple research strategies in studying a problem. This can be likened in some respects to a similar use of multiple research strategies by the Sprouts in their later work on Britain's declining role in the world. There one can find techniques ranging from interviews with high-level government officials to exhaustive examination of documentary materials to analysis of aggregate data. *East's* research on stratification in the international system is a continuation of work begun under the tutelage of the Sprouts and influenced greatly by their continual attempts to clarify and make more useful the concept of an international system. *Sapin's* thorough study of the role of "politico-military" personnel in the foreign policy process puts emphasis upon the impact of training and utilization of such persons for policy outcomes. In somewhat the same genre is *Davis'* study of the Office of the Secretary of Defense. Both of these studies parallel an early interest of the Sprouts in the organization and operation of the military component in the foreign policy process. *Black* has written an essay about perceptions of identifiable individuals, in this case the perceptions of world history held by three Russian historians. Although Black's work does not relate the perceptions of these three historians to a decisional setting, it is nevertheless a study focusing on a central concern of the Sprouts throughout their writings, namely, the relationship between individuals' perceptions and decisions.

In summary, it can be said that all the articles included in this commemorative volume have a close relationship to the work of the Sprouts. In some cases, it is the relationship of teacher to student; in others it is the influence of one scholar's ideas upon another; and in yet others it is the relationship between scholars sharing a common concern for the problems of world politics. In all of these ways, the Sprouts have made a profound impact upon several generations of international relations scholars and indeed upon the history of the discipline itself.

PART ONE

Theoretical Problems

CHARLES A. MC CLELLAND

On the Fourth Wave: Past and Future in the Study of International Systems

The assigned task of this chapter is to evaluate the status of the system approach in the theory of international relations. If some recent discussions in the literature are taken seriously, we face the possibility that we may be discussing spurious subjects. There are disorders in the understanding of basic terms: of theory, of system, and of international relations. The field of study—whatever its proper name might be—has been experiencing conceptual disturbances. Issues have been raised which call into question a number of conventional definitions and long-established orientations to the field.

It would be possible, of course, to overlook the ferment and to proceed as if the disturbances did not exist. Too many indications of change have arisen during the most recent five-year period to justify the resort to such an expedient. The ground beneath the study of international relations—or world politics or the global system—has been shifting and the context of the discussions that we called the theory of international relations in the decade between the mid-fifties and the mid-sixties has changed to an extent that we cannot safely ignore the new situation.

Change and Disorder in the Study of International Relations

It is no longer feasible to hold a review of the system approach in a narrow focus. The changing context must be taken into account and some historical perspective must be developed before we can begin to assess either the current status or the prospects of the system formulation. The

Notes and References for this selection will be found on pages 38–40.

first step to take, obviously, is to identify the nature of the conceptual disturbance. We can begin with the basic name for the subject.

Herbert Spiro in his text on—and here we encounter immediately the effect of a semantic displacement—"our subject"[1] has declared that the term *international relations* gave way to *international politics* in the 1950s, but now *world politics* is the correct designation. Spiro justifies his very careful and conscious shift in terminology this way: "The main reason for taking a global perspective upon what used to be called 'international relations' is that, today for the first time in history, a global community exists or, at any rate, is coming into existence in the consciousness of human beings."[2] His further reason for asserting that old concepts must be replaced is that the distinction between the studies of domestic and international politics no longer exists: "The approach of this book is based upon the thesis that the conditions which once brought about this divorce between the study of internal politics of states and the study of relations among states have evaporated. . . . No qualitative or 'essential' difference in political processes can be found between lower political systems and the all-encompassing global system to warrant the study of the two different levels of politics by different methods."[3] Spiro proceeds further from conventional understanding by rejecting the focus on power and the state and by contending that the political system should not be considered an operating component of the social system.[4]

One of James Rosenau's persistent interests in recent years has been to modify the outlook on the conceptual boundary between national and international systems. In his contribution to the symposium volume, *Approaches to Comparative and International Politics,* Rosenau cited recent events which, in his language, illustrate the increasing "obscuration of the boundaries" between national and international politics,[5] demonstrate the infiltrations into the "last stronghold of sovereignty,"[6] and reveal the obsolescence in "the tendency of researchers to maintain a rigid distinction"[7] between domestic and foreign affairs. He quotes with approval a statement attributed to Philip Mosely: "the difference between 'national' and 'international' now exists only in the minds of those who use the words."[8] More recently, Rosenau appears to have withdrawn somewhat from the position that national and international phenomena have become indistinguishable. In the introduction to *Domestic Sources of Foreign Policy,* he speaks of the need to give greater attention to a wide range of domestic factors entering "into the processes whereby internal variables condition external behavior"[9] and in work still awaiting publication he calls for the development of "linkage theory" to bridge between national systems and international systems.[10]

Similarly Andrew Scott accounts for a lag in the thinking of scholars of international relations and for their failure to grasp the significance in the recent "revolution in statecraft," the importance of "informal access," and the presence of the process of "penetration" in the scholarly addiction to the distinction between "domestic" and "international" fields and in the adherence to the historical approach. He notes that "One set of investigators has studied domestic politics while another has studied international politics, and each has overlooked that which is a mixture of both."[11] Scott blames the study of history for the lack of sensitivity on the part of scholars to new phenomena such as "penetration." His point is that anyone can always find evidence for any desired viewpoint in history, including data that informal access and penetration have always occurred in the relations of nations. This is an unfortunate argument however, since it can be brought to bear as readily against Scott's data in support of his thesis of a "revolution in statecraft."

J. David Singer has abandoned the term *international* and replaces it with *global*. His views are less extreme than those previously summarized. Singer merely wishes to provide conceptual room for numbers of "social entities" other than the nation-state in the future study of the field but at the same time he acknowledges that the nation-state is still a strong entity and will continue that way for a long time to come. The boundary between national systems and international systems continues to exist for him. He detects a trend toward the replacement of the nation-state as the prime international actor but it is not yet, in his view, a dominating influence. Singer's main point is that the state has received too much attention as the *only* important actor.[12]

Much more evidence of conceptual change and displacement occurring around the issue of what there is to study, analyze, and theorize about could be brought forward. Johan Galtung remarks in passing: "When we say 'trends in the international system,' what we really mean are trends in the *global* system, for we do not want to assume that this system is to remain, essentially, an inter*national* system. But nations are going to remain dominant still for some time to come, so we will also have to discuss trends in what happens inside these nations of relevance to the interaction between nation-states."[13]

In a recent and important inventory of the state of research in the field, E. Raymond Platig states that "international relations studies the distribution of power on a global scale and the interplay between and among power centers.[14] He defines the "substantive core" of the field in the "interaction of governments of sovereign states."[15] Raymond Aron relates that, in establishing the foundations of his book, *Paix et Guerre entre les Nations,* "I tried to determine what constituted the distinctive nature of international or interstate relations, and I concluded that it lay in the legitimacy or legality of the use of military force. In superior civilizations, these are the only social relationships in which violence is considered normal."[16]

The foregoing should be sufficient evidence to establish the fact not only that nomenclature has become unsettled but also that some uncertainty exists about what is meant and intended by any speaker or writer who employs terms such as international relations, international politics, world politics, global politics, and other variants or alternatives. This is the prevailing condition. Let us consider next the situation of "theory."

Presumably, everyone in the field—I am going to call it the field of international relations[17]—is aware that there are various meanings of theory.[18] In view of the situation, I proposed about a decade ago that a catholic definition of international relations theory be adopted to take in a wide range of meanings. This definition appears now to be obsolete; it was to the effect that international relations theory could be identified as the literature produced in "the struggle to lay down intellectual policy for the field"[19] and is to include both the discussions of issues and problems and "phenomena-centered" theories, the latter being what we would call now "empirical" theories.

In general, the current demand appears to be for definitions encompassing a narrower span of conceptualization. But, in addition, there are several discussions of theory in the recent literature that open other vistas on the entire theory effort of the past decade. They contain at least three basic interpretations, (1) that the theorizing effort has been a misconceived and fruitless attempt, (2) that it is being absorbed now into more comprehensive areas, and (3) that it has been not about theory at all but rather a long series of inquiries and preliminary discussions possibly leading toward theory. We may conclude either that we have not reached a theory stage or that we have passed through it. The arguments are interesting.

No less an authority than Carl J. Friedrich has let his views be known recently on international relations theory[20]:

Foreign and domestic policy in developed Western systems constitutes today a seamless web. . . . The division remains, of course, but it resembles that between agricultural and fiscal policy, calling for a distinct organization and a separate set of specialists, but certainly not calling for a separate kind of political theory. It is the more curious that just such a theory has been demanded in recent years by very able writers in the field of international relations. Such demands seem to spring from a certain lack of theoretical framework in the study and teaching of international relations and foreign policy.

More trenchant and, perhaps, more expected are Hans J. Morgenthau's evaluations of the worth of recent theoretical efforts[21]:

In the aftermath of the Second World War, reflections on international relations entered an entirely new phase. This phase is marked by a number of academic schools of thought—behaviorism, systems analysis, game theory, and methodology in general—that have one aim in common: the pervasive rationalization of international relations by means of a comprehensive theory. The new theories, insofar as they are new in more than terminology, are in truth not so much theories as dogmas. They do not so much try to reflect reality as it actually is as to superimpose upon a recalcitrant reality a theoretical scheme that satisfies the desire for thorough rationalization.

Elsewhere, Morgenthau has come more firmly to the point that he feels needs emphasis[22].

There is another function of international theory which is not so much intellectual as psychological in nature and it is of interest primarily to the sociology of knowledge. It is to provide a respectable shield which protects the academic community from contact with the living political world. That function is performed by much of the methodological activities which are carried on in academic circles, with sometimes fanatical devotion to esoteric terminology and mathematical formulas, equations, and charts, in order to elucidate or obscure the obvious. . . . By engaging in activities which can have no relevance for the political problems of the day, such as theorizing about theories, one can maintain one's reputation as a scholar without running any political risks. This kind of international theory, then, is . . . an innocuous intellectual pastime engaged in by academicians for the benefit of other academicians without effect upon political reality as it is unaffected by it.

It is plain to see, if we follow Friedrich and Morgenthau that current theoretical activity in international relations is something we ought to dispense with without delay. If we compare two notable statements, separated by thirteen years of time, we might conclude further that, having now reversed our aims, we are closing down the theory effort within international relations studies.

In 1955, Quincy Wright published in his *The Study of International Relations* a much-quoted passage on the objective and the difficulties in constructing theories of international relations[23]:

The discipline of international relations has developed synthetically and this has militated against its unity. Other disciplines have developed through analysis and subdivision of older disciplines, as did genetics from biology and classical economics from moral philosophy. These disciplines began with a theory and developed from an initial unity. In international relations, on the other hand, an effort is being made to synthesize numerous older disciplines, each with a specialized point of view into a unity.

Wright clearly envisaged theory-building as the task of weaving together the diverse abstract materials of a number of fields into a theoretical unity for the study of international relations.

In 1968, Chadwick Alger in his survey of the field for the *International Encyclopedia of the Social Sciences* interpreted the task in a quite different way. In a statement that will be taken widely as authoritative, Alger indicated that whatever conceptual materials we may have been borrowing from other fields for theories of international relations are now being put back where we got them[24]:

International relations research will in the near future be even more affected by the twentieth-century revolution in social science than it has been in the past. It is probable that a separate body of international relations theory will not be developed and that international relations will be a part of the broader theoretical framework of intergroup relations.

It is likely that aspects of international relations will be increasingly incorporated into the concerns of each of the social sciences. . . . The various kinds of human behavior which scholars have traditionally classified as diplomacy will be dissected and studied as cases of negotiation, legislative behavior, representative behavior, political socialization, communication, organizational behavior, etc. These developments will tend to inhibit the growth of a coherent discipline, but there will be pressure toward coherence as members of different disciplines collaborate.

One gathers that, in Alger's view, there will be a field of international relations but its theory will be distributed widely through many fields and for many different subject matters. As we face the prospect outlined by Alger, our anxieties may be allayed about the loss of progress already made toward theoretical integration and coherence by taking into account the judgments of James Rosenau and Oran Young on the actual status of international theory.

As is well known, Rosenau argues that the study of foreign policy is still in a pretheory stage. In a persuasive demonstration, he shows that foreign policy research has been nontheoretical and also that much preliminary construction work must take place before a theoretical stage can be reached. Meanwhile, "foreign policy analysis lacks comprehensive systems of testable generalizations that treat societies as actors subject to stimuli which produce external responses. Stated more succinctly, foreign policy analysis is devoid of general theory."[25] Young evaluates the "other level"—the systemic—in comparable terms. He, like Rosenau, finds that the preliminary steps toward theory for the international system have not yet been taken properly: "It is this general tendency to slide over the antecedent problems of approaches in systemic analyses of international politics that has produced much of the pervasive confusion and obscurity . . ."[26]

Young's diagnosis is that we have to deal with epistemological considerations before we can clarify approaches to analysis and that, even when we have the approaches well in hand, we will not yet have achieved theories.[27]

Some impression of what the "long road to theory" still entails a decade after Stanley Hoffmann called that phrase into being is conveyed by the commentaries cited above. The *theory of international relations* remains an indefinite topic with its tricky aspects: one can get caught in making severe criticisms of something that does not exist or, on the other hand, one might anticipate confidently forthcoming events of birth that turn out to be events of demise or vice versa. Perhaps enough has been noted to outline the uncertainties in the status of theory in the field; the remaining question is whether or not we have something meaningful to consider in the system concept.

The promise of the system approach or perspective for international relations has been hailed widely. Some views held are:

Harold Sprout (1959): "The study of international political systems has become, and seems likely to remain, one of the main foci of basic research in the field of international politics."[28]

Stanley Hoffmann (1960): System theory "is a spectacular development of the behavioral sciences. . . . In the case of international relations, I believe that 'system theory' is a huge misstep in the right direction—the direction of systematic empirical analysis. It is an effort that raises fundamental questions about the proper purpose and methods of the social sciences in general, and international relations in particular."[29]

James N. Rosenau (1961): "Of all the advances that have occurred in the study of international phenomena, perhaps none is more important than the ever-growing tendency to regard the world as *the international system*."[30]

Andrew Scott (1967): "The system approach will help overcome the sharp separation between domestic affairs and international politics, because it operates equally well at either level and can move between the two."[31]

There is, however, a less sunny and optimistic side to this picture of the potential of the system concept. Here the indication is that things have not gone well with the refinement and application of the system approach in the study of international relations. Again testimony to the fact is easily assembled:

Rudolph Rummel (1965): "This stagnation of general systems theory as currently used by social scientists had resulted largely from two aspects. One is the verbal edifice which now forms general systems theory. . . . A second aspect is the lack of a developed set of empirical methods—research techniques—through which the theory may have been developed."[32]

Charles McClelland (1965): "Yet, for all that promise, it should be kept in mind that the general-systems approach is neither a formula nor a doctrine, but a cluster of strategies of inquiry; not a theory, but an organized space within which many theories may be developed and related."[33]

Steven Brams (1966): "Unfortunately, the concept of an international system has had a singularly hollow ring in the works of many scholars who have employed the term . . . it is defined so abstractly that it would appear to have no specific empirical reference . . ."[34]

M.B. Nicholson and P.A. Reynolds (1967): "This discussion of the applicability of Easton's model to the global system has suggested that at almost every point the variables as he conceives them are in the global system so shadowy, and the systemic paths as he defines them so indeterminate, that the usefulness of his model as an aid to understanding the global system as it exists is questionable."[35]

Oran Young (1968): "The concept system has been widely but very loosely and confusingly employed in the social sciences. It is therefore impossible, at least at the present time, to formulate a lexical definition of the term."[36]

J. David Singer (1968): "In my judgment we have not yet developed a general system theory; hence the word 'approach'."[37]

Charles McClelland (1968): "If we had been less permissive in allowing almost any notion or viewpoint to be called a theory, 'international system theory' proabably would have been disallowed from the outset. . . . In the more exact sense, there has never been a system theory of international relations."[38]

These quotations again make apparent that confusion and disorder are affecting the study of international relations and that the concept of system as employed in the literature of the field has not escaped the malaise. Indeed, it is to be noted that a condition of confusion has prevailed in the field in the most recent years. There is some discouragement about the future and the enthusiasm for international studies along the broad front that includes foreign area studies has declined somewhat.[39] Some observers attribute the change to a shift of public interest in the United States from foreign affairs to urban pathologies and race relations. The course of recent American foreign policy has been held accountable for diverting academic efforts from research and analysis to the expression of indignation and action against that foreign policy. Whatever the causes, general conditions at the time of this writing are not good. Such external factors may be contributory, but they do not begin to account for the semantic and conceptual disorders of the kind that have been described here.

The Transition from the Third to the Fourth Wave

As was noted at the beginning of the discussion, important changes in perspective on international relations theory and research have been emerging. At the moment, we appear to be in some kind of transition; it is this situation that makes it particularly difficult to offer responsible appraisals of the conceptual and theoretical aspects of the study of international relations. To understand what is taking place, we need the advantages of historical perspective over as long a period as possible. Two interpretations of the history of international relations studies are especially useful for this purpose. One was written at the beginning of the period which we now appear to be leaving. The other was supplied very recently.

Kenneth Thompson, in a noteworthy survey in 1952 marked out several "relatively distinct stages or phases" in the history of the study of international relations. The first was the era of diplomatic history before and after World War I. The second and third periods between World War I and World War II had a double aspect: on the one hand, international organization and law were cultivated under a strong normative orientation and, on the other hand, a current events approach to international relations was much favored. The fourth phase, still prevailing in 1952, was concentrated on foreign policy analysis and international politics with political realism and political idealism being "the major competitors for recognition as the theory of international behavior."[40] But Thompson noted also the appearance of what he termed an "eclectic" approach. Two sentences in Thompson's survey forecast the developments that were to come: "Eclecticism in these terms asks the student to start without any *a priori* assumptions in making his inquiries in the field. The eclectic point of view has shown a preference for a sociological approach to the problems of world politics."[41]

Beginning in about 1954, a flood of candidate ideas for the ordering and interpreting of international relations poured in from "outside" fields. In a word, the response to the eclectic impulse was tremendous. We are harvesting now the fruits of that movement. The scope of the field of international relations has widened marvelously. It can be claimed that, in some respects, greater sophistication has been achieved. There have been costs that go with gains, however. As we have shown, some of the fruit is bitter, at least for the time being. One interpretation of the present situation is that the field, having experienced its eclectic phase is moving on into a new era. This is a thesis that Karl Deutsch has reinterpreted in a recent essay.

Deutsch suggests that the nature of a nation's international involvement has a bearing on the interest and support there is for developing knowledge about international relations. The present is a phase of low interest because of changes in the international environment adverse to American control or domination over that environment. He also relates this effect to four waves of advance in the history of the study of international relations[42]:

The first was the rise of interest in international law, symbolized by the two Hague Conventions of 1899 and 1907, and the many legal agreements and scholarly studies that followed. The second wave was the rise of diplomatic history after the opening of many government archives after World War I, and the simultaneous rise of interest in international organizations. . . .

A third wave of advance has been under way since the 1950's. It has consisted in the reception of many relevant results and methods from the younger of the social and behavioral sciences, such as psychology, anthropology and sociology, together with demography and the newer economics of development and growth. While this wave is still continuing, a fourth wave has begun to reinforce it. This is the rise of analytic and quantitative research concepts, models, and methods, a movement toward the comparative study of quantitative data and the better use of some of the potentialities of electronic computation.

Deutsch's definition of the situation is very helpful. As we look back on the third wave of advance in international studies during the behavioral decade—primarily, the period from the mid-fifties to the mid-sixties—and, at the same time take into account the coming of a fourth wave, we can begin to understand the rise of the present difficulties in the field. The prospects simply looked different on the crest of the third wave compared to the way they appear on the ascending slope of the fourth wave. In particular, shifts are occurring in the perspective on theory. Theoretical purposes, outlook, and aspirations are undergoing a change.

It is small wonder that expressions of discontent with the state of international relations theory have arisen. The very enlargement of the scope of the field—a major accomplishment of the behavioral decade—has made unsatisfactory the conceptual frameworks and theoretical formulations of that period. In addition, it now becomes clear that the orientation toward theory in the time of the third wave was very different from the emerging orientation of the fourth wave. If we wish to appraise the current status of the system approach, we must consider the difference between the third wave and fourth wave phenomena and compare the system perspective under two contrasting situations.

Theory During the Behavioral Decade

In the fifties, a number of approaches, perspectives, or ordering frameworks came to attention in the study of international relations. It seems most natural to call these importations to the field "theories" as was the common practice of the behavioral decade. The list is not exhaustive but the following were innovations in the international relations field: decision-making theory, field theory, system theory, capability theory, deterrence theory, communication or cybernetic theory, conflict theory, game theory, integration theory, development theory, environmental theory, and perceptual or cognitive theory. This is not the place to attempt to reconstruct the history of the advent of these ideas and the overlapping and crosscutting effects they produced. We can point to some effects of innovation, however.

The central problem seemed to be that of the integration of the new materials within the confines of the field. With almost perfect timing, Quincy Wright outlined the general nature of the task in 1955 in the passage of his book quoted earlier. The struggle of the behavioral decade was to establish some conceptual order in the field by defining, categorizing, comparing, shaping, reinterpreting, and combining the new abstract materials in an integrated framework. Thus, the greater part of the analytic effort of the decade went to the search for relationships among concepts. In the eyes of some scholars, the enterprise was the manifestation of wild-eyed radicalism. It was anything but that. Indeed, we can see now that the movement was conservative in that the general desire was to save the old learning, to incorporate its important theoretical elements, and to combine as many of the imported ideas as possible in the emerging conceptual structure. Competition existed between advocates of the various new approaches and a process of attempted cooptation can be detected in the literature of the field during the behavioral decade. Game theory was interpreted "as nothing more than" the old findings of diplomatic and military strategy and system theory was explained as "nothing more than" the ancient conception of the European state system.

Particularly important at the beginning of the behavioral movement within international relations was the relationship between the power and influence theory and the various candidate concepts.[43] The evidence is plainly in sight but the interpretation does not seem to have been advanced that the Morgenthau power and influence formulation was a major stimulus to the behavioral revolution and, in fact, an initial part of it. With the publication of *Politics Among Nations* in 1948, the field was given its first impressive demonstration of what a sustained and systematic *analysis* is like.[44] Further, by insisting with great force that we ought to look at the world as it really is rather than how it should be, Morgenthau stimulated interest in the motivational, situational, and behavioral aspects of international politics and foreign policy. *Politics Among Nations* can be shown to be based on a definite, if very limited, psychology of international relations.

Morgenthau held a steady focus on how nations act toward one another and in terms of basic, repetitive patterns of action—the balance of power process, for example. The realist formulation can be characterized as "behavioral" for the attention it directed toward political processes, system structures, situational factors, psychological influences, and actor behavior. In other respects, as is well-known, the label is inappropriate: Morgenthau's particular philosophical bent and his attitude toward inquiry do not belong with the behavioral science orientation.

Most important was the reaction to the power and interest theory. While it was generally agreed that the theory is a useful synthesis and covers *part* of international phenomena, it cannot be accepted as encompassing *all* the important aspects and features of international life and behavior and it does not probe as deeply as it should into the realities that it does cover. It is apparent that the Snyder decision-making formulation was, in origin, an attempt to deepen and elaborate the power and influence conception. In a word, Morgenthau's work was influential in opening the flood gates.

The role that the system approach came to play in the theoretical effort of the behavioral decade was that of providing a general perspective or orientation for all the candidate theories including power and interest theory. The idea of systems provided a terminology and a set of categories useful for identifying a wide range of phenomena and for relating a variety of names and concepts. Viewed in the light of the objective to construct a common framework of concepts, the works of Morton Kaplan[45] and Kenneth Boulding[46] were important mainly as a demonstration of the possibility of organizing widely diffused ideas and conventional insights into a coordinated discussion of systems. They showed that the conversions could be made—up to a point. The basic terms of systems—system, component, subsystem, environment, boundary, structure, relationship, process, transformation, etc.—are neutral and, therefore, advantageous for bringing ideas into association that otherwise would not seem to be compatible. The terms also are empty—like so many blank spaces to be filled in according to need or purpose. Until somebody specifies what the references—abstract or empirical—are to be for each of the fundamental terms, there is no way to know what a system is about.

References may be supplied in a large number of different ways, giving rise not to 9,045 international system identifications as Harry Ransom's query has it,[47] but to multitudes of possible systems far beyond that number. This is a complaint that arises as soon as interest turns to *research* and to the research needs for theory on international systems. It needs to be emphasized again that the chief preoccupation of the behavioral decade was to relate and calibrate different conceptual orders and that this complaint was, therefore, not then a relevant one. In the perspective of that period, if the system idea could show how decision-making theory, environmental theory, cognitive theory, and game theory might be brought together in fruitful conjunction, it would have demonstrated its validity and utility.

For a time in the early 1960s, the ambition to achieve a common conceptual framework, to be filled in by later theoretical improvements and by research, seemed almost to have been satisfied. The intellectual foundations for international relations appeared to be in the process of being laid down to "help people to think more clearly and fruitfully about the real world: what that world is like and how it functions."[48] Harold Sprout sketched out the essentials of a coordinated field according to main divisions of the study,[49] and Richard Snyder amplified the conception in more detail a short time later.[50] Sprout and Snyder spoke for those who were most interested in and had worked most persistently for a conceptual mapping of international relations.

The study of international relations would consist of two main branches, one of which would cultivate theory and research under a *foreign policy* heading and one which would develop the study of structures, relationships, interactions, and processes between nations under the label of *international politics* or international systemic relations. Sprout's description of how the "foci of basic research" could be established had the merit of clarity and simplicity. Snyder's exposition of the "lines of analytic development" was thorough and persuasive. The Snyder and Sprout proposals may be compared in the following lists:

Lines of Analytic Development (Snyder)

> *Society As the Acting Unit*
>   Decision-making and Policy
>   Values, Attitudes and Opinions
>   Quantifiable Indicators of Society-As-Unit Characteristics
> *Inter Unit and Interaction Foci*
>   System and Equilibrium Analyses
>   Internation System: Experimental Techniques
>   Intersocietal Conflict
>   Intersocietal Integration and Political Community

Foci of Basic Research (Sprout)

> *Foreign Policy Analysis*
> State Techniques
> State Policy Making Process
> State Capabilities
> *International System Analysis*

As it turned out, the potential in the Sprout-Snyder framework was not developed further. Almost immediately, a countering proposal was put forth in reaction against the two-branch solution. The objection was that a conceptual demarcation line was being drawn permanently between domestic and foreign affairs by this solution to the theory integration problem. Those who saw the advantages in the two-branch organization according to intra-unit and inter-unit foci recognized an integrating effect that could occur from a division of labor in theory development and empirical research. They conceived that at a later time after specialized investigations of both actor and interaction phenomena had clarified the two lines of theory, a movement would be effected to build a full integration. Meanwhile, the problem was defined as the tasks of carrying out needed research and of perfecting needed subtheories in each of the two branches of inquiry.

Those who disapproved of the two-branch approach did so according to one or more of three main criticisms:

1. Since actors and interaction are related in reality, the starting point for coherent theoretical development is this relationship or linkage. The critics saw a dividing line being proposed precisely in the place where they saw a territory to be occupied. Or, as Rosenau put it for a somewhat different context, boundaries were being proposed where there should be bridges.[51]

2. The traditional differentiation of foreign and domestic politics should be abandoned because many political phenomena usually thought to be "characteristically international" exist (or abound) in local and national environments and should be studied under the guidance of the crosslevel notion or of unified general political theory.

3. As was noted earlier, a change from "international relations" to "world affairs" has been detected to be taking place through a number of processes including that of "penetration." It is felt that this change makes obsolete and irrelevant the international relations theories based on a domestic-foreign dichotomy or on a strictly intergovernmental focus of attention.

It may be too early for a definitive interpretation but the present appearance is that the confrontation of the linkage argument and the plan for a two-branch organization of the field has produced not a great debate but a reaction of indifference and boredom. Weariness had begun to settle on the field by the mid-sixties from the exertions of a decade to manipulate large abstractions into preferred patterns. The drive for an integrated theory simply has dissipated. The change of attitude about conceptual integration probably marks the final transition to the fourth wave of inquiry in the study of international relations. The new outlook seems to be that it is better to accept theoretical disarray than to make further futile efforts to correct the situation.

Certain byproducts were produced in the quest for conceptual unification and these now have assumed greater importance than the main quest. Perhaps the most significant of these byproducts was the understanding of the multidimensional character of international phenomena. The vocabulary of systems had facilitated the discussion of multidimensionality.

At the beginning of the behavioral decade, the application of the system concept involved the identification of components of the international system simply as "nations" or sometimes more exactly as the governments of nations. The interactions of nations were considered to produce the system, itself, and the governing relationship in the system was taken, more or less automatically, to be power. Hence, patterns of interaction (i.e., processes) and arrangements of patterns (i.e., structures) both having to do with the power relationship in a system made up of nation-components was the design of the initial system formulation.

The next development was an expansion of the definitions and the general empirical referents for components and systems. Thus, the term "nation" tended to be replaced by "national system" to acknowledge the insight that the nation components in the international system are really complexes of intermeshed and interfunctioning subsystems, *some* of which are specialized or strongly related to external relationships and interactions. Similarly, the concept of *the* system gave way to the notion of several international systems (i.e., subordinate systems, regional systems, conflict systems, etc.).

The third elaboration was to open the prospect on a variety of possible international relationships over and beyond the power relationship. General change relationships (i.e., of development, of integration, or a widening gap between rich and poor nations, etc.) and social psychological relationships (of trust and suspicion, of threat, of mutual misperception as in the mirror-image effect, of rising expectations, etc.) were envisaged to be significant relationships in international systems.

The last conceptual development toward multidimensionality under the system perspective was the understanding that large numbers of concrete systems—national systems, international systems, extranational systems, subnational systems, and nonnational systems—all stand in numerous relationships to each other, that the flows of interactions within and between the systems take many directions including paths between international systems and subnational and nonnational systems, and that processes and structures produced in the flows of interaction are too numerous and varied to be classified adequately according to categories in general use.

At first the system approach to international relations was fairly simple, involved only a few factors, and was close in conception to the prevailing power and interests theory. In association with other behavioral science concepts that had been brought into the field, the system approach gradually increased in scope and took on more and more theoretical complexity. Thus, the role played by the system approach in the behavioral movement of the decade was first to hold out the promise of an integration of international relations theory and, ultimately, to expose the widening dimensions of the task, through progressive stages of inquiry, almost to the point of despair.

The lack of excitement on the part of those who had long followed the theoretical writings on international relations over the possible confrontation of the linkage and issue-area ideas, on the one hand, and the national system–international system formulation, on the other hand, can be accounted for on the ground that there existed already an intuitive grasp of the nature of the rising conceptual complexity of which linkages and issue areas are only one part. In any case, the response to the movement toward multidimensional complexity in the conceptual elaboration of international systems was to veer off in another direction. The current outlook—perhaps it is the "fourth-wave orientation"—is simply to abandon the conceptual unification problem.

Reshaping the Idea of International Systems

As Bruce Russett notes elsewhere in this volume[52] the current tendency is to put aside the manipulation of various conceptual schemes and to take up, instead, the testing of limited ranges of concepts against bodies of data. Theory is now being seen as a varied product that may be *built* from the results of research efforts more than something to be *consolidated* from combinations of existing conceptual systems. Russett argues that "inchoate theory" often is sufficient for *beginning* empirical research and that, if careful attention is given to matters of explanation and generalization *during* the research enterprise, some theoretical "payoffs" may result. When we look in the cupboard for explicit, well-developed international system theory to *use* in research and in the pursuit of new theory, we find it almost bare. What is to be found is a rich supply of inchoate theory that was accumulated for a purpose different from that of orienting specific empirical research. If international system theory currently has little to offer in the way of specific hypotheses for testing by research, it has much to offer by way of directing choices of areas of research and of limiting objectives in research undertakings.

The most important contribution of the past decade's discourses on international systems may be the insight into what needs to be done to make the system concept more useful to research. Very large numbers of international systems are conceivable. The idea of social multidimensionality leads to the realization that many actual, concrete systems are operating in the global environment, that many of them are coupled, and that they manifest reciprocal effects among themselves and in the environment. To test any propositions about an international system one must specify *which* international system is to be considered. The identification of concrete systems having components that work on one another (rather than simply sharing characteristics) will be most likely to be useful to empirical research. Thus, the future of international system theory appears to lie in conversions of the inchoate but general conceptualizations now available into very particular system formulations.

This conversion may be made in verbal accounts but it is equally possible that it will be accomplished by developing computer simulations. The designing of a model for computer simulation is, essentially, an exercise in system theory-building. To construct a simulation model of an international system for a computer, one must be entirely specific in identifying system components, boundaries, structures, processes, interactions, transformations, and relationships. Further, these specifications of system parts and functions must be amenable to "dynamic modelling" which is to say they must accommodate changes of "state" and the passing along of the effects of such changes through the system.[53] Future international system theory is most likely to focus on how certain systems operate in certain respects under certain circumstances.

Since virtually unlimited numbers of systems might be investigated, the system theory or computer simulation will have to be "about" something. The principle of selection will be developed in terms of certain fundamental relationships, processes, or properties of dynamic systems. It is probable that these relationships, processes, and properties will provide the names of particular system theories. Thus, alliance theory could be "about" a specific range of structural relationships among components of the system and about a range of processes active in the formation, maintenance, and dissolution of alliance systems.[54]

Some interesting *process* might be singled out to become the guiding consideration in the construction of a model, theory, or simulation. The penetration process which presently is recognized as a general idea around which are clustered some illustrations and anecdotal descriptions might be clarified and elaborated and then developed in more precise theoretical terms. The system components would then include government actors, subnational organizations, and individuals located within different sovereignties. The ways in which a penetration system operated in the interplay of demands and responses on the part of system components would be traced and analyzed, using, perhaps, "real world" data of observed interactions to set the limits of this interplay.

In other instances, specific system *relationships* might be made the basis of theories or simulations. A group of hypotheses might be constructed about the relationships of the occurrences of major public events and shifts of public attention between domestic and foreign preoccupations.

Then, the system components would be specified as certain strata of national populations identified by crossnational opinion responses and according to an attentiveness theory. The latter would show the expected shifts of attention between domestic and foreign problems according to some classification scheme for the occurrences of different types of public events.

Still another approach could use the idea of linkages. Certain patterned international interactions which are thought to couple with and respond to certain domestic processes could be investigated from the standpoint of some propositions about adaptability or error correction. Other hypothetical approaches could be set forth at some length. But it is not necessary to speculate more on what might be undertaken in reshaping the concept of international systems to accommodate research and modeling requirements. The "fourth-wave" reorientation of the system approach has proceeded already a considerable distance and evidence of this can be cited from published literature.

Despite the contention that differentiations of national and international systems are in error, researchers continue to find it useful to order data according to that distinction. A general hypothesis that has stimulated much research in recent years is that certain groupings of characteristics of national systems "predict to" behaviors in the international system. Stated otherwise, the proposition is that the attributes of a national social entity determine the patterns of that entity's external actions.[55] The research problem, under this orientation, is to isolate those groups of attributes that can be shown to relate to manifested external or international action.

Almost nobody believes in the absolute assertion of this formulation; the common sense view is that, from the standpoint of foreign policy, sometimes domestic characteristics are more determining than the nature of the international situation and, at other times, the nature of the international situation is more determining than domestic characteristics. But the common sense view is far less useful to research than the theoretical formulation. The latter gives a clear direction for the selecting and ordering of data and facilitates one stage of progress toward the ultimate goal of being able to specify on *which* occasions the balance is tipped more toward the domestic sources of behavior or more toward the international sources of behavior. The assertion of a theoretical position need not reflect one's insight or belief.

The idea that nation-attributes predict to international behavior is somewhat contrary to general system teachings. We would be predisposed to expect that attributes created by the operations and processes of numerous subsystems of a national entity would relate most often to internal needs and purposes rather than to external ones. Hence, we would not expect the attributes to correspond regularly to external phenomena. Further, it is more or less a general system principle that the attributes of subsystems are manifestations of specialized operations and are unlike the characteristics of the ensemble of the whole system. Nevertheless, we know little about the actual characteristics and operations of international systems but we suspect that they may not be very much like the highly articulated system that is the model for this principle. The series of research reports and articles by Rudolph Rummel and his students are the outstanding examples of the application of the attributes-determine-external behavior concept.[56]

A different theoretical direction can be taken by reversing the terms of the attributes-behavior formulation. Thus, it may be proposed that characteristics of external action predict to domestic attributes. An inventive research exploration that follows generally along this line of inquiry is to be found in the work of Raymond Tanter and Manus Midlarsky.[57] Limiting their system and theory to Latin American countries in a recent time period, they made the object of their research the complex process of revolution within countries, identified by a number of indicators of political instability, and they established with considerable success that some variable relationships may be shown to exist between the domestic manifestations of revolution and certain intrusive international activities (in the research, these were defined as the economic "presence" of the United States in Latin American countries).

Recently, Bruce Russett has employed the system approach to organize five different groupings of indicator data and to delineate groupings of political systems according to similarities in their characteristics and in comparison with geographical region concepts.[58] He has been working on a general theoretical problem in the system approach that was neglected mostly during the behavioral decade. This is the matter of accounting for the environments of systems. That environmental circumstances affect the operations of systems, both in shaping and limiting them, is well understood in principle but, in the study of international systems, it remained an empty concept. Russett's effort is to remedy this shortcoming by developing conceptualizations and research on the "ecology" of international political systems.[59] It is important to consider systematically the "outside" effects from environments on the political functioning of national and international systems.

Most fruitful of all the newer system formulations in attracting research applications and tests of hypotheses is Johan Galtung's structural theory of aggression.[60] Aggression may be a somewhat misleading descriptor of the theory since Galtung's definition of aggression is the "drives toward change, even against the will of others."[61] A particular characteristic in the structure of relationships among social entities (Galtung specifies relationships among individuals, groups, and nations) grounds the theory and establishes its structural aspect. This relationship is called rank-disequilibrium—the differential in status experienced in social intercourse. Rank-disequilibrium powers or motivates the actions undertaken by social entities in interaction, particularly with regard to the tendency to act against opposition. Stated most generally and absolutely for international systems, the theory is that rank position of a national system will determine what the behavior of that national system will be in the interaction flows of the international system.

Galtung conceives this hierarchical theory to be the foundation upon which numbers of other theoretical structures might be built. Different levels and aspects of system phenomena may be analyzed in empirical research applications. He has extended the fundamental notion of the structural theory of aggression in a recent essay. The inquiry takes a novel direction. Galtung's new formulation is especially noteworthy if for no other reason than that it identifies system components without locking them tightly to state or governmental actors—as is still the most common practice.

More a future-oriented discussion of trends than a theoretical discourse, the essay is too complicated for brief summarization.[62] Galtung's main emphasis is on change processes and change effects. The territorial nation-state is treated as a confined space within which various segments of one or more societies exist. These societal segments, which at first glance appear to be the operating components of the global system, squeeze out and beyond the nation-state space in some instances and have plenty of room within the nation-state space, in other instances. Nation-states are typed as more developed, less developed, large, and small.

Everywhere, Galtung contends, the value of development is being promoted and pursued. This leads to changing conditions within the societal segments and also between the societal segments as these are positioned variously within and across nation-states. The segments are in various stages and transitions of development (from primitive to traditional to modern to neomodern). Many of the changes wrought by the drive toward development are traced into the future in speculative explorations. Cross-national and cross-societal changes are also delineated in the same manner.

The really interesting aspect of this contribution toward international relations theory is found to be, upon careful study of the discussion, the designation of system components as social change *processes*. The societal segments are not the system components but only the loci of the components which are, to repeat, processes of change. The interplay of these change processes across and beyond the nation-state spaces as well as within them make up the global or international system. Thus, Galtung brings together ingredients of an international system theory consisting entirely of linked or coupled processes.

This kind of system formulation has not been seen before in the field. The usual concrete units that interact are not present in the formulation. The preoccupation with change within and between social locations and the incompatibilities of society and state are unusual features. It will be interesting to see if Galtung's ideas diffuse and attract theoretical refinement and research applications. The chances that interest will develop along these lines are increased by the publication of John Burton's *Systems, States, Diplomacy and Rules.*[63]

Although they are unlike in many respects, Galtung's and Burton's fundamental conceptions of the settings of present and future international relations are in resonance. Both respond to the widening, multidimensional prospects on the study of international relations and both take advantage of the vocabulary and orientation of general systems. Common in both Galtung's and Burton's recent inquiries is the importance attached to the differentiation of state and society. Where Galtung stresses state-society incompatibilites and the imperative for over-all social system transformations, Burton emphasizes the here-and-now crossfunctioning of system and state. Thus, those who find it difficult or impossible to follow along the trail that Galtung blazes may find Burton's formulation more congenial.

The fundamental idea presented by Burton is that we begin our inquiries with a conception of a world society comprised of vast numbers of systems of different types and functions[64]:

The map of this society would appear like millions of cobwebs superimposed one upon another, covering the whole globe, some with stronger strands than others representing more numerous transactions, some concentrated in small areas, and some thinly stretched over extensive areas. Each separate cobweb would represent a separate system. . . . This would be a world society without geographical boundaries, for systems have no such boundaries. There are points between which there are interactions or transactions.

Burton then invites us to bring into this picture of world society and the multitudes of systems the further idea of the State. States are *not* conceived to be systems but rather, clusters of system *effects* drawn apart and "organized by an administrative system responding and behaving within an environment. . . ."[65] The State relates to a geographical area and has geographical boundaries to maintain, unlike systems which do not (necessarily) have a singular geographical location and do not have fixed territorial boundaries but only functional limits.

An image is created of great networks of operating social systems, endlessly expanding, contracting, dying, creating, adjusting, failing, etc. but not doing all these things at the bidding or according to any absolute controls by States. The State, with its administrative apparatus can exert some partial control on some of the operations of some systems—it may, to an extent, direct, distort, nurture, shape, or modify the flows of interactions of the social system complex, both within and between the territorial boundaries. The general notion is that States sit astride the flows of world interaction, not absolutely but only contingently, and do not really command the world society. The rest of Burton's analysis, which cannot be followed here in detail, is concerned with the relationships between systems and states with special reference to the needs, power, conflicts, and the control resources involved in these relationships.

Other evidence exists in the very recent literature to show how the reshaping and redirecting of theory and research on international systems is beginning to take place. It may be unfair or, perhaps, misleading not to review all the manifestations of change in the fourth-wave stage of the study of international relations. On the other hand, it seems to suffice to give some indication—an inkling—at a very uncertain moment, of the apparent direction and movement of inquiry in the field. It has been shown, perhaps, that there are some positive and promising aspects in the current situation of theoretical disarray and confusion. Some demonstration has been made of the shifts in interest and in emphasis in the transition between the third and fourth waves of effort to produce more and better knowledge of international phenomena.

Some Estimates about Future Development

It does not seem entirely hazardous to offer a few concluding observations on how things may go in the coming decade:

1. The general system perspective will flourish. Indeed, the conception has diffused widely and self-conscious references to system approaches seem now to have a declining utility. The point about general system theory, frequently made in the past, will be more widely understood; it is not really a theory. As Anatol Rapoport has noted lately: "General systems theory is best described not as a theory in the sense that this word is used in science but, rather, as a program or a direction in the contemporary philosophy of science."[66] What we can anticipate is that the international system idea, having served a different purpose in the behavioral decade, will be the basis in the future of more specific and focused theoretical formulations that may not even bear the system label. The victory of a new idea is in no longer being recognized as new.

2. The scattering of international relations theory across the far reaches of the intellectual landscape will continue for a while. This effect can be accounted for by the relaxation of the demand for the integration of theory, by the shift of preoccupation toward empirical research, and by the vast widening of the horizon on what the study of international relations may include. Alger's prediction of the disappearance of international relations theory by absorption into general behavioral science theory is to be questioned. It will prove to be a nuisance and burden to pull along such a heavy theoretical apparatus; only a few special scholars are likely to keep a sustained interest across all the "levels" of human relations between the individual and the world community. The case is already being made, as we have seen, for a distinctive (if still somewhat impressionistic) approach to the world society or global system. Further, in about ten or fifteen years, some young theorist, some faculty group, some research center, or some research administrator will rediscover the fascinating problem of relating theories to each other and we can then expect a surge of interest in the conceptual unification of whatever the field, discipline, or emphasis is then called.

3. In the aftermath of the behavioral decade, the unsatisfied hunger now beginning to be indulged is for data, lots of data, for hard materials to be handled, ordered, and analyzed. Morgenthau's criticism of theory in the behavioral decade was correct in at least a single respect: one needs the direction of theory only in order to deal with specific details of the circumstances and occurrences in the world. Concrete theory, which is otherwise a ridiculous term, means theory that digs down into and orders the discrete materials of history. It is from historical materials, including today's world news, that most of the data of the dependent variable in research on international relations can be carved. A theory of aggression, for example, requires data—not just the information in reports—on what aggressors and victims *do* and on how behavior and interaction unfold in real cases. A single instance, e.g., the Soviet invasion of Czechoslovakia in 1968, for instance, may call for, under current standards and aspirations, actual data creation, ordering, and analysis of perhaps 50,000 historical items. The trend is to turn increasingly to history but in new ways.

4. One of these ways is to code, count, and compare data, even the data of historical events and occurrences. The computer requires this. Whether individuals resist it or approve it, the movement toward computerization in international relations research already has gone too far to be turned back. During the coming decade, too many purposes will be well served and too many problems of data will be coped with effectively to support the hope of heading off the movement toward the machine. We can anticipate, therefore, the rise of more and more computer applications and more and more computer-assisted analyses of data. Massive frustrations are also to be anticipated.

The learning of what are, in fact, very difficult attitudes, techniques, and approaches for such analyses is one source of coming frustration. A second source will be discovered in the shortages of needed, relevant data. To the present, most of the quantitative, machine-oriented international relations studies have simply requisitioned data already gathered and processed for other purposes. From here on, data acquisition will become more difficult; needed bodies of facts will have to be quarried by hand out of hard rock. This is the prospect especially if research tries to follow the lines such as those sketched by Galtung and Burton. The data needed to fit the many conceivable variables of the world society and global system approaches simply do not exist in most cases and would have to be created at great expense and labor.

A further prediction on the future direction of international system research arises from the consideration of the scarce data problem. Despite the widening scope of the field and the growing awareness of the social multidimensionality of national-international system phenomena, it is to be anticipated that most empirical research will continue to be done on official, interstate relations. From the present point of view, we know very little about these relationships, except in an impressionistic and imprecise way. But that is not the chief consideration: it is in the conventional area of international politics that data resources are rich and developed. It is here that reasonable expenditures will produce large amounts of new data.

Further, at least in the United States for the immediate future, the remaining source of funds for advancing basic international theory and research is governmental. However far-sighted, liberal, and light-handed government agencies become in their support of foreign policy and international relations research, they can hardly be expected to view international relations as anything very remote from governmental activity. Thus, it may be from abroad that the most interesting pathfinding work will come in the future. American scholars may become the foremost representatives of the old narrow focus on international politics. It is ironic, indeed, that the private American foundations, after a half century of intellectual nurture and financial support for the study of international relations, have withdrawn their interest and money at the precise time when the heart's desire of the foundations—new perspectives and bold intellectual innovations—have begun to come within immediate reach in the study of international or global society relationships.

Notes and References

[1]Herbert J. Spiro, *World Politics: The Global System* (Homewood, Illinois: The Dorsey Press, 1966), p. 1.

[2]*Ibid.*, p. 2.

[3]*Ibid.*, pp. 4–5.

[4]*Ibid.*, pp. 7–11.

[5]James N. Rosenau, "Pre-theories and Theories of Foreign Policy," in R. Barry Farrell (ed.), *Approaches to Comparative and International Politics* (Evanston, Illinois: Northwestern University Press, 1966), p. 53.

[6]*Ibid.*, p. 54.

[7]*Ibid.*, p. 53.

[8]*Ibid.*, p. 56.

[9]James N. Rosenau (ed.), *Domestic Sources of Foreign Policy* (New York: The Free Press, 1967), p. 5.

[10]James N. Rosenau (ed.), *Linkage Politics: Essays on the Convergence of National and International Systems* (New York: The Free Press, 1969).

[11]Andrew M. Scott, *The Revolution in Statecraft: Informal Penetration* (New York: Random House, 1965), p. vi.

[12]J. David Singer, "The Global System and its Sub-Systems: A Developmental View," in *Linkage Politics* (*op. cit.*), pp. 21–43.

[13]Johan Galtung, "On the Future of the International System," *Journal of Peace Research*, No. 4 (1967), pp. 307–08.

[14]E. Raymond Platig, *International Relations Research: Problems of Evaluation and Advancement* (New York: Carnegie Endowment for International Peace, 1966), p. 14.

[15]*Ibid.*, p. 19.

[16]Raymond Aron, "What is a Theory of International Relations?" *Journal of International Affairs*, No. 2 (1967), p. 190.

[17]An argument in behalf of the international relations label for the field can be found in Charles A. McClelland, *Theory and the International System* (New York: The Macmillan Company, 1966), pp. 16, 17.

[18]See Anatol Rapoport, "Various Meanings of 'Theory'," *American Political Science Review*, 52 (December 1958), pp. 972–88.

[19]Charles A. McClelland, "The Function of Theory in International Relations," *Journal of Conflict Resolution*, 4 (September 1960), p. 305.

[20]Carl J. Friedrich, "International Politics Foreign Policy in Developed (Western) Systems," in R. Barry Farrell (ed.), *Approaches to Comparative and International Politics* (Evanston, Illinois: Northwestern University Press, 1966), pp. 97–98.

[21]Hans J. Morgenthau, "Common Sense and Theories of International Relations," *Journal of International Affairs*, No. 2 (1967), pp. 208–09.

[22]Hans J. Morgenthau, "The Intellectual and Political Functions of a Theory of International Relations," in Horace V. Harrison

(ed.), *The Role of Theory in International Relations* (Princeton: D. Van Nostrand Company, Inc., 1964), p. 117.

[23] Quincy Wright, *The Study of International Relations* (New York: Appleton-Century-Crofts, Inc., 1955), p. 32.

[24] Chadwick F. Alger, "International Relations: The Field," *International Encyclopedia of the Social Sciences* (New York: The Macmillan Company & The Free Press, 1968), Vol. 8, p. 67.

[25] Rosenau, "Pre-theories and Theories of Foreign Policy," p. 32.

[26] Oran R. Young, *A Systemic Approach to International Politics* (Princeton: Center of International Studies, 1968), p. 6.

[27] *Ibid.*, pp. 4, 5.

[28] Harold Sprout, "International Politics and the Scholar," *Princeton Alumni Weekly*, 59 (January 23, 1959), p. 15.

[29] Stanley H. Hoffman (ed.), *Contemporary Theory in International Relations* (Englewood Cliffs, New Jersey: Prentice-Hall, Inc., 1960), p. 40.

[30] James N. Rosenau (ed.), *International Politics and Foreign Policy: a Reader in Research and Theory* (New York: Free Press, 1961), p. 77.

[31] Andrew M. Scott, *The Functioning of the International Political System* (New York: The Macmillan Company, 1967), p. 8.

[32] Rudolph J. Rummel, "A Field Theory of Social Action With Application to Conflict Within Nations," *General Systems Yearbook*, 9 (1965), p. 184.

[33] Charles A. McClelland, "Systems Theory and Human Conflict," in Elton B. McNeil (ed.), *The Nature of Human Conflict* (Englewood Cliffs, New Jersey: Prentice-Hall, Inc., 1965), p. 271.

[34] Steven J. Brams, "Transaction Flows in the International System," *American Political Science Review*, 60 (December 1966), p. 880.

[35] M.B. Nicholson and P.A. Reynolds, "General Systems, the International System, and the Eastonian Analysis," *Political Studies*, 15 (February 1967), pp. 12–31, 29.

[36] Young, *A Systemic Approach to International Politics*, p. 6.

[37] J. David Singer, "Man and World Politics: The Psycho-Cultural Interface," *Journal of Social Issues*, 24 (No. 3, 1968), p. 130.

[38] Charles A. McClelland, "Field Theory and System Theory in International Politics," forthcoming, 1971.

[39] Karl W. Deutsch, "The Coming Crisis of Cross-National and International Research in the United States," *American Council of Learned Societies Newsletter*, 19 (April 1968), pp. 1–7.

[40] Kenneth W. Thompson, "The Study of International Politics: Survey of Trends and Developments," *Review of Politics*, 14 (October 1952) p. 443.

[41] *Ibid.*, p. 449.

[42] Deutsch, "The Coming Crisis of Cross-National and International Research in the United States," p. 7.

[43] The attention to relating power concepts with the newly-imported ideas can be seen in Charles A. McClelland, "Applications of General System Theory in International Relations," *Main Currents in Modern Thought*, 12 (November 1955), pp. 1 27–34.

[44] Hans J. Morgenthau, *Politics Among Nations: The Struggle for Power and Peace* (New York: Alfred A. Knopf, 1948).

[45] Morton A. Kaplan, *System and Process in International Politics* (New York: John Wiley & Sons, 1957).

[46] Kenneth E. Boulding, *Conflict and Defense: A General Theory* (New York: Harper & Row, Publishers, 1962).

[47] Harry Howe Ransom, "International Relations," *Journal of Politics*, 30 (May 1968), pp. 345–71, 355.

[48] Harold and Margaret Sprout, *Foundations of International Politics* (Princeton: D. Van Nostrand Company, Inc., 1962), p. 68.

[49] Sprout, "International Politics and the Scholar," pp. 14, 15.

[50] Richard C. Snyder, "Some Recent Trends in International Relations Theory and Research," in Austin Ranney (ed.), *Essays on the Behavioral Study of Politics* (Urbana: University of Illinois Press, 1962), pp. 103–71.

[51] James N. Rosenau, *Of Boundaries and Bridges: A Report On a Conference On the Interdependencies of National and International Political Systems* (Princeton: Center of International Studies, 1967).

[52] Bruce M. Russett, "A Macroscopic View of International Politics," *infra*.

[53] For an indication of the dimensions of the problem see Morton Gorden, "Burdens for the Designer of a Computer Simulation

of International Relations: The Case of TEMPER," in Davis B. Bobrow and Judah L. Schwartz (eds.), *Computers and the Policy-Making Community* (Englewood Cliffs, New Jersey: Prentice-Hall, 1968), pp. 22–45.

[54]For a research-oriented theory inquiry on this topic see Bruce M. Russett, "Components of an Operational Theory of International Alliance Formation," *Journal of Conflict Resolution,* 12 (September 1968), pp. 285–301.

[55]Rummel, "A Field Theory of Social Action . . . ," p. 185.

[56]See Rudolph J. Rummel, "The Dimensionality of Nations Project," in Richard L. Merritt and Stein Rokkan (eds.), *Comparing Nations: The Use of Quantitative Data in Cross-National Research* (New Haven: Yale University Press, 1966).

[57]Manus Midlarsky and Raymond Tanter. "Toward a Theory of Political Instability in Latin America," *Journal of Peace Research,* No. 3 (1967), pp. 209–27.

[58]Bruce M. Russett, *International Regions and the International System: A Study in Political Ecology* (Chicago: Rand McNally & Company, 1967).

[59]Bruce M. Russett, "A Macroscopic View of International Politics," *infra,* and Bruce M. Russett, "The Ecology of Future International Politics," *International Studies Quarterly,* 11 (March 1967), pp. 12–31. It is heartening to see the growth of interest and research in an obviously important area of inquiry after a long period when Harold and Margaret Sprout were the major advocates and innovators among a very small group of scholars interested in the environmental foundations of international relations. See Harold and Margaret Sprout, "Environmental Factors in the Study of International Politics," *Journal of Conflict Resolution,* 1 (December 1957), pp. 309–28 and Harold and Margaret Sprout, *An Ecological Paradigm for the Study of International Politics* (Princeton: Center of International Studies, 1968).

[60]Johan Galtung, "A Structural Theory of Aggression," *Journal of Peace Research,* No. 2 (1964), pp. 95–119.

[61]*Ibid.,* p. 95.

[62]Galtung, "On the Future of the International System," pp. 307–27.

[63]J.W. Burton, *Systems, States, Diplomacy and Rules* (Cambridge: Cambridge University Press, 1968).

[64]*Ibid.,* p. 8.

[65]*Ibid.,* p. 232.

[66]Anatol Rapoport, "Systems Analysis: General Systems Theory," *International Encyclopedia of the Social Sciences* (New York: The Macmillan Company & The Free Press, 1968), Vol. 15, p. 452.

RAYMOND TANTER

Explanation, Prediction and Forecasting in International Politics*

This essay provides a glimpse at the epistemological setting within which terms such as explanation and prediction operate, discusses some of the principal techniques for their use, illustrates their substantive applications in international politics with particular reference to the seminal ideas of Harold and Margaret Sprout and draws out some policy implications.

Epistemology

Epistemology or methodology considers the logical ground for knowledge (Kaplan, 1964, p. 20). Its practitioners are philosophers of science, some of whom conceive of philosophy as logical analysis, i.e., ". . . as a clarification of the language which we speak in everyday life" (Bergmann, 1954, p. 2; Ayer, 1946). The explication of terms is an important aspect of logical analysis. Such explication concerns the specification of meaning—giving defining characteristics to concepts—and illustrating their use. A further characteristic of logical analysis is the clarification of so-called "topic heading" terms, such as explanation and prediction in addition to substantive concepts such as power and influence. Such clarification often involves making distinctions as illustrated by the debate over the similarity or difference between explanation and prediction.

*Acknowledgements to the National Science Foundation for support, to Milton Hobbs, Charles McClelland and Robert Young for ideas, and to Hazel Markus and Shafica Snider for assistance.

Note and References for this selection will be found on pages 54–57.

The Sprouts take up the debate in an imaginative way suggesting that an explanation of an historical event, *x*, is an answer to the question: *"How was it possible for x to occur?"* They admit that although explanation and prediction have the same logical structure, there are "some practical differences. . . ." (Sprout and Sprout, 1961, p. 61). Scholars who consider the principal aim of science the production of predictive theory sometimes assume the logical congruence of explanation and prediction. Carl G. Hempel and Paul Oppenheim, for example, contend that:

It is this potential predictive force which gives scientific explanation its importance: only to the extent that we are able to explain empirical facts can we attain the major objective of scientific research, namely not merely to record the phenomena of our experience, but to learn from them, by basing upon them theoretical generalizations which enable us to anticipate new occurrences and to control, at least to some extent, the changes in our environment (Hempel, 1953, p. 323).

George Lundberg agrees with Hempel stating that ". . . the primary function of all science (is) to formulate the sequences that are observable in *any* phenomena in order to be able to predict their recurrence" (Lundberg, 1963, p. 66).

On the other hand, scholars who do not consider prediction to be a central aim generally distinguish it from explanation. Israel Scheffler, for instance, opposes Hempel's view of science. Scheffler argues that:

Unlike our concern with control in practical affairs, our concern in science is not directed particularly toward the future, but frequently involves employment of general principles in the effort to substantiate past events on the basis of later events . . . (Scheffler, 1963, p. 54).

Hempel's and Scheffler's positions raise questions about the purpose of knowledge and the contrast between two approaches in philosophy: logical analysis and the history of science. Recall Hempel's view that the primary aim of science is to produce predictive theory. There are two reasons for his emphasis on predictive theory: it is a good test of its validity and it allows one to anticipate and partly control one's environment. This view is more typical of logical analysts. Scheffler's position is more akin to historians of science. Indeed, his assessment may reflect more accurately what scientists actually do! That is, scientists may explain more than they predict. Logical analysis, however, is not as concerned with the history of science as it is with the clarification of the language and aims of scientific method. This distinction approximates the difference between the positivist philosophers of the Vienna Circle who emphasize logical analysis and the Oxford analysts who stress the history of science, especially from the perspective of "ordinary language" (cf. Bergmann, 1954, pp. 1ff).

Now to the logic of explanation and prediction. Consider the following schema:

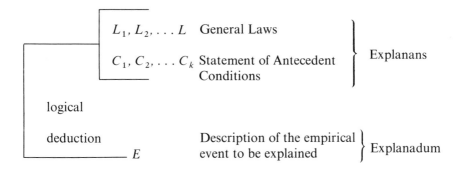

Hempel asserts this to be the basic pattern of scientific explanation. Moreover, if the explanation is sound, its constituents must satisfy logical and empirical conditions of adequacy. Logically, the explanadum or event to be explained must be a deductive consequence of the explanans—initial conditions and laws. Secondly, the explanans must have empirical content, e.g., it must be amenable to test by experience. Third, the explanans must contain at least one general law, which functions to derive the explanadum. Empirically, the sentences constituting the explanans must be true. This requirement is necessary because it is possible to deduce a true statement from false premises (Hempel, 1953, pp. 321–323).

Regarding prediction, moreover, Hempel contends that "... the same formal analysis, including the four necessary conditions applies to scientific prediction as well as to explanation. The difference between the two is of a pragmatic character. If E is given ... and a suitable set of statements $C_1, C_2 ..., C_k, L_1, L_2 ..., L_r$ is provided afterwards, we speak of an explanation of the phenomenon in question. If the latter statements are given and E is derived prior to the occurrence of the phenomenon it describes, we speak of a prediction. ... an explanation is not fully adequate unless its explanans, if taken account of in time, could have served as a basis for predicting the phenomenon under consideration" (Hempel and Oppenheim, 1953, pp. 322–323, footnote omitted).

How is this relevant to international politics? Consider the form of generalizations in international politics that might consitute the general laws for explanatory or predictive purposes. For example, the Sprouts suggest that "Democratic systems of government are less able than dictatorships to execute quick changes of policy" (Sprout and Sprout, 1961, p. 117). This appears to be a "tendency statement," e.g., about a statistical regularity rather than a universal general law. How does Hempel's scheme deal with such statements? He distinguishes between deductive arguments and statistical ones. Consider the following:

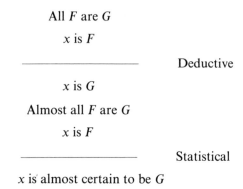

$$\text{All } F \text{ are } G$$
$$x \text{ is } F$$
$$\overline{} \qquad \text{Deductive}$$
$$x \text{ is } G$$

$$\text{Almost all } F \text{ are } G$$
$$x \text{ is } F$$
$$\overline{} \qquad \text{Statistical}$$
$$x \text{ is almost certain to be } G$$

In spite of an appearance of similarity, there is a fundamental difference between these two arguments. The deductive explanation accounts for the fact that x is G by showing that x has another attribute, F, which is uniformly associated with G by virtue of a general law. In the statistical explanation, however, x is *almost* certain to have G because it has a character, F, which accompanies G most of the time. The x could possess another feature which is almost always associated with non-G (cf. Hempel, 1962, pp. 125–126). Statistical statements thus do not guarantee that the event to be explained or predicted is a logical consequence of true statements. Statistical explanation or prediction is of extreme importance nevertheless. That is, it allows for knowledge of regularities to shed light on particular events or states of affairs in general. And as J.D. Singer asserts, "as our knowledge base expands and is increasingly integrated in the theoretical sense, the better our *predictions* will be . . ." (Singer, 1969, pp. 66–67).

Hempel's views on the congruence of explanation and prediction, whether deductive or statistical, are by no means the views of all philosophers of science. Ludwig Wittgenstein's *Tractatus* hints at the general problem saying that "We *cannot* infer the events of the future from those of the present" (Wittgenstein, 1961, p. 79). Michael Scriven, a recent critic, asserts that it is extraordinary to suppose ". . . that the contents of a prediction are logically identical to those of an explanation." He points out that a forecast is simply a description of an event given prior to its occurrence and identified as referring to a future time. He holds that explanation does more than describe because it uses laws. Predictions or forecasts do not require laws although they sometimes use them (Scriven, 1962, pp. 176–177).

How can one predict without laws? One way is to identify a pattern.

Indeed, Abraham Kaplan proposes that there are two modes of explanation: pattern and deductive. He suggests that laws play a part in pattern explanation but they are not necessary for prediction. The assumption that a pattern will continue, however, functions as does a law in Hempel's explanation and prediction logic. Furthermore, Kaplan claims that explanation without prediction and prediction without explanation are both more likely in the behavioral sciences than explanation *with* prediction (Kaplan, 1964, pp. 346–350; also cf. Singer, 1971, footnote 1; Meehan, 1965, pp. 36–37). But what does the fact of explanation with or without prediction have to do with whether they are logically congruent? It appears to depend on how one defines "logic." For example, May Brodbeck defends Hempel's position by using a more relaxed view of deduction. This perspective seems to include both cases that fit the various rules of logic as well as instances that concern inference from statistical regularity (Brodbeck, 1962, pp. 233 ff.).

What are some implications of this epistemological debate regarding explanation and prediction for the study of international politics? One consequence has to do with the possibility of a science in this area. Some who stress the logical dissimilarity of explanation and prediction sometimes hold to the "essential unpredictability of human nature" and thus to the impossibility of a scientific study of international politics. They overemphasize the contingencies of unique cases that they claim prevent predictions of immediate foreign policy decisions or long-term strategic forecasts (cf. Hula, 1963, p. 149).

These critics implicitly compare this alleged inability to predict human events to a very untypical branch of science—physics. Supposedly a physicist predicts any phenomena the scientist wishes. As Ernest Nagel rightly comments, however, ". . . we cannot predict with great accuracy where a fallen leaf will be carried by the wind in minutes because . . . we do not have the requisite knowledge of the relevant initial conditions. It is clear, therefore, that inability to forecast the indefinite future is not unique to the study of human affairs" (Nagel, 1963, p. 208; 1961, p. 461). In addition, perhaps physical events in a laboratory setting of tight experimental controls should not be compared with the social world of foreign policy decision-makers. Why not compare the physical world of earthquakes, mountain slides and epidemics to the social world of war, revolution and political integration? Natural scientists do not come off so well predicting to physical events in the world as they do in laboratory environments. Even where considerable control is present as in the aerospace industry, there is often a period where there is an inability to predict performance of new machines. Why should foreign policy scholars be expected to forecast the social future perfectly when natural scientists do not always succeed? Can we iron out our bugs with social experiments? Can we engineer performance in line with theoretical expectation? The possibility exists if we pay more attention to constructing predictive theory and using social engineering to revise such theory. (Also cf. Machlup, 1963, pp. 172–174.)

In short, the position of this essay is that there is not the kind of logical distinction between explanation and prediction that prevents a scientific study of international politics. The growth of a science needs empirical success as well as logical feasibility, however. The fact that there are ". . . some practical differences between explanation and prediction" (Sprout and Sprout, 1961, p. 66), moreover, suggests that appropriate techniques ought to be used given these differences.

In addition, the difficulty of developing explanatory and predictive theory should not lead to the acceptance of weak substitutes of the so-called functional variety.[2] Eugene Meehan, for example, considers the fact of explanation without prediction in political science to be a consequence of our inability to discover causal laws. Meehan gives up too quickly asserting that ". . . teleological explanations and functional explanations can fill a serious gap in our explanatory structure . . ." (Meehan, 1965, pp. 36, 37; 119–122). Hempel demonstrates that phenomena involving purposive behavior can be subsumed under deductive or statistical explanations. Motives and beliefs occur prior to action and can be classified among the antecedent conditions of a motivational explanation (Hempel, 1953, pp. 326–328). Such explanations can be used in conjunction with the following techniques.

Techniques

Methodology specifies criteria for concept formation, theory construction, explanation and prediction. For example, two criteria for accepting a theory are its explanatory and predictive powers. Hempel's deductive and statistical patterns of explanation are methods of inquiry. While methods are general across the sciences, techniques are not. Techniques vary with such things as the preferences of the scholar, his goals for the particular inquiry, and the nature of the problem at hand. The following discussion focuses primarily on techniques for anticipating the future.

A first step in presenting this brief overview of techniques is to specify more precisely the meanings of such terms as forecast, prediction and projection. As noted earlier, a forecast is a description of an event or a trend given prior to its occurrence and identified as referring to a future time. Moreover, a forecast is an estimate derived from a prediction, e.g., a predictive hypothesis and a projection of initial conditions. *A predictive hypothesis functions as does a general law in Hempel's explanation schema.* A hypothesis capable of yielding a forecast does not necessarily have a temporal relationship among the variables, though there can be a time lag between the independent and dependent variable. A projection of the initial conditions provides an estimate of the value of variables at some time given their values at an earlier time. (Also cf. T.J. Rubin, E.M. Krass, A.H.

Schainblatt, 1967, p. 53. Insofar as possible, the discussion below adheres to these distinctions and translates the work of others into this perspective.

Daniel Bell links his discussion of techniques for making forecasts with a keen awareness of the need for adequate explanation. He points out that a forecast without explanation is ". . . insight, experience or luck," and that "Only with adequate explanation . . . can one seek to control or transform a situation" (Bell, 1964, pp. 846, 847). Of the twelve modes that Bell identifies, consider a combination of two: trend forecasts and strategic analyses of alternative futures.

To forecast a trend, one requires the predictive hypothesis of a continuation of past trends and a projection of future values of the respective variables. Indeed, a simple technique is to assume no change over the period of the projection from the time of the last observation. A forecast on this basis is not very likely unless the change is very gradual, however. A second way is to derive a forecast by assuming the same direction and amount of change over the projection period as occurred over an equivalent period in the past up to the date from which the projection extends. For example, if the U.S. forces committed to South Vietnam increased by 50,000 between month $x - 10$ and x, it is forecast to increase by 50,000 between x and $x + 10$. This forecast recognizes a time trend; the particular rate of change almost reflects the negatively accelerating curve for U.S. troops committed to Vietnam 1965–1968. This curve assumes that the rate decreases through time with increases in the base such that the level of increase in each period remains the same.

A third way is to assume a constant rate of change over the projection period. Note that the third way yields changes of gradually increasing magnitudes as the size of the base changes through time. For example, if the rate of increase of U.S. forces committed to Vietnam is 10% per month, there is a higher magnitude of forces forecast each month as the base gets larger. A fourth way is to draw a curve onto a time series. A fifth way is to use a set of time series to forecast a dependent variable. For the single variable against time, derive the forecast by reading off the curve where it intersects the time axis at each forecast date. If there is very much fluctuation, however, this extrapolation technique is not too useful. Extrapolation fails to forecast structural changes that modify past trends.

This is where a theory is helpful. It might account for structural changes (also cf. D.F. Johnston, 1967, pp. 97, 98). For the single variable against a set of other time series, regression and simulation techniques are appropriate as suggested below under applications.

Forecasts based on projection of quantitative trends are a simple first step. These forecasts imply a predictive hypothesis and assume the possibility of a full explanation. Now combine the projection of trends with strategic analysis of political and military options. Whereas forecasts based on trends generally ignore the possibility of alternative paths to the future, strategic analysis explicitly addresses itself to these paths. Strategic analysis also provides for structural changes of past trends. The trend forecasts, in addition, provide the environmental opportunities and limitations within which strategic analysis maps out alternative futures and appraises various strategies (Also cf. Chapman, 1968; Knorr and Morgenstern, 1967 and 1968). Strategic analysis, moreover, does not produce forecasts of probable things to come; rather, ". . . it is an explication of possibilities," ". . . the construction of plausible profiles" (Bell, 1964, p. 866). A typical mode of expression for these profiles is the scenario or future history. While some authors feel constrained by limits from environmental forecasts, two leading exponents of scenarios assert that " 'Wild' speculation is also needed to provide an imaginative perspective within which alternate choices can acquire a deeper, if not necessarily more exact meaning" (Kahn, Weiner, 1968, p. 164).

As with trend forecasts, strategic analysis is dependent upon predictive hypotheses. Whereas the hypotheses for trend forecasts are quite narrow in scope, those for strategic analysis use the ideas from trend forecasts as well as some of the great notions from political thought. One body of ideas used in strategic analysis is that of pluralism. This is the belief that for the achievement of values like justice and welfare, society ought to be based on freedom of association and enterprise both nationally and internationally. John Chapman suggests that pluralists view politics from a *bargaining* perspective, e.g., as an endless series of negotiations. Compromise tactics thus are a part of the pluralist's operational code. On the other hand, Leninists see politics from an *optimizing* perspective because of their belief in the subordination of voluntary association and prevention of competition. These two alternative bodies of thought form bases for strategic analyses of alternative futures as the narrower hypotheses function for trend forecasts. In short, trend forecasts supplemented by strategic analyses provide an optimal combination when applied to world politics.

Applications

A principal thesis of the sections on Epistemology and Techniques is that explanation and prediction (forecasting) are similar in requiring hypotheses that function like general laws. Further, techniques such as trend forecasting and strategic analysis need predictive hypotheses in order to make forecasts and spell out alternatives. Indeed, as mentioned earlier, the trend forecasts provide an estimate of the environmental opportunities and constraints within which strategic analysis maps out and appraises alternative paths to futures. What are some theoretical bases for explaining and forecasting these futures in international politics? On what knowledge do theorists draw in applying trend forecasting and strategic analysis to world politics? One current theoretical orientation is "field theory."[3]

An early pioneer of the idea of field is Quincy Wright.[4] Writing in 1955, he points out ". . . that the study of international relations may be best approached through the concept of a field, constituted by the *relations* of the relevant *entities, forces, sentiments,* and *processes*". Wright hopes that the field concept will suggest lines of investigation for the development of theory in international relations (Wright, 1955, pp. 536–539). One of Wright's major assumptions is that national capability and value fields determine international behaviors. He specifies paths of influence relating six capability and six value factors to international behaviors such as war. Generally, he assumes that the capability and value factors have an independent effect on war. From Wright's diagram (1955, p. 564), one can infer 36 possibilities for the capability and value concepts to combine two at a time in determining war. Wright specifies only two direct value-capability combinations. Here is an illustration of his general idea:

In contrast to Wright, the Sprouts suggest that international behavior (foreign policy decision-making) is *not* a direct function of national capability. It is only through the psychological milieu that the capabilities have an effect on this behavior. There is a direct connection between the environmental capabilities and ultimate outcomes of international behavior; this illustration tries to reflect the Sprouts' view:

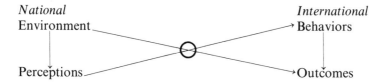

The diagram classifies environment and perceptions together under national attributes; outcomes and behaviors are under the international label. The Sprouts do suggest that factors external to the nation also are a part of the environment (Sprout and Sprout, 1961, p. 108). The general thrust of their work, though, indicates that the most important aspects of the environment are within the nation. Dina Zinnes, however, goes too far in interpreting the Sprouts' use of environment as referring solely to national attributes (Zinnes, 1971, in this volume). Zinnes' interpretation of the Sprout model contrasts with one of the original decision-making schemes pioneered by Richard Snyder and his associates. Here, the external setting consists of those factors outside the nation that decision-makers *perceive* to be important. The Snyder decision-making scheme is similar to the Sprout specification of relationships among environment, perceptions, behaviors and outcomes (cf. Snyder, Bruck, Sapin, 1961, pp. 189–190).

Building on the prior creations of Wright and the Sprouts, other theorists follow suit. For example, Rudolph Rummel and James Rosenau develop comparative foreign policy approaches. Drawing on Wright's work, Rummel constructs a "social field theory" of conflict behavior. He links a complex set of definitions, and tries to subsume system ideas under his field concept. Charles McClelland suggests that Rummel's attempt to subsume system under field is inadequate. McClelland, indeed, states that ". . . Rummel's definition of system is awkward and inadequate for the task of ordering the study of numerous recurring processes in international politics and that system definitions not tied so tightly to patterns of nation attributes are valid and useful" (McClelland, 1968b, p. 4; Rummel, 1965 a, b).

In contrast to Rummel, James Rosenau builds on the earlier effort of the Sprouts. Whereas Rummel does not admit international system attributes as determinants in his foreign policy scheme, Rosenau explicitly allows for the penetration of a polity by systemic forces. He proposes that foreign policy decision-making in small, less developed, totalitarian polities is a function of the following determinants in this order: systemic, idiosyncratic, role, societal and governmental. Rosenau's scheme allows for additive combinations *and* interaction effects among his variables; Rummel's approach only accommodates additive relations (cf. Rosenau, 1966, pp. 90, 91). While Rummel's approach fails to provide for perceptual variables, Rosenau explicitly refers to idiosyncratic attributes of particular foreign policy decision-makers. Rosenau, however, does not appear to take an explicit position on the relative paths of environment, perceptions, behaviors and outcomes as does the prior work of the Sprouts.

In short, the field approach accounts for much important theorizing in foreign policy analysis. This approach yields many testable hypotheses, some of which are useful for making forecasts. One body of ideas related to the field perspective is of particular relevance for forecasting. These are A.F.K. Organski's "power transition" notions. He suggests that over-all patterns of world politics are caused by sharp differences in social, economic and political modernization rates among and within nations. Differential modernization then causes shifts in the distribution of world power among states. It is these changes that underlie the wars and other conflicts of our era (Organski, 1968, p. viii).

Building on Organski's ideas, Robert North and Nazli Choucri hold that sharp changes in relative power capabilities lead to dissatisfaction and instability if the dominant power *perceives* itself as being challenged, overtaken or threatened by another power (North and Choucri, 1968, p. 126). In a subsequent paper they suggest that ". . . *differential* rates of population growth in combination with *differential* rates of technological growth contribute to conflict insofar as . . . societies and nations have *differential* . . . access to basic resources and general influences or control over their environments.

This state of affairs is dominated by the interplay of the actual and the perceptual—by 'reality' as it presents itself to national leaderships, and by leaders' perception . . . of the external environment" (Choucri and North, 1968, pp. 5–6). They link internal pressure, external competition, tension, and threat perception into a tentative model of international violence. An illustration of their ideas compares favorably with the Sprouts' perspective:

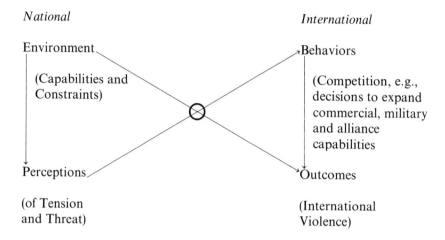

National

Environment
(Capabilities and Constraints)

Perceptions
(of Tension and Threat)

International

Behaviors
(Competition, e.g., decisions to expand commercial, military and alliance capabilities

Outcomes
(International Violence)

After a series of mathematical analyses (regression), they conclude that "under certain circumstances, the interactive effects of size and wealth (Environment) contribute directly to external conflict" (Outcome) (Choucri and North, 1968, p. 39). This suggests that there may be a direct link between the Environment and Outcomes as anticipated by the Sprouts.

An innovative use of mathematics allows Choucri and North to calculate alternative paths to past international violence. Through the use of path analysis, they explore a variety of routes linking the environment, perceptions, behaviors and outcomes assuming reciprocal as well as unidirectional causation. *Their utilization of path analysis introduces qualitative considerations and is equivalent to limited strategic analysis.* A primary difference, however, is that strategic analysis not only maps out alternative paths, but it appraises them from the viewpoint of policy preferences. Although Choucri and North explicitly prefer the option of peaceful competition to international violence, they do not systematically evaluate the costs and benefits of the two options as is done by some strategic analysts.

Another interesting aspect of the North/Choucri effort is its longitudinal design which facilitates forecasting. The other field research above, such as Rummel's and Rosenau's, is primarily cross-sectional. Building on the North/Choucri longitudinal work, Jeffrey Milstein and William Mitchell construct a computer simulation of the pre-World War I naval race between

Great Britain and Germany. A comparison of their "forecasts" with the actual results indicates a good fit (Milstein and Mitchell, 1968a, b).

These forecasts are primarily extrapolations of trends of *sets* of independent variables as they explain separate dependent variables. The forecasts assume a predictive hypothesis concerning a continuation of past trends. *In exercising the simulation, moreover, they bring to bear qualitative considerations.* Thus Milstein and Mitchell also combine trend forecasting via computer simulation with limited strategic analysis. They assert that "Policy-makers . . . might wish to determine probable outcomes of alternative strategies without actually implementing them on the battlefield or at the negotiating table. Simulation can be used to make forecasts of this kind so long as the relationships among the variables in the system remain constant." For example, they experimentally halt U.S. bombing of North Vietnam from January 1966 on and forecast that National Liberation Front defectors would increase, the NLF would decrease the killing and abduction of civilians and popular support for President Johnson would have been greater over-all (Milstein and Mitchell, 1968b), pp. 26–29).

Milstein and Mitchell also provide evidence regarding the links between the environment, perception, behavior and output. That is, their findings provide additional evidence for the idea that perceptions intervene between environmental changes and behaviors; moreover, the environment seems to be linked directly to outcomes. The work of North, Choucri, Milstein, and Mitchell on the whole appears to provide support for some of the Sprouts' ideas. In addition, their use of trend and limited strategic analysis affords estimates of environmental opportunities and constraints, alternative paths to futures and indications of some consequences of adopting different policy options. (See Zinnes' paper in this volume for further evidence regarding the Sprouts' ideas on environment, perception, behavior and output). [5]

Policy Implications and Conclusions

The attention to explanation and forecasting in academic circles lags behind the increasing interest given to the study of the future in policy circles. The U.S. National Intelligence Estimates are an example of institutionalized short-range forecasts. These estimates generally disregard the effects of changing environmental capabilities and constraints (Also cf. Friedlander, 1965, pp. 9, 10). The Long Range branch of the U.S. Joint Staff at the Pentagon produces forecasts in their Joint Long Range Strategic Study. These forecasts depend on projections of future environmental conditions. What is missing in both short and long range policy forecasting is an explicit awareness of the key role of perceptions intervening between environmental changes and decision-making behavior. As Singer notes, ". . . the behavior of . . . social systems may be *described*, and perhaps even *predicted* without recourse to such variables (perceptual); no satisfactory *explanation* is possible until we understand the psychological link which joins man to his sociopolitical environment, . . ." (Singer, 1968, p. 129). In addition to paying more attention to intervening perceptual processes, policy forecasts should close the gap between trend and strategic analysis.[6]

In summary, the similarity of explanation and prediction is sufficient to suggest the possibility of making valid forecasts. Forecasting is of value to the academy and to the polity. To the academy, it is a way of validating tentative models; to the polity, it provides information for policy planning. Academic and policy studies should take into account the insights of theorists such as the Sprouts regarding the intervening role of perceptions. Furthermore, planning should integrate information and knowledge from trend and strategic analysis.

Notes and References

[1] See how such assertions allow forecasts below under techniques.

[2] Singer also criticizes this premature explanation in his "Theorists and Empiricists . . ." paper in this volume.

[3] The authors that follow below differ in many ways from each other, but they share one field theory notion—foreign policy outputs are a function of national attributes.

[4] An alternative body of ideas is system "theory". In the late 1960s, more empirically based and policy relevant work falls under the field as opposed to the system label. The most significant theoretical payoff for explanation and forecasting, though, probably lies in the system ideas. The fresh system notions of Charles McClelland illustrate the great potential for this approach. His event interaction analysis is a breakthrough in measuring system performance. His working hypothesis regarding forecasting is deceptive in its simplicity and surprisingly fruitful in its application— the best estimate of the future performance between sets of nations is their record of prior interaction. That is, the short-range projection of a stream of events transpiring between countries need *not* refer to their national attributes at all (cf. McClelland, 1966; 1968 a, b, 1969).

[5] This review of the field approach literature is incomplete in many respects. Notably it omits the outstanding efforts begun by Karl Deutsch and continued by Bruce Russett and Hayward Alker. Illustrative of their contributions regarding trend analysis especially are the following: Russett, 1963, Russett, Alker, Deutsch and Lasswell, 1964; Russett, 1965; Russett, 1967; Taylor, 1968; Merritt and Rokkan, 1966; Deutsch, 1968; Alker, 1968; Alker and Puchala, 1968.

[6] The U.S. Office of the Assistant Secretary of Defense International Security Affairs supported policy studies at the RAND Corporation, Institute for Defense Analyses and the Hudson Institute. These studies contribute to strategic forecasting for the Defense Department Policy Planning Staff but do not adequately reflect the quantitative trend analysis going on principally in the universities. The Pentagon's Advanced Research Projects Agency supports research in the universities which acknowledges the key role of perceptions and is trying to close the gap between trend and strategic analyses. A next step is to translate the results of such inquiries into language understandable to those whose mission it is to produce forecasts. The U.S. State Department's Policy Planning Council does in-house studies of key problems utilizing a limited amount of strategic fore-

casting. Virtually no quantitative trend forecasting occurs at State except perhaps for some economic analysis. The Office of External Research and its parent Bureau of Intelligence and Research are in key positions to contract for such forecasting or to do it themselves were funds available.

Alker, Hayward R. Jr., "Causal Inference and Political Analysis," in C.L. Taylor (ed.), *Aggregate Data Analysis: Political and Social Indicators in Cross-National Research* (Paris: Mouton & Co., 1968), pp. 209–242.

Alker, Hayward, Jr., and Puchala, Donald, "Trends in Economic Partnership: The North Atlantic Area, 1928–1963," in J.D. Singer (ed.), *Quantitative International Politics* (New York: The Free Press, 1968), pp. 287–316.

Ayer, Alfred J., *Language, Truth and Logic* (New York: Dover Publications, Inc., 1946).

Bell, Daniel, "Twelve Modes of Prediction," *Daedalus*, 93, No. 3 (Summer 1964), pp. 845–880.

Bergmann, Gustav, *The Metaphysics of Logical Positivism* (New York: Longmans, Green and Co., 1954).

Brodbeck, May, "Explanation, Prediction, and 'Imperfect' Knowledge," in H. Feigl and G. Maxwell (eds.), *Minnesota Studies in the Philosophy of Science III: Scientific Explanation, Space, Time* (Minneapolis: University of Minnesota Press, 1962), pp. 231–272.

Chapman, John, "Strategic Forecasting and the Theory of World Power," (University of Pittsburgh, 1968). Mimeo.

Choucri, Nazli and North, Robert C., "The Determinants of International Violence," (Cambridge: Sixth North American Peace Research Conference November, 1968, mimeo), 44 pp.

Deutsch, Karl W., "Toward an Inventory of Basic Trends and Patterns in Comparative and International Politics," in C.L. Taylor (ed.), *Aggregate Data Analysis: Political and Social Indicators in Cross-National Research,* (Paris: Mouton & Co., 1968), pp. 29–46.

Friedlander, Saul, "Forecasting in International Relations," in B. de Jouvenel (ed.), *Futuribles II* (Geneva: Droz, 1965), pp. 1–112.

Hempel, Carl G., "Deductive-Nomological vs. Statistical Explanation," in H. Feigl and G. Maxwell (eds.), *Minnesota Studies in the Philosophy of Science III: Scientific Explanation, Space, Time* (Minneapolis: University of Minnesota Press, 1962), pp. 98–169.

Hempel, Carl G., and Oppenheim, Paul, "The Logic of Explanation," in H. Feigl and M. Brodbeck (eds.), *Readings in the Philosophy of Science* (New York: Appleton-Century-Crofts, Inc., 1953).

Holloman Air Force Base, Office of Research Analysis, *Long Range Forecasting* (New Mexico, July, 1968, mimeo).

Hula, Erich, "Comment," in M. Natanson (ed.), *Philosophy of the Social Sciences: A Reader* (New York: Random House, 1963), pp. 146–151.

Johnston, D.F., "Long Range Projections of Labor Force," United States Air Force, Office of Aerospace Research, *Long Range Forecasting Methodology* (A symposium at Alamogordo, New Mexico: October, 1967), pp. 97–128.

Kahn, Herman and Weiner, A.J., "Economics," in Foreign Policy Association (ed.), *Toward the Year 2000* (New York: Cowles Education Corp., 1968), pp. 148–164.

Kaplan, Abraham, *The Conduct of Inquiry: Methodology for Behavioral Science* (San Francisco: Chandler Publishing Co., 1964).

Knorr, K. and Morgenstern, O., "Designing Military Capabilities for Future Use: Politico-Military Inputs and Conjecture," (Washington, D.C.: Office of Naval Research, August 1967, mimeo).

———, "Political Conjecture in Military Planning," (Washington, D.C.: Office of Naval Research, March 1968, mimeo).

Lundberg, George A., "The Postulates of Science and Their Implications for Sociology," in M. Natanson (ed.), *Philosophy of the Social Sciences: A Reader* (New York: Random House, 1963), pp. 33–72.

McClelland, Charles A., "Field Theory and System Theory in International Politics" (University of Southern California, June 1968b mimeo), pp. 25.

———, "International Interaction Analysis in the Predictive Mode" (University of Southern California: January 1969 mimeo).

———, "Research Potentials and Rules in Predicting International Futures" (University of Southern California, Cal.: 1968a, mimeo).

——, *Theory and the International System* (New York: Macmillan, 1966).

Machlup, Fritz, "Are the Social Sciences Really Inferior?" in M. Natanson (ed.), *Philosophy of the Social Sciences: A Reader* (New York: Random House, 1963), pp. 158–180.

Meehan, Eugene J., *The Theory and Method of Political Analysis* (Homewood, Illinois: The Dorsey Press, 1965).

Merritt, Richard, and Rokkan, Stein, (eds.), *Comparing Nations* (New Haven: Yale University Press, 1966).

Milstein, Jeffrey S. and Mitchell, William C., "Dynamics of the Vietnam Conflict: A Quantitative Analysis and Predictive Computer Simulation," *Peace Research Society Papers*, X (1968a).

——, "Computer Simulation of International Processes: The Vietnam War and the Pre-World War I Naval Race" (Cambridge: Sixth North American Peace Research Conference, Peace Research Society (International), November 1968b, mimeo).

Nagel, Ernest, "Problems of Concept and Theory Formation in the Social Sciences," in M. Natanson (ed.), *Philosophy of the Social Sciences: A Reader* (New York: Random House, 1963), pp. 189–209.

——, *The Structure of Science,* (New York: Harcourt and Brace, 1961).

North, R.C., and Choucri, N., "Background Conditions to the Outbreak of the First World War," *Peace Research Society Papers* IX (1968), pp. 125–137.

Organski, A.F.K., *World Politics,* 2nd edition (New York: Knopf, 1968).

Rosenau, James N., "Pre-Theories and Theories of Foreign Policy," in R.B. Farrell (ed.), *Approaches to Comparative and International Politics* (Evanston: Northwestern University Press, 1966), pp. 52–71.

Rubin, Theodore J., Krass, E.M., and Schainblatt, A.H., *Projected International Patterns II* (Santa Barbara: General Electric Company–TEMPO, September, 1967).

Rummel, Rudolph, "A Field Theory of Social Action with Application to Conflict Within Nations," *General Systems Yearbook,* X (1965), pp. 183–211.

——, "A Social Field Theory of Foreign Conflict Behavior," *Peace Research Society Papers,* IV (1965), pp. 131–150.

Russett, Bruce, *Community and Contention* (Cambridge: MIT Press, 1968).

——, *International Regions and the International System* (Chicago: Rand McNally, 1967).

——, *Trends in World Politics* (New York: Macmillan, 1965).

Russett, Bruce; Alker, Hayward; Deutsch, Karl and Lasswell, Harold, *World Handbook of Political and Social Indicators* (New Haven: Yale University Press, 1964).

Scheffler, Israel, *The Anatomy of Inquiry* (New York: Alfred A. Knopf, 1963).

Scriven, Michael, "Explanations, Predictions and Laws," in H. Feigl and G. Maxwell (eds.), *Minnesota Studies in the Philosophy of Science III: Scientific Explanation, Space, Time* (Minneapolis: University of Minnesota Press, 1962), pp. 170–230.

Singer, J.D., "Man and World Politics: The Psycho-Cultural Interface," *Journal of Social Issues,* XXIV, No. 3 (1968), pp. 127–156.

——, "Modern International War: From Conjecture to Explanation," in A. Lepawsky, E. Buehrig, H. Lasswell (eds.), *Essays in Honor of Quincy Wright* (forthcoming, 1971).

——, "The Incompleat Theorist: Insight Without Evidence," in K. Knorr and J.N. Rosenau (eds.), *Contending Approaches to International Politics* (Princeton University Press, 1969b), pp. 62–86.

——, "Theorists and Empiricists: The Two-Culture Problem in International Politics," in this volume.

Snyder, R.C., Bruck, H.W. and Sapin, B., "The Decision-Making Approach to the Study of International Politics," in J.N. Rosenau (ed.), *International Politics and Foreign Policy: A Reader in Research and Theory* (Glencoe, Illinois: The Free Press of Glencoe, 1961), pp. 186–192.

Sprout, Harold and Margaret S., "Environmental Factors in the Study of International Politics," in J.N. Rosenau (ed.), *International Politics and Foreign Policy: A Reader in Research and Theory* (Glencoe, Illinois: The Free Press of Glencoe, Inc., 1961), pp. 106–119.

——, "Explanation and Prediction in International Politics," in J.N. Rosenau (ed.), *International Politics and Foreign*

Policy: A Reader in Research and Theory (Glencoe, Illinois: The Free Press of Glencoe, Inc., 1961), pp. 60–72.

Wittgenstein, Ludwig, *Tractatus Logico-Philosophicus* (New York: The Humanities Press, 1921).

Wright, Quincy, *The Study of International Relations* (New York: Appleton, 1955).

Zinnes, Dina, "Some Evidence Relevant to the Sprout Man-Milieu Hypothesis," in this volume, Chapter 13.

CHARLES F. HERMANN

Policy Classification: A Key to the Comparative Study of Foreign Policy[1]

I. Introduction

Harold and Margaret Sprout consistently have drawn a distinction between foreign policy analysis and capabilities analysis—the latter is a necessary perspective for the study of international politics.[2] In their own teaching and research they have sustained a balanced approach between the two areas of inquiry. The same cannot be said for the discipline as a whole. A decade ago Sondermann concluded that students of international politics devoted most of their energies to foreign policy analysis.[3] The pattern, however, has changed remarkably in the last ten years; now one can justly contend that—despite the evenhanded treatment of the Sprouts and a few others—it is the study of foreign policy that has become largely stagnant.

This contention does not imply a dearth of recent research on foreign policy. Continuation of old deficiencies, though, mars the contribution of such writing to any theoretical advance. A significant proportion of the literature remains devoted to the study of individual policy events, that is, to case studies. All too frequently this work substitutes a fascinating account of some historical occurrence for systematic insight into the general nature of foreign policy. Others have provided descriptive accounts of United States policy toward a given country or region. Still other analysts of foreign policy have joined those elsewhere in political science who "have focused their professional attention mainly on the processes by which public policies are made and have shown relatively little concern with their contents."[4] These studies seldom connect variations in processes with variations in policy. Critiques of policy makers and their policies together with prescriptions for the future comprise another part of the literature on foreign policy. Regardless of the particular kind of study, the overwhelming

Notes and References for this selection will be found on pages 76–79.

majority concern foreign policies of the United States. Whatever the merits of these foreign policy studies, they contribute little to the development of scientific theory. Those scholars in international and comparative politics committed to the development of networks of empirically reliable propositions appear to neglect foreign policy. Conversely, those scholars active in foreign policy display little interest in theory-building.

Advocates of the comparative study of foreign policy have stepped into this void. Although not entirely new, the current proponents possess two characteristics: (1) They seek to orient the study of foreign policy to all types of nation-states and other international actors; and (2) they wish to develop theories about foreign policy which yield empirically verifiable generalizations. In other words, the concept of comparison is used in two ways—to indicate the scope of inquiry is cross-national and to suggest the necessity for using the comparative method of analysis in scientific investigation. Some recent research of the Sprouts fits into the small group of comparative foreign policy studies. They employ the ecological perspective to consider the effects of environmental deterioration on resource allocations (i.e., policies) of different states.[5] One of their former students, James Rosenau, also appears in the vanguard of those exploring the comparative study of foreign policy. In a recent article, he asks whether such studies are a fad, a fantasy, or a field.[6] It is the contention of this chapter that the answer to his question, and in turn to the questions about the significance of the recent efforts by the Sprouts and others, depends upon our ability to establish meaningful ways of classifying different kinds of foreign policy.

More specifically, scholars who seek to include foreign policy as a central construct in theories about politics must offer theoretically relevant ways of identifying kinds of policies. One can conceive of various intriguing relationships incorporating foreign policy as a salient variable, for example, the effect of elements both internal and external to a nation on its policies, or the consequences of different kinds of policies on various actors in the international system including those that originated the action, or the effects of policy on the processes by which it is formed. The critical weakness lies in the absence of well defined foreign policy variables. In contrast to foreign policy analysts, students of comparative and international politics have taken some important first steps in their respective fields toward identifying interrelations of potential theoretical significance and toward the development of quantitative indicators. Presumably, hypotheses about foreign policy will draw upon the developments in these two fields. Consider as an example the scholar who wishes to look at the impact of domestic political factors on various kinds of foreign policy. He can find some leads in the comparative literature as to what political variables in what types of systems are considered salient. He may even be fortunate and find some data already collected on selected domestic variables for a substantial number of nations. But what about theoretically meaningful ways of classifying foreign policy or the existence of sets of data using such classifications? The scholar faces a high probability that he will find nothing; he must begin from scratch. In other words, students of comparative foreign policy may be able to borrow important concepts and even data banks for the variables to which types of policy might be related, but they must provide the ways of thinking about foreign policy.

To avoid subsequent disappointment the reader should be warned that no particular system will be advanced in these pages as a possible remedy to our need for better ways of identifying kinds of foreign policies. Instead more menial, but necessary, preliminary steps will be addressed including the types of classification presently in use, the requirements for a classificatory scheme, some alternative methods of constructing classifications, and the implications of research designs for foreign policy classifications.

II. *Current Types of Classification*

Various ways of describing and classifying foreign policies have been utilized for some time. Although a number of studies of foreign policy neglect the output or product almost completely, others have not. As a point of departure, we will review some of the most frequent kinds of classifications for distinguishing foreign policy as well as others that have been advanced, but less often used.

Geographical Region/Political Entities–One frequent means of classifying foreign policies rests upon the geographical region or political entities involved. Thus, we have studies of the policy of country X toward country Y or the policy of country X toward region Z.[7] The foreign target, or occasionally the initiating nation, provides the organizing concepts with little reference to the substance or content of policies. One common typology of foreign policies is formed by relating policies toward the countries in a region across several distinguishable periods of time. Analysts undoubtedly find geographical and political categories attractive for numerous reasons. They are fairly easy to identify; they can be assembled into an exhaustive set; they have been used by policy makers and journalists to the point that they seem a "concrete and natural" way of organizing the world. More abstract variations of these categories would permit analysis of classes of states rather than the individual cases. The classic distinction between authoritarian and democratic polities has provided the basis for some studies of foreign policy, but in these instances more attention has been devoted to differences in processes than policies. Abstract geographical categories, such as insular or landlocked, receive even less systematic use as ways of distinguishing types of policies.

Strategic or Grand Designs—Like the previous categories this system finds wide use by both policy makers and scholars. Unlike the prior classifications, the present one deals with the substance of policy conceived in terms of broad objectives or intentions of the initiating states. Each category in this scheme encompasses numerous discrete foreign policy actions. Examples include "containment," "Brezhnev Doctrine," "disengagement," "socialism in one country," and "maintenance of empire." Similar labels for strategic policies give rise to designations like "massive retaliation," "wars of liberation," and "flexible response." Despite the widespread use of such concepts for discussing foreign policy,[8] these descriptions often gain more currency as political symbols than as rigorous categories for distinguishing types of policy. They seldom constitute an inclusive set of categories that locate all foreign policies; instead one or two terms are used to characterize the dominant themes in a nation's foreign affairs.

Skills and Resources—Another means of identifying the substance rests upon the differentiation of capabilities and the specialization of tasks associated with various foreign policies. This procedure results in categories with modifiers like military, economic, cultural, propagandistic, diplomatic, and so on. In other words, the classification rests on the assumption that a military policy will involve individuals with special types of training and employing particular kinds of resources which will be different from those necessary for, say, an economic policy. Of course, many specific actions may fall into more than one category. Furthermore, distinctions become difficult at the boundaries of each grouping, but many analysts believe they can classify most policies into some set of these categories. Indeed, numerous books have been devoted to one or the other of these categories.[9]

Action Properties—In sharp contrast to the broad scope of categories in the preceding classifications, this method uses categories that codify discrete moves or actions made by actors within a nation. If one assumes that policy requires action, it becomes possible to group policies according to different types of acts. North and his colleagues select this method for the analysis of hostile and nonhostile acts.[10] One of the most extensive classifications of foreign policy according to action properties has been developed by McClelland whose scheme contains 63 categories grouped into major headings like yield, grant, deny, seize, and demand.[11] Some scholars regard the loss of the larger context which results from classifying discrete behaviors as a serious limitation on coding by action properties.

Relational Attributes—This system reduces the problem just described by establishing categories based on the connection between an action and some aspect of the context in which it occurs. Waltz uses the categories of continuity and innovation in comparing British and American policies; Deutsch and Pruitt both refer to the responsiveness of a state's policies; and Spiro proposes a classification using "procedural versus substantive" and "fundamental versus circumstantial" dimensions.[12] Other relational categories include duration, relative cost, reversals, and frequency of action. By definition, action cannot be codified by this scheme without reference to past action or some other aspect of the larger setting in which it occurs. Some of the recent explorations of program, planning, and budgeting applications to foreign policy involve the use of relational attribute classifications.

Basic Values—The great debate among many political scientists in the

1950s over idealism versus self-interest in foreign policy illustrates classification using basic values. The debate generated efforts to identify the value premises underlying a nation's foreign policy. This means of classification resembles both national goals (described below) and strategic or grand designs, but the distinctive feature consists of categories derived from standards as to how individuals or nations ought to behave. Policies can be grouped as approximating one of a set of principles. Efforts to discover operational codes in a state's policies offer an example as do Lasswell's set of eight fundamental values: power, respect, rectitude, affection, well-being, wealth, skill, and enlightenment.[13] With some modification the latter categories could be applied to foreign policies.

National Goals—Whereas values represent the principles that ought to guide a state's policies, goals constitute the ends toward which policy makers direct their nation. National goals represent abstract end-states applicable to a set of nations, but strategies or grand designs consist of programs that characterize a particular nation. Wolfers' familiar three-way division of national goals—national self-extension, national self-preservation, and national self-abnegation—illustrates a simple set of categories by which foreign policies might be classified.[14] The Sprouts are developing a more extensive system of categories based on national goals.[15]

Communication Characteristics—Categories in this classificatory system identify aspects of the process by which a policy is conveyed from the initiating nation to the recipients. The fundamental distinction between verbal and nonverbal behavior, or what Schelling describes as the difference between tacit and verbal communication,[16] illustrates the type of classification involved. The channels employed to convey a message offer another basis for grouping foreign policies according to their communication features. Presumably information theory could be applied to foreign policy to determine the number of "bits" of information contained in a particular foreign policy communication. Osgood identifies still another potential set of communication categories. Regardless of culture, he finds that all communicative behavior can be analyzed on three dimensions: evaluation (good/bad), potency (strong/weak), and activity (active/passive).[17] All these ways of classifying policy require the examination of extremely discrete foreign policy behaviors.

Pattern Variables—According to Parsons and Shils "a pattern variable is a dichotomy, one side of which must be chosen by an actor before the meaning of a situation is determinate for him, and thus before he can act with respect to that situation."[18] Parsons contends that there are five basic pattern variables:

> Affectivity—Affective neutrality
> Self-Orientation—Collective-orientation
> Universalism—Particularism
> Ascription—Achievement
> Specificity—Diffuseness

Although not necessarily adhering to the formulation of Parsons, others introduce the concept of pattern variables as a means of classifying policies.[19] Such schemes bear considerable resemblance to what we described as relational attributes. At least in Parsons' work, however, pattern variables purport to constitute an exhaustive set of interrelated dimensions. Relational attributes, on the other hand, are theoretically limitless and ad hoc.

Issue-Areas—Dahl suggests that the elites engaged in the governing process vary with the field of public policy involved.[20] Rosenau has developed this approach with respect to foreign policy. Policies are placed in the same or different categories depending on whether the actors and the processes used in formulating the policy are similar or different. He tentatively advances issue areas for policies dealing with status, territory, human resources, and nonhuman resources.[21] Though he does not refer to them as issue-areas, Huntington's distinction between strategy and structure rests upon two separate processes concerned with different types of issues in military affairs.[22]

Other means of classifying foreign policy could be added, but the present list reveals the diversity evident in current studies. In addition to the variety of classifications based on the substance of policy, our review identifies classifications derived from the initiating state or the recipients, the processes and principles for establishing policy, and the purposes toward which policy is directed. With this wide range of options for classifying foreign policy, why is the examination of kinds of foreign policy so retarded? To answer that question we must consider the requirements for classification schemes.

III. *Requirements for Classification*

Like most social scientists, students of foreign policy know that requirements for classification include mutually exclusive and exhaustive categories as well as they know the techniques for skirting these standards. A set of categories can be exhaustive by adding a catch-all, miscellaneous category labeled "other." Nonexclusive classifications can be excused because they are exploratory. The neglect or casual treatment of these standards seriously undermines the utility of some of the classification systems in current use. Beyond these logical standards, an examination of requirements depends on the purpose for which a classification is undertaken.

Many classifications act as organizational devices; they enable users to locate a single item or a kind of item from a much larger number with a minimum of search. The classification system of books in a library offers an example. The usual practice of arranging most bureaus or departments of a foreign ministry according to geographical areas most likely results from organizational considerations and long tradition.[23] Although bureaucratic politics may intrude upon the logic of the geographical arrangement, such divisions provide a mutually exclusive and exhaustive system for the delegation of tasks. Thus, the geographical origin of an incoming cable provides a foreign ministry's communication center with a relatively unambiguous indicator as to which bureau should be assigned the "action" copy.

The development of theory serves as another broad reason for establishing classifications. A classification entirely satisfactory for organizational requirements may have little to offer in the generation of theory. Studies of foreign policy, even those that profess some theoretical interest, have tended to rely on means of classifying policy that were originally introduced as organizational devices.

If we specify that our interest is in scientific theory, then further requirements for classification take form. Two of major significance are the identification of relationships and the establishment of measures. The categories in a classification system should relate to numerous other characteristics. Kaplan treats the categories of classification as concepts and then distinguishes between those classificatory concepts that identify many relationships (natural) and those that do not (artificial).

A significant concept so groups or divides its subject-matter that it can enter into many and important true propositions about the subject-matter other than those which state the classification itself. Traditionally, such a concept was said to identify a "natural" class rather than an "artificial" one. Its naturalness consists in this, that the attributes it chooses as the basis of classification are significantly related to the attributes conceptualized elsewhere in our thinking. Things are grouped together because they resemble one another. A natural grouping is one which allows the discovery of many more, and more important, resemblances than those originally recognized. Every classification serves some purpose or other (the class-term has a use): it is artificial when we cannot do more with it than we first intended. The purpose of scientific classification is to facilitate the fulfillment of any purpose whatever, to disclose the relationships that must be taken into account no matter what. [24]

One cannot insure in advance that the classification scheme he constructs will yield numerous valid relationships with other concepts or variables. Therefore the development of a scientific classification becomes an act of formulating hypotheses. "Any decision as to which classification scheme is best is itself a hypothesis, which subsequent investigations may lead us to reject." Copi continues this argument for treating scientific classifications as hypotheses by noting that the position applies to human events in social sciences: "Just as the biologist's classification scheme embodies his hypothesis as to which characteristics of living things are involved in a maximum number of causal laws, so the historian's decision to describe past events in terms of one rather than another set of properties embodies his hypothesis as to which properties are causally related to a maximum number of others." [25]

The treatment of classifications as hypotheses that must be tested with empirical data leads to the requirement that the categories be measurable. "There is a direct line of logical continuity from qualitative classification to the most rigorous forms of measurement, by way of intermediate devices of systematic ratings, ranking scales, multidimensional classifications, typologies, and simple quantitative indices. . . . An operation which must precede any sort of actual measurement is the formation of the categories in terms of which the objects under study are to be classified or measured."[26] The reference by Lazarsfeld and Barton to the formation of categories is not simply to any categories, but rather to those which can be reliably used by any investigator who applies the category definition. The categories must permit the classification of directly or indirectly observable phenomena in such a way that the same items always fall in the same categories regardless of when the sorting occurs or who does it. In short, the categories must be operational.

In concluding this section, it is well to reiterate the implications of the alternative uses of classifications. Such systems devised for organizational purposes may have little theoretical worth, and may even obstruct the development of theory. A simple organizing classification which distinguishes between living organisms that fly in air and those that swim in water would group bats with birds and whales with fish. Biologists employ another classification scheme which identifies both bats and whales as mammals because categories in the latter system appear to be associated with many more theoretically important characteristics. To return to the example of geographical bureaus in a foreign ministry, it may be that the organizational utility of such a scheme exceeds its value for theory-building. Of course, such an assertion contains little merit until we establish what phenomena we seek to explore. Geographical categories may be useful for theories relating climate, physical location, contiguity of borders, or spatial distance to foreign policy. But few political scientists who use such categories indicate much interest in theories dealing with these and related topics. And those that do, like the Sprouts, tend to employ more abstract geographical concepts.

IV. *Alternative Methods of Classification*[27]

Having examined requirements, let us consider some alternative methods for classification relevant to the construction of scientific theory. Presumably these alternatives apply to any content, but we shall discuss them with special reference to foreign policy.

Nominal Categories—This approach might be labeled the "shopping list" method of classification. The researcher recognizes a number of distinctive kinds of foreign policy which he believes to have theoretical interest. These types of policy become nominal categories in the classification system. Although he knows the categories create mutually exclusive classes, the researcher has no knowledge of whether, or how, the categories relate to one another. Moreover, he may be able to divide some or all of the categories into subcategories, but the subcategories cannot be ordered or scaled in any meaningful way. Most likely, the categories result from an inductive process during which the investigator observes a large number of policies and notes that they differ with respect to some properties.

Many classifications follow this approach. It appears satisfactory for organizational purposes and possesses an undeniable attraction for initial explorations in theory-building. For example, one might define one category for policies involving the use of military forces, another for policies that involve the exchange of nonmilitary goods, a third for meetings between diplomatic representatives, and so on. Presumably, the scholar has a hunch that such categories lead to important differences in the processes by which policies are formed, or in the impact on other countries, or some other set of variables. The categories need not be derived on the basis of accumulated observations. For instance, one might try to classify foreign policies using the zero-sum and nonzero-sum concepts from the theory of games.

Even if nominal categories are mutually exclusive, we often have no assurance that the concepts are parallel or deal with the same level of analysis. As an obvious example consider the following set of mixed-level categories: Europe, Asia, Africa, Latin America, the United States, and Canada. Mixed-level categories become a problem when drawing theoretical generalizations about the classificatory scheme. More important, the multiple-levels problem indicates a more basic difficulty with nominal categories; namely, we have extremely little information about the set of defining concepts. We do not know how the categories may be ordered with respect to one another. Often with ad hoc categories we do not know if they exhaust the universe of phenomena under examination unless we affix a remainder (i.e., "other") category. With more information another method of classification would likely be used. The minimal information requirement makes nominal categories good candidates for exploratory inquiries, but minimal information also makes theory development more difficult.

Single Dimension—This form of classification assumes that the researcher has information that will allow him to arrange all phenomena of interest at different values along a single variable. The underlying dimension provides the basis for sorting out the policies according to "more" or "less" or some other ordering principle. The variable may be discontinuous, in which case separate categories along the dimension will be discernible, or it may be continuous. A continuum might have categories or scale points for purposes of reference or organization, but they would be intrinsically no different from any other location on the dimension except for value.

Scholars concerned with the problems of war and peace have been among the users of the single-dimension method of classification. Some have classified foreign policies according to the amount of conflict or violence. In an effort to overcome the large number of policies clustered at or near the "no conflict" end of the dimension, other researchers have used the degree of positive or negative affect (hostility-friendship) expressed in foreign policy statements. Economics provides another potential dimension in the form of the cost of various policies in dollars or some other monetary unit.

The single-dimension approach offers a number of benefits, not the least of which is the statistical advantages offered by forms of measurement beyond nominal categories. By selection of a single dimension, the researcher can concentrate his attention on the careful refinement of his variable. With a given amount of time and resources, he should be able to collect more data than the investigator using numerous dimensions or categories. These assets must be weighed against certain liabilities. The problem of adequate coverage plagues several methods of classification, but it appears most severe in the single-dimension approach. Some policies may cluster at "zero" or in some neutral category; they may not even be classifiable on the dimension. (The users of nominal categories can usually surmount this problem by adding new categories.) The old problem of placing all one's eggs in the same basket may be an acute difficulty for this classificatory method given the present state of knowledge about foreign policy. Does the investigator have enough anecdotes, analogies, and speculative hunches about the possible theoretical significance to risk the investment in a single-variable formulation of foreign policy. Finally, the question must be raised as to whether the proposed dimension actually is unidimensional. Often the effort to generate broad, comprehensive dimensions leads to conceptualizations which constitute fragments of many different dimensions.

Multiple Dimensions—This approach is a logical extension of the single-dimension classification where policy is conceptualized in terms of more than one variable. If we establish dimensions that permit every policy to be located on each dimension, then we create the opportunity for various cross-classifications. The familiar four-fold table involving two dichotomized variables represents the simplest form. Cross-classification of continuous variables produces a multidimensional space in which each policy represents a point in that space located by its position on each dimension. Elsewhere the author illustrates such an arrangement using the dimensions of threat, decision time, and surprise.[28] Wright gives a dynamic quality to his multi-dimensional field theory by tracing the movement of nations across time with respect to a series of policies.[29]

Of course, cross-classification is possible only when the same policies are located on all dimensions. The problem of inclusiveness and adequate distribution across each variable exists with this method as with the single dimension. In addition, the danger of nonindependent dimensions exists. Although the concepts may seem different to the researcher, analysis may reveal them to be highly intercorrelated. Finally, too many dimensions can become unwieldy. Even though computer-assisted means of data analysis reduce the mechanical difficulty, the desire for parsimony in theoretical development remains.[30]

Progressive Differentiation[31]—A fourth approach to classification, which extends the nominal category method, remains unused in political science, but has played a significant role in biology. Beginning with a broad subject like organisms or foreign policy, one divides the subject into a small number of distinct classes such that each class has a characteristic shared by all members of that class but by none in any of the other classes. Each of the classes is then subdivided using the same procedure. The dividing or branching may continue through a number of levels. Students of biology and zoology will recall that biological classification begins with the broadest category, kingdom (plant and animal), and proceeds through the increasingly differentiated categories of phylum, class, order, family, genus, and species. For example, the animal kingdom divides into the subkingdoms of *Protozoa* (one-celled animals) and *Metazoa* (many-celled animals). One of the phyla into which *Metazoa* are classified is *Chordata* which in turn contains three subphyla including *Vertebrata*. The vertebrate subphylum contains seven classes one of which is *Mammalia* and so on. Strictly for purposes of illustration an extremely tentative classification of foreign policy using this same method appears in Figure 1. The broadest heading of policy is divided into positive, neutral, and negative classes. A negative policy is hostile to the intended recipient, whereas a positive policy is friendly and a neutral policy is indifferent to the recipient. Explanations of further divisions appear below the figure.

The striking characteristic of this method of classification is not the presence of subclasses, but rather the distinctiveness of a class from those in other branches together with its commonality with all broader classes in the same branch. Since each class yields a number of statements about its similarities and differences with other classes in the system, progressive differentiation represents a significant theoretical exercise in a way not required by other approaches. As one moves down in the classification, the homogeneity of class members increases and the scope of theoretical assertions decreases. This approach also deals explicitly with the level of analysis problem by identifying one or more characteristics which differentiate each level from those above it.

Of the four methods of classification this one requires the most information about the subject. The distinctive characteristic of each class, subclass, sub-subclass, and so on, demands extensive knowledge about the properties of all elements in the system. Students of foreign policy may discover that they can conceive of numerous first divisions of policy: verbal-physical, unilateral-bilateral-multilateral, procedural-substantive, and so on. Before going very far, however, they are likely to find the necessity for more information than is available or the creation of classes that apply equally to several divisions already formed. Further, the differentiation is limited by the use of nominal scales. Some attributes do not appear as sharply defined

FOREIGN POLICY

Figure 1. A classification of foreign policy using progressive differentiation. Note: Categories are defined in terms of the recognized intent of the initiating state and not the perceptions of the recipients or the actual effects as judged by independent observers. Items not defined below are discussed in the text. *Force*: obstructive actions actually initiated to block an objective of the recipient; *Obstruct*: measures to block an objective of the recipient; *Threat*: obstructive actions warning of conditional future measures to block an objective of the recipient; *Object*: measures indicating disapproval of the objectives or actions of the recipient; *Demonstrate*: objections accompanied by hostile physical behavior which is not obstructive; *Protest*: objections involving only verbal statements of disapproval; *Indifference*: measures involving no discernable effects to specific political actors; *Environment*: indifferent actions directed at non-human environment; *Nondirect*: indifferent actions addressed to unspecified or vaguely defined other actors; *Declaration*: measures deliberately designed neither to aid nor to hinder recipients; *Impartiality*: declarative actions designed to maintain neutrality by noninvolvement or by just compensation for any damages; *Procedure*: declarative actions considered to be devoid of any substance having a significant effect on other actor's objectives; *Approval*: measures affirming the desirability of other actor or its goals; *Respond*: approval actions elicited by sources external to the initiating state; *Volunteer*: approval actions that originate within the nation; *Support*: measures endorsing another actor or its objectives through the commitment of resources; *Exchange*: support actions involving trade in which resources are paid for in money or goods by the recipient; *Loan*: support actions for which the recipient promises to repay in the future; *Grant*: support actions for which no payment is required.

groups, but as a matter of degree or "shading." Although arbitrary categories can always be formed, this has the ironic effect of discarding information that would permit more sophisticated methods of measurement and analysis.

V. *Research Considerations Influencing Classification*

Even though we can describe the requirements and methods of classification, we cannot specify rules to insure that a particular system will assist in the development of theory. Other factors than the desire to be theoretically significant will influence the construction of a classification. This final section interprets these factors in a manner that promotes research preferred by the author. We must emphasize that other research interests will lead to alternative choices in building a classification system. Whatever his decision, the social scientist intending to classify foreign policy must confront these issues.

Definition of Foreign Policy—By now many readers must impatiently wonder in what sense this chapter uses the concept of foreign policy. It is an important concern because no agreement exists on the meaning of foreign policy. The serious investigator must stipulate his own definition which, in turn, influences his system of classification. A review of definitions indicates the range of choice and the issues involved.

Concerned specifically with an evaluation of United States' external activities, Seabury contends: "American foreign policies comprise the totality of purposes and commitments by which the United States, through its constitutionally designated authorities, seeks by means of influence, power, and sometimes violence to deal with foreign states and problems in the international environment."[32] Modelski offers a more generalized definition which reflects his interest in systems analysis. "Foreign policy is the system of activities evolved by communities for changing the behavior of other states and for adjusting their own activities to the international environment. Within it, two types of activities may be singled out for special attention: the inputs flowing into it, and the output it produces."[33] In contrast to Modelski's conception of foreign policy as the product of a system's processing of inputs, Furniss and Snyder emphasize the decision-makers within the system and their selective attention to the external setting.

Decision makers must be thought of as acting upon, and responding to, factors and conditions which exist outside themselves and the governmental organization of which they are a part. . . . Relevance will depend primarily on the attitudes and purposes of the decision makers, on the problems and threats which confront them —in short, on the perceptions and judgments of the decision makers. . . . To have a policy means that a course of action or set of rules or both have been selected with respect to some problem, contingency, or event which has occurred, is occurring, or is expected to occur.[34]

Finally, consider Rosenau who defines the unit of analysis in foreign policy as an undertaking. "An undertaking is conceived to be a course of action that duly constituted officials of a national society pursue in order to preserve or alter a situation in the international system in such a way that is consistent with a goal or goals decided upon by them or their predecessors."[35] A comparison of these definitions raises a number of critical questions.

1. Who are the foreign policy actors? Are they constitutionally designated authorities, the national community, the decision makers, or somebody else? Can other than the constituted officials, for example, elites, interest groups, etc., be actors in foreign policy?

2. What occasions foreign policy? Is it the fulfillment of a previous commitment, an input from the external system, the perception by decision makers of something that may or may not exist, or the achievement of national goals?

3. What is the unit of analysis? Is it an output of the system, an undertaking, or a course of action together with rules for action?

4. Who is to be affected by foreign policy? Can it be foreign states, other sectors of foreign societies, the international environment, a problem or situation, or the community initiating the policy? (The latter option is particularly intriguing. Is it appropriate to designate as foreign policies actions addressed to external actors but initiated solely for the purpose of changing all or part of the government's own society?)

5. Is foreign policy more than intended effect? Is foreign policy the effort to deal with selected recipients or the actual results, both intended and unintended, that follow from action?

Beyond these questions lies another—perhaps even more fundamental— inquiry. Is foreign policy actually different from other kinds of domestic or public policy? With increasing frequency scholars have given voice to their doubts about the validity of the long proclaimed distinction between domestic and foreign policy.[36]

Other than reaffirming the uniqueness of foreign policy in the tradition of past students of the subject, several positions are possible. One can argue that foreign policy differs from domestic policy, but not in the ways we previously believed. For example, the specific property that accounts for the difference between foreign and domestic policy may vary from nation to nation depending on the nature of the political system, the level of economic development, and so on. Alternatively, one can contend that the difference is one of degree and that fundamental changes in nations or the international system make the distinction greater or smaller. Of course, the null difference position asserts the commonality of the two kinds of policy. An advocate of this position might note that in the past the distinction between domestic and foreign policy resulted almost exclusively from observations of policy in the United States. As one enlarges the study of foreign policy beyond western, industrialized democracies, the exceptions to the observed differences multiply rapidly.

This chapter rests on the premise that it is theoretically useful to distinguish foreign from domestic policy. In part this decision is based on the apparent inadequacy of current classifications of other kinds of public policy for foreign affairs. In part it is based on the subject matter of interest to the author and which he seeks to understand. Several caveats with respect to this position must be noted. Certainly the similarity or difference between foreign and other policies depends upon the properties to be examined and the level of generality of the constructs. Furthermore, with reference to a given property or set of properties, the final determination of difference depends upon empirical investigation.

In response to the other questions about the nature of foreign policy, the following definition is offered: Foreign policy consists of those discrete official actions of the authoritative decision makers of a nation's government, or their agents, which are intended by the decision makers to influence the behavior of international actors external to their own polity. The recipient international actors are individuals acting on their own behalf or as decision makers or as agents for organizations (governmental or private) including the governments of other nations. Foreign policy results from the decision makers' perceptions of present or expected problems in the relationships between a nation and its international environment (both human and nonhuman) including the consequences of the initiating state's own prior actions.

This definition contains a number of implications for the five questions raised earlier. A bias toward the decision-making and problem-solving approaches appears throughout the definition. All actors are individuals although only the authoritative decision makers of a nation (the state) initiate foreign policies. Certainly actors other than states act directly in international affairs, but the contention is that their behavior should be sharply distinguished from state behavior. Although the perceived consequences of state behavior serve as feedback, the distinctions noted by the Sprouts are maintained as critical (see footnote 2); therefore, foreign policy actions concern the intended influence, not the actual effect. The choices in the definition reflect judgments (perhaps "hunches" would be less presumptuous) about theoretical significance and about the practical problems related to empirical research. Because this definition is proposed for a particular kind of research rather than as a reference point for all those who study foreign policy, we need not review it here point by point. Consideration of one feature, however, will illustrate the interplay between the definition of foreign policy and classification.

Policy as Discrete Actions—We contend research on foreign policy is needed that treats policy as an operational concept on which empirical data can be gathered for all nation-states. This means that the unit of analysis must be defined so that it can be reliably identified by any careful analyst and that it occurs with sufficient frequency to permit statistical analysis. Therefore, we want cross-national foreign policy data which are publically accessible for all nations. Moreover, the basic unit of analysis should be sufficiently limited so that we can construct a profile or distribution for each nation incorporating a period of time not much in access of one year. (More will be said about this point below.) These requirements suggest that initially our classification should deal with discrete foreign policy actions (e.g., the announcement of a trade agreement, an official state visit, or the breaking of diplomatic relations) rather than broader formulations frequently associated with the concept of policy (e.g., all actions designed to obtain a Middle East settlement, the various efforts to maintain a friendly regime in power, or the totality of measures to prevent the expansion of an undesired political system). In short, our definition of foreign policy should recognize the discrete action as the fundamental building block or unit of analysis.

A number of problems arise from the use of discrete foreign policy actions. An argument against this choice maintains that most meaning is lost by consideration of an isolated act separate from the context and sequence of events of which it is a part. Without doubt this argument contains substantial merit. Although some nuances may be lost, one would hope to assemble discrete acts into sequences or larger groupings (moving up in progressive differentiation classification, for example). It is easier to assemble discrete actions into alternative broader clusters than to decompose a larger unit of analysis; unless, of course, all the individual acts are separately recorded in the larger unit, in which case one actually is beginning with discrete actions.

Although the concept of action has received considerable attention,[37] it cannot be accepted as a primitive, undefined term. A practical aspect of this problem is the separation of acts or the level at which acts are defined. Does one count as a single action the entire Paris Peace talks on Vietnam or each individual session or each point at a given session? It will be necessary to construct guidelines based on some criteria of relevancy to cope with this difficulty. Possibilities include the exclusion of redundant acts involved in administering the same decision, or alternatively, the inclusion of acts only when they involve some redistribution of human or nonhuman resources between international actors.

In all likelihood the application of these or comparable criteria still will yield extremely large numbers of foreign policy actions. From the perspective of statistical analysis the quantity is desirable, but beyond some point the task of recording actions may become unmanageable. Systematic sampling procedures could be used to limit the problem. Sampling procedures also provide a means of coping with the overreporting of actions for some states. Most American sources of foreign policy report actions of the United States more completely than they do for other countries. In general, closed societies and less developed countries receive less attention regardless of the source. Use of supplemental regional sources and national newspapers may provide some assistance, particularly in establishing baselines for states underreported in more general materials. With baselines established, nations for which actions are less frequently reported in the basic sources can be oversampled. Not only types of nations, but also certain kinds of actions are underreported. We can speculate about the kinds of actions that appear less regularly in public sources—intelligence-gathering activities, sensitive political negotiations, and so on—but we cannot reliably ascertain their frequency of occurrence. This problem remains a significant one in constructing profiles of a nation's foreign policy actions.

Profiles of Foreign Policy Actions—The previous references to profiles or distributions of foreign policy actions introduce a basic purpose of the research envisioned in this chapter. The researcher records the frequency of occurrence of every kind of policy in the selected classification scheme using a systematic sample of all foreign policy actions initiated by a state in a given period of time. He forms additional profiles for the nation using different time periods. For example, he might construct frequency distributions for the Soviet Union at five-year intervals since the end of World War II—1945, 1950, 1955, 1960, 1965. Alternatively he might elect to examine profiles for consecutive years.[38] Similar profiles using the same classificatory scheme and time periods would be prepared for other states. With data collected and classified in this manner, the investigator could answer questions like the following:

1. What does the configuration or profile of a given state's foreign policy actions look like? For a given state and time period are some kinds of actions initiated far more frequently than others?

2. How does the profile of a given state vary through time? Does a given state's frequency distribution change gradually over a number of years or does it shift abruptly?

3. How do the profiles of different states compare? What states appear to have approximately equivalent kinds and distributions of foreign policy behaviors and which states contrast sharply with one another? What states experience parallel changes in their distributions?

4. What is the combined configuration of foreign policy actions for all states in the international system at a given time? Does this over-all pattern change across time? What is the profile for different blocs or alliances?

These are essentially descriptive questions. They provide the bases, however, for a major theoretical undertaking which begins with the inquiry "why"? Why do states *A, B,* and *C* experience frequent and sudden changes in their dominant kinds of foreign policy action? Why do seemingly dissimilar states *E, I,* and *Q* have similar patterns of foreign policy? Some may protest that this highly inductive approach to theory building is less likely to be successful than a formal mathematical model that establishes relationships between a small set of constructs from which one derives propositions that can be tested against reality. As a rejoinder one might observe that a descriptive phase—mapping the terrain of a subject area—provides a necessary first step through which almost every field of science has passed.

In addition one should note that the inductive-deductive choice reflects the skills and temperament of the investigator.[39]

The character of the proposed research contains implications for the method of classification to be used. Given the survey quality of the needed study, the single dimension approach offers a system with too narrow a focus. We want to canvas the range of actions not one particular kind or quality of action. The exploratory nature of the research invites the use of nominal categories. If we are dealing with a wide variety of seemingly unrelated substantive attributes of foreign policy action, that method may be the best we can do. However, given the restrictions on theory building with nominal categories, it seems desirable to hold the approach in reserve as a minimum fallback position. Its ordering properties and the possibilities for cross-classification and correlation give the multiple dimension approach certain advantages. Similarly the clear delimitation of levels and the accumulation of distinguishing characteristics in the progressive differentiation method have significant value in theory building. Should the needed information for progressive differentiation prove too difficult, it could be collapsed into a nominal categories approach. An initial strategy for the research discussed in this section might involve the use of several alternative classifications, each offsetting the weaknesses of the other. One classification might use multiple dimensions and another progressive differentiation.

The critical point remains that we now have no adequate classification of the kinds of foreign policy actions pursued by various states. Accordingly, we have not gathered data on policy actions. The development of such classificatory systems and the collection of data on policy remains an essential first step, not for the purpose of organizing the array of actions (viz., finding a "pigeon hole" for all possible actions), but for the construction of comparative theory about foreign policy. This step must be followed by the testing of relationships selected to investigate the hypotheses advanced as explanations for the profiles of foreign policy actions.

Notes and References

[1] In addition to the Sprouts, a number of individuals influenced the ideas expressed in this chapter. These include my former colleague, Harry Eckstein, the graduate students who participated in my seminar on the comparative study of foreign policy (particularly Norman Frohlich, Edward Morse, and Stephen Salmore), and my associates in the project on the politics of adaptation headed by James N. Rosenau. Upon completing this manuscript, I received a copy of David H. Blake's "The Identification of Foreign Policy Output: A Neglected But Necessary Task" (Midwest Political Science Association, Ann Arbor, Michigan, April 24–26, 1969). Although it came too late to be commented upon in the body of this chapter, Blake's paper constitutes an important companion to the present work.

[2] This distinction is a major, recurrent theme in their writing. See, for example, Harold and Margaret Sprout, *The Ecological Perspective on Human Affairs* (Princeton University Press, 1965), pp. 222–223, and their "Environmental Factors in the Study of International Politics," in James N. Rosenau (ed.), *International Politics and Foreign Policy* (New York: Free Press, revised edition 1969), pp. 41–56.

[3] Fred A. Sondermann, "The Linkage between Foreign Policy and International Politics," a paper presented at the Annual Meeting of the American Political Science Association in 1958 and reprinted in James N. Rosenau, (ed.), *International Politics and Foreign Policy* (New York: Free Press, 1961), pp. 8–17.

[4] Austin Ranney, "The Study of Policy Content: A Framework for Choice," in Austin Ranney (ed.), *Political Science and Public Policy* (Chicago: Markham, 1968), p. 3.

[5] See Harold and Margaret Sprout, *An Ecological Paradigm for the Study of International Politics* (Research Monograph No. 30, Princeton University, March, 1968); and their "The Dilemma of Rising Demands and Insufficient Resources," *World Politics,* XX (July 1968), pp. 660–693.

[6] James N. Rosenau, "Comparative Foreign Policy: Fad, Fantasy, or Field," *International Studies Quarterly,* XII (September 1968), pp. 296–329.

[7] An example of the country to country approach is Edwin O. Reischauer, *The United States and Japan* (Cambridge: Harvard University Press, 3rd edition 1965). The country to region approach is illustrated by John S. Badeau, *The American Approach to the Arab World* (New York: Harper and Row, 1968).

[8] For example, see John W. Spanier, *Amer-*

ican Foreign Policy Since World War II (New York: Praeger, 3rd edition 1968).

[9]From the hundreds of possible titles, a small sample illustrates the point. David A. Baldwin, *Foreign Aid and American Foreign Policy* (New York: Praeger, 1966); Frederick C. Barghoorn, *Soviet Foreign Propaganda* (Princeton: Princeton University Press, 1964); Phillip H. Coombs, *The Fourth Dimension of Foreign Policy: Educational and Cultural Affairs* (New York: Harper and Row, 1964); Raymond L. Garthoff, *Soviet Military Policy* (New York: Praeger, 1966); and E.A.J. Johnson (ed.), *The Dimension of Diplomacy* (Baltimore: Johns Hopkins Press, 1964).

[10]See Ole R. Holsti, Richard A. Brody, and Robert C. North, "Affect and Action in International Reaction Models," *Journal of Peace Research*, 3–4 (1964), pp. 170–190; and Ole R. Holsti, Robert C. North, and Richard A. Brody, "Perception and Action in the 1914 Crisis" in J. David Singer (ed.), *Quantitative International Politics* (New York: Free Press, 1968), pp. 123–158. Dina A. Zinnes has contributed some of the most advanced work in scaling the intensity of hostility. See her "The Expression and Perception of Hostility in Prewar Crisis: 1914" in J. David Singer (ed.), *Quantitative International Politics* (New York: Free Press, 1968), pp. 85–119. Rudolph J. Rummel treats conflict as an action property, but his unit depends upon the interaction of two or more parties and, therefore, has significant limitations as a foreign policy category. See his "The Relationship Between National Attributes and Foreign Conflict Behavior" in J. David Singer (ed.), *Quantitative International Politics* (New York: Free Press, 1968), pp. 187–214.

[11]Charles A. McClelland, "The Quantity and Variety of Events, 1948–1963" in J. David Singer (ed.), *Quantitative International Politics* (New York: Free Press, 1968), pp. 159–186; and Barbara Fitzsimmons, Gary Hoggard, Charles A. McClelland, Wayne Martin, and Robert Young, "World Event/Interaction Survey Handbook and Codebook," Department of International Relations, University of Southern California, January, 1969 (mimeo). For an independent effort to code a variety of action properties, see Erik V. Nordheim and Pamela B. Wilcox, *Major Events of the Nuclear Age,* ORNL-TM-1830, Oak Ridge National Laboratory, Oak Ridge, Tennessee, August, 1967.

[12]Kenneth N. Waltz, *Foreign Policy and Democratic Politics* (Boston: Little, Brown, 1967); Karl W. Deutsch and others, *Political Community and the North Atlantic Area* (Princeton: Princeton University Press, 1957); Dean G. Pruitt, "An Analysis of Responsiveness Between Nations," *Journal of Conflict Resolution,* VI (March 1962), pp. 5–18; Herbert J. Spiro, "Foreign Policy and Political Style," *The Annals of the American Academy of Political and Social Science,* 366 (July 1966), pp. 139–148.

[13]See Harold Lasswell and Abraham Kaplan, *Power and Society* (New Haven: Yale University Press, 1950).

[14]Arnold Wolfers, "The Pole of Power and the Pole of Indifference," *World Politics,* IV (October 1951), pp. 39–63.

[15]In a preliminary classification of goals, the Sprouts organized them under three broad headings: (1) promoting the national entity; (2) promoting subunits within the nation; and (3) promoting goals pertaining to areas or entities external to the nation. The Sprouts further reflection on national goals is in their forthcoming text, *Toward a Politics of the Planet Earth,* to be published by Van Nostrand Reinhold.

[16]Thomas C. Schelling, *The Strategy of Conflict* (Cambridge: Harvard University Press, 1960).

[17]Charles E. Osgood, George J. Suci, and Percy H. Tannenbaum, *The Measurement of Meaning* (Urbana: University of Illinois Press, 1957).

[18]Talcott Parsons and Edward Shils, *Toward A General Theory of Action* (New York: Harper and Row, 1962), p. 53.

[19]See, for example, Edward L. Morse, "A Comparative Approach to the Study of Foreign Policy," Department of Politics, Princeton University, October 1968 (mimeo); and Samuel Beer and Adam Ulam (eds.), *Patterns of Government* (New York: Random House, 2nd edition 1962).

[20]Robert A. Dahl, *Who Governs?* (New Haven: Yale University Press, 1961).

[21]James N. Rosenau, "Pre-theories and Theories of Foreign Policy" in R. Barry Farrell (ed.), *Approaches to Comparative*

and International Politics (Evanston: Northwestern University Press, 1966), pp. 27–92; and James N. Rosenau, "Foreign Policy as an Issue Area" in James N. Rosenau (ed.), *Domestic Sources of Foreign Policy* (New York: Free Press, 1967), pp. 11–50.

[22]Samuel P. Huntington, *The Common Defense* (New York: Columbia University Press, 1961), pp. 3–7.

[23]Although most foreign ministries have some functional sections—administration, legal services, and public-press relations—geographical divisions dominate the arrangement in most countries. The Soviet Union makes use of geographical bureaus in the Ministry of Foreign Affairs, but a more basic division occurs between sections handling affairs with communist party states as opposed to those dealing with non-party states. See Jan F. Triska and David D. Finley, *Soviet Foreign Policy* (New York: MacMillan, 1968), pp. 35–38.

[24]Abraham Kaplan, *The Conduct of Inquiry* (San Francisco: Chandler, 1964), pp. 50–51. The terms "natural" and "artificial" are frequently used in discussions of classifications, but they can be misleading if one assumes that "natural" refers to systems that have an existence in nature independent of the observer. See A. Broadfield, *The Philosophy of Classification* (London: Grafton, 1946).

[25]Irving M. Copi, *Introduction to Logic* (New York: Macmillan, 2nd edition 1961), pp. 409–411. With reference to social science, it might be preferable to refer to strongly related variables rather than causal laws.

[26]Paul F. Lazarsfeld and Allen H. Barton, "Qualitative Measurement in the Social Sciences: Classification, Typologies, and Indices" in Daniel Lerner and Harold D. Lasswell (eds.), *The Policy Sciences* (Stanford: Stanford University Press, 1951), p. 155.

[27]My thinking on this subject has been influenced considerably by Harry Eckstein. I have adapted one of his conceptions of alternate methods of classification; and although we might differ on the evaluations, I am indebted to him for aspects of the other three.

[28]Charles F. Hermann, "International Crisis as a Situational Variable" in James N.

Rosenau (ed.), *International Politics and Foreign Policy* (New York: Free Press, revised edition 1969), pp. 409–421.

[29]Quincy Wright, "The Form of a Discipline of International Relations" in James N. Rosenau (ed.), *International Politics and Foreign Policy* (New York: Free Press, revised edition 1969), pp. 442–460.

[30]Emphasis on parsimony, however, is not always justified. Other things being equal, a classificatory system with the fewest categories to cover the largest number of observations and relationships is to be desired over a classification with many categories. But in classification, as in theories, premature insistence on parsimony may substantially limit the utility of the system. Furthermore, "categorizing a given population into a few types or subtypes may reduce validity if the variance within single categories or types is thereby unduly increased." Edward A. Tiryokian, "Typologies," *International Encyclopedia of the Social Sciences,* 16 (New York: Macmillan-Free Press, 1968), p. 178.

[31]The term is Harry Eckstein's. In his graduate seminar on comparative politics, where he develops alternative methods of classification, Eckstein compares "progressive differentiation" with "progressive generalization." The latter method reverses the former by beginning with the smallest or most homogeneous class and by becoming more inclusive at each subsequent level. A somewhat similar discussion of classification as alternative processes of subdivision or accumulation appears in Baruch A. Brody, "Glossary of Logical Terms," *The Encyclopedia of Philosophy,* 5 (New York: Macmillan-Free Press, 1967), p. 60.

[32]Paul Seabury, *Power, Freedom and Diplomacy: The Foreign Policy of the United States* (New York: Random House-Vintage, 1965), p. 7.

[33]George Modelski, *A Theory of Foreign Policy* (New York: Praeger, 1962), pp. 6, 7.

[34]Edgar S. Furniss, Jr., and Richard C. Snyder, *An Introduction to American Foreign Policy* (New York: Rinehart, 1955), pp. 6, 28.

[35]James N. Rosenau, "Moral Fervor, Systematic Analysis and Scientific Consciousness in Foreign Policy Research" in Austin Ranney (ed.), *Political Science and Public*

Policy (Chicago: Markham, 1968), p. 222.

[36]See the opening paragraphs of Bernard C. Cohen's essay, "Foreign Policy," in the *International Encyclopedia of the Social Sciences,* 5 (New York: Macmillan-Free Press, 1968), p. 530. See also the various distinctions between domestic and foreign policy discussed in Chadwick F. Alger, "Comparison of Intranational and International Politics," *American Political Science Review,* 58 (June 1963), pp. 406–419.

[37]For explorations of the concept of action, see Talcott Parsons and Edward Shils, *Toward A General Theory of Action* (New York: Harper and Row, 1962), p. 53; Harold and Margaret Sprout, *The Ecological Perspective on Human Affairs* (Princeton: Princeton University Press, 1965), p. 23; and Richard C. Snyder, H.W. Bruck, and Burton Sapin (eds.), *Foreign Policy Decision Making* (New York: Free Press, 1962), p. 64.

[38]Of course, the selection and organization of the time units depends upon the research design. Most likely, time periods will be chosen to permit the investigation of some prior hypotheses about variables expected to affect the distribution of foreign policy actions. For example, time periods might be selected to determine the influence of changes in a country's regime, shifts in the level of international tension, or the configuration of the international system.

[39]A pair of barnyard analogies, which the author somewhat reluctantly attributes to a conversation with Harold Sprout, reminds us of the pitfalls present in excessive use of either approach. On the one hand, the excessive user of the inductive approach can be likened to the foolish farmer who piles manure higher and higher in the hopes that this action alone will cause a rose to spring forth. On the other hand, the excessive user of the deductive approach can be likened to the inefficient farmer who seeks to feed the sparrows by feeding the cows.

J. DAVID SINGER

Theorists and Empiricists: The Two-Culture Problem in International Politics

One possible way in which we can judge the progress of a newly emerging discipline is to look at the size of the gap between the "theorists" and the "empiricists." For all too long and in all too many of the social sciences, we have tended to accept—and perpetuate—the belief that certain scholars will do the theorizing and others will do the experimental or empirical work. In the field of international politics, however, we seem to be moving away from that unfortunate dichotomy. If a personal note be permitted, one of the more telling reasons for my eagerness to participate in this tribute to Harold and Margaret Sprout was precisely this factor: that someone like myself, generally identified as an enthusiastic empiricist (if not a data-obsessive!) could be invited to write on theory. Let me, therefore, take up the assigned task by first discussing some of the dangers, as I see them, of perpetuating the theorist-empiricist distinction.

The Two-culture Problem

In noting and popularizing the "two-culture problem," C. P. Snow (1961) has rendered a most important service to the academic as well as to the governmental community. He reminds us that the intellectual style of the humanist is, in certain critical aspects, very different from that of the scientist, and as any international politics scholar who has worked with foreign ministry people can readily attest, the observation is all too accurate. But this is by no means the only setting in which the two-culture problem rears its head. Even *within* the various scientific communities we

Notes and References for this selection will be found on pages 94–95.

find these manifestations: between micro- and macro-economists, between psychologically and ecologically oriented sociologists, between organicists and reductionists in many disciplines, and, of course, between empiricists and theorists.

In my view, all of these cleavages should be viewed with concern. We cannot, of course, get along without specialization, but specialization within a coherent context is one thing, and specialization in an isolated vacuum is quite another. Whether it is the biochemist who cares not a whit for physiology, or the psychiatrist who remains utterly innocent of social structure, the result is likely to be a diminution in relevance, a lower frequency of meshing discoveries, and a serious retardation in their cumulative effects. The same would seem to hold true for the cleavage between the empiricist and the theorizer, even though it is natural that some of us will make more of a contribution by working nearer to one end or the other of this particular continuum, due to our interests, skills, and research facilities. Theorizing without data, or data-gathering without theory, can be—and have been—equally sterile.

Let me expand on this assertion. In the first place, this division of labor and attention permits, and encourages, the theorizer to stay in his armchair, neither aware of past data-based findings nor concerned with the way in which his concepts might be measured in the referent world or how his propositions might be put to the inductive test. Further, and all too often, those who style themselves "theorists" have only the foggiest understanding of epistemology, and therefore lack sufficient appreciation of the total range of processes by which knowledge is acquired and codified.

At the other extreme (and we are dealing here, of course, with "ideal" types) are the barefooted empiricists. These are the scholars who, for a variety of reasons, of which some are all too compelling, turn their back on the "big picture." Skeptical about the endless verbiage which presumes to be theory, and baffled by those who merely substitute mathematical notations for polysyllabic meanderings, this sort of researcher longs to pin something down. Even if it is nothing more than a single variable time series, a cross-sectional bivariate correlation, or worse yet, a "simulation" in which naive and transient students act out their folkloristic notions of diplomatic behavior, they are at least generating data. What these data lack in validity, they make up in reliability; and whatever they may lack in relevance, they are at least tangible bits of knowledge.

In my judgment, neither of these orientations by itself is likely to carry us very far, and even though the two streams do periodically converge, it happens much too infrequently and only in the most inefficient manner. As I suggested above, there are now some encouraging signs of a trend toward greater interdependence and interpenetration between theorizing and empiricism, and the purpose of the following remarks is to suggest one possible orientation toward a more fruitful synthesis of the two types of activity. In short, the view taken here is not only that atheoretical empiricism is much less useful in the acquisition of knowledge than empiricism guided by theoretical concerns, but that successful theorizing depends heavily on rigorous empiricism, along with the two other strategies discussed below.

The Acquisition and Codification of Knowledge

Having enumerated some of the problems which arise out of a scholarly division into the theoretical and the empirical subcultures, let me now move on to matters of a more affirmative nature. But rather than turn directly to what I mean by theory and the purposes for which we need theory, let me come at the matter in a more oblique fashion, via a discussion of the major purpose of all scientific research: the acquisition and codification of knowledge. As I see it, every bit of knowledge comes in the form of an assertion or proposition about the past or the future, expressed via some sort of shared symbols, be they verbal, numerical, pictorial, or any other form. If the proposition cannot be so expressed, and therefore communicated within the relevant scientific community, it is not knowledge; thus, until a hunch or insight is so expressed, it falls short of our definition. Every bit of knowledge may, in turn, be evaluated and appraised in terms of two distinct sets of considerations. One set concerns its *substantive relevance* for the problem at hand, and that is not only a function of the individual scholar's concern, but lies beyond my assignment here. The other set concerns the *epistemological quality* of our knowledge, and is largely indifferent to its empirical referents and its substantive relevance. These qualitative aspects of our knowledge, regardless of empirical domain and substantive relevance, may be evaluated in terms of three criteria: accuracy, generality, and explanatory power.

The Qualitative Dimensions of Knowledge—The first, or *accuracy,* dimension reflects the degree of confidence which the relevant scientific community can have in any assertion at a given point in time; this confidence level is basically a function of the empirical or logical evidence in support of the proposition, but may vary appreciably across time and among different scholars and schools of thought at any particular moment. The second dimension reflects the *generality* of the proposition, ranging from a single fact assertion (of any degree of accuracy) to an assertion embracing a great many phenomena of a given class. The third reflects the *explanatory* dimension: whether a proposition is merely descriptive, essentially correlational, or largely explanatory. With these three dimensions, we can construct some sort of epistemological profile of any proposition or set of propositions, and can classify and compare a given body of knowledge with another, or with itself over time. It should, however, be emphasized that all three dimensions are rough and merely ordinal in nature, and that there is no intention of treating them as interval or ratio scales, at least for the present. Let me now discuss each in turn.

As to the confidence level, or *accuracy* dimension, little needs to be added. For any proposition to qualify under the knowledge rubric it must be stated in relatively operational terms in order that it may, in principle, be verified by empirical or by logical procedures. Now some will contend that there is no need for an accuracy *continuum;* taking the binary view, they will hold that every proposition either is or is not true. This may be a defensible position for a logician or a mathematician, but would be disastrous for a social scientist. While many social science propositions are indeed either true or false, the great bulk of them are probabilistic. As our propositions are refined and as our knowledge increases, more of the latter will be classified as either true or false, but many will always be probabilistic. This prediction is based on two considerations: (a) the more we know, the more difficult and complex and rephrased propositions we will put up as hypotheses to be tested, and we will *never* be able to examine all of them; (b) as our knowledge increases and is extended to more of the people whose behavior we try to describe in lawful terms, the more likely these people are to act in ways which confound the generalizations.[1]

Thus I take the position here that determinism is not a property of the conditions and events which we study, but of the propositions we employ in that study, and that the amount of our knowledge which is deterministic will, and should, increase with the development of our discipline; nevertheless a formidable sector will always remain probabilistic. That is, many generalizations which embrace future as well as past conditions and events will have only a certain probability of being correct and only some fraction (however large) of the subsumed cases will turn out to match the hypothesized pattern. For propositions embracing only the past, we will of course come closer to deterministic knowledge, but it is quite safe to assert that our curiosity will always outrun our knowledge, leaving the inevitable residue of uncertainty.

Now, some will argue with my position regarding knowledge of the *future*, and assert that we have here a contradiction in terms. Following what seems to be a corollary of the binary view of knowledge, they will assert that there is no such thing as knowledge of the future; until the events or conditions have actually unfolded, we may make *predictions* about them, but can have no *knowledge* about them. This position strikes me as untenable because it presumes too great a discontinuity between past and future, and ignores the constancy—and therefore the predictability—of many classes of social, as well as biological and physical phenomena.

To sum up, very little about international politics is now really "known" in the simple and certain sense, and much will always remain uncertain and partially unknown; *all* propositions (regarding either past or future) are, therefore, best treated in a tentative fashion. And, short of joining the agnostics, the most efficient way of expressing that tentativeness and uncertainty is to assign some measure of confidence or probability to any given proposition.

A final point in regard to our confidence or accuracy dimension is, unhappily, in order. Many social scientists, after laborious and careful research on a given set of propositions will have their findings greeted with the comment that "we knew *that* all along" and "it doesn't take *x* years and *y* dollars to tell me that!" While recognizing that some research *is* trivial in the sense that it tends to confirm the obvious, three counter-retorts are called for. First, it is almost impossible to have too much evidence in support of a given proposition; the more often we replicate a study, either in the same or different spatial-temporal domains, the greater the confidence level we can assign to the proposition and the more refined and precise we can make it. There are so many ways in which social research, scientific as well as pre-scientific, can go wrong that it behooves us to remain ever skeptical, with rigorous and independent replication serving as one of our most effective measures against spurious or ill-founded conclusions. Second, while it may be well-known that there is a positive or negative relationship between two particular variables, only correlational analysis will tell us the *magnitude* of the relationship. And when we move from bivariate to multivariate models, of course, it is mandatory that we find out not only the *direction* of the inter-variable relationships, but the extent to which each contributes to the outcome. Third, if I may be permitted a rhetorical question, how is it that so many scholars "know" so many things in one passage or chapter and so many contrary things in other passages? Those who have high confidence in those assertions which have yet to be tested against evidence might do well to "tease" such propositions out of the pre-scientific literature and then check them against one another. They will, I suspect, be amazed not only by the difficulty of finding explicit propositions, but by the inconsistencies between and among them once they *are* found. So much, then, for "knowledge" which is unconfirmed, incomplete, or based on the prestige of the source rather than the credibility of the evidence. [2]

Turning now to the *generality* continuum, the end at which we choose to work is one possible indicator of whether we are likely to contribute to a science of international politics or not. That is, if we dedicate ourselves to the making—or even the testing—of single fact assertions, the chances are that even while adding these high confidence, but small-sized, bits of knowledge to the storehouse, they will not be sufficiently comparable to permit us to combine them. Unless we make our assertions in fairly general form, and test all of the subsumed cases (or a representative sample of them) simultaneously, we end up with non-cumulative *facts* rather than empirical generalizations; such facts may be interesting and illustrative, but the knowledge they convey is scientifically negligible. One of the most dramatic differences between what are called the ideographic and the nomothetic types of study is seen in what might be called the N/V ratio: (Deutsch, Singer, and Smith, 1965). [3] The historian, the psychiatrist, and the traditional political scientist will usually take a single case at a time ($N = 1$) and then try to describe, analyze, and even explain the case in terms of a large (even exhaustive) number of variables ($V = \pm \infty$). The scientist, on the other hand, realizing that generalization is the *sine qua non* for cumulative knowledge, and that he cannot possibly handle all relevant variables at once, defines a class of cases (N is considerably more than 1, with a practical minimum for statistical purposes seldom under 20) and decides which variables he will examine in which order, until he has discovered which combination of them best accounts for the distribution of observed outcomes within that class of cases.

Looking at the *descriptive-explanatory* continuum, we have the most elusive of the three qualitative attributes of any piece of knowledge. Scholars generally agree on the criteria for establishing the accuracy and the generality of a proposition, but explanation has remained a major source of contention. Without getting too deep into the epistemological quagmire, then, let me assert that there are three discernible sectors along this particular dimension. At the low end are mere *descriptive* statements; without description, science cannot exist, but description is not enough. Such propositions may describe a single event or condition, or an entire class of events or conditions, may deal with the past or the future, and may embrace from one to many variables by which these phenomena are described. In the middle sector are bivariate and multivariate *correlational* propositions. Such statements assert the extent to which any two or more phenomena have been observed to co-vary, or might be expected to do so, within a given spatial-temporal domain. These assertions of statistical association gradually shade over, in turn, into the third, or *explanatory*, sector of this axis. What differentiates descriptions, correlations, and explanations from one another is their epistemological complexity and their scientific aspirations; the familiar distinction between correlation and causation is what differentiates the latter two sectors. But just as increasingly complex descriptions shade over into correlations, so do increasingly complex correlations shade over into explanations.[4]

In sum, what is proposed here is the notion that we can evaluate and compare bits of knowledge in terms of their epistemological profile and that the most significant dimensions of any such profile are those of accuracy, generality, and explanation.

Where Do We Go for Knowledge?—Having suggested three major criteria by which our knowledge might be appraised, let me turn now to some possible sources of those propositions which constitute scientific knowledge. Again, the number is three. The first and most obvious source is direct *observation* of, or more likely, inductive inference from, the referent world. A second source of knowledge is that of *deduction,* in which our descriptive, correlational, or explanatory knowledge is deductively inferred from some larger body of theory. At certain stages in the growth of a scientific discipline, deduction is the most efficient and reliable route to knowledge, but when almost no theory worthy of the name is available, a major share of the burden must be carried either by induction (as noted above) or by *analogy,* to which we turn first.

If we bear in mind that all knowledge of any generality must be based on empirical referents which are not exactly identical, but only similar enough to fall into the same class of phenomena, this proposed reliance on analogy will not seem too outrageous. Suppose, for example, that we want to test the proposition that foreign policy decision-makers experience a contraction in the number of options they perceive, as the time pressure on them increases. The most reasonable setting within which to put the hypothesis to the test would be that of the actual decisional setting, in a representative sample of governments, over a period sufficiently long to embrace a range of time pressures from leisurely to crisis. But that would only permit us to generalize about the contemporary setting. To achieve greater generality, we might try to reconstruct the decision processes and the associated perceptions for earlier, historical periods, thereby providing settings which may be only partially similar to the contemporary one, and which may turn out to be quite *dis*similar in fact.

Given the lack of complete identity among the decisional settings across time and space, how much worse off would we be if we studied the effects of this time pressure variable in the decision making of such other organizations as business firms, labor unions, other types of governmental agencies, political parties, or universities? Or, perhaps in the small-group laboratories where the sociologists and social psychologists address themselves to precisely this sort of question? Or perhaps, in a simulated decision-making session in which the experimental subjects are instructed to act *as if* they were foreign policy officials? Would all of these offer as useful a source of knowledge as the referent world itself? Clearly not, but in science we must always make tradeoffs between what is desirable and what is possible, and it may well be, furthermore, that there is indeed a *general* social law which applies to all collective decision-making on certain classes of problems under such conditions. My view, then, is that in the absence of access to the contemporary governmental setting, or in the event that we do not have the resources required for researching the historical past and content analyzing the relevant documents, we might well be satisfied with the knowledge based on examination of these analogous settings.[5]

Not all of the alternatives are equally attractive, however. First of all, there may already exist a fair amount of research on the problem in these *non*-foreign policy settings, or in the experimental laboratory, in which case it would be uneconomical to set up a new field study. Perhaps least satisfactory would be the all-man or man-machine simulation, in which some experimental controls are almost inevitably weak and in which the confounding effects of transitory role-playing could be severely misleading[6]

Consideration of these alternative sources leads to a closely related issue, bearing on the inductive road to knowledge. One of the more debilitating notions found among educated people is that science is something done in laboratories, and that if you cannot put the relevant materials into a test tube, under a microscope, or in a centrifuge, you cannot do scientific research. Admittedly, it is much easier to do laboratory research, but systematic observation and analysis is quite possible in a variety of other settings as well. As I see it, there are three basic types of experiment, depending upon the setting in which they are carried out. First, there is the familiar *laboratory* experiment, in which similar observations may be carried out over and over, modifying various conditions as necessary. Most laboratory experiments (be they crucial or routine) permit a high degree of manipulability of variables and are therefore known as controlled experiments. The controlled laboratory experiment need not be confined to cells or particles, however; much of the best work in individual and social psychology is also carried out in laboratories.

However, since the laboratory experiment often lacks in "realism" what it gains in controllability, social scientists often engage in *field*, or natural, experiments. Here, they go into a more or less natural social setting, and at the appropriate time, and under pre-designated conditions, wait for or inject some new element or set of conditions. One might, for example, persuade a foreign ministry to change the decision-making procedures in several of its bureaus or offices in order to help the researcher ascertain whether, under the revised procedures, more suggestions came from junior staff than under the normal procedures. In astronomy, a science which has made impressive strides based heavily on field experiments, the researcher waits, for example, until three planets are in a certain spatial relationship to one another in order to ascertain whether that configuration produces the hypothesized shift in the orbit of a fourth planet. He cannot control the movement of his objects of analysis, but he has nevertheless achieved a controlled experiment of sorts. The same may be said for the meteorologist or the oceanographer.

Finally, and in my judgment most important for us, there is the ex post facto, *historical,* experiment. Here, the researcher can neither control the way things developed in the past nor wait for the desired configuration of conditions, but he can nevertheless conduct a moderately controlled experiment. What he tries to do is ascertain whether, in the past, certain sequences of events followed as he hypothesizes. If his observational procedures are sufficiently imaginative, he can locate and measure a wide variety of historical traces, and if his analyses are sufficiently rigorous he can do almost as well as either the field or laboratory experimenter. Despite what the purists tell us, I find absolutely nothing wrong with an experiment in which the outcome (in the narrative sense) is already known to the investigator. The major purpose of operational procedures, after all, is to minimize or eliminate those pre-investigation biases which make traditional research so unproductive of generalized, high confidence knowledge, and so ephemeral in its scientific effects.

Having discussed the qualitative dimensions of knowledge, and analogy and induction as two of the sources to which we might turn in its pursuit, let me now try to relate knowledge to theory, and then move on to some of the difficulties which seem to plague us these days as we seek to develop coherent theory in international politics.

Theory and Knowledge

In my judgment, the word "theory" is one of the most casually used ones in the scholarly and lay lexicon, and I would therefore like to propose a more restrictive use of the term before its currency is further debased. One way of doing this is to differentiate between it and other forms of knowledge —or hunch—with which theory is often confused. Once that risky chore is out of the way, I can move on to the ways in which theory and knowledge are or might be related, as well as the uses to which theory may be put.

Taxonomies, Models, and Theories—In the process of ordering and codifying our knowledge, whatever its quality or its source, we make use of several conceptual tools. One of these is the *taxonomy*, which is nothing more than a delineation and ordering of the variables which describe one's empirical domain, along with the way in which the key variables are operationalized. The sort of taxonomy we use will not only reflect the state of our knowledge and our predictions as to which factors will turn out to be most critical in accounting for certain classes of outcomes, but will also exercise a profound effect on the kinds of new knowledge we generate and the kinds of theories that will emerge. Despite the frequent, and often justified, charge that taxonomy building is seldom more than "packing one's bags for a trip that never starts," I would contend that the nature of our taxonomies in the social sciences is largely to blame for the appalling state of our theory, and will therefore return to this shortly.

As we go beyond mere specification and measurement of our variables, and begin to postulate the causal or correlative relationships among them, we move from a taxonomy to a *model* or paradigm. While mathematicians, and those who work closely with the language and notation of that discipline, may prefer to define model more stringently, or to equate it with theory, we must recognize that we often use, and badly need, some sort of conceptual scheme which lies somewhere between a taxonomy and a theory. For that role, when our knowledge is insufficient in accuracy, generality, or explanatory power, it seems appropriate to use the notion of model or (since they are often used interchangeably) paradigm.

When a model has been sufficiently refined, partially tested against existing knowledge, and assigned a fairly explanatory mission, it begins to look more and more like a *theory*. Thus, theory is defined here as a fairly large (but unspecified) amount of descriptive, correlational, and explanatory knowledge which has been assembled into a logical and coherent whole. The propositions which constitute this whole must meet two other conditions: (a) they must be completely consistent and compatible with one another, and (b) some of the central ones must have been put to the empirical test and found to be quite accurate; the exact number will depend on the advanced or retarded state of the discipline, with the threshold rising as the discipline develops. Theories may and do vary in their usefulness and value, according to their generality, their accuracy, and their explanatory power, but if their component parts do not satisfy certain minimal requirements of logic and of empirical testability, they should not be called theories. They may be called theoretical formulations, or frameworks, or conceptual schemes, or perhaps models, but not theories.

Likewise, I would not apply the label of theory to a bivariate, or even a multivariate correlation, whether that correlation be hunch or hypothesis, speculative or confirmed. At the minimum, a theory must attempt to *explain* some particular *class of outcomes,* and not merely deal with one set of variables that do, or might, correlate with such outcomes. For example, propositions to the effect that a specified age range and occupational role will usually tell us whether a man belongs to one political party or another, or that nations withdraw from war when their fatalities exceed some fixed per cent of the population, may constitute correlational knowledge, and may be essential *components* of a theory, but are not themselves theories. The predictor variables may account for a large percentage of the variance in these outcomes, but the statements do not explain or attempt to explain in anything like a complete sense. They do not describe the way in which a *variety of phenomena combine and interact in a given sequence to produce the outcome in question.* Note, then, that just as descriptive knowledge eventually shades into explanatory knowledge by virtue of increasing completeness and generality, all knowledge eventually shades into theory by virtue of increasing coherence. Theory may be grand or modest, depending upon how many classes of phenomena it attempts to embrace and to explain, and how large a spatial-temporal domain it covers, but there remains a very large sector of scientific knowledge which falls short of this august status.

We must recognize, however, that the standards we apply to distinguish knowledge in general from theory must inevitably be a function of the state of the discipline. When the discipline has produced few taxonomies that are coherent and operational, very few observed correlations, and little data on the basis of which we can go from description to correlation to explanation, our criteria must of necessity remain modest and reasonable. Conversely, any attempt at theory-building which pays no attention to the relevant data and correlations which are already at hand is laboring under a self-imposed handicap and is less likely to be useful than an attempt which is self-consciously committed to both the codification of existing knowledge and the acquisition of future knowledge.

Some Uses of Theory—What is a theory good for, and why is it so highly valued an objective? In the view taken here, a theory has two major functions. First, it offers the most systematic and parsimonious means of codifying what we *already* know. If a theory is good, it brings together the more powerful concepts and insights and the more relevant knowledge that has been generated via induction, analogy, and deduction. Second, and equally critical, it provides the foundation from which we can move in the acquisition and codification of *future* knowledge. In sum, a good theory provides *an intersection between what we already know* (with some degree of confidence) and *that which we seek to know*. With it, we can describe, predict, and explain in a more reliable and economical way than without it, and identify the more promising questions and research strategies. Without it, or with a poor one, our descriptions are likely to be erroneous or misleading, our predictions are less likely to be accurate, and our explanations become either a maze of confusion or a conglomeration of plausible folklore.

Some Pitfalls on the Road to Theory

Most contemporary scholars will have little to quarrel with in what has been said so far in this paper, even though some would disagree with certain of the emphases and formulations. Let me now shift, however briefly, to a number of more controversial observations, and try to indicate some of the pitfalls and wrong turns we have made, or are likely to make, in developing theories of international politics. All of us have our pet pre-occupations and concerns in this regard, and the three which follow strike me as particularly relevant at this stage in the development of our discipline.

Normative Theory?—From both a scientific and an ethical point of view, one of the more dangerous pitfalls confronting us is the likelihood that we will accept the distinction which several other disciplines make between *empirical* and *normative* theory. This distinction, in my view, is not only confusing, but pernicious. First of all, every social science theory has normative implications; anything that helps to describe, explain and predict social phenomena may also be used to influence or control such phenomena. The purposes to which such knowledge may be put, and the ways in which it may be applied are brimming with ethical and normative implications; thus, *all* theory is, to some extent, normative.

Secondly, in making the distinction, we somehow imply that we need not apply the same criteria to normative problems as we do to empirical description and explanation—that scientific method is for the world as it *is* (or was), but not as it might be or *should* be. To put it another way, the distinction suggests that we must be rigorous and disciplined when addressing ourselves to things that can no longer be changed, but that we can be quite casual and poetic, or merely hortatory, when addressing ourselves to things that still remain partly within our control. I think this is a dangerous joke, and the double standard which it reflects has contributed mightily to the ethical shambles and human suffering which marks much of man's social history.

I realize, of course, that this is not the only implication which flows from the normative-empirical distinction, and that in game "theory," for example, it is convenient to distinguish between the strategies which are allegedly dictated by the logic of the expected values in a payoff matrix and those which are actually followed by experimental subjects. But I see no need to confer the status of theory on a purely deductive paradigm. Likewise, one hears of "positive" economics as opposed to "normative" economics. And even in political science we find the literature—and most academic departments—making a sharp intellectual and organizational distinction between the two via the use of "theory" when we speak of ethical concerns and the history of ideas, and not when we deal with knowledge about the substantive fields of the discipline.

Truthfulness and Usefulness—Another possible pitfall, from my point of view, concerns the question as to whether a theory needs to be true, or merely useful. Because a number of physical science theories which were not "true" turned out to be useful in guiding empirical research or in generating new hypotheses, many social scientists have leaped to the conclusion that our theories need not be, in even the crudest sense, isomorphic with the referent world to which they allegedly apply. Using such precedents as the frictionless inclined plane, the pure vacuum, or the perfect elliptical path, social scientists have confused the modest discrepancy between the ideal types and the referent world of physical science with the absence of *any* need for veridicality in their own formulations. It is one thing, it seems to me, to build a model or a theory which *abstracts* from and simplifies the referent world, and quite another to construct a scheme which is not—and cannot be—laid alongside and compared to the results of systematic empirical observation.

It does not, of course, follow that a theory which *is* highly representational will necessarily turn out to be scientifically useful. Such isomorphism may well be a necessary condition, but it is far from a sufficient one. That is, even while satisfying this requirement, it may be relatively unproductive for a variety of other reasons. It may focus on variables which have a minimum of explanatory power, or which are relevant only under very restricted conditions of time and place; or it may lead away from—rather than toward—that crucial experiment which might "wrap up" a given set of issues and open up a whole new set of critical and researchable problems.

Premature Explanation—Of the several traps into which we might fall, perhaps the most likely and most menacing one is that of premature explanation. What makes this pitfall most alarming is that it is the one toward which our most rigorous and creative scholars seem particularly drawn. What are some of the markers along this path of good intentions?

First, a good many modern researchers in international politics seem to be embracing, consciously or otherwise, the teleological models found in the work of Parsons, Bales and Shils (1953), Easton (1965), and Deutsch (1963) for example. Under the rubric of "systems analysis" and similar labels, we develop taxonomies and models which *assume* that which remains to be *ascertained*. The essential theme in these models is that individuals behave "in order to" accomplish one or another specific goal, or worse yet, that the international system and its various sub-systems have certain attributes which exist "in order that" the system survive or carry out some particular "function." Apparently coming out of the "structural-functional" models of social anthropology (Radcliffe-Brown, 1952), via the "systems of action" orientation, these formulations ask us to believe that political man is a purposive and goal-seeking animal, that he creates and modifies social systems largely in order to help in the realization of such goals, and that these systems also pursue rationally selected goals. As an assumption, this *may* be well founded (although I strongly doubt it), but to assert or imply the accuracy of the idea is extremely premature. In our haste to develop explanatory theories, I fear that we have embedded into our taxonomies and models a major inarticulate premise which is more prudently treated as an open empirical question.

Second, and closely related, is the range of constructs we employ when dealing with individual and collective behavior. One finds little effort to develop relatively theory-free taxonomies here, but rather a host of constructs which not only *describe* certain classes of behavior, but allegedly *explain* them at the same time. That is, instead of recognizing that a major preoccupation of social science research is to discover the causes and the consequences of different classes of individual and collective behavior, our behavioral constructs tend to assume that which remains to be demonstrated. Consider, for example, these oft-used concepts: task-fulfilling, pattern-maintaining, integrative, cooperative, loving, ego-gratifying, defensive, aggressive, information-seeking, supportive.[7] In each of these cases, there is nothing neutral about the behavioral descriptor; it is almost invariably explanatory. That is, rather than separate classes of behavior from those factors which lead to such behavior, or those consequences which flow from it, our constructs all too often try not only to *describe,* but to *account for,* many classes of action.

Third, all too many of the models in current fashion carry with them the implication that behavior occurs in either an environmental vacuum, or in a largely impotent environment. Thus, even as we insist (when speaking in policy-relevant terms) that foreign policy decision-makers enjoy little latitude in the behavioral alternatives facing them, our taxonomies and paradigms are often bereft of any relevant ecological variables. Of course, they take cognizance of other actors in the system, and appreciate that incompatibilities of goals and interests may constrain the actor whose behavior is under scrutiny, but how often do they specify the physical, structural, and cultural attributes of the systemic setting itself? By tending to ignore such variables, we attribute an inordinate degree of autonomy to our units of analysis, and once again assume the accuracy of implied propositions which have yet to be demonstrated. That is, in our eagerness to explain behavioral and interactional patterns, we often leap-frog the essentially descriptive phase of research in which we might identify a number of ecological variables and ascertain their potency in helping, along with other behavioral variables, to account for the behavior with which we are, at a given moment, concerned.[8] And until we have systematically described both the behavioral regularities *and* the conditions which are statistically associated with them, any claims to explanation must be characterized as unwarranted and premature.

Summary

The theme of this paper is fairly simple. Starting with the argument that empiricism is too important a factor in theory building to be separated from the latter enterprise, I move on to urge that good theory represents the intersection between the knowledge which we have and the knowledge we seek to acquire. To qualify as good theory, our knowledge must be in the form of propositions which are operational and consistent, and must satisfy certain criteria of accuracy, generality, and explanatory power. As critical as the latter criterion is, the taxonomies and models which undergird our theoretical attempts often lead us astray in their tendency to bypass systematic description and move on to very premature efforts at explanation.

As suggested in the discussion of normative versus empirical "theory," our problem is to make a clear discrimination between speculation and exhortation on the one hand and scientific theory on the other, even while paying close attention to the normative implications and consequences of whatever theoretical knowledge we generate. If civilization commits suicide in the next several decades (as seems all too possible) it is likely to be as much due to the ignorance of the few as to the avarice of the many, and while there is little that our discipline can do about the latter, we may be able to markedly reduce the former. The most promising route, in my judgment, is to begin taking theory much more seriously. And by that I mean paying as much attention to evidence as to speculation in the construction of taxonomies, models, and theories.

Notes and References

[1] I should emphasize that these exceptions need not be thought of as scientific nuisances, to be eliminated as quickly as possible so that we can pile up an increasing number of lawful propositions. Deviant cases, idiosyncratic behavior, and counter-examples constitute much of the stuff of science, and in addition to being fascinating in their own right, can often lead us to important new insights.

[2] In a classic review of Stouffer's *American Soldier*, Lazarsfeld (1949) begins by summarizing a number of propositions which are so obvious as to be dismissed as trivial: better educated men show more neurotic symptoms during training, Southerners withstand tropical climate better than Northerners, white soldiers are more eager for promotion than Negroes, and so forth. He then summarized the evidence showing that each of them was completely wrong.

[3] Most statisticians, whose notational criteria continue to elude me, use K (rather than V) to represent the number of variables in a model as well as several other concepts.

[4] An alternative formulation might be to differentiate among three types of knowledge: existential-factual, correlational, and explanatory.

[5] In fact, all general knowledge rests ultimately upon analogies, since no two phenomena are ever identical in *every* respect. We immediately recognize, and assail, an analogy between inter-person and inter-nation events, but often fail to note many evident, but equally risky, ones.

[6] The all-machine, or computer, simulation is of course another story. When built around referent world inputs, it provides a powerful vehicle for testing a wide range of alternative models, and it may eventually approximate our major goal, i.e., a mathematical theory which is also machine-readable. On the weaknesses of role-playing simulation as a research device, see Singer (1965).

[7] For the sake of brevity, only the adjectival forms are used, and the many possible antonyms are omitted.

[8] Those to whom this volume is dedicated have, of course, made a major contribution to an understanding of this problem, and represent an unfortunately small minority of international politics scholars; see Sprout and Sprout (1965 and 1968). Taking some of the classical notions of geopolitics and combining them with a great deal of modern social science, they have brought considerable clarity to the relationship between hehavior and the setting within which it occurs.

Deutsch, Karl W., *The Nerves of Government* (New York: Free Press, 1963).

Deutsch, Karl W., J. David Singer, and Keith Smith, "The Organizing Efficiency of Theories: The N/V Ratio as a Crude Rank Order Measure," *American Behavioral Scientist* 9/2 (October 1965), pp. 30–33.

Easton, David, *Systems Analysis of Political Life* (New York: Wiley, 1965).

Lazarsfeld, Paul, "The American Soldier— An Expository Review," *Public Opinion Quarterly* 13 (1949), 337–404.

Parsons, T., R.F. Bales, and E.A. Shils, *Working Papers on the Theory of Action* (Glencoe, Illinois: Free Press of Glencoe, 1953).

Radcliffe-Brown, A.R., *Structure and Function in Primitive Society* (New York: Macmillan, 1952).

Singer, J. David, "Data-Making in International Relations," *Behavioral Science,* 10/1 (January 1965), pp. 68–80.

Snow, C.P., *Science and Government* (Cambridge, Mass.: Harvard University Press, 1961).

Sprout, Harold and Margaret Sprout, *The Ecological Perspective in Human Affairs* (Princeton, N.J.: Princeton University Press, 1965).

Sprout, Harold and Margaret Sprout, *An Ecological Paradigm for the Study of International Politics* (Princeton, N.J.: Center of International Studies, March 1968).

MORTON A. KAPLAN

Freedom in History and International Politics

Harold and Margaret Sprout have been long concerned with problems of man-milieu relations and environmental possibilism. Thses subject matters involve a host of problems concerned with interpretation of the environment and power of choice that are vital to the study of international relations. That their scope of importance extends even further is evidenced by the fact that political science generally and more specifically political theory and political philosophy must cope with issues arising in these areas. When, for instance, President Kennedy faced the Cuban missile crisis, he undoubtedly had advisers who differed in their assessment of Russian motivation and potential response patterns. To what extent did empirical evidence warrant acceptance of any of the plausible interpretations? To what extent did strategic considerations or perhaps rules of prudence override behavior based upon at least some plausible interpretations of Russian behavior? To what extent was Kennedy's behavior free and to what extent was it governed by character and institutional constraints? And, if we were to decide that in some sense the entire pattern of behavior was determined by empirical constraints, then what does this mean with respect to human freedom?

These questions deserve examination from the standpoint of micro-empirical analysis, in which hypotheses and evidence are carefully weighed; from the standpoint of political theory in which models are constructed and used hypothetically in the exploration of macropolitical questions; and from a philosophical standpoint in the exploration of the meaning of many of the assessments we make and of the value judgments that we form. The gamut of considerations is beyond the scope of this paper, but some of the more philosophically oriented aspects of these questions will receive brief treatment. Thus the present discussion will apply generally to the broadest questions relevant to the field of political inquiry, as does much of the work of the Sprouts, but its broader relevance makes it even more central to some of the more specific and more important questions of international relations, as some of the examples used later in the paper will make clear.

I

There is an old philosophical debate as to whether man's choices are free or are fully determined. It is true, and no reasonable man would question this, that a number of constraints upon freedom of choice do exist. The constraint, and the only such, recognized by Hobbes is physical constraint. A man bound to a post by iron chains is not free to leave that spot, according to Hobbes, but a man threatened by weapons is free to disregard the danger and to move. Although there is a sense in which we are absolutely constrained by physical constraints, few of the actual physical constraints absolutely preclude contrary action. A Houdini could slip out of his chains, while another individual paralyzed by fear might remain unable to elude the constraint imposed by a toy gun. Still other individuals might be so constrained by habituation, perceptive delusion, moral fanaticism, or strategic inhibitions that their behavior in given types of situations becomes completely stereotyped, predictable, and uniform. Looked at from the obverse perspective, some individuals may appear to themselves to be able freely to choose from among alternatives; other individuals may have the oppressive sense of being completely constrained either by external circumstances or by internal inhibitions.

Some at least of the classic philosophers defined freedom as the recognition of necessity, by which they meant that man was free when he acted in harmony with his own nature. Others responded that this freedom was an illusion if it followed that man's actions were products of his biological being and of his social and psychological upbringing. Choice was an illusion because man was constrained to do that which he was psychologically motivated to do and those who understood the motivations could predict the actions. Others questioned what use freedom might be if use of it did not respond to a man's character and nature, for if it were not related to these in what sense would the action "belong" to the man?

In both the case of determinism and that of indeterminism then freedom might appear an illusion. In the one case, the act would be determined by circumstances, by constitution, and by upbringing; in the other case, the action would be the product of chance or of accident and thus unrelated in any meaningful way to choice. In the one case, freedom is the working of inexorable necessity; in the other, freedom lies in the chance attrition from the norm produced by the flux of events in a complex world. In the one case, the world is completely ordered; in the other the world contains surds that deviate from any statable rule and that produce discrepancies between class and individual. Yet an accident, or a deviation from a rule, is always an event that eludes control and that therefore, although free in this sense, is a restriction on the freedom of the chooser. Thus the philosophy of Peirce, or the earlier one of Heraclitus, which includes chance and accident would seem on superficial examination to exclude freedom as much as fully deterministic worlds.

The difficulty with such discussions is that they occur at such a high level of abstraction that they do not distinguish between different kinds of systems. A railroad train may be said to have two degrees of freedom because it can move only backwards or forewards along the track. It cannot travel off the track or even onto other tracks for which the rails have not properly been set. A bus has many more degrees of freedom for it can be driven onto any existing road and even across some surfaces that are not roads. An amphibious vehicle can travel on the ground and in the water as well. It thus has a degree of freedom that the bus does not have. An automatic lathe has the freedom only to pursue a preset schedule of operations. Industrial equipment containing negative feedback has the capacity to reset or reschedule operations if certain deviations in the external environment are noted by the indicators of the system. An ultrastable machine has the capacity to change its mode of response to the environment by correcting its own internal programs if feedback indictates that its scheduled mode of operation for variations in the environment produces unanticipated and undesired results. The lower animals have a freedom to respond to psychological considerations that is not possessed by machines. Man has a freedom to respond to intellectual and to moral considerations. Two men may be said to differ in their degree of moral freedom if one of them is incapable of adapting moral rules to circumstances and the other is capable of this. The former has lost the capacity to use negative feedback in this important area of activity. He thus may be said to have reduced freedom, a condition often, although not invariably, accompanied by consistent internal feelings. The psychopath, on the other hand, adjusts to circumstances not by adapting moral rules but by disregarding them. He has lost his capacity for moral action and has thereby reduced his freedom in a quite different way from that of the moral fanatic.

In our usage, freedom is related to the capacity for and the quality of action of different kinds of systems. Freedom is related to the types and numbers of responses the system has available for any environment, to its capability to use negative feedback, and to its possession of ultra- or multistable capabilities. This usage is much closer to the classical definition of freedom as necessity than might at first appear to be the case.

Freedom is a relational concept and not an absolute concept. Freedom thus has restraint and constraint as its reciprocals. As the equality of the freedom becomes extended and complex and multifarious, so does the quality of the system of constraints and restraints become extended, and multifarious. The freedom of a ball to roll in any direction is dependent on its globular shape. The freedom to act morally depends upon a framework for and a capacity for moral choice. Thus just as the freedom to roll is inconsistent with a square or rectangular shape, so is the freedom to act morally inconsistent with immoral or amoral character or nonmoral constitution. Every freedom requires a set of consistent constraints. These constraints are not merely limitations on the specified types of freedoms but are the very grounds for their existence. That they are inconsistent with other modes of existence and with their particular freedoms, whether greater or lesser or of a higher or lower mode, is tautological. The quest for absolute freedom of revolutionaries and of anarchists is a romantic and illogical attempt to recapture infantile feelings of omnipotence. The quest for Godhead or for absolute freedom on earth is a disguised death wish, as was so clearly pointed out by Hegel, for in the historical world, if not in the fantasy world, freedom is always related to constraint.

II

In part at least the confusions surrounding the subject of freedom stem from failures to distinguish between closed and open systems and between choice, prediction, and retrodiction. Every prediction partaking of the character of law is made in terms of a closed system. As Charles Sanders Peirce pointed out, we cannot know whether the laws of physics may not be changing. The world system is open; our predictions are made entirely within the framework of closed and bounded theories, models, or systems, or whatever other term one prefers to use.

Knowledge concerning the world is always ineradicably limited. Knowing is always a stage removed from the known; the knowing self observes the known but is not itself known. Although any act of observing may itself be relegated to the realm of the known by raising the level of examination or of knowledge, there is ineluctably a metalevel at which one knows and is not known. At the simplest and most general level of the distinction between subject and object there is always a subject that is not itself part of the knowledge equation. Although a subject may observe itself or be observed by another subject, the metalevel of subjectivity is never entirely brought within the realm of the known.

Thus, even apart from uncertainty principles and the problems arising from measurement error, the world is never inherently a completely knowable phenomenon. Of course, matters do not have to be pushed to this extreme, for it is also the case that theoretical depth is purchased at the price of the restriction of the variables considered in a theory; depth of knowledge is pursued by increasing the number of variables external to one's theories or propositions that may affect behavior. Increasingly as one moves from simple subjects, the individual as an item of knowledge departs from the uniformity that would be imposed by putatively lawful formulations. Increasingly surds and novelties assert themselves.

Yet to call these surds and novelties free creations would be to confuse their lack of predictability with their degree of freedom. Conversely, to assert that the predictable is unfree is to confuse its predictability with its degree of freedom. Would we assert than an unpredictable mutation is a freer act (it is, of course, not an act at all but an occurrence or event) than a predictable act by an honest man not to steal money?

The freedom of a "free" action depends on the choosing and not on the choice. Our subjective awareness of freedom is an awareness that accompanies the act of choosing. Retrospectively the act may appear even to the chooser as completely determined. And so it may be, except that in the act of choosing, the display of alternative ends and of alternative means reveals the scope and range of the decision framework and therefore acquaints the chooser with the array of alternatives that he is physically and biologically and perhaps even socially and psychologically free to choose from, although perhaps constrained upon deeper examination by intellectual or moral considerations to merely a single one of the alternatives. As the choice is made, the range of alternatives is increasingly narrowed until finally reduced, often to one only. Yet, to make the choice less determined as in the case of the ass torn between two bales of hay, where the choice may depend upon a number of accidental considerations, having little or nothing to do with the healthful or aesthetic qualities of the food, such as closeness to or original attention to one of the bales, does not increase the freedom of the chooser. On the contrary, to the extent that the choice depends upon such accidental circumstances, it appears as externally constrained and less subject to freedom of choice. Where these external constraints or considerations are almost evenly balanced and dominant, the chooser does not feel free; he feels ambivalent and imprisoned by external circumstances. The higher or greater freedom of man is more fully made manifest the more his decisions rest upon the ultrastable reasoning processes, both intellectual and moral, and the less they depend upon fortuitous external, physical, or physiological constraints.

The undetermined type of freedom that we appear to have during the process of choosing arises from the contemplation of choice independently of the parameters that constrain it. Thus, the apparent freedom to steal of the honest man arises from contemplation of the act of acquiring money. "I could steal this money and purchase those things that I need or want," he thinks, "if it were not for my moral code." "I could do my enemy in if I did not have to tell a lie." "I could climb that rope if I were less tired." "I would eat that ice cream cone, as I am tempted to do, except that I wish to lose weight." Each of these statements reveals how, in the process of choosing, an end is considered in the absence of given constraints and then rejected as the appropriate constraint is recognized. Moreover, most of these acts are physically possible and thus may be committed if the motivation to do so is strong enough. Thus, "I ate the ice cream cone although I knew it was bad for me." "I stole the money although I knew it was wrong and did injury to others." Yet most people who commit such acts usually do not feel free; they rather feel themselves in the grip of a powerful emotion over which they lack ego control. In both sets of cases, the action is determined by the, at least momentarily, strongest motivation. In both, it is the closure of the open system as it was contemplated during the act of choosing that produces action. But in the latter set, and not in the former, the action is controlled by inputs from outside the ultrastable regulatory subsystem of the human system that dominate it. Another form of this phenomenon arises when a rigid superego controls the ego process. In neither case do individuals usually feel free.

III

Both historical predictions and retrodictions have to cope with the nature of the uncertainties arising from the open character of the historical process. Both predictions and retrodictions involve uncertainty. Thus, in the oft-used example of Cortes's third expedition to Baja California, it is sometimes argued that although it would not have been predictable that Cortes would have discovered the Pacific on the basis of his ambition, it is retrodictable that it was his ambition that led Cortes to the third expedition. This assertion is false. It was surely not predictable that Cortes's ambition would have led him to the third expedition, unless, of course, one also were able to fill in all the other circumstances and conditions that led to the choice. At best one might have predicted that Cortes would have been led to exploration or perhaps alternatively to armed conquest. On the other hand, the retrodiction that Cortes was led to the third expedition by ambition is at best plausible. His characteristic of ambition is consistent with an activity such as the third expedition. Ambition, however, is not necessarily or clearly the motivation that led to the discovery. Prior to the third expedition the known datum consists of the characteristic of ambition. The consequences of the ambition remain open. With respect to the retrodiction, we start with the third expedition. We find a plausible motivation for the discovery in Cortes's known ambition. But it is only knowledge of the outcome that gives rise to false confidence in the known personality characteristic as the cause. Just as other discoveries or other self-assertive activities might have been predicted from Cortes's ambition, so other motivations or causes might be hypothesized for the known third expedition. In the prediction, the anterior event is known and the posterior inferred. In the retrodiction, the posterior event is known and a known anterior characteristic asserted as the cause. Although the retrodiction has at least two knowns, it is primarily a form of mental habituation that leads us to transform the certainty of the posterior even into the high likelihood that the known anterior characteristic functions as cause in a satisfactory explanation. There is too much that we do not know and that we probably cannot know with respect to complex events and human motivations to view retrodictions as essentially different from predictions.

Historical explanation sketches almost invariably depend upon perspectives which are poorly articulated. A sketch of an explanation involves a choice of evidence from an almost unlimited array of potential evidence. Even the best of historical explanations are so selective in the use of evidence that they barely escape caricaturing the events they are designed to explain. Our interpretations of the evidence are themselves subject to doubt. Our weaving of the strands of evidence into an explanation sketch is too complicated for complex events for us to examine the logic of relationships and the structure of inference in detail. It is only in the roughest and most precarious form that we know how our conclusions are related to our assumptions. We employ generalizations in interpretation that may be wrong, misunderstood, or misapplied. We deal with partial accounts only partially understood.

Even the most plausible interpretations of events constitute but a fragile house of cards ready to collapse at the first strong wind. Often a single piece of unexpected information may force us to revise or even to reverse the most convincing interpretations. Even the most solid evidence may serve to support a contrary hypothesis when reevaluated in the light of other evidence or new hypotheses. To illustrate how fragile our hypotheses may be and how fragile the conclusions for policy we derive from them, consider such a typical event as the Czechoslovak coup of 1948. Did Russia plan the coup as early as 1944 or 1945? Even were we to discover documentary evidence that Russia did in 1944 or 1945 plan a subsequent coup, it would not follow inexorably that the later coup occurred because of the earlier plan. Even the discovery of a document written in late 1947 or early 1948 calling for the coup in implementation of an earlier plan of 1945 would not preclude the possibility that the coup was decided upon for entirely different reasons but that it was rationalized in terms of earlier decisions because of a human motivation to project a continuity not present in the events themselves.

The firmest proof that the coup was decided upon for immediate reasons pertaining to the state of the world in early 1948 could not be used to demonstrate that an American reaction, based upon an interpretation that assumed that the coup was merely the culmination of a plan initiated in 1945, was an irrational or improper response to the circumstances of the coup. Nor could the discovery of proof that the coup was the fruit of a long-prepared careful plan prove the rationality and reasonableness of an American response based upon a similar conception of the coup. Prudential responses to events may be based on interpretations that are less probable on the basis of available evidence than alternative hypotheses. Yet acting on a less probable hypothesis may deserve the characterization of "prudent" if acting on the alternative hypotheses entails greater risks. Moreover, the complicated relationship between prudential intrepretation, motivation, knowledge of one's own motivation, and so forth involves a feedback process that may be very difficult if not impossible for the historian to disentangle.

There is a tendency, perhaps ineluctable given the needs of human beings for orientation in the world, to impose upon the pattern of events hypotheses whose unilinear dimensions deny the possibility of novelty and emergent levels of organization. Thus, with respect to the Soviet bloc, for instance, theories of permanent purges alternate with those of progressive societal changes toward freedom or even, in some cases, toward democracy. The intellectual difficulty of such theories lies not in the incorrectness of either, for either may turn out to be fortuitously correct, but in the almost casual assignment to reality of a prediction that pertains only to a model, whether implicit or explicit, that neglects many of the variables that will affect the real world outcome and that is blind to the sports that produce novelty.

It is amazing how often overly simple models are offered as conventional wisdom even in the face of contrary evidence. Thus, for instance, the Kennan -Fulbright thesis proposes that the way to produce favorable change in the Soviet bloc is to be friendly to individual bloc countries and to aid them. Yet Yugoslavia broke with the Soviet bloc in 1948 during the period when American hostility toward Yugoslavia was even greater than its hostility toward the Soviet Union; China broke with the Soviet Union during a period in which American hostility toward China was greater than to- ward the Soviet Union; Rumania developed autonomy during a period in which American citizens were not even permitted to travel to Rumania; Poland, of all the Communist bloc nations, has been the most retrogressive since 1956 and it has been the recipient of large amounts of American aid and friendship.

The Kennan-Fulbright thesis is usually buttressed by the seemingly commonsensical argument that the advocated policy provides Communist governments with alternatives. But what kinds of alternatives does it provide them with? Did American aid perhaps reduce the Polish need for increased economic productivity, for the consensus underlying such productivity, and therefore for less repressive measures? Did acceptance of American aid increase the political need to stress Communist orthodoxy? Did American aid reduce internal opposition by showing American support for the regime, thereby removing a leadership incentive for reform? These questions, and numerous others that could be asked, suggest that at least some historical generalizations are based upon models, whether implicit or explicit, that are so simplified that they are worthless for any purposes of extrapolation. They assert a simple determinism in the world not warranted by any existing evidence. As guides to action, they circumscribe multistable freedom of choice in a thoroughly dys- functional fashion. Those who have the responsibility for making decisions in the world cannot afford to assume a high degree of control over a deter- mined and predictable simple world; such a world does not present itself in the historical realm. Decisions cannot simply be deduced from formulas; multistable self-regulation is a more complex process.

IV

To the extent that freedom can be regarded as multistable self-regulation at the rational and moral levels of analysis, majority rule or rules of equality in politics would merely be means toward the attainment of such ends. Although procedures are enormously important, for liberties are maintained in the interstices of procedures—a datum of social and political life not understood by the New Left—the concept of freedom as multistable self-regulation is basically substantive. The concept therefore suggests that to the extent that equality is desirable, it should be obtained by levelling up-wards rather than by levelling downwards and that, to the extent that a choice must be made between freedom and equality, the preservation of freedom somewhere in social and political life is preferable to equality. Freedom as multistable self-regulation implies that it is achieved not by the mere satisfaction of desires, as in a prototypical welfare state, but in the self-regulating attainment of desired ends. In this sense, both the pampered sons of the rich and the products of the dregs of the slums may be deprived of large areas of personal freedom through a process of education or of acculturation that deprives one of the need, and the other of the capability, for behaving freely.

The attempts by totalitarian governments and by supporters of the New Left to legislate or to coerce the moral beliefs of the general population involve (not necessarily conscious) attempts to destroy freedom of the individual, to suppress the diversity of life, and to force social and political processes within the world to conform to sets of narrowly choosen tenets: the moral equivalents of simplistic historical theories. Stasis, absolute freedom, and absolute death meet at Kelvin zero, at which all motion stops.

In Thomas Mann's *Magic Mountain,* the intellectual duel between Herr Naphta and Settembrini is a clash between opposing schemes for death, which differ from each other only in their intellectual guise. Peeperkorn, who ignores this dialog but lives, represents the life principal that breaks through all attempts to impose rigid logical structures upon the world. Mann, however, achieves no synthesis, for Peeperkorn lacks the degree of intellectual control which is necessary for operating in the world and for recognizing that degree of order that temporarily exists and without which life would be impossible.

Individual freedoms exist, but they are relative and constrained by necessities. Order and disorder, freedom and rule, structure and process, are obverse faces of a common existence in which freedom can increase and reach higher levels of performance as the world becomes increasingly complex. Man's neuronic and biological structure provides the framework within which multistable moral and rational self-regulation are possible. The psychopath and the obsessive compulsive are opposite dysfunctions of self-regulating systems. Both dysfunctions diminish the freedom of multistable systems, one by removing that framework of order within which freedom has meaning and the other by increasing the level of order to the point where all choices are uniformly determined regardless of environmental differences. Thus freedom too has its left and its right deviations. Self-regulation, the cybernaut, is a helmsman or steersman who must navigate the narrow route between the Scylla of absolute disorder and the Charybdis of absolute stasis. Order and disorder, freedom and control, are polarities bound in a symbiotic nexus, false opposites whose meanings are reciprocally revealed and whose limitations are overcome developmentally through appropriate synthesis in complex systems.

PART TWO

Conceptual Foci

BRUCE M. RUSSETT

A Macroscopic View of International Politics*

The Environment of Politics

The thrust of this paper is simple and direct: it expresses my growing conviction that political research, and especially research on international politics, has too much neglected the *environment* of politics. That is, we have often failed to study the role of social, economic, and technological factors in providing the *menu* for political choice. Relatively speaking, too much effort has gone into examining the ways in which choices are made, the political process itself, rather than into asking, in a rigorous and systematic way, what possible choices were in fact available and why those possibilities and not some others were available.

It is this emphasis on looking at the wider environment within which political decision-makers act that I mean by the title, a macroscopic view. A microscope is of course an instrument for looking in great detail at a tiny portion of tissue or other material, ignoring the whole of a large organism or system for the sake of a painstaking examination of the structure or processes of one element. The term macroscope is meant to refer to just the opposite kind of tool, one for examining, in a gross way, the entire system or at least large portions of it. The fine detail available from the microscope is lost, but compensation comes from an image of the

*This chapter in part discusses empirical work done by the World Data Analysis Program of Yale University, and the writing of the paper was facilitated by the Program. I am grateful to the National Science Foundation, Grant GS 614, and to the Advanced Research Projects Agency, Contract No. N0014-67-A-0097-0007, monitored by the Office of Naval Research, for their support of these efforts. An early version of the paper was presented to a conference at the University of Texas.

Notes and References for this selection will be found on pages 123–124.

interrelationships of the parts. I deliberately use the word macroscope in place of telescope as the opposite for microscope. A telescope is of course used for making distant objects appear close, for bringing out the detail of distant objects that one cannot approach physically. In this sense its function is not so different from that of the microscope. Like the latter it implies a relatively narrow view; one chooses to focus upon a particular star rather than on the entire galaxy that is visible to the naked eye in the night sky. So what I will be referring to is more nearly analogous to a wide-angle lens for a camera than to a telephoto lens.

The other aspect of this approach that I would emphasize here, as preface, is the interdisciplinary implication. To investigate these environmental questions political scientists have had to seek out a great deal of information from other sciences, physical as well as social. Because we are interested in social, economic, and technological factors, however, does not mean that we must become amateur sociologists, economists, or engineers so as to do original research in those disciplines. If we did we would certainly do it badly. But we have had to learn enough to understand their major findings, and to use their data. We have to know what the major nonpolitical trends are or may be so that we can develop some sense of how they may widen or limit the range of political choice.

Data Bases for Taxonomy and Hypothesis-Testing

I will try to justify this view in greater detail below, with comments –that will be deliberately sweeping and provocative. First let me sketch very briefly some developments in theory and research on international politics in the past few years, identifying the rise of what has been called a quantitative, or behavioral, or self-consciously social-scientific study of international politics. This scientific mode is crucial to the rigorous, as compared with the merely stimulating, use of the macroscopic model. Some of the theoretical and conceptual breakthroughs necessary for the emergence of such an approach are apparent in some articles and a few books of the middle and late 1950s, with the primary impetus traceable directly to the work of Quincy Wright just before World War II. But it was only about eight years ago that major research results, the really quantitative books with findings, appeared in sufficient number as to mark the emergence of a science.[1] First came the development of taxonomies and explicit models, sometimes using simple mathematics, but largely limited in application to a few case studies or pilot efforts. Then came a more widespread effort at hypothesis-testing as contrasted with description, however careful and rigorous. And finally, by the mid-1960s, we saw the deliberate search for large-scale data bases, with many comparable observations for many variables.

This tends to become a "historical sociology" approach, with roots in the work of Weber or, if one is searching for a legitimator, perhaps even

Aristotle. The approach makes use of a wide variety of data on the components of international systems, both present and historical systems. Such large data bases are essential for systematic comparison and hypothesis-testing about the behavior of nations. They are also essential for continuing the taxonomic efforts. This classificatory or mapping exercise in fact establishes the operational definitions of many of our variables. The original classifications of nations, or of foreign-policy influences, or of behavior patterns, were based largely on deductive theory and impressionistic evidence. Now, however, we can check and supplement these classifications with inductively based taxonomies from examining these large data bases to find the patterns of similarity and cleavage. Thus nations can be categorized in terms of similar patterns of attributes or interdependence. On many grounds, for instance, Japan can be grouped with the Western European nations, a fact that could have been suspected but not satisfactorily established without a great deal of information. Furthermore, we can now go beyond the taxonomies to look for the *relationships* between the boxes, or variables, so identified.

These developments impose no restrictions on *where;* that is, at what level of analysis, to develop powerful hypotheses. Many studies, for one example, have focused on the personality characteristics or life experiences of *decision-makers*. Much of the most interesting theory of the 1950s applied to this level, and led to a number of important cross-national elite studies. Secondly, we are just now beginning to see important studies of the patterns of *interactions* among nations. Charles McClelland, for instance, is compiling a complete mapping of governments' verbal and physical acts toward other governments in the current international system, and has begun to publish some very important analyses of recent patterns that show unsuspected ways in which the sequence of events in crises is different from that in "normal" times.[2] Other analyses have been concerned with comparative foreign policies, in the sense of how differences in *national* characteristics affect national policies. These may be relatively small differences, such as between parliamentary and presidential systems, or changes in the structure of particular countries over time. The large-scale comparisons, however, require larger data bases and more gross, more aggregated national characteristics. Thus it is possible to investigate what difference being economically developed, or democratic, or European makes for behavior. Finally, at this same level of aggregation are the patterns of *linkages* among nations. Included here are the studies of trade ties, bonds of communication, and frequency of membership in international organizations. Such studies lead on to comparisons of *international systems,* defined by a combination of the pattern of linkages plus certain characteristics of the states being linked. Thus a comparison of bipolar with multipolar systems depends on measures of the relative size of the major nations making up the systems, and the linkages among states that signify the bonds of alliance.

In my own work I have largely concentrated on the gross, aggregated characteristics of states and their linkages for explaining nations' behavior. I started out with that approach largely as a matter of hunch, and since then have retained it because of the good predictive (or retrodictive) power that in fact seems to be available with it, for very many kinds of problems. Study at lower levels of analysis is critical for quite a large number of situations and issues, however, and it is not at all true that effort should be *confined* to the aggregated level. In fact, some real limits to the utility of aggregate data analysis are becoming very clear, and the rapid progress of the macroscopic approach actually brings us nearer to those limits. So all the returns are certainly not in.

The Menu of Choice in Foreign Policy

Whatever its utility, the basic characteristic of this approach is in asking what are the *limits* of political choice, and here I return to my opening comments about the environment of politics. What determines the choices available to (or perceived by) national decision-makers? What are the limits *within which* personality differences, or different role conceptions, or alternative styles of bargaining and negotiation, can affect choice? This distinction between the process of selection among alternatives ("competition for scarce resources"; "the sharing of values") and the set of choices offered is perhaps crucial to an understanding of the current United States foreign policy dilemma. If you walk into a restaurant, what you order of course depends on how hungry you are, what your tastes are, and how much money you have. It also depends on what the menu offers. Dinner at a pizza palace offering dozens of varieties of pizza is not likely to be very satisfactory if you don't happen to like pizza.

Not many people are very happy about the menu that has been provided to us in Southeast Asia. Neither escalation nor withdrawal, in any of their possible permutations, nor continuing to slog on somewhere in between, looks like a very attractive policy. There *is* no "good" solution to the predicament, only a selection of bad options, some of which are less bad than others. Now of course there are some differences among Americans on just what the possible range of choice offered really is. Or rather, there are different perceptions of what the consequences of selecting various options would be. The right-wing or hawk opposition to current policy sees more opportunities for the use of military force than the government probably sees. The hawks do think that a wider and more intense application of violence could bring a meaningful military victory. The left-wing or dove viewpoint, on the other hand, stresses the irrelevance of events in Southeast Asia to American vital interests. They maintain that an American withdrawal in South Vietnam and communist victory would not seriously endanger other Asian nations' security or, even if there should be a domino effect, that even all of Southeast Asia is not so critical to the distant and powerful United States as to be worth the price we are paying.

The American government, presumably somewhere in between these dissenting views, for some time expressed what was really a rather broad United States consensus. It maintained that neither the alleged alternative put forth by the right, nor that of the left, was a real one; that each would have undesired consequences that its protagonists did not anticipate. More recently perspectives, both of some people in government and in wide segments of the populace at large, have changed. But strong opposition to the war did not spread far beyond intellectual circles before 1968, a fact the latter tend to forget. And even in the middle of 1968 the range of realistic choice, as generally perceived, was not wide. While Gallup poll respondents had become as likely to refer to themselves as doves as hawks, few favored a unilateral American withdrawal from South Vietnam.[3] Though many would have preferred a somewhat different policy by their government, most had in mind matters of style and emphasis rather than a drastic shift. They still saw their nation as distressingly bound by previous acts to a short and not very varied menu.

The Power of Macroscopic Prediction

I suggested that the aggregate macroscopic view could be shown to have a good deal of power for predicting policy, that it works well in a great number of instances. This is so because both perceptions and policy are quite stable for most nations, as I will now try to demonstrate. My initial example will be from the work Hayward Alker and I have done, individually and together, on voting behavior in the United Nations.[4] First, we found that a very wide variety of *particular* issues and roll-calls— about the Congo, Korea, Chinese representation, disarmament, South Africa, West New Guinea, and many others—are in fact usually concerned with one of the *major broad* issues of contemporary world politics. Three great cleavages or "superissues"—the Cold War, colonialism, and the role of the United Nations organization itself—account for about 60 per cent of the variance in roll-call voting. This in itself was a surprising regularity, and provided a basis for an empirical typology of issues. And I think most observers would agree that these are truly the issues around which the entire globe (as contrasted with more parochial regional disputes) currently does divide.

From there it was easy and appropriate to try to predict the voting behavior of particular nations on these superissues. For instance, Alker found that on cold war issues he could predict most of the variation in voting position (75 per cent of the variance) by knowing only a few basic facts. Simply categorizing the various states according to regional or caucusing groups would do that well, as would knowing a few facts about the military and economic bonds among nations (their alliance commitments and their receipt of trade and aid from the United States and the Soviet Union.) This too was surprising, to us as well as to others. We had been given many predictions that nothing resembling this level of regularity would emerge; that delegates' voting decisions depended too heavily on the vagaries of instructions from home, or upon volatile interests of the delegations, or interdelegation bargaining, or upon what nation's representative happened to be sitting next to a delegate on a particular day. Furthermore, we found that we could "predict" more than 80 per cent of the variance in states' voting by knowing their *past* voting behavior. Even data on positions taken ten years earlier provided that kind of predictive power.

Votes on smaller, more parochial, and more transient issues are of course more difficult to predict. But on these three continuing and salient cleavages we could do very well at the aggregate, macroscopic level without knowing anything about changing conditions or decision-processes *within* individual governments. Changes of personnel in the delegations; changes in the leadership of the home governments; alternation of parties; all had little effect. Even changes of regime or governmental structure, as caused by coups or palace revolutions, made little difference to the leaders' perceptions of choice in the United Nations, or at least to their actual choices of behavior.[5] In all but a literal handful of cases it took a virtual social revolution, with an impact on the level of that occuring in Iran with the overthrow of the Mossadegh regime or Guatemala and Arbenz in the 1950s, to produce a very marked shift. Furthermore, we can specify what we mean by a marked shift. Cuba's change of polarity from Batista to Castro was by far the greatest national flip-flop over the past decade and a half. On a scale of Cold War issues, Guatemala and Iran shifted their UN voting by an amount that is roughly one-third of Cuba's change, and there are but six other states that moved by even a fifth as much as Cuba did (not necessarily in the same direction).[6] In most instances one could "map" the political differences and concurrences of nations in a very stable way.

Similarly, in my recent work on regional groupings[7] I found that I could predict about 80 per cent of the variance in patterns of membership in the world's more than 150 international organizations, or patterns of trading relationships, or UN voting behavior, or social and cultural similarities, by knowing what any *one* of those patterns looked like. Finally, knowing international organization memberships ten years previously, or trading patterns ten years previously, allowed one to predict between 85 and 95 per cent of the variance in the later period. In the case of trade, one could even predict more than three-quarters of the 1963 variance from the 1938 pattern, despite World War II, the Cold War, and decolonization. Thus these influences, and we include here the very important regional and other bonds of community among nations, change at a glacial pace in this international system. The stabilities of our world are, on examination, very impressive.

Finding these continuities contrasts very sharply with the task of day-to-day journalism and impressionism. The journalist's job is to tell us how today is different from yesterday, and to do so in a sufficiently vivid manner to attract and hold our attention. When writing about Anglo–American relations, for instance, a good journalist like Drew Middleton changes his evaluation constantly. He looks not at the system level but at political events, personalities, and personnel changes in decision-making positions. Anglo–American relations are good one day following a meeting of chiefs-of-state, and bad the next day as a consequence of a new disagreement. It is precisely against this participant's-eye view that I am reacting, trying to back up and gain perspective both on how the relations between two states fit into the global pattern of relationships and how they perform over a much longer time-span. The journalist's view is, at best, like confusing the business cycle with the long-term secular trend in the economy. And at that it is not likely to be analogous to a concentration on the depression and inflation ends of the business cycle, but only on the numerous rather mild fluctuations in between.

It is of course true that the macroscopic kind of approach is not *very* good for explaining why the United States acted as it did during a specific period of stress like the Suez crisis of 1956—though it is not bad even for that—but it *is* quite good for explaining why, after 1957, the drift of British alliance (NATO) policy was one way and France's leaders moved in another direction.[8] The basic underlying bonds of the relationship with America were very much stronger in one case than in the other, as revealed by macroscopic analysis. And a more detailed, microscopic, examination shows that the British elite, after overcoming their bitterness at American inconstancy, drew the lesson that Britain could never again afford to take a critical policy decision in conflict with the United States position; their dependence on this country was too great. The French, on the contrary, concluded that they could not again afford always to depend on the support of a United States that had independent interests; thus they must prepare the basis for action that might be independent of or even in major conflict with America.

Note, incidentally, that neither of these countries' directions since 1956 can be traced to the idiosyncrasies of single parties or decision-makers. Britain's decision for dependence was made by a Conservative government and has been carried out, to the point of virtual obsequiousness, by a Labour government. France's review of its commitments was begun well before De Gaulle took office. Alliances and alignments of various sorts thus are rooted in longterm influences and in environmental factors over which politics does have some control, but only over the passage of substantial periods of time. This sounds like a very general affirmation, but in fact the data are there to document it.

Such a perspective on the stabilities of world politics has crucial policy implications. Too often observers and policy-makers take alarm at every coup or change of government. The Chicken Little syndrome (The sky is falling! Run and tell the President!) is widespread. But if important policy reversals in these countries are rare, expensive attempts to affect the composition of the next governing coalition in Boonistan are at best unnecessary, and more likely a dangerous waste of resources that will ultimately weaken the United States both abroad and domestically. The roots of an interventionist foreign policy lie in the faulty intellectual understanding that is unaware of the gross stabilities.

Political Variables as Predictors to Political Outputs

Such constancy reminds us again of the limits of politics, of the degree to which future choices are controlled by past choices, and of the restricted degree to which the available menu is set by political choice in any case. Differences among types of political systems, for example, are *poor* predictors, on the aggregate level, to most variations in the outputs of economic and social systems. Some examples, drawn from within the United States as well as from cross-national studies are:

1. Type of *political* system (authoritarian vs. competitive) is often only a moderately good predictor to international political behavior. In the UN General Assembly political system type explained only about a quarter of the variance of voting on East-West issues, and was essentially unrelated to voting on North-South issues. With some economic and cultural attributes, on the other hand, one could account for as much as half of the voting variance.[9]

2. Political system *outputs,* such as public spending in various functional categories, can on one level be very well explained by such *environmental* characteristics of a system as its level of income, degree of urbanization, racial composition, and average level of educational attainment. This has been effectively demonstrated by comparing budgetary data on cities and on American state governments. But the outputs are very *poorly* predicted by political system characteristics such as governmental structure, relative party strength, or electoral competition.[10]

3. On another level, however, these system outputs can be equally explained by knowing what the proportionate expenditures were in the *past.* A simple model predicting that the relative allocation in the future will be the same as it has been gives extremely good results.[11] In this sense the irrelevance of politics to *change* stems from the strength of political organizations to maintain themselves against the competing claims of other organizations in a bargaining situation. This constancy has been found in American cities, at the level of the federal budget, and even apparently in the national budget of the Soviet Union, where current spending on ballistic missile defense can be seen as largely the bureaucratic inertia of previous purchase, now virtually saturating the country, of anti-aircraft equipment.[12]

These conclusions at the aggregate level are of course controversial.

It is still appropriate to maintain that other variables, more sophisticated indicators, or more interesting multivariate models will produce better results, in the sense of higher explanatory power for the political variables. But the results so far are intriguing, and perhaps help to meet an accusation that is frequently made against certain kinds of political scientists—that they are not interested in politics. Being interested in political outcomes does not necessarily require being interested in the political process.

A Limited Defense of Induction

Many of these findings have been obtained from testing, on large data bases, some relatively simple hypotheses about the interrelation of political and environmental variables. Others nevertheless should not be dressed up with the appearance of hypothesis testing, but have been obtained essentially from taxonomic or other inductive efforts. Inductive uses of various techniques, such as multiple regression, factor analysis and multi-dimensional scaling, "causal modeling," and "curve fitting," have proved extremely valuable at the macroscopic level. Their productivity in research to date provides a powerful defense of induction, or fishing expeditions, at that level and at this stage in the growth of the science.

Now certainly even the inductive political fisherman needs some theory to guide him. You have to know what pools and streams to fish in, how to select tackle, and how to manipulate the tackle. Some inchoate theory must specify what the most promising variables for the inductive exercise are to be, and you had better understand the kind of functional relationships that your procedures are seeking. It is hardly worthwhile to use statistical procedures that search for additive relationships among variables if an adequate theoretical system specifies multiplicative relationships. If revolutionary potential is a curvilinear function of income you will not discover it by using only a linear regression model. And surely you need the ability to formulate a set of alternative hypotheses so as tentatively to "explain" the results. Only with that much theory can you then go on to understand more about the relationships, to formulate further and more explicit hypotheses about what the causal mechanism is and under what circumstances it applies. Doing political analysis without it is like fishing with a bent pin in a laundry tub, and likely in the long run to be about as profitable.

But induction *per se* has been much maligned. Whatever the approach, the aim is to arrive at nonobvious propositions. Our natural science colleagues may *now* be more heavily deductive than we, but that is in part made possible by *past* inductive successes which are now part of their knowledge (e.g. much of the work of Galileo, Newton, and especially Kepler). Because our international politics discipline is so sorely lacking in good, deductive, formal, rigorous theory, we often are forced to be rather heavily inductive, and can often achieve substantial payoffs despite the handicap of weak theory. And since we are in any case speaking in terms of probabilistic hypotheses, the deviant cases are subject to careful microscopic examination. We first need the macroscopic studies to identify the deviant cases as such, but in no sense can we dispense with detailed analysis.

Yet there is one critical limit to the kind of knowledge we derive from induction, and it concerns the difference between prediction and explanation. Inductively discovered patterns can be used for substantial periods of time to predict political behavior. If we know empirically that A is associated with B, we may derive important policy benefits from predicting changes in B as a result of changes in A, without knowing *why*. But however exciting and important the discovery of high aggregate correlations may be, prediction without "understanding" is vulnerable to system changes; when we do not understand why two variables are related our predictions are vulnerable to shifts in the relationship. Historic determinants of alliance formation may not hold in the nuclear era; where power considerations once brought nations together in military pacts, nuclear proliferation now is associated with the *absence* of formal alliances. (In the 16 years since completion of the 42-nation western security system in 1955, no other nations have aligned themselves with either the United States or any major Western European state.) Or, in the nineteenth century the degree of alliance aggregation in the international system was negatively correlated with the magnitude and severity of war, suggesting a causal relationship in that greater predictability of national behavior implied by the alliances kept the system more stable and less war-prone. A prediction from this observation into the twentieth century, however, would have gone badly astray, since after 1900, with the increasing rigidity of European power relationships, alliance formation became positively associated with the outbreak of war.[13] A failure to explore the *political* mechanisms beneath the correlation would have led to an eventual failure of prediction.

Similarly, the high degree of association discussed previously between environmental variables and political ones could be very deceptive in future international politics. Since 1945 the international system has been remarkably stable in the continued dominance of two superpowers (one significantly stronger than the other) with a substantial gap between them and the other major states. The relative gap between superpowers and others may have narrowed slightly in recent years, and together with Russian consolidation of an invulnerable second-strike nuclear force the system has changed somewhat, modestly in the direction of greater multipolarity. But these changes are very moderate when compared with the kind of dramatic system change that has in the past resulted from great war or from revolution in a major state. They are also moderate compared with the kind of system change one can imagine from a technological breakthrough that made cheap nuclear weapons available to all. Only new theory, not the continued extrapolation of inductively derived patterns, could tell us which past regularities would hold and which would be shattered in the new system. Some of the old constraints on political choice would surely be broken.

In this respect our present understanding of international politics is perhaps comparable to the understanding of American voting behavior reached by the early survey analyses. They established that certain demographic characteristics, such as religion, income, and occupation, were highly correlated with partisan choice.[14] These correlations were fairly stable over time, but enough individuals, typically less than 20 per cent, changed their votes and so could reverse the outcome of the preceeding election. Induction and knowing the gross correlations were not enough to know the dynamic elements—who would change, and whether the changes would be enough to make a major shift in the state of the system. Yet it is hard to imagine these later questions being studied in the absence of the earlier inductive findings. In many respects, then, this paper is more of a retrospect than a prospect. It expresses a certain amount of satisfaction with where we have been, but tells us less surely where we should go next.

Wherever we go, it is important to press ahead both on the empirical front and on that of abstract theory. The advocates of a purely deductivist social science often point to modern economics as proving the power of deductive theory. To a degree they are right. But deductive theory-building has characterized much work in economics for a century or more, with but limited accomplishments for much of the time; the greatest successes of economics date only from World War II. No more than 30 years ago did the data necessary to test or apply macro-economic theory become available to scholars and planners. Only then was the Keynesian revolution solidified, and the opportunity for proper theoretical refinement presented.

Some find it tempting to reject not only induction but even the necessity to put deductively-derived propositions to the test. The later Greek philosophers have been described as,

... led away by their intellectual triumphs into the conceit that it ought to be possible to think out the whole structure of the natural world from a few axioms. Recourse to experiment was in their view a sign of an inferior mind, a view which was no doubt reinforced by the fact that in Greece most of the manual work was done by the helots, an inferior class, so that the manual work of an experiment would be well below the dignity of a philosopher.[15]

This mistake, the author observes, was fatal to Greek science. He further characterizes the mandarin civil servants of China: "As they stewed in their own intellectual juice, their imagination was not given the jolting stimuli that arise only from contact with the new experience gained from experiment."

Even when deductive theory is tested and not refuted, one still must raise probing questions about the theory. Careless testing, on inadequate data or small samples, can mean that a variety of deductively-derived systems will "work" if no demands are made that the initial premises be politically relevant. Thus the ideal position—that only the deductions, not the premises, need be plausible—cannot be widely accepted in a social science with serious data problems.[16]

Irreversible Choices

As children of modern psychology we all are well aware of the limitations on our personal choice as individuals—limitations of genetic endowment, of environment, and of experience. Without accepting a rigidly deterministic model of human action, we nevertheless comprehend the severe restrictions within which our *private* choice is able to move. But I think we perceive less clearly what are the bounds on the *public* choice exercised by leaders of nations, we too often fail to consider their real options, either as might be seen by an objective observer or as seen by the decision-maker himself.[17]

If it is true that political choice is severely circumscribed, we must focus special attention on a particular kind of choice node, on those decisions which sharply restrict the menu of future options. Often choices are not irreversible, and one may at least approximate, at a later point, an option that was rejected earlier. For this kind of situation the adage about *any* decision being better than *no* decision, or a paralysis of will, is especially appropriate. But this happens less often than we may like to think. In too many circumstances the model of the decision tree is all too relevant; as we proceed from one node to another previous options become ir-recoverable. Japanese leaders in 1941 found that successive choices cost them so many alternatives that in the end the decision to fight the United States, in a war they did not really expect to win, seemed unavoidable.[18] The American decision to develop atomic weapons brought technical knowledge that cannot be unlearned, immensely complicating disarmament efforts. The Red Army, whose incursion into Central Europe for the defeat of Hitler we applauded, became less welcome in a changed inter-national system. The decision to fight a "limited" war now may be at the expense of later economic growth, with the consequence that a nation's material power base is forever smaller than it might have been had arma-ments not taken the place of capital investment.

This is an especially serious problem in international politics because we know so little about the articulated consequences of our decisions. Neither the best theorist nor the most confident man of action can really know what the ramifications of an act will be. And the danger is compounded by the *speed* with which decisions are forced upon leaders before even whatever inadequate analytical tools we have can be brought to bear on the choice. Scientific and technological advances that bring the entire world within reach of instantaneous communication, or any target on the globe within 30 minutes of destruction, can leave little time for reflection.

When population natural increase rates are two per cent a year, total population doubles in thirty years. A world whose population has once reached three billion will never again be the natural, uncrowded environment that our ancestors knew. The further environmental consequences of a jump from 3 billion to 6 billion on earth are far different from those of a jump from 3 million to 6 million. There are also unimagined consequences of the *level* of power available to change our environment. One manifestation is the potential destructiveness of nuclear warfare, but another ostensibly more constructive manifestation is in the changes that modern industrial processes and urban living patterns are inflicting on the environment. Scientists warn us about an "ecological crisis" from pollutants that could quite literally make the globe uninhabitable.

Hence the old virtues of any decision being better than none become transmuted. The avoidance of a decision that would work irreversible changes looks attractive if there is some chance that our science can, given time, help us better to evaluate the consequences of decision.

Japan's 1941 policy is a good example of how hard it may be to recognize critical decision nodes when they do appear. America's incremental creep into the Vietnam quagmire is another. Regrettably, there is no automatic warning signal to flash before the decision maker. Until our science becomes better developed, perhaps all one can do to identify such nodes before they are passed is always to have someone ask explicitly, "What will it cost if this decision turns out badly? How, if at all, could we turn back?" This scepticism might help prevent seduction by alternatives that seem to carry fairly high probabilities of favorable outcomes, and high benefits if they work, but disastrous costs should they fail. The acquisition of very expensive weapons systems (because their costs will foreclose other military or civilian options) is an especially relevant class, as is the procurement of systems with very greatly enhanced capabilities. So, in this world, is a superpower's decision actually to use military force. And so, perhaps unfortunately, would be a decision to implement a major disarmament measure. In the last case, however, our foreign policy making system is well supplied with cautionary voices; for the others the devil's advocate has too often been reticent or unwelcome.[19]

Karl Marx showed us some economic foundations of politics. However flawed the glass through which he saw his vision, the image it projects remains a vibrant one. To give that view perspective, we must equally see the social and technological bases of choice. Politics, it sometimes seems, has become the arena for avoiding cataclysm. Political gladiators can destroy far more readily than they can create; their task is one of avoiding error. But they are human, and in repeated encounters ultimately they do blunder. In the spirit of Marx, it may be more fruitful to ask what shapes the arena than what determines each stroke of their blunt swords.

These final comments may perhaps suggest some needs, and also suggest how the many elements of new and traditional political theory must be combined. To make wise political choices in an era of rapid technological and social change requires a great variety of pieces of information.

1. We must know our own values. Here, in defining what we want to achieve, remains the central role of traditional normative political philosophy.

2. We also must know the consequences of various alternative actions. This must be specified in an involved and complex way, using such modern theoretical perspectives as general systems theory.

3. In the role of political engineers, we must know too about the processes of our own American political system and how it works, so as to be able to use and strengthen those elements that will support the action we desire.

4. Finally, we must discover the environmental constraints, what choices are actually available, what the options really are. The farther ahead we can see the greater is likely to be our choice.

Notes and References

[1]Quincy Wright, *A Study of War* (Chicago: University of Chicago Press, 1942, 2 vols.). Some later empirical contributions whose importance is now apparent are the content analysis studies of Ithiel Pool, Daniel Lerner, and Harold Lasswell: *Symbols of Internationalism* (Stanford: Stanford University Press, 1951), *Symbols of Democracy* (Stanford: Stanford University Press, 1952), and *The Prestige Papers* (Stanford: Stanford University Press, 1952); William Buchanan and Hadley Cantril, *How Nations See Each Other* (Urbana: University of Illinois Press, 1953); Karl W. Deutsch, *Nationalism and Social Communication* (Cambridge and New York: M.I.T. Press and Wiley, 1953); Karl Deutsch and Lewis Edinger, *Germany Rejoins the Powers* (Stanford: Stanford University Press, 1959); and Lewis F. Richardson, *Arms and Insecurity* (Pittsburgh: Boxwood Press, 1960) and *Statistics of Deadly Quarrels* (Pittsburgh: Boxwood Press 1960). In 1963 were published Harold Guetzkow, et al., *Simulation in International Relations* (Englewood Cliffs: Prentice Hall); Robert North *et al.*, *Content Analysis: A Handbook with Applications for the Study of International Crisis* (Evanston, Ill: Northwestern University Press); and my *Community and Contention: Britain and America in the Twentieth Century* (Cambridge: M.I.T. Press), although the first two are essentially how-to-do it volumes discussing the techniques behind the important substantive articles published elsewhere. The ten-year gap between *A Study of War* and the publications of Pool, Lerner, Lasswell, Buchanan, Cantril, and Deutsch may well mark the damage done to the nascent science of international politics by the intellectual as well as material disruption wrought by World War II and its aftermath, when almost all scholars were pressed into applied work. On the other hand, the enormously enhanced funding recently available for research is largely due to war and cold war.

[2]Charles A. McClelland, "Access to Berlin: The Quantity and Variety of Events, 1948–63," in J. David Singer (ed.), *Quantitative International Politics: Insights and Evidence* (New York: Free Press, 1968) is a preliminary study of these data. See also McClelland and Gary A. Hogard, "Conflict Patterns in the Interaction Among Nations", in James N. Rosenau ed., *International Politics and Foreign Policy* (New York: Free Press, 1969, 2nd ed.).

[3]American Institute of Public Opinion press release, April 30, 1968.

[4]Hayward R. Alker, "Dimensions of Con-

flict in the General Assembly," *American Political Science Review*, 58, No. 3 (September 1964), pp. 642–57; Alker and Russett, *World Politics in the General Assembly* (New Haven, Conn.: Yale University Press, 1965); and Russett, *International Regions and the International System* (Chicago: Rand McNally, 1967), chs. 4 and 5. See also R. J. Rummel, "Some Empirical Findings on Nations and Their Behavior," *World Politics*, 21, No. 2 (1969), pp. 226–41.

[5]Cf. also David H. Blake, *Leadership Succession and Foreign Policy* (Ph.D. dissertation, Rutgers University, 1968).

[6]Russett, *International Regions*, pp. 90–91.

[7]*Ibid.*, chapters 6–11. Also Russett, "'Regional' Trading Patterns, 1938–1963," *International Studies Quarterly*, 12, 4 (December 1968), pp. 360–79.

[8]Cf. Russett, *Community and Contention*, *op. cit.*, and "The Calculus of Deterrence," *Journal of Conflict Resolution*, 7, No. 3 (June 1963), pp. 97–109.

[9]Alker and Russett, *op. cit.*, Chapter 11.

[10]Thomas R. Dye, *Politics, Economics, and the Public: Policy Outcomes in the American States* (Chicago: Rand McNally, 1967); John Patrick Crecine, *Governmental Problem Solving: A Computer Simulation of Municipal Budgeting* (Chicago: Rand McNally, 1969); and a forthcoming study by Stephen V. Stephens of Johns Hopkins University.

[11]Crecine, *op. cit.*, and Otto A. Davis, M.A.H. Dempster, and Aaron Wildavsky, "A Theory of the Budgetary Process," *American Political Science Review*, 60, No. 3 (September 1966), pp. 529–47.

[12]On the latter, see Graham T. Allison, *Conceptual Models and the Cuban Missile Crisis* (Boston: Little Brown, 1971). It should be noted that Allison makes a strong case for knowing, especially in the analysis of crisis situations, about bureaucratic politics as well as system-level variables.

[13]J. David Singer and Melvin Small, "Alliance Aggregation and the Onset of War, 1815–1945," in Singer (ed.), *op. cit.*

[14]Paul Lazarsfeld, Bernard Berelson, and Hazel Gaudet, *The People's Choice* (New York: Columbia University Press, 1944) and Bernard Berelson, Paul Lazarsfeld, and William McPhee, *Voting* (Chicago: University of Chicago Press, 1954).

[15]R. V. Jones, "Science, Technology, and Civilization," *Bulletin of the Institute of Physics and the Physical Society* (April 1962), p. 97. See also my "The Ecology of Future International Politics," *International Studies Quarterly*, 11, 1 (March 1967), pp. 12–31, on the need for imagination, data, and rigor.

[16]See the Appendix on mathematical arms race models by Peter A. Busch in my *What Price Vigilance?* (New Haven, Conn. Yale University Press, 1970).

[17]For a similar perspective see Harold and Margaret Sprout, *An Ecological Paradigm for the Study of International Politics* (Princeton: Center of International Studies, Research Monograph No. 30, 1968). The renewed attention to spatial variables in macroscopic analyses also owes much to the Sprouts' long work on the subject.

[18]Bruce M. Russett, "Pearl Harbor: Deterrence Theory and Decision Theory," *Journal of Peace Research*, 2 (1967), pp. 87–104. There was *finally* a general consensus, among Japanese of many political persuasions, on this step. Robert North and his Stanford associates seem to be reaching a similar judgment about the German decision for war in 1914.

[19]If this sounds like an argument for always trying to avoid any possibility of the worst outcome, I do not mean it to be. It can be argued that American involvement in Vietnam stemmed from such a strategy—an attempt to prevent the very bad consequences, however unlikely, of the domino effect. If so, the strategy's proponents ignored the risks of an outcome very nearly as bad, and more probable—the quagmire.

ORAN R. YOUNG

The Actors in World Politics*

Most contemporary discussions of world politics[1] are based squarely on the postulate that the state, in its modern form, is the fundamental political unit in the world system[2] and that, therefore, it is possible to analyze world politics largely in terms of interstate relations.[3] It is true that there has been, from time to time, a certain amount of controversy concerning the essential characteristics of statehood.[4] And it has seldom been denied that various types of non-state actor exist and play secondary or peripheral roles in world politics.[5] Nevertheless, the postulate of the state as the fundamental unit of world politics has enjoyed a remarkably unchallenged position in the twentieth century. Interestingly, this orthodoxy appears to be just as firmly entrenched in scholarly writings as it is in the more popular literature in the field.

A variation on the postulate of the dominance of the state which deserves mention stems from the concept of the nation-state. The term "state" is generally applied to central political institutions without regard to the internal makeup of the society in which they exist. The concept "nation," on the other hand, is commonly used to refer to an integrated community held together by some combination of ethnic similarity, linguistic compatibility, shared traditions, and common culture.[6] The concepts of nation and of nationality came into common currency considerably later in time than the notion of statehood. In brief, emphasis on the nation emerged in the wake of the French Revolution and came into

*This is a much-revised version of a paper originally circulated in mimeographed form in 1967. I am grateful to Norman Frohlich, Helmut Handzik, Karl Kaiser, Edward L. Morse, Joe A. Oppenheimer, and Harold Sprout for their helpful comments on the original version.

Notes and References to this selection will be found on pages 140–144.

common currency largely as a result of political developments in Europe during the nineteenth century. Moreover, it was only incorporated into a kind of international orthodoxy with the emergence of the Wilsonian philosophy of self-determination for nations during the peace conference following the First World War. Especially in the western world, however, it has since become fashionable to insist on a coincidence of boundaries for the state and the nation and to express skepticism concerning the viability of multinational or nonnational states.[7] Under the influence of this intellectual movement, many writers pass beyond the initial concept of the state to insist on the nation-state as the fundamental unit of world politics.

The postulate of the dominance of the state focuses attention, in the first instance, on essentially homogeneous political systems (with regard to type of actor) in contrast to heterogeneous systems.[8] Beyond this, however, the postulate has several further implications and is generally linked with several corollaries which require specification. First, the notion of external sovereignty is incorporated in the modern concept of state.[9] And the notion of external sovereignty leads both to an emphasis on the *formal* equality of all states and to the idea that there can be no higher authority over the states, at least with regard to basic political functions. Second, the principle of territoriality, which is also incorporated in the definition of state, implies that the map of any given world system can be divided into neat geographical compartments without the ambiguities of overlapping jurisdictions.[10] Third, the idea that a wide variety of human activities (both political and nonpolitical) can be defined spatially in terms of state boundaries is also commonly assumed as a corollary of the postulate of the dominance of the state. This notion will be referred to in this essay as the corollary of functional congruence.

These concepts and definitions add up to a powerful set of assumptions in analytic terms. In effect, they operate to limit sharply the range of variables considered in analyses of world politics by holding a number of important factors constant. This procedure facilitates the analysis of essentially homogeneous states systems. At the same time, however, it precludes the analysis of a wide range of *logically* possible and *empirically* interesting models of world politics. Thus, most recent analyses of international politics have dealt with only a small segment of the broader field subsumed under the heading of world politics in this essay.

The concepts and assumptions incorporated in this state-centric view of world politics are remarkably entrenched in contemporary thinking in this field.[11] A few examples will suffice to indicate the extent of this entrenchment in practical terms. First, the very notion of *international* politics, which is common currency today, subsumes the postulate of the nation-state as the fundamental unit of world politics.[12] And since this orientation leads, in turn, to various corollaries such as those of state sovereignty and nonoverlapping jurisdictions, it is frequently necessary to make extensive efforts to fit reality into this conceptual schema. Second, orthodox views concerning human loyalties focus on the state or the nation-state as the highest repository of such loyalties. Though reality appears to be diverging in important ways from this conception at the present time (more on this below), there is no doubt that it holds an influential place in the basic imagery in terms of which people conceptualize world politics. Third, the predominant conceptions of international law in the contemporary period start from the postulate of the state as the fundamental unit of world politics both in ascribing the attributes of sovereignty only to states and in establishing states as the only subjects (in contrast to objects) of international law.[13] Fourth, prevailing views of international organization incline in the same direction in the common thesis that membership should be limited to states. This thesis is presently enshrined in formal terms, for example, in Articles 2 and 4 of the United Nations Charter.[14]

Given the entrenched quality and far-reaching implications of these orthodox conceptions of world politics, it is particularly interesting to note that they actually reflect quite recent developments in the longer flow of history and that a good case can be made for the argument that they have never described the realities of world politics very accurately. Over the bulk of recorded history man has organized himself for political purposes on bases other than those now subsumed under the concepts "state" and "nation-state."[15] After prolonged competition with the Papacy and the Holy Roman Empire, the state in its modern form crystalized as the leading pattern of political organization in the Western European arena during the fifteenth and sixteenth centuries.[16] And, as indicated above, the more restrictive concept of the nation-state is of considerably more recent vintage. Moreover, even after the development of the European states system during the seventeenth and eighteenth centuries,[17] a number of non-state actors continued to play significant roles in the politics of the system. Examples such as the Papacy, the Holy Roman Empire, and the various semi-autonomous principalities of Central Europe make this point clear.

At the same time, the modern conception of states, let alone a states system, is even more recent in the contexts of Asia and Africa. The traditional political empires, tributary relationships, and loose cultural links in these areas were followed closely by the establishment of externally imposed colonial arrangements that lasted (in most cases) well into the twentieth century. As a result, the state in its modern form is only now achieving prominence as a political unit within the Asian and African arenas. Moreover, the existence of extensive discontinuities between the boundaries of states and nations is presently one of the principal sources of political upheavals throughout Asia and Africa.

A. *Attacks on the State-Centric World View*

To what extent is the picture projected by the state-centric world view
an accurate reflection of the contemporary realities of world politics?
It seems clear, to begin with, that the degree of correspondence between
key concepts and reality has fluctuated considerably over time. In addition,
a persuasive argument can be made for the proposition that the correspondence has always been quite poor, at least outside the confines of the
European arena. A little reflection on the dimensions of contemporary
world politics, however, suggests that the discrepancies between the state-
centric world view and reality are currently especially large and growing at
a substantial pace. Precise and systematic efforts have not yet been made to
pin down and assess these discrepancies. But a number of distinguishable
groups as well as individual scholars have begun to develop evidence concerning particular aspects of these discrepancies and to formulate limited
attacks on the state-centric view of world politics. In the absence of more
systematic work, it seems useful to turn first to these limited attacks on the
orthodox views outlined in the preceding section.

An increasingly significant group whose concepts, images, and activities
constitute an explicit challenge to the orthodoxies of the state-centric
view of world politics might be labeled the integrationists. The fundamental
theme of this group is that rapid and continuing developments in a variety
of areas such as communications, transportation, and military technology
have caused an effective shrinking of the world and have led to a situation in
which the state, nation-state, and states system are increasingly obsolescent
and ineffective structures for the achievement of human security and
welfare.[18] Pointing to the continued growth of interdependencies among the
units of the world system, the integrationists argue that the only alternative to the spread of disorder and chaos in world politics is the development of an effective worldwide political community to replace or supplement
the existing multiplicity of national political communities.[19] Under the
circumstances the integrationists generally go on to maintain that a shift
from the dominance of the state in world politics to the supremacy of some
type of "world state" is necessary (and in their view feasible) in the foreseeable future.[20]

A second important group whose activities challenge the orthodox
formulations of the state-centric world view might be labeled, in general
terms, the transnationalists. While the challenge in this case is largely
tacit, its influence is both substantial and spreading rapidly. Broadly
speaking, the theme of the transnationalists is that the boundaries of established states and nation-states are too confining for the activities they
consider important. In other words, it is increasingly viewed as inefficient
and uneconomical to allow one's activities to be defined or disrupted by
the intervention of the political boundaries of states.

Beyond this basic theme, however, the transnationalists divide into a variety of subgroups. Some of these subgroups can be categorized usefully under the heading of pragmatic transnationalists. Among those included under this heading would be: groups designed to engage in economic ventures requiring organizations cutting across state boundaries;[21] groups geared toward hard-core revolutionary activities on some basis such as socioeconomic class or political status which has transnational significance, and groups based on transnational professional interests such as associations of lawyers, educators, or scientists. Many of the other subgroups can be placed under the general heading of idealistic (or visionary) transnationalists. This category of transnationalists would include, *inter alia,* the less pragmatic ideological movements, many of the so-called peace groups, and a wide range of more particularistic organizations concerned with some specific problem of well-being or morality on a transnational basis.[22]

Interestingly, transnationalism appears to be reemerging as a pervasive element in world politics in the contemporary period. While transnational concepts and activities permeated world politics in earlier eras such as the Middle Ages and the early modern period,[23] transnationalism declined substantially during the late nineteenth and early twentieth centuries as the doctrines associated with the modern state and, especially, the nation-state developed into a pervasive intellectual preoccupation in European circles.[24] There is a good deal of evidence to suggest, however, that the second half of the twentieth century is witnessing a new upsurge of trans-nationalism on a wide variety of fronts.[25] In fact, it would be difficult to avoid such an upsurge of transnational activities (both intentional and unintentional) in the contemporary period given the rapid growth of interdependencies in the world system associated with far-reaching developments in such diverse areas as communications, transportation, and military technology.

At the same time, a number of individual scholars have begun to mount attacks on various aspects of the state-centric world view in recent years. John Herz, for example, has elaborated at some length on the theme of "the decline of the territorial state."[26] Herz's work is primarily a reaction against the more extended implications of the principle of territoriality, which is elevated to a position of central importance in the state-centric world view. Specifically, his work challenges the current applicability of two of the conceptual images that arise from this elevation of the principle of territoriality. In the first instance, Herz questions the relevance of the image of states as relatively hard-shelled and impermeable units demarcated by clear-cut territorial boundaries. In this connection, he points both to the relative ease with which states and their subsidiaries are able to penetrate each other for various purposes[27] and to the extensive ambiguities concerning political boundaries in many parts of the contemporary global system. And this line of reasoning leads Herz to question, in addition, the so-called billiard-ball conception of world politics as the limited interactions among hard-shelled units. In brief, the realities of world politics now seem closer to a complex pattern of interpenetrations among various types of actor within the world system than to the simple and clearcut dichotomy between international politics and domestic politics which flows directly from the billiard-ball conception.[28]

Kenneth Boulding has also developed an interesting, albeit less persuasive, challenge to the state-centric world view with his conception of "viability."[29] Boulding's challenge rests essentially on an argument about the technological context[30] in which the actors in world politics currently operate. His fundamental proposition is that the state in its modern form can remain the basic unit of world politics only as long as military technology is such that at least some states can remain viable no matter what the other states in the system do (i.e., unconditionally). The practical explication of Boulding's proposition contains several steps. An international system in which no state enjoys unconditional viability will be actively unstable. The contemporary revolution in military technology, however, has generated a situation in which unconditional viability is impossible for any state. Therefore, the state can no longer fulfill its key roles as the producer of human security and welfare with any confidence since the performance of these roles requires the existence of an overall system that is at least minimally stable.[31]

Though Boulding's argument is an interesting and provocative one, it needs to be tempered with several additional observations. First, there have been few periods during the whole sweep of modern history in which any states have enjoyed a situation of unconditional viability for any length of time. While the unique qualities of world politics in the contemporary period are significant, therefore, they should not be overemphasized. Second, even though a shift from a system of unconditionally viable units to a system in which the units are only conditionally viable clearly constitutes a major change, it is not self-evident that the latter system will necessarily be unstable *as a system* or that the adaptations required to keep such a system stable will not take place in the course of its emergence. Whether they will take place appears to depend on various intervening variables such as the nature of the actors in the system and the prevailing rules of the game[32] as well as changes in the technological context.

These challenges to the state-centric world view have been sufficient in recent years to precipitate some interesting speculations among scholars. However, they have not yet significantly undermined the postulate of the state as the fundamental unit of world politics as far as most observers are concerned. In short, most observers still find it satisfactory to treat these challenges in terms of *ad hoc* exceptions not requiring any substantial realignments in the orthodox views of world politics.

B. *Additional Discrepancies*

The challenges reported in the preceding paragraphs, nevertheless, do not indicate the full extent of the growing discrepancies between the images·of the state-centric world view and the realities of world politics. In the first instance, current usage of the concepts "state" and "nation-state" is stretching these notions to the point where they are becoming ambiguous and beginning to lose their core meaning. In previous periods, the focus on the European states system in discussions of world politics operated to restrict these problems of meaning to manageable proportions. In the European context, it was possible to pin down with some clarity both the consolidation of the modern state in the fifteenth and sixteenth centuries and the growing shift toward the idea of nation-states in the nineteenth and twentieth centuries. Moreover, it was possible to regard most of the states of the European system not only as well established political entities but also as entities that were quite similar in many respects.[33] And with this focus went a marked tendency to elevate the European arena to a position of primary importance in world politics and, therefore, to deemphasize the other areas of the world which clearly were not organized on the basis of modern states, let alone nation-states.

However, the shift to an increasingly interdependent and global world system,[34] together with the emergence of a large number of "new states,"[35] in the twentieth century has created a situation in which the core meanings of the concepts "state" and "nation-state" are much less clear than they were when applied primarily to the European arena. If the basic attributes of statehood are taken to be such things as a clearly demarcated territorial base, a relatively stable population, more or less viable central institutions of government, and external sovereignty, the contemporary situation immediately begins to appear unclear and confusing. Many of the "new states," for example, are of doubtful viability in political terms, poorly integrated as communities, geographically fluid, and sufficiently dependent upon other states and organizations (albeit often on an informal basis) to compromise seriously their external sovereignty.[36] Moreover, the growth of interdependencies and, therefore, of interpenetrations among the units of world politics in the contemporary period is producing a wide range of developments, affecting both the "new states" and the more established states, which are breaking down and obscuring the traditional characteristics of external sovereignty to the point where most generalizations on this subject have become hazardous and suspect.[37]

Second, the state-centric world view suggests not only that the state is a relatively hard-shelled unit, but also that most human activities (both political and non-political) can be defined with reference to the boundaries of states. In the first instance, this accounts for the insistence on a clearcut dichotomy between international politics and domestic politics which is generally incorporated in the state-centric world view. But the corollary of functional congruence is also employed with reference to many human activities that are not solely or even primarily political. An individual, for example, may travel widely in the world but only as a national of a specific state and without much independent standing in international law. Similarly, the orthodox view allows corporate entities to operate internationally but only as state-chartered organizations that can be subjected to national regulations. In short, state boundaries acquire special significance in the state-centric world view not only because they mark breaking points for straightforward political purposes, but also because they have been conceptualized as watersheds in marking a simultaneous shift in the status of a great many different types of human activity.

The contemporary period, however, is marked by a striking growth in divergences and discontinuities with regard to the spatial definitions of various human activities. There is no doubt that the state remains an important unit in world politics or even that it is increasingly important in some parts of the world and with respect to some purposes or functions. What appears to be changing, in this connection, is the role of state boundaries in marking a simultaneous shift in the status of most important human activities. As a result, a vertical layering effect is increasingly replacing the simple horizontal pattern, projected by the state-centric world view, in terms of which a two-dimensional map was sufficient to describe the basic dimensions of international relations. Thus, the grids formed by the maps of the various layers of human activity in the world system no longer constitute such a neat package that a single two-dimensional map is sufficient to describe the fundamental dimensions of all the layers. Moreover, the incongruities among the various layers are presently increasing at a substantial pace rather than decreasing.

Next, the emergence of this layering effect or third dimension in world politics and the partial attenuation of the territorial principle which it has caused have facilitated an expansion of the roles of various non-state actors that cannot be thought of wholly as subsidiaries of states with respect to their involvement in world politics. Several broad classes of these actors are distinguishable. To begin with, the human individual is slowly acquiring (or reacquiring) independent influence in world politics despite the fact that the concept of nationality and the basic postulates of international law constitute substantial barriers to developments along these lines.[33] Then, as indicated previously, there is the growing assortment of transnational organizations whose purposes are political, economic, cultural, and so forth and whose membership is based on some criterion other than statehood or nationality. In addition, there are the international and regional organizations that are composed of states and fundamentally oriented toward political activities but that frequently operate as semi-autonomous actors in world politics.[39]

With respect to the two types of organization distinguished in the previous paragraph, the twentieth century has witnessed expansions of such striking proportions that it deserves to be designated as one of the great ages of organization at levels other than that of the state.[40] These expansions have taken place, moreover, despite the severe restrictions placed upon such developments by the various concepts, assumptions, and prescriptions associated with the state-centric world view. While prevailing doctrines suggest that only states can acquire the attributes of external sovereignty, achieve the standing of subjects in international law, or gain formal diplomatic recognition, for example, the contemporary history of the development of nonstate actors constitutes a striking record of tacit and *de facto* chipping away at these doctrines.[41]

A fourth, and related, trend in world politics which constitutes a challenge to the state-centric world view arises from the development of new patterns of human loyalty in the current era. It would certainly *not* be accurate to argue that we are presently witnessing a decisive shift away from patterns of human loyalties in which the state is a major focal point. In fact, in some areas of the world it is possible to discern movements toward an intensification of loyalties focusing on the state and on various loose conceptions of the nation-state. Particularly among the "new states" developments that might be subsumed in a loose sense under the heading of the growth of nationalism are evident in the contemporary world. Taking the world system as a whole, nevertheless, the picture that emerges can best be described in terms of a fractionation of human loyalties together with the development of important new patterns of multiple loyalties.[42]

The phenomenon of multiple loyalties is not, of course, a new one. In earlier periods, however, the critical axis of fractionation with respect to human loyalties centered on the tension between various local institutions or communities on the one hand and the state or nation on the other. This tension is a familiar one, and it has been dealt with in various ways at different times and in different places. But the point of interest in the present discussion arises from the fact that the critical axis of fractionation with respect to human loyalties now appears to be shifting more and more to a tension between individual states or nation-states on the one hand and various non-state actors, transnational units, or the over-all world system on the other hand. Several separate developments evidently account for this shift including: the increasing supremacy of the state in the contest between local institutions and the state for human loyalties; rapid developments in the technology of communications and transportation which have substantially broadened the scope of human concerns; the growth of interdependencies and interpenetrating relationships among the units of world politics, and the emergence of widespread feelings to the effect that the state is no longer an adequate vehicle for the achievement of basic security and welfare requirements of the human individual.[43]

Though this shift is an important one, it is also a somewhat confusing one at the present time. While the state or the nation-state constitutes a relatively clear and unambiguous repository for human loyalties, the development of a wide variety of non-state actors together with the current weaknesses of transnational and global organizations means that there is no single alternative to the state as a focus of loyalties. As a result, the critical axis of fractionation with respect to loyalties is not clearly defined at present, and multiple loyalties tend to be scattered over a series of alternative focal points. Nevertheless, the implications of these developments for the state-centric world view are far-reaching. Should this shift continue, the state-centric world view would almost certainly devolve, at some point, into a competitor among several alternative world views, thereby losing its present status as a reigning and largely undisputed orthodoxy.

A review of current trends in world politics, therefore, throws up a variety of indications of growing discrepancies between the nature of reality and the picture projected by the state-centric world view. It is possible to argue that these developments still have not undermined the empirical applicability of the state-centric world view in any decisive sense. But it seems clear that the world system has now reached a point where there are great difficulties in constructing satisfactory explanations of various important aspects of world politics in terms of this world view and where decisive undermining is by no means unlikely within the foreseeable future. Under the circumstances, it seems important to consider the conclusions that can be drawn from the situation and to begin thinking, at least in rough terms, about the kind of world view that may begin to supplement or replace the state-centric world view in the foreseeable future.

C. *Systems of Mixed Actors*

Perhaps the most common reaction to the trends described in the preceding sections, among those who have thought about them at all, might be described as the monist interpretation. The basic outlook of the monists, which appears ultimately to stem more from unhappiness with the alleged deficiencies of states systems than from an analysis of current trends in world politics, contains several principal elements as follows.[44] The state in all its forms is increasingly inadequate for the achievement of human security and welfare and, therefore, increasingly anachronistic in the contemporary world. Moreover (according to the monist argument), growing interdependencies in the world, symbolized by a wide range of developments from new communications systems to the emergence of new transnational communities in the European arena, indicate that the predominant role of the state has begun to decline in any case. Under the circumstances, what is now impending is a decisive shift toward some new pattern of organization for the world system based on the supremacy or predominance of some unit other than the state. In this connection, the great majority of the monists argue that the new pattern of organization both can and should focus on some form of "world state."[45] And to lend weight to this view an hypothesis to the effect that man has moved steadily toward larger and larger units for the achievement of political functions is frequently adduced to make the shift to a "world state" seem almost inexorable.

The monist interpretation is superficially attractive because it encompasses a set of analytic assumptions just as powerful as the one it replaces as well as giving the appearance of adaptation to the changing realities of world politics in the contemporary era. On further reflection, nevertheless, this interpretation seems extraordinarily weak on both logical and empirical grounds. Logically speaking, there is no reason why any given world system should be dominated by one class or type of actor. Indications that the status of the state in world politics is undergoing significant changes, therefore, need not necessarily imply an impending shift of supremacy from the state to some other single type of actor. In addition, there is no logically persuasive reason to conclude that a world system based on a multiplicity of actors, even if they are only conditionally viable vis-à-vis each other, cannot remain stable over time. Furthermore, it is far from clear that an alternative form of organization based on some type of "world state" would have a comparative advantage over a states system with respect to the achievement of human security and welfare. To argue in this fashion appears, at least to some extent, to ascribe to faulty organizational patterns phenomena that might be explained just as satisfactorily in terms of basic qualities of human nature.[46]

At the same time, the monist interpretation is vulnerable in empirical terms. Above all, there is every indication that states and nation-states are still remarkably resilient both in some areas of the world and in terms of the performance of some important functions. As experience even with such relatively successful ventures as the European communities makes clear, the modern state cannot be superseded with ease even under comparatively favorable circumstances.[47] And in many other parts of the world, there is every evidence that the state is only now coming into its own as the dominant form of political organization. Even nationalism, with its thrust toward the idea of nation-states, is still a potent and rising political force in many areas of the world despite (or perhaps because of) the fact that developments in the middle decades of the twentieth century such as the imperial activities of various great powers virtually destroyed, at least temporarily, the independent political bases of a number of important nations.[48] Beyond this, the monist hypothesis concerning the shift toward larger and larger political units cannot be validated by any systematic empirical analysis.[49] In brief, conclusions in this area are heavily dependent upon the segment of human history that is selected for analysis, and virtually any hypothesis can be "supported" by means of a careful selection of time periods.[50]

The monist interpretation, therefore, does not provide either a persuasive explanation of the developments discussed in the preceding sections of this essay or a very useful conceptual framework in terms of which to think about the future of world politics. How then are these developments, which have stretched the state-centric world view to its limits, to be conceptualized? The thesis of this essay is that it is necessary, under the circumstances, to relax a major assumption that is common to both the state-centric world view and the monist interpretation. In particular, it seems desirable to think increasingly in terms of world systems that are heterogeneous with respect to types of actor (i.e., mixed actor systems) in the analysis of world politics. While a shift along these lines will introduce some new complexities into this field, it seems likely that it will allow for more satisfactory explanations of many of the changes that are now taking place in world politics.

The basic notion of a system of mixed actors requires a movement away from the assumption of homogeneity with respect to types of actor and, therefore, a retreat from the postulate of the state as the fundamental unit of world politics. Instead, the mixed-actor world view envisions a situation in which several qualitatively different types of actor interact in the absence of any settled pattern of dominance-submission (or hierarchical) relationships. In such a system, questions concerning political stature, competencies, rights, obligations, and so forth cannot be dealt with in terms of a simple rule indicating the supremacy of one type of actor and, therefore, they must be worked out on some *ad hoc* basis with different results for different types of relationship.

As a result, the interstate relations of the state-centric world view give way, in a mixed-actor world view, to a situation in which the totality of world politics is made up of a number of distinguishable patterns of political relationships. In the first instance, this suggests two overarching categories of relationships, which should be separated clearly. First, there are relationships involving two or more representatives of the same type of actor *inter se*. This would produce as many different patterns of political relationships as there are types of actor in any given system. Second, there are the various patterns arising from relationships involving two or more different types of actor. This category would produce an even greater number of patterns of political relationships under the broad heading of world politics.

Beyond this, it would seem desirable to consider the possibilities arising from the relaxation of the various corollaries associated with the postulate of the state as the fundamental unit of world politics. Within the context of mixed-actor systems, therefore, it would be possible to consider the analytic consequences of the existence of relationships not characterized by sovereign equality; the development of functional discontinuities in the spatial definition of various human activities, and the emergence of actors not based directly on the principle of territoriality. While it would no doubt be generally undesirable for analytic reasons to vary all these factors simultaneously, the range of potential conceptions of world politics opened up by the possibilities of relaxing these corollaries of the state-centric world view would be great.

Given the diversity of the component units, the qualitatively different types of political relationships, and the prospects for extensive interpenetrations among actors in systems of mixed actors, it is to be expected that such systems will be highly dynamic ones. That is, while the quality of the system itself as a mixed-actor system might remain the same, a relatively large amount of shifting with regard to both the existence and the significance of specific types of actor and political relationships would be predictable. In this sense, also, the mixed-actor world view tends to involve greater complexity than the state–centric world view. In effect, the state–centric world view sets up certain postulates concerning the role of the state as unchanging axioms and deals with variations from the resultant norms in terms of *ad* hoc exceptions. The mixed-actor world view, on the other hand, suggests the occurrence of somewhat more extensive dynamic shifts within the parameters of the system itself and, therefore, poses greater requirements of intellectual flexibility for those who endeavor to use it to explain and assess specific phenomena in world politics.

D. *Some Implications of Mixed-Actor Models*

If present trends in the world system unfold in such a way as to make mixed-actor models increasingly relevant, what will be the implications for the analysis of world politics? To begin with, it should be reemphasized that: (1) developments along these lines would leave room for a continuing role of major proportions for the state and, in many cases, the nation-state in world politics, and (2) mixed-actor situations are not entirely *de novo* in the history of world politics.[51] As indicated in the preceding section, there is every reason to suppose that both states and nation-states will continue to occupy positions of importance in the world system. The point at issue in this essay, therefore, is the empirical proposition that states are currently in the process of receding from their earlier role as the dominant units in the system to a new role as important, but *not* dominant, actors in world politics.

Interactions among the political units in the Mediterranean arena during the sixth through fourth centuries B.C.[52] and during the fourth and fifth centuries A.D.[53] exhibited the fundamental characteristics of mixed-actor systems. There are, moreover, relevant examples of systems of this kind in the history of more recent periods. The European system that prevailed from approximately the tenth through the fourteenth centuries was a mixed-actor situation of almost classic proportions. The mainsprings of this system consisted of the complex interpenetrations and dynamic shifts among: (1) the Papacy, an essentially religious and non-territorial actor, (2) the Holy Roman Empire, an actor whose strength was based fundamentally on secular but nonterritorial relationships, and (3) the various regional states whose secular and territorial foundations indicate their antecedent relationship to the state in its modern form.[54] Similarly, the relationships among the principal actors in east and southeast Asia during most of recent history (prior to the imposition of European dominance) have exhibited the qualities of a mixed-actor system. Here the bases of a mixed-actor system arose from a combination of the pervasive mystique of the Chinese Middle Kingdom, the efficacy of various loose tributary relationships, and the ability of local rulers to retain considerable freedom of action within the framework established by the preeminence of China.

Despite these elements of continuity with the past, the contemporary movement in the direction of a system of mixed actors contains far-reaching implications for world politics. And the fact that the state-centric world view is still deeply entrenched in most thinking about world politics tends to magnify the consequences of this evolution of realities. A few examples should indicate the scope of these implications. First, since most of the reigning schemes for the analysis of world politics are based squarely on state-centric assumptions, movement in the direction of a system of mixed actors tends to make these conceptions of *international* politics increasingly outmoded (in terms of empirical relevance) in a number of important respects. In terms of the language employed in an earlier section of this essay, for example, most of these schemes offer two-dimensional explanations of a world system that increasingly involves three-dimensional phenomena. Second, movement toward a mixed-actor system tends to undermine some of the major tenets of the principle of state sovereignty which occupies the position of a basic assumption in the state-centric world view. As a result, the accepted derivations of standards and norms with respect to such matters as legitimacy, recognition, international representation, the control and use of force, and intervention in the affairs of other actors are becoming harder and harder to square with the realities of world politics. Third, these developments are also beginning to call into question some of the basic postulates of prevailing orientations toward international law and international organization. Among other things, therefore, the requirements of adaptation go right to the core of the normative substructure of political relationships in the world system. For this reason, superficial adjustments in the prevailing world view are likely to produce only *ad hoc* compromises that will give way to more fundamental changes over time. Fourth, all the factors outlined above suggest that there are serious deficiencies in the "foreign policy" apparatus of most of the relevant actors in world politics. In brief, the formulation of foreign policy presently tends to be organized on a somewhat narrow and formalistic interstate basis, even though some of the important problems of foreign policy are increasingly difficult to deal with in these terms. Interestingly, this applies both to the foreign offices of states, which find it hard to deal effectively with nonstate actors, and to the various nonstate actors themselves, which are apt, at present, to approach their problems of "foreign policy" only on a sketchy, uncoordinated, and *ad hoc* basis. In general, therefore, the implications of the movement toward a system of mixed actors are not only far-reaching in conceptual terms, they also impinge on important matters of a practical nature.

In the light of the analysis set forth in this essay, however, it should hardly come as a surprise that there is great resistance at the present time to any shift from a state-centric world view toward a mixed-actor world view. There are at least three distinguishable elements in this general pattern of resistance. In the first place, the orthodoxies of the state-centric world view are deeply entrenched. While they have recently been challenged from several quarters, there is little doubt that their dominance remains essentially unshaken at this time. Next, the changes involved in such a shift of world views would be both extensive and ultimately quite fundamental. In such matters it is difficult to make major modifications without calling into question some of the basic tenets of a prevailing world view. Finally, the particular shift in question would run counter to the goal of maximizing conceptual simplicity. That is, the principal concepts, definitions, and postulates of the state-centric world view are characterized by an attractive simplicity, and the assumptions of this world view are powerful in analytic terms. Despite the fact that the conceptions of a mixed-actor world view offer a wide range of interesting possibilities for the analysis of world politics, therefore, resistance to movement in this direction is hardly surprising.

E. *Conclusion*

The current era is witnessing a movement away from a world system dominated by a single type of actor and toward a system characterized by extensive interactions among several qualitatively different types of actor. Moreover, a survey of major trends in world politics suggests that this movement is presently gathering momentum. So far, however, these developments have been conceptualized and explained primarily in terms of isolated exceptions to accepted orthodoxies and *ad hoc* deviations from the prevailing images of world politics. As a result, the basic postulates, assumptions, and prescriptions of the reigning state-centric world view have not yet been seriously or systematically questioned.

Nevertheless, the shift toward a system of mixed actors has already reached a stage in which many new developments in the world system are difficult to explain satisfactorily in terms of orthodox assumptions and doctrines. If movement in this direction continues at a substantial pace, the world system may well reach a threshold, within the foreseeable future, at which the whole edifice of the state-centric world view begins to crumble. All this clearly does *not* imply that states and nation-states are likely to become unimportant as actors in world politics within the foreseeable future. It does, however, indicate the current importance of efforts both to assess the implications of contemporary trends affecting the actors in world politics and to explore the nature of alternative conceptual schemes and world views that may become increasingly influential in the wake of these trends.

Notes and References

[1]The term politics is employed in this essay to refer to all phenomena associated with relationships of power between or among actors in sociopolitical systems. "Power" refers to the changes one actor causes in the actions of others whenever these changes are: (1) the result of conscious intent on the part of the first actor, and (2) achieved by the first actor at a relatively low cost in terms of its own values.

[2]The expression "world system" is employed in this essay in place of "international system," which is the dominant expression in the literature. As the present essay demonstrates, the notion of an international system assumes the postulate of the state or nation-state as the fundamental unit of world politics. An international system, therefore, is a special case of the category "world system" within the conceptual scheme of this essay.

[3]A perusal of the standard texts in the field will make this point clear. Consult, for example, Hans Morgenthau, *Politics Among Nations* (New York: Alfred A. Knopf, 1949); Ernst Haas and Allan Whiting, *Dynamics of International Relations* (New York: McGraw-Hill, 1956); Harold and Margaret Sprout, *Foundations of International Politics* (Princeton: Van Nostrand, 1962), and K. J. Holsti, *International Politics: A Framework for Analysis*

(Englewood Cliffs, N. J.: Prentice-Hall, 1967).

[4]This controversy cannot be settled definitively since this would require an ontologically correct definition of the concept "state." In this essay, the term "state" will be defined nominally as a political entity characterized by: (1) centralized institutions of government organized on a formal and secular basis, (2) the capacity to interact with other actors in the world system on a formally equal (i.e., sovereign) basis, (3) a relatively fixed and clearly delimited territorial base, and (4) a clearly definable core population. While this definition allows for substantial variation with respect to size, power, and so forth, it does set definite limits on the empirical applicability of the term "state."

[5]An actor in world politics will be defined for this essay as any organized entity that (1) is composed (at least indirectly) of human beings, (2) is not wholly subordinate to any other actor in the world system in effective terms, and (3) participates in power relationships with other actors. Within this framework, actors can vary greatly with respect to such matters as: size of population, territoriality, geographical size and dimensions, functional specificity, criteria of membership, type of organization, and so forth.

[6]For an excellent brief discussion of the ambiguities surrounding the concept "nation" consult Rupert Emerson, *From Empire to Nation* (Cambridge: Harvard University Press, 1960), Chapter V. For some useful points on the differences between the concepts "state" and "nation" see also J. P. Nettl, "The State as a Conceptual Variable," *World Politics,* XX, No. 4 (July 1968), pp. 559–592.

[7]For a recent example of skepticism along these lines see Walker Conner, "Self-Determination: The New Phase," *World Politics,* XX, No. 1 (October 1967), pp. 30–53.

[8]The terms homogeneous and heterogeneous as applied to world politics have recently become highly ambiguous because they have been utilized to refer to a number of different phenomena without specification. In particular, they have been applied willy nilly to the existence of ideological divergences, differences in the internal political arrangements of states, geopolitical asymmetries, and so forth. For a clear-cut example of the resultant confusion see Raymond Aron, *Peace and War* (New York: Doubleday, 1966). The two terms are employed in this essay only to distinguish between world systems in which one basic type of actor is predominant and systems encompassing several basic types of actor.

[9]For a thorough exploration of the notion of external sovereignty see F. H. Hinsley, *Sovereignty* (New York: Basic Books, 1966), Chapter 5.

[10]For a discussion of the principle of territoriality, including some interesting historical comments, see John Herz, *International Politics in the Atomic Age* (New York: Columbia University Press, 1959), Chapter 2–4.

[11]These comments should not be taken to imply that there are no exceptions whatsoever to the state-centric views in current usage. Nevertheless, it seems reasonable to describe the resultant conceptual schema for the analysis of world politics as a "world view" that is widely prevalent and largely unquestioned.

[12]The term world politics is used in this essay to refer to the political interactions between and among all the actors in any given world system. In this context, inter-national politics becomes a subset of world politics. It refers to relations between states or nation-states in a world system. When a system is composed entirely of states or nation-states, the two terms naturally become fully congruent.

[13]This is one of the main reasons why international law has been somewhat difficult to adapt to the various roles of organizations such as the United Nations and the European Common Market in the contemporary period.

[14]Article 2 (1) of the United Nations Charter reads:
"The Organization is based on the principle of the sovereign equality of all its members. . . . "
Article 4 reads in part:
"Membership in the United Nations is open to all . . . peace-loving states which accept the obligations contained in the present Charter. . . . "

[15]In particular, various forms of empire and unstructured community relationships have been prevalent. For a general survey of this subject consult Adda B. Bozeman, *Politics and Culture in International History* (Princeton: Princeton University Press, 1960).

[16]It is, of course, difficult to pin down multifaceted developments of this kind with any precision. For relevant historical material consult Bozeman, *op. cit.,* Chapter 13, and Hinsley, *op. cit.,* Chapter 3 and 4.

[17]The date 1648 (the Peace of Westphalia) is frequently employed as a shorthand reference to mark the emergence of the European states system. But see also Hinsley, *op. cit.,* Chapter 5, for an argument to the effect that some of the important attributes generally ascribed to the European states system did not crystalize until the eighteenth century.

[18]For a sophisticated summary of these arguments see Amatai Etzioni, *The Active Society* (New York: Free Press, 1968), especially Chapter 19.

[19]Interestingly, this argument can be thought of as a special case of the problems that arise when the level of interdependence among the units of any sociopolitical system increases rapidly. In general, rising levels of interdependence increase the scope and importance of public (in contrast to private) goods in sociopolitical systems.

And assuming rationality on the part of the actors, this will lead to a growing incentive to increase the level of systemic organization. For the theoretical arguments underlying these relationships consult Mancur Olson, Jr., *The Logic of Collective Action* (Cambridge: Harvard University Press, 1965), Chapter 1.

[20] For a sensitive expression of this line of argument see Richard A. Falk, "On Minimizing the Use of Nuclear Weapons: A Comparison of Revolutionary and Reformist Perspectives," in Richard A. Falk, Robert C. Tucker, and Oran R. Young, *On Minimizing the Use of Nuclear Weapons* (Princeton, N.J.: Princeton Center of International Studies, 1966).

[21] On this subject see George Modelski, "The Corporation in World Society," pp. 64–79 in *The Yearbook of World Affairs 1968* (New York 1968), and Richard N. Cooper, *The Economics of Interdependence* (New York: McGraw-Hill, 1968).

[22] The Red Cross constitutes a particularly interesting case in this category. For a somewhat dated but still useful discussion see L. Ledermann, "The International Red Cross," *The Yearbook of World Affairs 1947* (London: Institute of World Affairs, 1947), pp. 248–64.

[23] Transnationalism in these periods had several distinguishable bases including: (1) religion (e.g., the activities of the Papacy), (2) trade and commerce (e.g., the Hanseatic League), (3) dynastic relationships (e.g., intermarriages), and (4) the diffusion of loyalties (e.g., the cosmopolitianism of the upper classes). For useful information on all these forms of transnationalism see Bozeman, *op. cit.,* Parts III and IV.

[24] The point here concerns a relative decline in transnationalism; such phenomena did not of course disappear entirely during this period. In general, however, the decline was a marked one, particularly in Europe where the rise of nationalism led to a growing emphasis on national self-sufficiency, political symbols of local origin, and clearcut national loyalties. It is true that the older habits of the nobility stood against these trends at first. But in the end the growth of nationalism was one of the factors that undermined the effective power of the nobility all over Europe.

[25] For useful information on the rise of transnational organizations consult, *inter alia, Annuaire de la Vie Internationale* (Paris: L'Office Central des Institutions Internationales); *Handbook of International Organizations* (Geneva: The League of Nations), and *Yearbook of International Organizations* (Brussels: The Union of International Associations).

[26] The principal arguments are developed in Herz, *op. cit.,* Chapter 6. Herz himself has recently begun to modify his views on this subject—see, for example, his "The Territorial State Revisited," *Policy,* I (1968), pp. 12–34. The concepts employed here, however, are derived primarily from the 1959 book.

[27] On the growth of interpenetrating relationships consult also Andrew Scott, *The Revolution in Statecraft* (New York: Random House, 1965).

[28] These developments also make it increasingly difficult to employ a black-box image of the state in analyzing interactions among states.

[29] Kenneth Boulding *Conflict and Defense* (New York: Harper, 1962), Chapters 4, 12, and 13.

[30] For a discussion of the term "context" (rather than the term "environment") in this connection, see Oran R. Young, *A Systemic Approach to International Politics* (Princeton, N.J.: Princeton Center of International Studies, 1968), pp. 22–24.

[31] This argument can also be conceptualized as a special case of the problem of achieving the production of public goods in an increasingly interdependent system (see note 19 on this point). Under the circumstances, the regulation of highly destructive military technology becomes a public good since no actor could be excluded from experiencing the consequences of such regulation.

[32] For an effort to conceptualize the notion of the "rules of the game" along these lines consult Young, *op. cit.,* pp. 32–33.

[33] For a useful discussion of this point see Emerson, *op. cit.,* especially pp. 103–104. The force of this argument was especially strong in the period following the unification of Germany in 1870–1871.

[34] On the emergence of a global system see Aron, *op. cit.,* Part III.

[35] For an interesting commentary on the

impact of the "new states" on the world system see Peter Calvocoressi, *World Order and the New States* (London: Institute for Strategic Studies, 1962).

[36] For an excellent though brief discussion of these issues consult Emerson, *op. cit.*, Chapter V.

[37] For a discussion of these issues which arrives at somewhat different conclusions see Hinsley, *op. cit.*, Chapter 6. Note also the growing gap between the boundaries of formal sovereignty and the boundaries of effective autonomy which plagues many actors in world politics. For a helpful commentary on this point see Cooper, *op. cit.*, Chapter 1.

[38] For evidence of the conceptual problems hampering efforts to relate these developments to the state-centric world view see Wolfgang Friedmann, *The Changing Structure of International Law* (New York: Columbia University Press, 1964), Chapter 15. For an interesting specific case consult the decision of the Shimoda Case and the discussions of its implications printed in Richard A. Falk and Saul H. Mendlovitz (eds.), *The Strategy of World Order* (New York: World Law Fund, 1966), I, pp. 307, *et seq.*

[39] For an effort to conceptualize the United Nations as a semi-autonomous actor in world politics see Oran R. Young, "The United Nations and the International System," *International Organization*, XXII, No. 4 (Autumn 1968), pp. 902–922.

[40] For information on this subject consult the references cited in note 25.

[41] For some interesting examples consider the activities of the United Nations as illustrated in the Reparations Case and the negotiations of status of forces agreements with Egypt in 1956 and the Congo in 1960 as well as the activities of the European Common Market in negotiating with non-members.

[42] On the concept of multiple loyalties see Harold Guetzkow, *Multiple Loyalties: Theoretical Approach to a Problem in International Organization* (Princeton: Organizational Behavior Project, 1955).

[43] For an interesting set of comments on current developments in this area see Johan Galtung, "On the Future of the International System," *Journal of Peace Research*, 4 (1967), pp. 312–318.

[44] For a brief summary of the principal strands of the monist interpretation see Richard A. Falk and Saul H. Mendlovitz, "Toward a Warless World: One Legal Formula to Achieve Transition," in Falk and Mendlovitz (eds.), *op. cit.*, II, pp.10–17.

[45] For a good summary of the arguments for a world state see Etzioni, *op. cit.*, Chapter 20.

[46] For a review of the various substantive arguments in this area see Kenneth Waltz, *Man, the State, and War* (New York: Columbia University Press, 1959).

[47] For an excellent discussion of this problem see Stanley Hoffmann, "Obstinate or Obsolete? The Fate of the Nation-State and the Case of Western Europe," *Daedalus* (Summer 1966), pp. 862–915.

[48] Starting in the 1930s, the activities of Germany (outside the German-speaking area), Japan, Italy, the Soviet Union, and (more recently) the United States have tended to disrupt the empirical manifestations of the idea of the nation-state as the fundamental unit of world politics. Despite the continuation of wide-spread support for the doctrine of self-determination in formal terms, therefore, the record of the nation-state has been a highly checkered one in the twentieth century.

[49] For a discussion leading to the same conclusion see Karl Deutsch *et al.*, *Political Community and the North Atlantic Area* (Princeton: Princeton University Press, 1957), pp. 22–28.

[50] For example, if one started either with the Roman Empire or with the various organizations of the Middle Ages in Europe, it would be possible to "support" the opposite hypothesis that man has moved toward smaller political units.

[51] For a helpful general survey of a number of mixed-actor situations see Bozeman, *op. cit.*

[52] Especially important in this case were the relations among the Persian Empire, the Greek city states, the various Hellenic leagues, and (toward the end of the period) the rising power in Macedonia.

[53] The principal actors in this case were the Roman Empire (with its two foci at Constantinople and Rome), the Church, and the various tribes of the European and Central Asian hinterlands.

[54]Two other qualities of this system are particularly interesting in the present context. First, it was characterized by a complex (and shifting) division of functions among the major actors. Second, this European system as a whole engaged, from time to time, in relatively extensive interactions with the Byzantine Empire, the Muslim Empire, and the Mongolian Empire in the East.

JAMES N. ROSENAU

The External Environment as a Variable in Foreign Policy Analysis*

The behavior of any human system, whether it be a single person or a complex society, results in part from the cumulative weight of past experience and in part from the impact of current stimuli. Anyone who has ever enjoyed the task of raising a small child can provide ample testimony on the interplay of the historical and the environmental—the habits and characteristics that have been shaped by previous conditions and the impulses and responses that are evoked by new circumstances. Indeed, child development becomes most intriguing when prevailing demands and established habits come into conflict. For these are the times when unexpected behavior occurs as the child achieves a new synthesis between the past and the present.

The characteristics and behavior of social systems can also be seen, at any moment in time, as products of both their cultural tradition and their changing environments. Consider societies undergoing rapid economic and political development. The dynamics of development alter the objective circumstances of a society and, in the process, they also equip individuals with new skills that give rise to new attitudes which, in turn, foster new institutions. These new circumstances, skills, attitudes, and institutions, however, do not necessarily replace the old patterns that prevailed prior to the onset of the developmental process. The cultural norms and historical traditions passed down from earlier generations may continue to operate upon the members of the society. An American engineer is a U.S. citizen as well as a skilled technician. An African physicist has tribal ancestors

* In preparing this paper I have been substantially aided by the suggestions and criticisms offered by Norah Rosenau.

Notes and References for this selection will be found on pages 164–165.

as well as complex knowledge. An Asian economist may be as familiar with the teachings of Buddha as he is with those of Keynes. But which are the dominant forces, those derived from national culture or those inherent in industrialization? Do new circumstances, skills, attitudes, and institutions compete with and ultimately replace the old ones? Or do they coexist and eventually yield a new synthesis that is a blend of the historical and the environmental? Are the educated African and the educated American more like each other in their attitudes toward, say, political involvement and public issues than the former is like uneducated Africans and the latter like uneducated Americans? Even more specifically, if a sample of 2000 persons consisting of 500 Africans with a Ph.D. in political science, 500 Africans with no more than a sixth-grade education, 500 Americans with a Ph.D. in politcal science, and 500 Americans with no more than a sixth-grade education were asked to respond to questions that probed their sense of competence as a citizen, would their responses be distributed as follows?

	high competence	low competence
African Ph.D.'s	500	0
6th-grade Africans	0	500
American Ph.D.'s	500	0
6th-grade Americans	0	500

Or would the American democratic heritage and the lack of one in Africa result in a distribution that looked more like this?

	high competence	low competence
African Ph.D.'s	200	300
6th-grade Africans	0	500
American Ph.D.'s	500	0
6th-Grade Americans	400	100

At the foreign policy level, too, the forces of the past and those of the present can conflict, coexist, or synthesize. The choices and activities of foreign policy decision-makers can be guided by the cultural norms and historical precedents that governed the behavior of their predecessors; or the choices and activities can be guided by the changing demands that emanate from the international system or from the decision-makers' own society. Consider severe international crises. These can generate demands that uncover previously unrecognized values which, in turn, can channel behavior in new directions. Yet these new behavior patterns do not necessarily supplant the historical ways of conducting foreign policy. A Russian decision-maker is a Russian as well as a skilled diplomat. His United States counterpart is an American as well as an adroit politician. But which of these factors are the dominant ones? Do past precedents operate in situations? Or do crises evoke a momentum of their own, a momentum in which the historical norms and characteristic forms of behavior give way? Or does some combination of these factors shape the undertakings through which decision-makers relate their societies to their external environments? Even more specifically, if a sample were compiled of 200 well documented foreign policy actions, 100 undertaken by the Soviet Union and 100 by the United States, with half of each group being a response to intense crises and half being a response to routine situations, would their distribution in terms of the amount of ideological rhetoric that accompanied the behavior be as follows?

	high rhetorical content	low rhetorical content
USSR in crisis	0	50
USSR in noncrisis	50	0
U.S. in crisis	0	50
U.S. in noncrisis	50	0

Or would the formal character of Soviet ideology and the unstructured nature of American ideology result in a distribution that looks like this?

	high rhetorical content	low rhetorical content
USSR in crisis	45	5
USSR in noncrisis	50	0
U.S. in crisis	5	45
U.S. in noncrisis	50	0

I. *Horizontal, Vertical, and Diagonal Analysis*

Although some empirical evidence bearing on the interaction of historical and environmental stimuli is available insofar as behavior in national political systems is concerned,[1] no systematic data have been developed on their respective roles in foreign policy. Indeed, except for the Sprouts' effort to delineate five basic approaches to the causal relationship between foreign policy officials and their environments,[2] the conceptual problem has not been confronted by students in the field. One is hard pressed to hazard even a reasonable guess as to which of the two distributions of the 200 foreign policy actions in our example is likely to prove most valid, much less to offer a rationale for a third distribution that may reflect even more accurately the dynamics of foreign policy. To be sure, attention has long been paid to the role of historical precedent and style—or, in the terminology of an earlier era, of national character—and lately foreign policy behavior in crises has increasingly been the subject of conceptual and empirical investigation.[3] Other than the studies bearing on crisis behavior, however, foreign policy analysts have not made environmental variables the focus of theoretical inquiry. As a consequence, their literature contains neither propositions nor data bearing on the interaction and relative strength of the demands that arise out of past experiences on the one hand and out of present circumstances on the other.[4] This is not the occasion to generate data that would clarify the problem, but an exploratory discussion of some of its conceptual dimensions would seem to be in order. Such is the purpose of this paper.

Doubtless there are a number of reasons why aspects of the prevailing environment have not served as an analytic focus. In the first place, there is a compelling simplicity about the task of uncovering the precedents and style born of past experience—what we shall call "vertical" analysis since it involves tracing trends down through history. The external actions undertaken by societies can always be seen as the extension of some previous pattern. The citizens of every society share a history that is not experienced by any other peoples; and embedded in this history are cultural norms that are refined and passed on from one generation to the next, culminating in the predispositions shared by the present generation. The residue of the past can thus be seen as differentiating the behavior patterns and attitudinal tendencies of any society from those of every other society. Moreover, since the norms that sustain a nation's culture are not entirely consistent with each other, contradictions among the external policies that a society may pursue can be easily explained as reflecting the diversity inherent in the society's culture. If, for example, a society avoids involvement in one situation abroad and becomes deeply involved in another, a perusal of its past would probably yield enough evidence of flexible orientations to permit one to posit the contradictory behavior as expressive of a pragmatic style.[5]

Secondly, while vertical analysis is not simple, it certainly appears more manageable than the task of coherently organizing all the diverse stimuli that may emanate from the many situations extant at any moment in time—what we shall call "horizontal" analysis, since it involves tracing trends across a range of concurrent behaviors. The identity of the situations that comprise the external environment of any society toward the end of the 20th century may continuously change, but their number will always be high; and since each situation has unique antecedents and dynamics, the foreign policy behavior required to cope with all of them would appear to be so variable as to render hopeless any attempt to analyze it in terms of properties that may be common to some situations and not to others. And the variability of the behavior is broadened further by virtue of the fact that certain situations may also embrace developments within the society and that, in any event, internal conditions may shape the response to some external ones and not to others. Hence, with the possible exception of characteristics that follow from the distinction between crisis and non-crisis situations, the challenges posed by the environment would seem to be too disparate in terms of the responses they evoke to justify the use of horizontal analysis. Instead of the compelling simplicity of vertical analysis, environmental variables present a seemingly incredible complexity—or at least enough complexity to reinforce the analytic inclination to emphasize historical commitments and experiences as the basis of present choices and behavioral styles.

If horizontal analysis thus appears unmanageable, the task of combining it with vertical analysis—what we shall call "diagonal" analysis, since it involves discerning trends across situations in terms of predispositions acquired down through history—seems even more hopeless. For in order to assess the extent to which historical precedents are offset by environmental demands, the foreign policy behaviors of at least two societies confronted with similar external problems need to be compared. Such a procedure seems to defy mastery because the circumstances that confront different societies are never exactly the same, thus making it difficult for the researcher ever to be certain that the environmental stimuli he has compared are sufficiently similar to justify his assessments of the relative strength of vertical and horizontal factors. It is little wonder, in short, that diagonal analysis has not become common practice among foreign policy researchers and that the vertical mode of inquiry remains the dominant approach to the subject.

II. *Conceptualizing the Environment*

Notwithstanding the accuracy of the foregoing explanations of why vertical analysis dominates the study of foreign policy, they hardly amount to a sufficient set of reasons for the lack of horizontal and diagonal analysis. Assuming that horizontal variables are no less important empirically than vertical ones, and that therefore diagonal analysis ought to characterize researchers in the field, it seems highly unlikely that students of foreign policy avoid this form of analysis simply because they are fearful of its complexity. Foreign policy researchers are no less venturesome than those in other fields. On the contrary, they are often quick to point to the complexity of their subject and to avoid simplistic approaches to it.

So there must be more to the neglect of horizontal and diagonal analysis than the compelling simplicity of vertical inquiry. Reflection about other possible reasons for the neglect leads to the realization that little work has been done on the concept of the environment, that for the most part it is treated as merely the source of stimuli rather than as an organized set of processes, and that consequently analysts have found it more clarifying to explain the conduct of foreign relations in terms of the policy commitments and value orientations acquired from the past. As noted, these commitments and orientations are the product of organized processes. Their shape and contents can be traced from one generation to the next and any foreign policy behavior can thus be seen as the most recent expression of a coherent, over-all, and self-sustaining pattern. For the most part, however, an equivalent conception of the environment at any moment in time has not developed. At worst the environment is conceived to consist of an unspecified variety of objects, actors, and situations with which the environed society copes by drawing upon its past experience and utilizing its present resources. At best the environment is conceived to consist of specific objects, actors, and situations, each of which has distinct characteristics that can serve as stimuli to action on the part of the environed society. Yet there is more to the environment than the specific situations to which a society is linked. It also consists of self-sustaining processes that arise out of the interdependencies of the various objects, actors, and situations, quite apart from any connections these may have with the environed society. That is, the environment constitutes a generalized context besides comprising specific situations, just as history consists of a cumulative experience as well as of particular episodes. And it is with respect to the environment as a generalized context that conceptualization is lacking, thereby holding back the development of horizontal analysis. Rare indeed are conceptualizations of the external environment that posit and trace patterns of interaction which, in the process of unfolding, become independent variables in relation to the behavior of the environed society's foreign policy officials.

In other words, it is not enough to categorize various environmental phenomena and to analyze them separately as sources of foreign policy. To proceed in this manner is not to specify the interdependencies among the phenomena that sustain and give coherence to the environment and that, in so doing, also serve as sources of foreign policy. The interdependencies also operate as policy determinants because they form a generalized context that conditions both the content and style of the responses to specific situations. Consequently, the categorization and analysis of specific situations must be supplemented by concepts which delineate types of environmental contexts that can result from different degrees and forms of interdependencies among the actors, objects, and situations in the environment. Once various types of environmental contexts are identified, propositions about the relationship between each environmental type and the behavior of foreign policy decision-makers can be developed.

It must be stressed that both the generalized contexts and the specific situations of the environment shape the conduct of foreign policy and that they do so independently of each other. An environmental context consists of attributes of the interdependencies of foreign objects, actors, and situations and not of the attributes of particular objects, actors, or situations. At any moment in time, therefore, a society's total environment has structural and behavioral characteristics of its own and these, being the cumulative result of all the extant objects, actors, and situations, are different from any of them.

Although it follows that both the specific situations and generalized dimensions of the environment contribute to the external behavior of societies, this is of course not to imply that they are equally potent as independent variables. This may or may not be the case, and under some circumstances specific situations may be more potent while under other circumstances greater potency may accrue to certain generalized dimensions. Determining their relative potencies is an empirical problem that cannot be addressed until after conceptualization of the structural and behavioral characteristics of the environmental context is undertaken. Thus here it is only asserted that both the specific and generalized dimensions operate as independent variables.

It is also important to emphasize that while the environed society is directly connected to specific situations of the environment that shape its foreign policy style, such is not the case with respect to the interdependencies of the environment that operate as independent variables. The interdependencies unfold irrespective of the nature and behavior of the environed society. They serve to condition the society's behavior, to be sure, but their status as independent variables is in no way dependent on a connection to the society. Obviously, on the other hand, the operation of a specific situation as an independent variable is entirely dependent on a connection between it and the society. The earlier analogy to a child serves to clarify this point. The behavioral characteristics of a first-grader are in part a result of the specific teacher assigned to teach his class. The connection is direct in the sense that the teacher's treatment of the child is to some degree a consequence of how the child behaves even as it also contributes to the nature of the child's responses. At the same time developments in the community that shape the goals and structure of the school system contribute substantially to the behavioral characteristics of the child even though, being a first-grader, he has no direct connection to the general affairs of the community. Thus both specific and generalized dimensions of the child's environment at age six contribute to who he is and how he behaves. Furthermore, the analogy highlights the relevance of vertical as well as horizontal factors: obviously the child's behavior is also a consequence of his experience over the previous six years.

An illustration of these distinctions drawn from the foreign policy field is provided by the recent conduct of United States policy toward Cuba. While U.S. policy is in large part a consequence of the advent of a Cuban Communist regime that, being different from its predecessor, provoked direct U.S. responses, the Cuba-oriented activities of the United States are also a result of the interdependencies of Latin American countries and of a number of other developments in the international system to which the

United States did not contribute. In addition, of course, United States behavior with respect to Cuba arises out of a long history of relations with that country.

Interestingly, the relevance for foreign policy style of the distinction between the specific and generalized dimensions of a society's environment can also be illustrated by noting that a similar distinction operates with respect to the consequences of past experience. History yields both specific and generalized guides to present behavior. The conduct of American foreign policy in Latin America, for example, is in part a consequence of the reiteration of the Monroe Doctrine throughout the 19th and 20th centuries. The Doctrine and its frequent reiteration set specific precedents that continue to guide the behavior of American officials. At the same time the cumulated experience of the American past has resulted in characteristic ways of approaching problems and this pragmatic style— if that is what it is—also underlies the behavior of officials toward Latin American situations.

III. *The Search for Conceptual Equipment*

In sum, diagonal analysis of foreign policy behavior requires that conceptual equipment be available for the analysis of the relationship between such behavior and each of the types of phenomena embraced by the cells of the following matrix:

sources of *foreign policy stimuli*	*nature of* *foreign policy stimuli*	
	SPECIFIC	GENERAL
HISTORICAL EXPERIENCE	1 *policy commitments*	2 *value orientations*
PRESENT ENVIRONMENT	3 *situations*	4 *contexts*

It does not take much reflection to recognize that extensive conceptual equipment is available for the analysis of the phenomena embraced by Cells 1, 2, and 3. Foreign policy analysts have long focused on such phenomena and have developed a number of concepts and methods for examining them. For example, the concept of the national interest, the decision-making approach, and game or strategic theory are but a few of the tools that are used to probe the interaction of past policy commitments and present situational dynamics in the determination of the external behavior of a national society. Similarly, analysis of the contribution that the major value orientations of a society make to the conduct of its foreign policy has been facilitated by the concepts of role, national style or character, and political culture—to mention but a few of the available tools.

But what about Cell 4 of the matrix? Have environmental contexts also been subjected to close scrutiny? Have any conceptual tools been developed for linking them to the conduct of foreign policy? Have practitioners in other areas of inquiry perfected tools for contextual analysis that can be refashioned for application to foreign policy phenomena? Anticipating our answers to these questions, the search for relevant concepts was only minimally rewarding. Some conceptual equipment has been developed, but it is still crude and limited in scope. Certainly environmental contexts have not been explored as fully as the other phenomena in the foregoing matrix and there is even some evidence of a tendency to avoid focusing on the interdependencies that sustain the environment. At the same time the possibility of adapting concepts should not be discounted. In particular, the concept of change appears promising as a connecting link between environmental interdependencies and foreign policy behavior.

That the conceptual equipment available for environmental analysis is not extensive—and, indeed, that the main tendency is to avoid conceptualization of the interdependencies that sustain the external environments of societies—can be readily illustrated. Consider the work of David Easton. Although his efforts to delineate the nature of political systems and the boundaries between them and their environments are probably more extensive than those undertaken by any other student of politics, Easton devotes more attention to the processes of the system than to those of its environment. To be sure, he does not deny that the political processes of a society are responsive to developments that unfold in the world beyond its borders. Yet he does not indicate any systematic ways in which the developments abroad may be interdependent and thereby generate environmental patterns which may in turn condition societal processes. Rather he distinguishes between the intra- and extra-societal environments of a political system and notes that the latter consists of international political systems, international ecological systems, and international social systems. International political systems are conceived to consist of such entities as other political systems and international organizations like NATO, SEATO, and the United Nations. Similarly, the international cultural system, the international social structure, the international economic system, and the international demographic system are offered as examples of international social systems.[6] One can hardly quarrel with the utility of categorizing the environment of any society along these lines. Such entities do exist and their functioning does have consequences for the society. Yet in a basic sense they are little more than categories and subcategories. Nowhere in Easton's discussion are the phenomena embraced by his categories posited as interdependent. Nowhere are they conceived as self-sustaining processes which, like the cumulative impact of historical experience, lead to predictable forms of behavior. To know that the external environment of a society consists of other political, economic, and social systems is not to know anything about how that society may respond to them. To assert that specified categories of phenomena are the source of inputs into a system is not to suggest the way in which behavior might be a function of the particular attributes of the interdependencies encompassed by the environmental categories. Categorization, in short, is not conceptualization, and thus Easton offers no help to the researcher interested in horizontal forms of analysis.

Another example of the problem is provided by the decision-making approach to foreign policy. Again the external environment is posited as a major source of stimuli to action on the part of those responsible for the conduct of foreign policy. And again aspects of the environment that can lead to activity on the part of decision-makers are differentiated. One formulation, for example, elaborates the "external setting of decision-making" in terms of the nonhuman environment, other cultures, other societies, and other governments.[7] Here again, however, the view is essentially one in which the environment consists exclusively of specific objects, actors, and situations. Notwithstanding the assertion that "the external setting is constantly changing,"[8] the differentiated aspects of the environment are not posited as interdependent. No suggestion is made as to the generalized dimensions of the prevailing environment that might condition the behavior of decision-makers. Indeed, the only cumulative phenomena stressed by the authors of the decision-making approach are the societal norms and values passed on by one generation to the next that serve to guide the behavior of foreign policy officials.[9]

A seemingly more promising lead in the search for concepts that allow for a causal treatment of environmental contexts is provided by recent attempts to view the environment as a complex of issue-areas. An issue-area is conceived to consist of a variety of conflict situations that may differ in numerous ways, but that are similar in the sense that the same values serve as the focus of conflict. One formulation, for example, posits the external environment of any society as consisting of four basic issue-areas— status, territorial, human resources, and nonhuman resources—that are differentiated by the fact that the different values they encompass will trigger different responses on the part of its foreign policy officials.[10] Theoretically, therefore, this approach allows for an environment with both specific and generalized dimensions. In each issue-area it posits the existence of environmental interdependencies and, in so doing, it suggests how the external behavior of a society may be linked to the processes that are sustained by different types of conflicts. Once the researcher identifies the core values at stake in a situation and classifies it in the appropriate issue-area, he should theoretically be in a position to compare how historical precedent in different societies is modified by the common issue-area values involved in the situation. That is, it should be possible for him to engage in horizontal and diagonal analysis. Unfortunately, however, the clusters of values that generate similar behavior have yet to be worked out conceptually and the causal processes that differentiate the areas have yet to be traced empirically.[11] As of now, the issue-area approach is only a hunch that situations sustained by common values generate common responses. Unless and until this hunch can be given theoretical coherence and supported by empirical evidence, therefore, it remains little more than another collection of categories.

Conceptual equipment that more closely approximates the kind that is needed to facilitate environmental analysis is to be found in the work of Morton A. Kaplan.[12] Concerned about stability and change in the international system, Kaplan posits six "states" of the system—balance of power, loose bipolar, tight bipolar, universal, hierarchical, and unit veto—each of which has certain "essential" rules that must be followed by the national actors comprising the system for the state to persist through time. Among the essential rules for each system state, for example, are stipulations that specify the conditions under which its national actors should negotiate, mobilize resources, fight, stop fighting, join alliances, contest some changes, and accommodate to other changes. Although Kaplan's rules for each system state are highly abstract, he does not make their existence dependent on the behavior of any national actor. A single actor might alter the system state by breaking one or more of its rules, but the rules themselves derive from the over-all patterns of interaction among the actors. From the perspective of a single national actor, therefore, the essential rules are a part of its environment. Irrespective of the policy commitments and value orientations that the decision-makers of a society acquire from the cumulative experience of their predecessors, and irrespective of the specific situations with which they must cope, their actions must conform to the systemic requirements if the prevailing state of the system is to endure.

This is not to imply that Kaplan's formulation is free of defects. The *if* clause that ends the previous paragraph is of course a large one. The state of the international system is not permanent. Its interdependencies can undergo transformation, and while Kaplan acknowledges this point, his formulation does not deal with the processes whereby the system is transformed from one state to another. Even in Kaplan's terms, therefore, during periods of transformation decision-makers will presumably have difficulty adjusting their behavior to the systemic requirements. Furthermore, there are many areas of foreign policy behavior for which the essential rules of Kaplan's model are irrelevant. His formulation of environmental interdependencies is essentially addressed to the issue-area bounded by questions of military and national security which, while extremely important, are far from a predominant majority of the external problems with which societies must contend.

Notwithstanding the limitations in the scope of his model, Kaplan does highlight the relevance of environmental contexts and suggests ways in which horizontal analysis might be undertaken. Indeed, by distinguishing between democratic and authoritarian regimes (what he calls "nondirective" and "directive" actors),[13] at one point Kaplan even suggests a way in which this horizontal approach can be extended into a diagonal form of analysis. The presumption here is that the historical commitments and value orientations of the two types of regimes are likely to lead to different interpretations of how adherence to the essential rules of a particular system should be achieved. Kaplan's analysis here is abstract and sketchy, to be sure; but at least it allows for the interaction of environmental and historical factors as stimuli to foreign policy behavior.

As previously indicated, still another set of conceptual tools that might facilitate horizontal analysis can be found in the efforts to probe whether crisis situations give rise to distinctive forms of behavior.[14] Hermann's work is particularly illustrative in this regard. He posits three characteristics as distinguishing crisis from noncrisis situations—high threat to national goals, short decision time, and lack of anticipation. The joint presence or absence of these three characteristics is hypothesized to have a variety of consequences for the way in which foreign policy is conducted. Among the behavioral consequences that Hermann hypothesizes to be linked to crises, for example, are the tendencies of decision-makers to increase the rapidity of responses to stimuli, to reduce the number of cooperative responses, to increase the number of exploratory responses, to reduce the search for alternative solutions, to increase the search for support of their position, to reduce the number of participants in the decision-making process. Quite apart from the empirical question of whether this line of reasoning is affirmed by the available evidence,[15] the conceptual utility of the crisis/noncrisis distinction is that tendencies such as the foregoing are posited as operating irrespective of historical circumstances. Whatever the policy commitments made by their predecessors, and whatever the value orientations that normally guide their policy-making conduct, decision-makers in crisis share a readiness to respond to stimuli in similar ways. That is, their behavior is seen to be primarily a consequence of concurrent rather than past events in their external environments.

While the crisis concept can thus serve as a valuable tool in the horizontal analysis of foreign policy behavior, it is not free of difficulties. Like Kaplan's formulation, it tends to be confined to phenomena in one issue-area, namely, to situations in which military considerations predominate. The three characteristics associated with crisis do not preclude the possibility that economic or social situations may develop into crisis proportions, but the combination of high-threat, short-decision time, and lack of anticipation is certainly most likely to occur when political situations reach the point where actors are ready to resort to the use of force. Secondly, the crisis formulation is weakened by its dichotomization of the environment and the fact that the dichotomy is not conceived in variable terms. Crises are conceived to have certain characteristics, but these are treated as attributes of situations that always induce the same form of behavior rather than as variables that can generate several types of responses. Unlike Kaplan's formulation, in other words, the crisis concept as developed so far does not take formal account of the processes and interdependencies of the environment, thus limiting its utility as a tool to analyze the contents of the external undertakings of society.

IV. *The Concept of Turbulence*

The search for conceptualizations of the environment yielded one other formulation, developed by students of organizational theory, that is sufficiently different from those outlined above to warrant notation. Although organizational theory is much more advanced than foreign policy theory,[16] it too is lacking in formulations that treat the environment as a dynamic pattern. Organizational theorists recognize that organizations must, like societies, adapt to their external environments. Yet only recently have they developed an appreciation of the need to conceive of organizational behavior as a response to self-sustaining interdependencies within the environment as well as to interdependencies within the organization and to exchanges between it and its environment.[17] Thus, for example, drawing upon general systems theory as a means of clarifying the role of environmental interdependencies, two organizational theorists have suggested four "ideal types" of environments in which organizations can be located.[18] Their basis for differentiating between the four types is the degree of *system connectedness* that prevails among the components of the environment. The environment with the least connectedness they have called the *placid, randomized environment,* in which the value attached to the objects that constitute the environment are relatively unchanging and are randomly distributed. Amoebas, human foetuses, and nomadic tribes are posited as existing in such an environmental context, but it is difficult to conceive of a modern nation-state being located in a placid, randomized environment. However, the foreign policy behavior appropriate to such an environment can be theoretically deduced. In such a context a society would not distinguish "between strategy and tactics," but would instead come to regard "the optimal strategy . . . [as] the simple tactic of attempting to do one's best on a purely local basis."[19]

Moving up the scale of system connectedness, the next context to be differentiated is the *placid, clustered environment.* This is a more complex environment in the sense that some of its objects "hang together in certain ways,"[20] but it is nevertheless placid in the sense that the values attached to the objects are relatively unchanging. The environments of human infants or of plants that are subjected to seasonal cycles are offered as illustrative of this type. Again it is hard to imagine a modern society in such a context, though perhaps it prevailed in earlier eras when classical diplomacy sustained international relations. Should such a context exist for a society, however, its foreign policy would distinguish between strategy and tactics, since the clustering of the objects in the environment means that short- and long-range calculations have to be made if the society is to achieve its goals.

The third ideal type, called the *disturbed-reactive environment,* involves a significant qualitative change over the previous two. It is characterized by the existence of at least one—and usually many—other systems similar to the one that is environed. While the two placid environments do not contain any other objects comparable to the environed one, the disturbed-reactive environment does, and this difference is of considerable import. It means that there are other objects in the environment that may have the same goals with respect to the environment as the environed object, thus compelling the latter to act on the knowledge that what it knows can also be known by the others. Such knowledge can lead all the objects in the environment to seek to thwart the others, and every object, knowing such is the case, will have to foster and react to disturbing events in their environments. That is, it will have to launch undertakings that combine strategy and tactics in such a way that the behavior of other objects is anticipated and countered, thus facilitating the procurement of goals in the environment. Examples of systems that exist in this type of environmental context can readily be cited. Certainly the disturbed-reactive environment is descriptive of the context in which the human being that survives infancy and the interest group or business organization that persists through time must operate. And frequently it would also appear to be characteristic of the context in which modern societies find themselves. Their environments consist of other societies also seeking to realize external goals. Since the goals sought by societies are often mutually exclusive, their environments are bound to be pervaded by disturbances with which they become strategically and otherwise interdependent.

Further reflection on the structure and functioning of organizations, however, led the authors of the foregoing distinctions to a fourth ideal type of environment, one that they call a *turbulent field environment,* and that they claim "is new, at least to us, and is the one that for some time we have been trying to identify."[21] A turbulent field environment is conceived to consist of even more system connectedness and complexity than the disturbed-reactive type. This greater complexity is seen to stem from dynamic processes that arise not only from the interactions of the component organizations in the environment, but "also from the field itself." That is, the actions of the environmental components and linked sets of them "are both persistent and strong enough to induce autochthonous processes in the environment. An analogous effect would be that of a company of soldiers marching in step over a bridge."[22] In other words, in contrast to the other types of environments, the accelerating rate and complexity of change in the turbulent environment "exceeds the component systems' capacities for prediction and, hence, control of the compounding consequences of their actions."[23] Uncertainty thus becomes the dominant characteristic of the turbulent environment and, the organizational theorists contend, such a characteristic is increasingly the condition in which modern organizations find themselves. The behavioral response to the conditions imposed by turbulent environments, they imply further, is the convergence, either formally through legal mergers or informally through the emergence of shared values, of the environed unit with comparable units in its environment. The individual organization recognizes that it cannot rely exclusively on its own strategy and tactics to cope with the turbulence of the environment and thus it joins, as it were, with parts of its environment. The recent trend toward mergers of business corporations, colleges, and interest groups are illustrative in this regard.

It hardly needs documenting that much the same can be said about the environments of modern societies. These also appear to be turbulent as well as disturbed-reactive. Treating the Soviet Union as the environed unit, recent trends in Eastern Europe exemplify the point, albeit at this writing it could be argued that the Russians are coping with the turbulence by contesting rather than joining with other societies in Eastern Europe.[24] Indeed, it is not unreasonable to view the existence of "mergers" in the international system—such as the European Common Market and regional arrangements like the OAS, SEATO, and the OAU—as expressive of the predicted responses to a turbulent field, namely, the postwar environments of national societies.

Suggestive as this typology of organizational environments is, its application to foreign policy behavior is necessarily limited. While it serves to identify one important way in which societies react to the interdependencies of the international system, cooperative efforts to build supranational institutions are not the only bases of foreign policy. Unlike the crisis approach, the concept of the turbulent field does posit environmental interdependencies and links them to a specific form of foreign policy behavior, but, like Kaplan's formulation, it does so only with respect to behavior in a narrow range.

V. *Change as an Organizing Concept*[25]

The search for conceptualizations of environmental interdependencies has not been fruitless, but neither has it turned up a formulation which delineates: (1) types of foreign policy behavior that may be a response to (2) varying forms of environmental interdependencies across (3) a wide range of issue-areas. All three of these dimensions emerge as desirable features of any attempt to explore the role of environmental contexts, but even the most promising of the formulations examined above include only two of these dimensions. Moreover, none of the formulations allows for the operation of interdependencies that are external to the deliberations of foreign policy decision-makers but internal to their society. Easton and the authors of the decision-making approach do posit an internal as well as an external environment, but they merely categorize the two environments rather than treating them as a series of self-sustaining processes. Thus there would appear to be plenty of room for additional efforts to conceptualize the environment in which foreign policy behavior occurs and it is not a rejection of the foregoing formulations to suggest still another. While the one developed below must be viewed as sketchy and tentative, it seeks to incorporate the three desired conceptual dimensions and, in addition, to allow for the distinction between internal and external interdependencies.

The central concept in the ensuing formulation is that of change. Change is measured by alterations in the occupants and requirements of the governmental and nongovernmental leadership statuses and roles in the environed society and in its environment. When the passage of time results only in deaths and retirements that alter the occupants of the leadership statuses and roles, then the degree of change that occurs during this period is considered to be low. Under these conditions the identity of leaders will be different, but their behavior will be responsive to the same requirements and thus will be essentially undifferentiated from that of their predecessors. When the passage of time is accompanied by the emergence of new social, political, economic, and technological conditions that alter the requirements as well as the occupants of the leadership roles and statuses to which new requirements are attached, the behavior of leaders in and out of government, at home and abroad, will tend to vary from that of their predecessors. If these variations are extensive, the degree of change is considered to be high, amounting, in effect, to a turbulent environment.

If for analytic purposes the innumerable degrees of change that societies experience are dichotomized into low and high, and if allowance is made for the possibility that both degrees of change can occur either at home or abroad, then four basic types of environmental contexts in which foreign policy is conducted can be distinguished (see the matrix below). More significantly, it seems reasonable to hypothesize that these four types of contexts will foster four very different modes of foreign policy behavior—what we shall call, respectively, the habitual, spirited, deliberative, and convulsive modes.

The *habitual* mode refers to the condition in which the degree of both internal and external change are low; and it is so designated because, with not much changing either at home or abroad, the routinized decision-making processes of governments will suffice to cope with the course of public and world affairs. There is no need for top level officials to deliberate over the most appropriate responses to internal demands and external pressures. Change is so minimal that the lower levels of a society's bureaucracy can—and are authorized to—handle any demand or pressure that may arise by resorting to established policies and applying established procedures. The international behavior of Switzerland during the 1920's might be expected to exhibit this mode if data depicting it were to be gathered.

		EXTERNAL CHANGE	
		High	Low
INTERNAL CHANGE	High	CONVULSIVE	SPIRITED
	Low	DELIBERATIVE	HABITUAL

The *deliberative* mode is a response to the condition in which internal change is low and environmental change is high; it is so designated because the absence of new internal demands on government allows officials to weigh carefully the appropriate course of action to follow in meeting the rapidly changing scene abroad, but at the same time the high degree of environmental change involves too much responsibility for the bureaucracy to handle alone and the top level of officialdom must thus participate in the decision-making process. Their participation and the presence of high uncertainty and change abroad means that recourse to established policies and procedures will not be sufficient and that therefore top officialdom must informally deliberate over the choices to be made as well as formally ratify them. The behavior of the United States during the first years immediately following World War II is perhaps illustrative of the deliberative mode. Between 1945 and, say, the school desegregation decision of the early 1950's, developments at home were slow to unfold, but considerable change was occurring abroad, with the result that top leaders of the State Department and the Congress joined with the President in prolonged and wide-ranging calculations of how to cope with such developments as a blockade of Berlin, a collapse of Europe's economy, a military threat to Western Europe, an attack in Korea, and a reemergent Japan. Accounts of these episodes reveal a highly reasoned and innovative quality in American foreign policy behavior,[26] with perhaps the epitome of the deliberative mode being achieved during the fifteen weeks in 1947 when extended assessments and discussions of the decaying European economy culminated in the Marshall Plan.[27]

The *spirited* mode is conceived to characterize foreign policy behavior in the condition in which internal change is high and external change is low; it is so designated because the high degree of change at home leads to demands that officials act quickly and energetically to alter the unchanging environment in such a way as to render it more compatible with the unfolding variations in the society's essential structures. Officials are not free to handle these domestic demands as deliberatively as they can when the pressures of change arise in the environment. For these demands require them to promote, rather than to cope with, new situations abroad; and whether the changes are such as to lead to demands that involve aggressive military conquest of parts of the environment or whether they give rise to a peace movement that demands efforts to disarm the environment, they require officials to act precipitously abroad and to do so in a much more spirited way than is the case when the internal scene is relatively unchanging. The foreign policy behavior of Germany during the 1930's exemplifies this spirited mode. Arising out of the economic and political dislocation of Germany, it was characterized by persistent diplomatic claims and insistent military threats that were justified in moralistic and vigorous terms.

Finally, the *convulsive* mode is hypothesized to arise out of the condition in which both internal and environmental change are high; it is so designated because, with a great deal transpiring at home and abroad, the top leadership of governments must respond quickly to societal demands and external pressures that are often contradictory and that thus necessitate erratic, unpredictable, and agitated efforts to keep the interdependencies of the external environment in balance with the shifting structures of their societies. The combination of high change at home and abroad tends to make established policies and procedures unreliable and compels policymakers to fall back on hasty and makeshift judgments that give rise to sudden shifts in external behavior which may, in turn, heighten internal tensions that foster the need for further shifts in policy. The convulsive mode is thus marked by more of a self-sustaining quality than the other modes. It is also a primary source of tension in the international system. Mainland China's external behavior in the 1960's is perhaps the most recent and clearcut example of the convulsive mode and some would say that the United States also exhibited this mode during the latter half of the 1960's. Certainly it is true that both societies underwent considerable change during this period and that constancy did not mark the foreign policy behavior of either.

VI. *Conclusion*

All of this does not imply that the concept of change resolves the problem of how horizontal and vertical factors combine to shape the external behavior of societies. The tasks of diagonal analysis, however, are essentially empirical ones. They involve comparisons of the external behavior of societies with different historical experiences located in similar environmental situations and contexts; or, conversely, societies with common pasts coping with different stimuli in the present. The concept of change does seem to provide a needed supplement to the conceptual equipment available for horizontal analysis. With it, it becomes possible to probe the contexts as well as the situations that comprise the external environments to which societies are responsive. Notwithstanding the many difficulties that will be encountered in the measurement of change, the concept does seem to create equipment with which to analyze, in a wide range of issue-areas, the links between interdependencies that sustain the environment and different forms of behavior that constitute the conduct of foreign policy. As developed here, the concept is still crude and unwieldy, but it would appear to offer a new means for engaging in the kind of horizontal analysis that must precede the empirical task of ascertaining the specific manner in which a society's external behavior is a result of yesterday's experiences and today's circumstances.

Notes and References

[1]See, for example, Gabriel A. Almond and Sidney Verba, *The Civic Culture: Political Attitudes and Democracy in Five Nations* (Princeton: Princeton University Press, 1963).

[2]Harold and Margaret Sprout, *The Ecological Perspective on Human Affairs— With Special Reference to International Politics* (Princeton: Princeton University Press, 1965), esp. Chapters 3–7.

[3]For example, see Charles F. Hermann, *Crises in Foreign Policy: Simulation Analysis* (Indianapolis: Bobbs-Merrill, 1969), and Charles F. Hermann, "International Crisis as a Situational Variable," in James N. Rosenau (ed.), *International Politics and Foreign Policy: A Reader in Research and Theory* (New York: Free Press, rev. ed., 1969), pp. 409–21.

[4]For a discussion of what foci are contained in the literature on foreign policy, see my "Pre-Theories and Theories of Foreign Policy," in R. Barry Farrell (ed.), *Approaches to Comparative and International Politics* (Evanston: Northwestern University Press, 1966), pp. 27–92, and my "Moral Fervor, Systematic Analysis, and Scientific Consciousness in Foreign Policy Research," in Austin Ranney (ed.), *Political Science and Public Policy* (Chicago: Markham, 1968), pp. 197–236.

[5]For an analysis of American foreign policy that follows this procedure, see Herbert J. Spiro, "Foreign Policy and Political Style," *The Annals*, Vol. 366 (July 1966), pp. 139–48.

[6]David Easton, *A Framework for Political Analysis* (Englewood Cliffs, N.J.: Prentice-Hall, 1965), Chapter V. For more elaboration of Easton's formulation, see his *A Systems Analysis of Political Life* (New York: John Wiley, 1965).

[7]Richard C. Snyder, H. W. Bruck, Burton Sapin (eds)., *Foreign Policy Decision-making: An Approach to the Study of International Politics* (New York: Free Press, 1962), pp. 67–72.

[8]*Ibid.*, p. 67.

[9]*Ibid.*, pp. 156–60.

[10]James N. Rosenau, in Farrell (*op. cit.*), pp. 71–88; also see my "Foreign Policy as an Issue-Area," in James N. Rosenau (ed.), *Domestic Sources of Foreign Policy* (New York: Free Press, 1967), pp. 11–50.

[11]However, for one successful effort to empirically trace issue-area differences in foreign policy, see Ole R. Holsti and John D. Sullivan, "France and China as Nonconforming Alliance Members," in James N. Rosenau (ed.), *Linkage Politics: Essays on the Convergence of National and International Systems* (New York: Free Press, 1969), pp. 147–98.

[12]See, in particular, his *System and Process in International Politics* (New York: John Wiley & Sons, 1957), Chapter 2.

[13]*Ibid.,* Chapter 3.

[14]Hermann, *op. cit.*

[15]Although Hermann has found considerable support for most of his hypotheses (*ibid.*), his data were derived from situations simulated in the laboratory and thus further tests of the hypotheses need to be made.

[16]For a thorough review of the substantial progress that has occurred in organizational theory, see J. G. March (ed.), *Handbook of Organizations* (Chicago: Rand McNally, 1965).

[17]Cf. Shirley Terreberry, "The Evolution of Organizational Environments," *Administrative Science Quarterly,* Vol. 12 (March 1968), pp. 590–613.

[18]F. E. Emery and E.L. Trist, "The Causal Texture of Organizational Environments," *Human Relations,* Vol. 18 (1965), pp. 21–32.

[19]Emery and Trist, *op. cit.,* p. 24.

[20]*Ibid.,* p. 25.

[21]*Ibid.*

[22]*Ibid.,* p. 26.

[23]Terreberry, *op. cit.,* p. 593.

[24]On the other hand, if one equates the Soviet Union with the leadership of its Communist Party, its recent behavior becomes quite consistent with that predicted by the presence of a turbulent environment. For the tides of upheaval in Eastern Europe have connected the Soviet party leaders even more firmly to their counterparts in control of several other East European societies (particularly East Germany and Poland).

[25]The ensuing formulation draws heavily on James N. Rosenau, "Foreign Policy as Adaptive Behavior: Some Preliminary Notes for a Theoretical Model," *Comparative Politics,* Vol. 2 (April 1970), pp. 355–74.

[26]See, for example, W. Phillips Davison, *The Berlin Blockade: A Study in Cold War Politics* (Princeton: Princeton University Press, 1958); Glenn D. Paige, *The Korean Decision: June 24–30, 1950* (New York: Free Press, 1968); and Bernard C. Cohen, *The Political Process and Foreign Policy: The Making of the Japanese Peace Settlement* (Princeton: Princeton University Press, 1957).

[27]See Joseph M. Jones, *The Fifteen Weeks* (New York: Viking Press, 1955).

ROBERT GILPIN

Has Modern Technology Changed International Politics?

T here is a striking divergence of opinion today regarding the impact which modern technology has had upon the nature of international politics. In fact, the differing viewpoints on this subject mark one of the most fundamental cleavages among contemporary students of international politics and no doubt among its practitioners as well. On the one hand, it is postulated that the technologies of atomic energy, rocketry, and electronics, among others, have produced the first true revolution in the nature of international politics. According to this view, these contemporary developments, in contrast to all previous innovations in weaponry, have had strategic and not merely tactical consequences, altering the nature of war itself and not solely the nature of the battle. War can no longer be contained on the battlefield, but is total and may be suicidal for society itself.

In disagreement with those who hold this, shall we say, radical view (radical in the sense that they believe a fundamental change has taken place) are others who retain a conservative view of the unchanging nature of international politics. Although cognizant of the horrible possibilities inherent in modern warfare, these observers point to the competition of nations for individual advantage in a state of international anarchy as the essential and unalterable characteristic of international politics.

The conservative argument was given its most cogent and still relevant expression by Thucydides in his *History of the Peloponnesian War*. In the conclusion to his introductory chapter, Thucydides stated that he had written his history for "those inquirers who desire an exact knowledge of

Notes and References for this selection will be found on page 174.

the past as an aid to the interpretation of the future, which in the course of human events must resemble if it does not reflect it. ... I have written my work, not as an essay which is to win the applause of the moment, but as a possession for all time." [1] The purpose of the *History* was not to examine a unique historical phenomenon, but to reveal the underlying and unalterable dynamic of history.

The key to international politics, Thucydides believed, was the differential growth of power within a state system. To substantiate this, he gives a brief history of the relationship of the Lacedaemonian (Spartan) confederacy and the Athenian empire; he concludes this history with the observation that the real cause of the war was the expansion of Athenian power. "The growth of the power of Athens, and the alarm which this inspired in Lacedaemon made war inevitable." [2]

In the language of contemporary social science, what Thucydides believed he had advanced was a general theory of international relations. He expected that the phenomenon he had observed would repeat itself over and over again. As in the case of Athens, the power of one state in an internation system would grow until it threatened the position of the other states in the system. The fear of the threatened states would produce a reaction which inevitably would lead to war and the founding by the victor of a new international system. And over time the foundations of this new system would be eroded as new powers arose within the international system. [3]

One can understand Thucydides' argument and self-confidence only if he comprehends Thucydides' concept of science and his view of what constitutes explanation. [4] Whereas modern students of international relations tend to take theoretical physics as their model, Thucydides took as his model the method of the great physician Hippocrates. Disease, the Hippocratic school argued, had to be understood not as the manifestation of some supernatural influence but as a consequence of the operation of natural forces. Through dispassionate observation of the symptoms, one could understand the nature of the disease. One "explained" the disease from the genesis of the disease through its periods of crisis and at its resolution.

Similarly, Thucydides wrote the *History* to fulfill the same prognostic function; namely, to enable men to recognize war as a recurrent phenomena. War, or what he refers to as "a great war," he sought to show, follows a recurrent and discernible course. The initial phase is the slow growth of power of the most dynamic member of the state system. As its power grows, it comes into conflict eventually with the hegemonic state of the system. The struggle between these two states and their respective allies leads to crisis and war. And, finally, there is the resolution of the war in favor of one state or the other.

Following this model, Thucydides begins his history of the war between the Peloponnesians and the Athenians by stating why, at its very inception, he believed the War would be "a great war"—the greatest yet fought in human history and, therefore, one worthy of attention. To substantiate his claim for the greatness of the War, Thucydides proceeds to analyze the growth of power in Hellas from ancient time to the eve of the War. In his choice of the factors which he considered explanatory, Thucydides is strikingly modern.

The first set of factors he discusses to explain the rise of Athenian power is geographic and demographic. Because of the poverty of its soil, Attica was envied by no other peoples and enjoyed freedom from conflict. "The most powerful victims of war or faction from the rest of Hellas took refuge with the Athenians as a safe retreat."[5] As the population swelled, Athens became too small to hold them and sent out colonies to other parts of Greece.

The second and, in Thucydides' view, key set of factors underlying the War was economic and technological: The Greek, and in particular, the Athenian mastery of naval power. This led to the rise of the Greek city-state, the development of commerce among these states, and the establishment of the hegemony of Hellas in the Eastern Mediterranean.

After the defeat of Troy, Hellas attained "the quiet which must precede growth."[6] The Greeks turned to commerce and the acquisition of wealth. With the rise of a wealthy commercial class in cities like Athens, the old form of government—hereditary monarchy—was overthrown and tyrannies representing this aggressive and enterprising class were established. Although the emerging sea powers such as Athens grew "in revenue and in dominion," there was no great concentration of power prior to the War with Persia. "There was no union of subject cities round a great state, no spontaneous combination of equals for confederate expeditions; what fighting there was consisted merely of local warfare between rival neighbors."[7]

The third set of factors leading to the War was political: the rise of the Athenian empire at the end of the war with Persia. As a consequence of the War, the Hellenes became divided into two great blocs. "At the head of one stood Athens, at the head of the other Lacedaemon, one the first naval power, the other the first military power in Hellas."[8] The former—commercial, democratic, and expansionistic—soon inspired alarm in the conservative and historically more powerful Lacedaemons. It was the latter's fear of growing Athenian power that led to the outbreak of the War.

In modern parlance, Thucydides would be included among those writers who are interested in the linkage between domestic and international politics. Though the underlying causes of the War can be traced in large part to geographical and technological factors, the major determinant of the foreign policies of Athens and Sparta was the differing characters of their regimes or political cultures. Athens was a "democracy"; its people were energetic, daring, and commercially minded; its naval power, resources, and colonies were expanding. Sparta, the traditional hegemonic state of the Hellenes, was a kingdom; its population was regimented and cautious; its foreign policy was conservative and attentive merely to the narrow security interests of the kingdom. They had little interest in commerce and empire.

In the last analysis, therefore, it was the nature of the Athenian state and the qualities of its citizenry that resulted in the growth of Athenian power and brought the two city-states into conflict. The Athenian character was the tragic element that led Thucydides to believe that the War was inevitable and that he was witnessing a phenomenon which would repeat itself throughout time. In future ages there would be other "Athenians" who would spark a growth that would then challenge "Spartas" and thus give rise to wars and subsequently to new eras of human history.

The basic assumption of Thucydides' cyclical view of international politics was that man's nature is a constant. Driven by greed, pride, and fear, men seek to increase their wealth and power until other men out of their fear try to stop them. While political knowledge, and this was the intent of his history, could assist men to understand the world and adjust to it as well as possible, the advance of knowledge could not change the fundamental character of international politics as defined in the *History*. Forerunning contemporary realists such as Hans Morgenthau, Thucydides saw reason (and science) as the instrument of man's passions and not as their master.[9] If he were alive today Thucydides would no doubt cast a skeptical eye on those political scientists who hope to find in the science of international relations the key to eternal peace. Nor, as he shows in the introduction to the *History,* did Thucydides believe that advances in wealth and technology would change the nature of international politics. Through increasing man's power, wealth and technology only bring men into conflict with one another and enhance the magnitude of war. Wealth and technology, like reason, do not transform man but are the slaves of his primitive drives.

In contrast to the Thucydidean view that man's knowledge would not change the cyclical nature of history is the modern belief in progress through a science of politics. Through his reason man is believed to be able to learn how to control the forces of the natural world as well as the wild passions within himself. Writers as early as Machiavelli believed that man could acquire political knowledge which would enable him to escape the operation of *fortuna*. In its "multiciplicity of states," Machiavelli saw that feature which distinguished Europe from other civilizations and, in the words of F. H. Hinsley, "enabled him to reach an early, if imperfect, formulation of the modern principle of the balance of power."[10]

The theory and practice of the balance of power were developed by theorists and statesmen of the sixteenth and seventeenth centuries in response to the great growth and concentration of power in the nation-state. Created out of the necessity to bring order, calculation, and moderation into international affairs, and to resist the hegemonic designs of first the Hapsburgs and then the French, the balance of power theory reflected the intellectual climate and practical needs of post-Renaissance Europe. And while we may regard it as a primitive "science" of international relations and a pernicious system through which to order human affairs, it represented a major advance in man's understanding of and control over international relations.[11]

The establishment of the balance of power system in the seventeenth century and its survival into the twentieth was a fortuitous outcome of the relatively low level of technology prior to the Industrial Revolution. Until the twentieth century no single state was capable of generating sufficient power within its own borders to dominate the rest of the states in the system. As a self-regulating system, the European balance of power broke down with the advent of the railroad and the emergence of a unified industrialized Germany at its geographical center. Only the entrance of a non-European power, the United States, in the first and second World Wars saved the Europeans from being dominated by Germany. And now in the view of many Europeans, two great non-European empires—the American and the Russian—have divided Europe into two spheres of influence and contest one another for world supremacy.

In addition to political and technological circumstances several seventeenth-century intellectual innovations as well underlay the classical balance of power system. The first was the concept of the international system as a framework for analysis and diplomatic action; as numerous writers have suggested, this reflected undoubtedly the transfer to the political realm of the mechanistic concepts of Newtonian physics.[12] The second concept was the shift from dynastic to national interest as the basis of foreign policy;[13] while the concept of *raison d'état* has led to abuses in its own right,[14] it has also served to moderate the behavior of states and, in contrast especially with ideological goals, has provided a basis for the negotiated settlement of interstate disputes. And, thirdly, the balance of power system rested on the assumption that the international system was composed of units whose power could be measured; this Newtonian mechanism for estimating power provided a basis for rational calculations and the settlement of disputes in a manner which kept the system in equilibrium.

The fundamental purpose of the system was to insure the survival of individual states through preserving the system of which they were a part. As Edward Gulick brings out in his excellent analysis of the balance of power system, the means to this end become highly formalized.[15] In its classical period the theory provided a basis for rational calculation in the formulation of policy and a means for the negotiation and settlement of disputes. While this primitive science did not insure peace, for this was not its purpose, it did moderate the behavior of states and preserved the independence of most, if not all, the members of the system.

Among the more important arguments that modern technology has transformed the nature of international relations is one which holds that nuclear weapons have undermined the efficacy of the traditional tools of statecraft. To put the point in more specific terms, this position argues that nuclear weapons have destroyed the traditional instruments which were basic to the operation of the balance of power system. The question to be asked, then, is the following: What has been the effect of nuclear weaponry upon war, diplomacy, and alliances as the basic instruments of foreign policy? The issues in the debate between the "conservatives" and "radicals" will be examined in order to elucidate the type of question which the contemporary technological revolution poses for the student of international relations.

The radical view that military power is no longer a rational instrument of statecraft and that consequently a qualitative change has taken place in international affairs has been expressed most emphatically by Hans Morgenthau. Morgenthau writes: "I think a revolution has occurred, perhaps the first true revolution in foreign policy since the beginning of history, through the introduction of nuclear weapons into the arsenal of warfare. [In the past] a statesman could [and did] ask himself whether he could achieve what he sought for his nation by peaceful diplomatic means or whether he had to resort to war . . . the statesman in the prenuclear age was in the position of a gambler who is willing to risk a certain fraction of his material and human resources. If he wins, his risk is justified by victory; if he loses, he has not lost everything. His losses, in other words, are bearable. This rational relationship between violence as a means of foreign policy and the ends of foreign policy has been destroyed by the possibility of all-out nuclear war."[16]

Paradoxically, however, as the conservative would doubtlessly reply, as war has declined as an instrument of national policy, the threat to wage war has been enhanced as an instrument of policy. He would point to threats of massive retaliation and of nuclear blackmail as continually a part of the Cold War scene. And the foremost task of the statesman apparently has become that of convincing an opponent of the credibility of his nuclear threat. It was for such a reason, it is pointed out, that the then Vice President Lyndon Johnson pledged "our Lives, our Fortune, and our sacred Honor" to the defense of West Berlin.

The lesson of the Cuban missile crisis of October 1962 as the first direct confrontation of two nuclear powers is inconclusive with respect to this issue of the efficacy of nuclear weapons as policy instruments. To the radical the episode revealed the absurdity of the nuclear threat. He sees both the United States and the Soviet Union as having been unwilling to take matters to a conclusion. The possibility of mutual destruction itself was what placed severe limits on the action of both and provided the basis for a sensible compromise. In short, the circumspect behavior of nations in a situation of imminent nuclear war exposes the inefficacy of modern weaponry as instruments of national policy.

The conservative, on the other hand—and the late President John F.

Kennedy apparently took this position—drew a different lesson. According to this view, the American policy objective of having the Russian missiles removed from Cuba was achieved precisely because the United States was able to couple its overwhelming conventional superiority in the South Atlantic with the credibility of its massive nuclear threat. The use of the traditional instrument of military threat did succeed. The missile crisis thus reinforced an operating assumption of those persons who believe that a primary responsibility of the statesman and strategist today is to manipulate the opponent's psychological set with respect to one's military intentions, and thereby to control his behavior. Such statecraft requires for its effectiveness the uniting of threats of punishment to deter "undesirable" behavior and promises of self-restraint to reward "desirable" behavior.

Obviously it is impossible to determine the merits of these arguments and different people draw conflicting lessons from the October crisis. Similarly, turning to a consideration of diplomacy as a policy instrument, men differ in their opinions of the effect of modern technology. For some, diplomacy—here, meaning the search for compromise solutions—has now been made the only rational course for state action. Compromise is obviously the lesser evil when nuclear holocaust is surely the only alternative. From this premise, some thinkers conclude that negotiation and compromise will come to replace violence in international politics as they have largely displaced violence in domestic politics.

A more conservative view is that though the modern technology of warfare has placed limits on international violence, the consequence has not been an upgrading of diplomacy as an instrument of national policy. On the contrary, this position would argue that the impasse evident with respect to the settlement of outstanding Cold War issues such as that of divided Germany is due precisely to the limits nuclear weaponry has placed, at least temporarily, on interstate violence. In the prenuclear age, they point out, diplomats were able to resolve interstate disputes because of the high probability that deadlock at the negotiating table would lead to decision on the battlefield. Today, on the other hand, the total destructiveness of war has decreased the probability that war will result from diplomatic impasse. From this perspective, the continuing Cold War and the failure of the many attempts to settle East-West differences in Europe, for example, are the result of the unwillingness of either the United States or the Soviet Union to use force in support of its diplomatic demands. For some conservatives, therefore, diplomacy can only succeed to the extent that nations are willing to use limited violence and the threat of total violence in the pursuit of foreign policy goals. Some look forward, although not with pleasure, to the time when arms control and disarmament measures may once again make the world safe for war in support of diplomacy.

The third instrument of statecraft whose efficacy is now questioned by some as a result of modern technology is the alliance. Traditionally, states threatened by a third state, or group of states have agreed to support one another in the event of war. Again, it can be argued that the advent of nuclear weapons has seriously eroded the basic assumption underlying this tool of foreign policy. In the prenuclear age, one nation coming to the support of another risked relatively little compared to the evil of seeing a third enhance its power through conquest. Today, on the other hand, the consequence of coming to the aid of an ally threatened by a nuclear power may mean complete and irrevocable destruction. The calculus of risks has changed—or so it is argued. Most certainly it is such reasoning that underlies the desire of Charles DeGaulle for an independent nuclear deterrent and the belief of many in peace through universal deterrence.

A more conservative view would grant much of the argument above but would take it one step farther. Though nuclear weapons have produced a crisis of confidence within such alliances as NATO, the intercontinental missile has taken the world into an even newer age where a different logic from that of DeGaulle applies. Here the missile with its great speed, decisiveness, and manageability actually dictates more tightly integrated alliances, and unity of command and control of the alliance's deterrent. Given the destructiveness and swiftness of missile warfare, individual members of an alliance simply cannot have national strategies which may conflict with one another. One member of an alliance must not have a strategy which seeks to limit damage by avoiding nuclear attacks on cities in the event of war. Such, however, is the situation today in NATO with respect to the American and French strategies. At issue in the Paris–Washington dispute, therefore, are differing conceptions of the fundamental nature of alliances in the contemporary world.

What has been the consequence of modern technology for international politics? One answer would appear to be that atomic weaponry and rockets have indeed had a significant impact on the nature and instruments of statecraft. On the other hand, these changes may not be nearly as fundamental in character as many observers would argue, nor do these changes appear to be as benign as the most optimistic would have us believe. Yet, there may be some ground for cautious optimism in that the threat of thermonuclear weapons to national survival gives nations, for the first time in history, a strong overriding common interest in avoiding war. The pursuit of this common interest, therefore, in terms of formulating appropriate international institutions and codes of behavior becomes one of the foremost challenges modern technology poses for the statesman today if mankind is to escape the fate foreseen by Thucydides.

Notes and References

[1] Thucydides, *The Peloponnesian War* (New York: Modern Library, 1951, pp. 14–15.

[2] *Ibid.*, p. 15.

[3] The use of the term "system" to describe international politics in ancient Greece must be understood to differ from the contemporary usage. The nature of the state system is treated by Victor Martin, *La Vie Internationale dans la Grèce des Cités* (Sirey, 1940).

[4] This discussion is based on John H. Finley, Jr., *Thucydides* (Ann Arbor: University of Michigan Press, 1963), p. 70.

[5] Thucydides, *op. cit.*, p. 4.

[6] *Ibid.*, p. 9.

[7] *Ibid.*, p. 11.

[8] *Ibid.*, p. 12.

[9] Hans J. Morgenthau, *Scientific Man versus Power Politics* (Chicago: University of Chicago Press, 1946).

[10] *Power and the Pursuit of Peace* (Cambridge: Cambridge University Press, 1963), p. 157. . . . .

[11] Charles Dupuis, *Le Principe d'Équilibre et le Concert Européen* (Perrin, 1909), p. 13.

[12] Alfred Vagts, "The Balance of Power: Growth of an Idea," *World Politics* (October 1948).

[13] On the innovation of the concept of "national interest" see Charles Beard, *The Idea of National Interest* (New York: Macmillan, 1934), chapter one.

[14] See Frederick Meinecke, *Machiavellism* (London: Routledge and Kegan Paul, 1962).

[15] *Europe's Classical Balance of Power* (New York: W. W. Norton, 1955).

[16] Hans Morgenthau, "Western Values and Total War," *Commentary* (October 1961), p. 280.

KLAUS KNORR

Notes on the Analysis of National Capabilities

Capability analysis has been one of Professor Sprout's main scholarly interests throughout his distinguished career. It seems to me fitting therefore that, in order to contribute to this volume dedicated to him, I discuss some aspects of capability analysis which came to my attention while reading his and Margaret Sprout's recent monograph entitled *An Ecological Paradigm for the Study of International Politics.* [1] One major point made by the Sprouts is that capabilities can be discussed sensibly only within some framework of objectives, strategies and contingencies. In the following, I will develop this theme and somewhat qualify the Sproutian proposition in the process of doing so.

I

The Sprouts observe that questions regarding national capabilities for future achievement "... pose a further question: capability for what? One can estimate capabilities *only within some frame of GIVEN facts or assumptions regarding objectives* (what is to be accomplished), *strategies* (by what course of action), and contingencies (against what adversaries, where, under what operating conditions, etc.). That is to say, a capabilities analysis takes the logical form of a prediction: if conditions are as specified, then such-and-such will probably occur." [2]

The Sprouts' proposition seems to me to be true. Certainly the observer of the real world has no difficulty in concluding that the relationship between objectives, strategies and capabilities is close. If objectives change in kind, their achievement is apt to call for or presuppose changes in

Notes and References for this selection will be found on page 186.

strategy and capabilities; and changes in capabilities will affect the range of feasible strategies and objectives. The student of history can observe these relationships in past patterns and use them for explaining past events. On the normative level, government leaders are disposed, or advised, to pay due attention to these relationships since they affect the outcome of policy action. It is equally clear, not to say obvious, that the feasibility of objectives, and the effectiveness of strategies and capabilities, depend on the nature of contingencies. I wish to develop this conceptualization somewhat further, and will do so with reference to military capabilities to which the Sprouts refer repeatedly. There is, of course, a gross sense in which existing military capabilities can be quite unsuited to particular objectives and contingencies. In the contemporary world, for instance, a strategic nuclear capability may serve the purpose of deterring another nuclear power from attack, but is clearly useless for attack or defense in conventional war; a capability for waging conventional war is not well suited, in terms of training and equipment, to conducting guerrilla war or to combating guerrilla forces. This lack of fit is readily understood. It is nothing new, since the training and equipment of military forces have always limited them to certain kinds of fighting and physical environment. I assume that the Sprouts' proposition is concerned with less obvious relationships resulting from the extremely varied patterns which may characterize future conflict situations. Taking as an example Great Britain in 1968, how should its government organize its naval forces alone, even after the scheduled retreat from a military presence in the East reduced the range of conceivable military missions? Several naval roles are distinguishable in relation to various possible future conflicts. One is the strategic nuclear deterrent role; a second is defense against attacks on maritime shipping; a third a blockading mission; a fourth an amphibious counter to limited land-based threats; a fifth a contribution to defensive missions guarding NATO's northern flank, etc. Looking toward the future, British planners could develop a large number of scenarios, each one favoring a different proportioning of British naval forces. How should the planners decide? Clearly, such considerations call attention to extremely difficult relationships between capabilities, objectives, strategies and "operating conditions." In order to explore these, it is necessary to give further definition to the main concepts.

Whatever the particular goals of foreign policy, whenever military capabilities come into play, if only by the recognition of their existence, the instrumental objective is to derive, or to concede, advantage in international politics from the possession and use of military means designed for coercion and for the sheer forcible seizure or defense of valued objects. The strategy is a plan for employing these capabilities to these kinds of effect in particular contingencies. Military capabilities are the military forces maintained by a nation-state.

At this point, I find it convenient to introduce the concept of "power" which the Sprouts dislike and seek to avoid in recent writings because of the ambiguities which have resulted from the uses of the term.[3] I do so because the mere concept of "capabilities" does not specify which range of various instrumental means in the real world it may refer to. In the military area, military capabilities defined as existing military forces do not exhaust the means of military coercion available to a state. Military power is the more inclusive term. In a study published elsewhere[4], I have distinguished between *putative* and *actualized* military power. Putative power is a means. Actualized power is an effect. The effect is to achieve influence through military coercion, or to take or defend a contested object. Putative military power consists of military capabilities, as defined above, *plus* the ability to increase these capabilities (i.e., military potential), *plus* the military reputation of the state concerned. Military reputation is based on a state's previous military and crisis behavior, and exists in the expectation among the governments and elites of other states that this past behavior is indicative of behavior in future disputes and crises.

Putative military power can be transformed into actualized power by means of three mechanisms. One is resort to war or warlike acts; the second is the threat of military action, which may be war or warlike acts or the expansion of an ongoing war; the third is through the anticipation by the governments of other states that the country in question may proceed to use its military forces in the event of a serious dispute, in order to make specific coercive threats or go to war. Although it has little, and often no, salience whatever, the third mechanism is very important in interstate relations. Its operation is more pervasive than resort to war or specific military threats. The government of a militarily weak state, in shaping its policy toward a state perceived to be militarily stronger, may take this difference tacitly into account even though no military threat has been made or considered. Thus, the putative power of the militarily stronger state may become actualized even though no deliberate attempt at achieving coercive influence has been undertaken.

This conceptual framework permits the construction of various models identifying the variables which determine the transformation of putative into actualized military power, and accommodating all outcomes including the extreme result of a complete failure in making putative power effective. For example, a relatively simple model identifying the conditions which determine the effectiveness of a military threat might be drawn up as follows. Assuming a severe crisis between states A and B, and assuming furthermore that all other means of influence have been exhausted, the effectiveness of a military threat by A against B would depend upon:

1. The estimate of B's government of
    (a) the ability of A to execute the threat,
    (b) the probability that A will execute the threat,
    (c) the disutility of the threatened action compared with the disutility of compliance,
    (d) the character of domestic and foreign support for B's alternative courses of action;

2. The skill of A's and B's governments in the bargaining process;
3. The propensity of B's government to accept military risks and behave rationally.

This model could be made more complicated by the introduction of subvariables, for instance, in order to clarify the conditions affecting A's ability to execute the threat, and B's evaluation of this ability. Similar models could be designed to analyze the transformation of putative into actualized military power by the other mechanisms. In each case, the number of variables is optional. For some purposes, scholars will find it convenient to be parsimonious in their choice; others will strain after exhaustiveness. The rational statesman must, however informally, seek to consider all variables that are important in a particular situation.

It is in any case apparent that the Sprouts' proposition refers to a very complex reality. To begin with, military capabilities are themselves very complex and variable phenomena. The mobilized military forces of each nation undergoes more or less rapid changes in size and composition, leadership and equipment, training and morale, doctrine and mobility. Rapid advances in technology lead to the development and production of new weapons which are often untried in combat, whose performance is subject to uncertainty, and which tend to become obsolescent as better weapons or defenses against them are invented and deployed. The military potential of nations is subject to similar variations in kind and magnitude. The effectiveness of military capabilities depends obviously on the comparable capabilities available to an opponent. But it also depends upon a varying number and pattern of contingencies, e.g., the type of military conflict which might arise or has arisen; the location and characteristics of the theater of operations; the kind of military strategy adopted; the need to reserve forces for other purposes; the readiness to inflict and receive military destruction which, in turn, depends upon the stakes involved in the conflict and other conditions affecting resolve at the time and over the longer run; the behavior of other states, etc. Military potential as a capability is relevant chiefly in the event of prolonged conflicts or arms races. This list of factors, which could be easily lengthened, explains the conditionality of actualized military power. As the Sprouts note, achievements "reflect capabilities to achieve. . . ."[5] In fact, the intervening variables can be many and several of them can be of crucial importance in the determination of the outcome.

The use of fairly elaborate models which order the variables, including contingencies, that intervene between objective, strategy, and capabilities on the one hand, and achievement on the other, should be helpful to the historian concerned with explaining past events. It should also be useful to governments preparing capabilities for future use. However, historians are known to disagree about the explanation of past events because of differences in the intricate patterns of capabilities and contingencies which they seek to trace, and in attributing weight, in terms of determining outcomes, to various parts of the pattern. Government planners cannot hope to predict the shape of the pattern and the weight of its parts with respect to *single* future events in which objectives, strategy and capabilities encounter the complex of particular circumstances. It is, of course, true that the actualization of power always takes place in single events which are unique in the full configuration of the conditions determining outcomes. But the question "capabilities for what?" does not imply that capability analysis is worthwhile only if it provides the predictions which would permit the precise fitting of capabilities to particular future uses. Capability analysis, directed to the future, must inevitably cope with uncertainty.

In planning capabilities for future use, governments will necessarily make assumptions about future contingencies, as is also done in the employment of various aids to military planning such as maneuvers, war games, and simulation exercises. The assumptions that are actually made by governments and the military may, of course, reflect various and conflicting purposes. In the military area, for instance, assumptions about future contingencies may be designed more or less openly or covertly to serve the career and business interests of people who profit from a change in over-all or particular military capabilities. To the extent that the focus of planning is that of meeting future exigencies arising in relations with the outside world, the assumptions about the future may in fact often be crude and unrealistic as, for instance, if it is simply assumed that, in all relevant aspects, the future will be essentially like the past or present, or that only the worst possible set of imaginable future contingencies will form a sound basis for capability planning. The three kinds of cognitive limitations deriving from perceptual or apperceptual behavior, which the Sprouts discuss,[6] apply here. However, if provided with adequate resources of expertise, forward-looking capability analysis, assisted by a study of past and present trends, one can conjecture about *types* of contingencies that will probably be encountered in the future, that is to say, types of crises, military conflicts, threats of war, opponents, alliance relationships, etc. Concerning particular singular opponents or situations of supreme interest, the same techniques can be used to design a set of possible *alternative futures.* If capabilities are designed to fit several possible alternatives, they are more likely to accomodate future events than if the planner picks a single set of contingencies. The hallmarks of useful conjecture are that it accepts the element of uncertainty about future events, that it recognizes differences in the conjecturability of different objects, and that it is analytically reasoned and hence capable of criticism.

It seems therefore inescapable that the question "capability for what?" cannot usually be answered with precision and a high degree of confidence. Nor does the problem reside only in the fact that future contingencies or "operating conditions" are only more or less conjecturable. To a considerable extent, the worth of military capabilities is also unknown even for kinds of employment for which they were specifically designed. Furthermore, since the production of many military capabilities involves a long lead time, objectives and strategies may change more or less as these capabilities are being generated. The presence of uncertainties hovers over all capability planning, and all capability analysis. Yet to say that the Sprouts' question permits of no high-confidence answer is not saying that capability analysis is impossible or useless. Since planning is impossible without assumptions about the future, such assumptions will be made, and they can be made well or badly. The social sciences can contribute substantially to the inputs which will determine the quality of this kind of statecraft although their appropriate utilization will remain a responsibility of government. Recent work on the nature of projection and prediction, and on the development of cost-effectiveness analysis, indicates the lines along which progress in the social sciences should prove fruitful to this purpose. These lines are especially the systematic conceptualization of hitherto neglected problems, the refinement of hypotheses about relevant relationships among relevant variables, and the discovery or construction of indicators suitable to statistical analysis. Advances in these directions will greatly improve the present capacity for capability analysis and thus provide a richer tool kit for the cultivation of what, as an exercise of statecraft, must nevertheless remain an art.

The annals of history bear strong testimony to the fact that, in trying to match capabilities with future contingencies, or more broadly, to match changing capabilities with changing objectives, strategies, and operating conditions, governments confront a hazardous task. The rate of failure is impressive. However, as these annals likewise reveal, this task is not as hopeless as the difficulties of relevant prediction, or the Sprouts' cognitive limitations, seem to suggest. And good capability analysis, which is based on reasoned conjecture about uncertain future events, though no doubt itself a key capability, is not the only resource on which government leaders can draw in attending to the matching job. There are ways, in fact time-honored ways, to adapt to the irreducible limitations to the "capabilities-for-what" analysis.

First, one common practice of governments is to maintain military capabilities for a variety of contingencies. Although small states, especially if facing political threats from much larger powers, are obviously limited in developing much built-in flexibility out of their own resources, this limitation is a lesser handicap for the great powers—which are militarily great precisely because they possess versatile military capabilities and are equipped to meet a broad range of military contingencies. And many lesser powers are, after all, concerned mainly with the military posture of neighboring states of comparable military potential. To be sure, the maintenance of a flexible military posture imposes costs. With a given volume of resources available for the military sector, the costs of being prepared for several contingencies is to be less well prepared for any one. With more available resources, more possible contingencies can be covered, or more solid preparations made for a limited number of contingencies. In this case, the opportunity costs are foregone uses of the extra resources for nonmilitary purposes. But though flexibility is not costless, it is—as in other areas of human problem-solving—a rational way of coping with uncertainty.

Second, if we look, beyond mobilized military forces, to other components of putative military power, military potential appears important because it may come into play in the event of a protracted military effort either in an arms race or in a prolonged military conflict; and precisely because it may come into play under these particular circumstances, the very recognition of this potential may affect the conflict behavior of other states. Resources capable of being mobilized for military purposes afford another element of flexibility in meeting various, and perhaps unforeseen, "operating conditions" in the outside world. This holds true not only of such obvious resources as technological sophistication and industrial capacity, but also of administrative skills that can be brought to bear on making sure that industrial and technological capacity is employed toward providing the right kinds of military outputs; and it is true also of the political will which a national community, whatever its regime, is able to muster in order to allocate additional resources to the military sector. These *general* capacities for developing or expanding the military capabilities of a state are extremely important whenever circumstances allow time for their mobilization. If one studies the performance of militarily successful states, one is struck by the weight of these less proximate conditions—government skill, and the war-related determination of the elites and influential publics—in facilitating adaptation to changing and unforeseen sets of contingencies. Rome's achievement in the two Punic Wars is a telling example. In the first war, though the Romans had not been a seafaring nation before, they built navies and resolutely continued to do so, despite initial failures, until they had beaten the greatest naval power in the Mediterranean. In the second war, staggering under a series of defeats administered by Hannibal, Rome never stopped to form new legions and eventually prevailed. Polybius, a contemporary Greek historian, attributed this achievement mainly to the Roman political constitution.[7] He exaggerated the weight of this one "capability," but he was perceptive in concluding that it was the noneconomic capabilities from which the Roman armies and navies were created, rather than economic resources and the military forces themselves, which made Rome prevail in the face of changing and surprising contingencies. This was precisely because these kinds of capabilities, unlike specialized forces, were not limited to perform under a particular or small set of "operating conditions."

Third, calling on the assistance of other nations is clearly another way for a state to cope with a larger range of contingencies than it could if limited to its own resources. Formal alliances are evidently meant to accomplish this effect. Even in the absence of alliances, however, states are often able to avoid situations in which they have nothing but their own capabilities in order to match objectives, strategy and contingencies. They are often able to solicit or accept help from others in the hour of need.

Fourth, the matching of national capabilities, on the one hand, and changing objectives, strategies and contingencies, on the other, is achieved frequently, and for compelling reasons, by adapting objectives and strategies to capabilities, and by avoiding situations, if at all possible, when "operating conditions" are highly unfavorable, or too exacting in relation to available capabilities. To do so has always been the object of prudent statecraft. In this sense, the actual use of capabilities, including military forces, is always a matter of opportunism, that is, of exercising an option when capabilities seem to fit objectives and circumstances. Even a state threatened militarily by a far superior power has, after all, the choice of a conciliatory approach. And even great powers, although they are able to match objectives, strategies and operating conditions with capabilities more easily than smaller powers can, are limited in this respect.

Finally, in pursuing objectives under variable circumstances, states dispose of several kinds of capabilities (e.g., military, political, economic) which permit them to use a variety of noncoercive as well as coercive means of influence. As already implied, they may resort to diplomacy in order to obtain assistance from other states, or to avoid or terminate conflicts in which their military capabilities are inadequate. Whenever different means of international influence can be combined in order to achieve given objectives, the composition of these combinations is adaptable to changing operating conditions. In many international situations, one capability becomes thus, at least marginally, a substitute for another.

However, this kind of substitutability is limited by objectives, strategies and operating conditions. For instance, these may rule out, or render unproductive, the association of coercive, and especially military, means with noncoercive means for influencing outcomes of certain international disputes. For this reason, the Sprouts are right in complaining of the tendency to estimate and compare the capabilities of nations mainly in terms of winning military wars. The traditional focus on military capabilities was understandable in view of the abundantly observable fact that non-military capabilities are a poor counter to hostile armies and that, historical-ly speaking, war has figured preeminently as the final arbitrament in inter-national conflict. But it was never the only arbitrament, and it is clear that the nonmilitary capabilities of states have been, and are, of pervasive importance in shaping international politics, and hence deserve more attention in capability analysis than they received. Indeed a thorough anal-ysis of the relationships between the various means of international influence, on the one hand, and various state objectives and strategies, and various configurations of international contingencies, on the other hand, should yield a body of theory which is sorely needed for explaining international relationships, and might also benefit statecraft.

One may conclude that capability analysis need not be related too closely to particular patterns of usually unpredictable contingencies, although whenever power is actualized, the fit between capabilities and operating conditions is an important determinant of the outcome. I see a greater difficulty with capability analysis in the bewildering complexity of variables with which it must cope if it is to be more than superficial and fragmentary. National capabilities are the product of many kinds of resources at the disposal of a society, and behind these resources is a complex of political, economic and social forces and structures, attitudes, cultural values, and so on. And excepting economics and demography, the social sciences have not so far developed the models and data on which capability analysis in depth should be able to draw.

II

The Sprouts also suggest in their essay that, in the contemporary world, military capabilities are becoming less important in structuring interstate relationships.[8] They attribute this trend to two concomitant factors. One is that states are experiencing an "insufficiency of resources to cover all commitments and desirable projects that are potentially attainable with the knowledge and skills available.[9] They mention seven concurring conditions which have made this over-all resource limitation "increasingly restrictive in recent decades."[10] Conspicuous among these seems to be the rising level of demands and expectations by the less privileged segments of political communities. The other factor is the rapidly escalating costs of military capabilities.[11]

The insufficiency of economic resources in relation to social demands made on them has been, of course, a perennial problem with which all human communities have had to cope. No community can for long consume more than it produces except to the extent that it forcibly exploits other communities or secures voluntary assistance from them. Excess consumption entails a decline in production. A community which is unable to maintain equilibrium over time will probably disintegrate in the face of progressive impoverishment. Whatever its political regime, every community will divide the available produce in accordance with politically effective preferences. The share-out is capable of substantial revision over time, and substantial changes in the distribution of income are usually preceded, accompanied, or followed by political turbulence. If it is not worried by possible international repercussions, a community is free to reduce or even eliminate military outlays in order to employ more resources for other purposes.

Available statistical data do not indicate that, as a whole, the existing state members of the international system cannot make ends meet. International differences in military expenditures bear a remarkably close relationship to differences in national incomes.[12] A good number of countries suffer from persistent and substantial price inflation. Although this results from excessive spending, price inflation has in these countries become an accepted method for correcting the imbalance between demand and supply. Some countries also experience occasional balance-of-payment problems; but sooner or later they will be compelled to make the adjustments necessary for a correction. The available statistical records do not indicate either that, as a whole, states have been reducing their military expenditures, in recent years or decades, either in absolute amounts or as a share of national income. A few individual states have done so, though not by radical cuts, in recent years. But it seems clear in most instances (e.g., western Europe) that the perception of a diminished security threat preceded the decision. Even though a felt insufficiency of resources, and repeated balance-of-payments disequilibria, probably contributed to Britain's gradual withdrawal from a world-wide military role, the main considerations were probably that postwar decolonization sharply reduced and changed the nature of British interests overseas, and that the remaining British interests (largely economic) outside Europe are not, in today's world, susceptible to promotion or protection by national military power. But even after deciding to withdraw its forces beyond the Suez Canal, the United Kingdom is still spending on defense a proportion of its national product which is about average for the more developed countries.

It is true that the costs of military ships, aircraft, personnel, etc., have risen very sharply in absolute terms ever since World War II. I am not aware of any comparative statistics on the matter, but I doubt that these cost increases have been of an appreciably higher order than those for many other goods and services such as medical care and factory construction. On the whole, there is no reason why military technology should be very different in this respect from comparable civilian technologies. If the cost of a particular kind of military system—for example, aircraft— rises disproportionately, there is a tendency to make do with a smaller number than were maintained before. Of course, it is technologically possible for countries to spend far more on military capabilities than they do at any one time. This has always been so. Yet since all governments experience pressures arising from the demand for resources for other uses, and since their military efforts are related to one another, it is not difficult for them, quite without formal negotiation, to arrive at bearable levels. There is no evidence that, at this time, the mounting costs of military hardware are pricing "military power out of the market," in a manner of speaking, and thus causing military capabilities to be of lesser account in international affairs.

I have argued elsewhere, however, that there is a contemporary tendency for the utility of military power to diminish as an instrument for settling international disputes, and I examined several conditions which may explain this phenomenon.[13] Most interesting as contributing factors are new, or, if not new, tightened restraints on the use of military power in particular kinds of contingencies, and also a decreasing attraction of some of the values on behalf of which military power has been used frequently in the past, i.e., territorial conquest. One should not exaggerate these changes in the utility of military power, nor assume that they impinge equally on all states. But these changes are taking place, and they can explain why military capabilities are declining as a factor in international relations. The restraints involved work, to the extent they do, because disregarding them imposes costs on governments and states. But these are political and moral costs. These factors are different from any restraint resulting from new and powerful pressures, which, in turn, are induced by insufficiency of resources and the escalating rise in the costs of weapon systems.

If the trend toward a lessening utility of national military power is correctly perceived, and especially if it persists, the consequence could be an appreciation of the nonmilitary means of international influence. Indeed, an interesting question is whether similar restraints are not developing regarding the use of other coercive means of international influence. Another possible consequence might be that the governments of states become less subject to international influence, and that the level of influence attempts made by governments will fall throughout the international system. Should this happen, it need not, of course, apply to all kinds of international conflicts of interest but express itself only, or mainly, with reference to certain specific international functions of governments. An example might be changes in the nature of international responses to defaults on financial debts, or the nationalization of foreign private enterprise. Around the turn of the nineteenth century, it was still customary for governments of creditor nations to employ military threats, and sometimes to execute these threats, against defaulting countries. In the first half of the present century, this practice was gradually replaced by resort to financial or economic reprisal. It is quite possible, in view of more recent behavior patterns in these cases, that the use of any coercive action is losing legitimacy. It is, of course, possible that a decline in the usability of international sanctions will cause some shrinking of transactions which gave rise to these kinds of disputes. In any event, traditional modes of international order will change substantially if such developments are in the making or gathering momentum. And such developments would also have interesting implications for capability analysis.

Notes and References

[1] Research Monograph No. 30, Center of International Studies, Princeton University (March 1968).

[2] *Ibid.*, p. 35.

[3] Cf. Harold and Margaret Sprout, *Foundations of International Politics* (Princeton: Van Nostrand, 1962), p. 141.

[4] Klaus Knorr, *Military Power and Potential* (Lexington, Mass.: Heath, 1970), Ch. I.

[5] *An Ecological Paradigm, op. cit.,* p. 33.

[6] These are lack of opportunity to perceive the limiting condition; misperception resulting from selectivity; and misinterpretation of what is perceived. *Ibid.*, pp. 38–41.

[7] Polybius, *Histories,* Book VI.

[8] *An Ecological Paradigm . . . ,* p. 35.

[9] *Ibid.*, p. 41.

[10] *Ibid.*, p. 42.

[11] *Ibid.*, pp. 42–44.

[12] For data on recent national defense expenditures, see United States Arms Control and Disarmament Agency, *World-Wide Military Expenditures and Related Data* (Calendar Year 1965, Washington, D.C., 1967).

[13] Klaus Knorr, *On the Uses of Military Power in the Nuclear Age* (Princeton: Princeton University Press, 1966), esp. Chapters II and III.

RICHARD A. FALK

*Zone II as a World Order Construct**

*H*arold and Margaret Sprout
write that "In any period of history, the results of international statecraft
exhibit more or less clearly discernible patterns of coercion and submission,
and influence and deference, patterns reflected in political terms with
strong geographic connotations: such as balance of power, bipolarity,
political orbit, satellite, bloc, coalition, alliance, the Monroe Doctrine,
the Atlantic community, the Near East, and many others." [1] In this chapter,
I propose to make out a case for regarding the relationships between the
United States and its dependent allies in Central America and between
the Soviet Union and its dependent allies in Eastern Europe as exhibiting
a discernible pattern of statecraft.

Part of the argument of this chapter is that these patterns of control
over certain categories of dependent countries contribute to the confinement
of conflict and violence within tolerable limits, given the present character
of international society. In fact, that indulgence of the claims of superordinate actors to exert control is one critical safeguard against the occurrence
of more general warfare. The ordering role of these patterns of control
is important, partly because modern military technology makes it imperative that nuclear rivals achieve some kind of reciprocal understanding

* I would like to thank several colleagues who have commented helpfully on an earlier draft
of this chapter: Gabriel Almond, Lewis Coser, Vincent Davis, William Frankena, Ernst
B. Haas, Ulf Himmelstrand, Albert O. Hirschman, Rajni Kothari, Leon Lipson, Pierre
Noyes, Lawrence C. Petrowski, Nadav Safran, Charles Tilly, and O. R. Young. My revisions
have been strongly influenced by their various suggestions, and although I may not have
done all they would have had me do, I have tried to take account of their principal points.
This chapter is part of a longer study of this same subject-matter.

Notes and References for this selection will be found on pages 202–205.

as to their tolerance range with respect to their behavior. The fact that this tolerance range departs from the positive law of international society has many undesirable consequences, especially for the dependent societies, but it still seems less undesirable than would vagueness about reciprocal tolerance ranges.[2] There are additional superordinate–subordinate patterns of relationship in international society. China, India, Indonesia, Ghana, and the United Arab Republic each enjoy to varying degrees the status of superordinate actor in relation to certain subordinate countries, and these patterns both resemble and contrast with the dependency relationships maintained by Soviet and American behavior. However, these secondary patterns have a less dramatic relationship to international society because the consequences of challenge and error are more locally confined. It is the interconnection between nuclear bipolarity and the assertion of superordinate status that establishes the world-order focus of this inquiry.[3]

Let me, however, be clear. The existence of external structures of domination is a very costly form of order in the present international system. Such structures rely upon the threat and actuality of military power. Reliance on military power to sustain the full domain of political authority tends to preclude any kind of drastic disarmament or move toward a less dangerous, more humane kind of world order system. These principal structures of domination are a major, perhaps a decisive, impediment to the achievement of much needed social and institutional change in international society. So long as these structures exist in a world of nuclear rivalry it remains nevertheless desirable that their boundaries be defined with the same clarity that pertains to national boundaries. Above all else, it is essential for the maintenance of world order to avoid overlapping pretensions of authority and commitment on the part of principal rival states.

My endeavor to clarify these relationships between dominant and subordinate states in international society draws on the work of several principal authors in the area of international relations. The idea of Zone II is adapted, in particular, from theoretical material associated with conceptions of "spheres of influence" and "bipolarity."[4] In this chapter the particular effort is to consider the relevance of normative considerations to a set of hegemonial relationships between states. Most approaches to these problems discern the conflict between the normative premise of sovereign *equality* and the political actuality of *hegemony*, and infer from this conflict the conclusion that such relationships are based on *power* rather than *norms*. My contention is that such a disjunction is not useful and that a principal role of norms is to clarify and sustain established patterns of power that are generally acceptable, or at least tolerated, by the relevant political community.

This essay offers a geopolitical interpretation of one set of important relationships that have emerged in the early decades of the nuclear age.

These are the relationships between the two preeminent states—the United States and the Soviet Union[5] and certain states of a secondary character that are subordinate to one or the other of these states, but *not* to both simultaneously. This set of relationships is differentiated from those between the superpowers *inter se* and between the superpowers and weaker states where no direct chain of subordinate affiliation is consistently visible. A primitive set of terms is supplied so as to simplify description, to establish the basis for more comprehensive lines of interpretation, and to show the links between hegemonial relationships and other categories of relationship in international society. The intellectual claims on behalf of this analysis are modest:

1. a primitive taxonomy more useful than alternative modes of analysis in designating dependency relationships in international society;
2. a level of awareness about the pattern of relationships at the center of inquiry that should make one more sensitive to expected patterns of action and reaction than one would be without the analysis.

No claim is laid that it is possible to predict behavior on the basis of the presentation that follows, although with some refinement of the analysis, a kind of forecasting, comparable to early weather forecasts, should be possible.

The United States and the Soviet Union are identified as Zone 1 actors; secondary states subject to supervisory domination by *either* the United States or the Soviet Union are identified as Zone II actors; secondary states subject to no clear line of hegemonial subjection by either Zone I are identified as Zone III actors.[6] States which enjoy national autonomy in the sense of being reasonably free from the prospect of military interference by either Zone I actor are identified as Zone IV actors. France, Switzerland, Japan, and Sweden are examples of states belonging in Zone IV. The countries of East Europe and of Central America are clear instances of Zone II actors, whereas most of the ex-colonial states of Asia and Africa are examples of Zone III actors.

The main patterns of relationship can be put in the form of a simple diagram[7]:

	Mandatory Alignment	Discretionary Alignment or Non-Alignment
Major States	I	IV
Minor States	II	III

To be entitled to Zone I status requires both capability, intention and conduct.[8] The distinction between Zone II and Zone III is mainly a jurisdictional one. Membership in Zone II is determined by the unit possessing the formal attributes of sovereignty and being subject to supervisory intervention, either without the consent of its government or without the option to establish a government that might withhold its consent, by a Zone I actor. These conditions do not necessarily involve geopolitical proximity between the Zone I and its sector of Zone II, but such proximity is a characteristic of the present interzonal relationships. As control over proximate territory diminishes in importance for security purposes, one might expect that Zone II status will diminish in importance, if not altogether disappear. However, other socioeconomic, ideological, and psychological factors may continue to motivate the preeminent actors in international society to maintain their control over political developments in neighboring small countries. It is also possible that an expansive Zone I actor would extend its sector of Zone II to encompass countries situated in other parts of the world. It would be quite conceivable, for instance, to imagine the United States intervening in Dominican fashion to prevent a Castroist-takeover of a country in the northern portions of South America or to prevent the emergence of a radical left regime in one of the smaller countries of the Pacific. At present, a Zone II setting is only established if there is a reasonably clear line of dependence by the target country and an expectation that a supervisory intervention in defiance of the government of the dependent country might occur. When Zone II is so narrowly defined it becomes fairly clear that as of 1968 only the countries of Central America (including the Caribbean area) and Eastern Europe qualify as Zone II actors. States in Zone II are clearly subject to hegemony and potential intervention by one and only one Zone I actor, whereas states in Zone III may be subject to periods of hegemony and military intervention by states in either Zone I, or quite possibly by states in Zone IV, or even by states, usually geographical neighbors, belonging to Zone III. A sector of Zone II is usually identifiable through a process of claim, control, and geopolitical access maintained over time by the Zone I actor. The process is not, in this postcolonial age, translated into juridical form, although the regionalist mantle may be used to obtain a quasijuridical basis for relegating certain smaller countries to Zone II status. It is interesting to note that the Soviet reliance on the consensus of "the socialist Commonwealth" to justify its 1968 action in Czechoslovakia is quite parallel to the United States' claims of "collective responsibility" in the Caribbean theater of operations.[9] One further way to comprehend Zone II is to consider it an extension, in diluted form, of the domestic jurisdiction, of a Zone I actor. That is, the Zone I actor treats its sector of Zone II as if, on certain limited occasions, it were part of its national domain.[10] The critical variable that distinguishes a Zone II situation from other varieties of dependent country relationships is the assertion by the Zone I actor of its military power despite the absence of an invitation from the constituted government. Such military assertions may be censured and a Zone I actor may even renounce its own interventionary competence, but there is no serious external effort to challenge the assertion in the event that it does occur, provided it occurs within the boundaries of an acknowledged sector of Zone II. There is an intentional circularity here: the conditions that identify a country as belonging to Zone II are a consequence of its being in Zone II. The circularity arises from the fact that the boundaries of Zone II are drawn as a consequence of the claims and behavioral patterns of the Zone I actor and of the limits placed on counterclaims and countervailing behavioral patterns by its opponents in international society.

The fundamental character of world order reflects the degree and form of consensus prevailing among principal national governments as to the standards governing the threat or use of military power in pursuit of external goals.[11] The consensus may produce collective procedures as it did in the period during which the Holy Alliance functioned in Europe following the Congress of Vienna; the consensus may be based on allocational procedures whereby the principal states allocate spheres of exclusive concern, as occurred with respect to the colonization of Africa by virtue of the Congress of Berlin (1885). In the period since 1945 only the nuclear superpowers have been in a position to shape the basic jural order by agreeing with one another. Their intense rivalry on moral, and ideological grounds has prevented effective recourse to either collective procedures or to explicit allocational arrangements. At the same time, neither state has often wanted to challenge the jural order in such a way as to produce or even seriously threaten general war. Therefore, low-visibility consensus-generating devices have evolved, such as "the hot-line," assuring rival governments the means for communication during periods of crisis. Such a facility for communication tends to facilitate the coordination of policy, and helps induce tacit patterns of deference to allocational arrangements within Zone II. As suggested earlier, the perimeters of Zone II have been reasonably stable with respect to those marginal situations where the jural order was itself being challenged by opposing revisionist movements each sponsored by a Zone I actor—the divided country situation for states of Zone II rank.[12]

In this section an argument will be made to show that Zone II deserves to be included in a description of the contemporary system of world order. It should be underscored that "world order" neither implies the maintenance of world peace, nor the justice of the system in being. The character of world order at any given time is created by the rules, procedures, and institutions of both a formal and informal character that attempt to regulate behavior and confine conflict within tolerable limits, as well as to minimize the risk of large-scale, irreversible violence occurring in the relations among principal states. In the present historical period a central concern of world order is to prevent the use of nuclear weapons, especially in the relations of Zone I actors with one another. Part of this concern is expressed through the tacit acceptance of Zone II relationships, even when these relationships result in the violent suppression of a group adhering to the ideology of the rival sector of Zone I.

Henry Kissinger writes of "a generally accepted legitimacy" as characterizing the procedures used to moderate conflict in the period of European history after 1815. Zone II appears to possess such "a generally accepted legitimacy" within the present international system. Kissinger points out that his use of legitimacy "means no more than an international agreement about the nature of workable arrangements and about permissible aims and methods of foreign policy."[13] Legitimacy, then, can be said to pertain to an international arrangement, whether explicit or implicit, that allows a careful observer to explicate its contours and define the nature of tacit consensus as it creates an orbit of effective authority in geographical space. Zone II appears entitled to be considered, under these ideas, a component of the current world order system, representing an area of tacit agreement, the implicit rules of which are part of the process by which world order is maintained.[14] A "violation" of these "rules" would be likely to make it difficult to confine conflict; for instance, this difficulty might arise if the United States used force to interfere with Soviet policing efforts within the sector of Zone II controlled by the Soviet Union. Normative taboos associated with an absolute respect for national sovereignty and for national self-determination of all states, regardless of size or geopolitical locus, prevents any formal acknowledgment of Zone II by Zone I actors. France, during the debate of August 1968, in the United Nations on the Czech crisis, referred to the facts of Soviet occupation as the outcome of "the policy of blocs" that had dominated the European scene since the end of World War II. Only an opponent of a prevailing pattern of control is likely to identify its existence in such explicit and derogatory terms; the practitioners of Zone I diplomacy share an aversion to any overt acknowledgment of a symmetrical pattern and, instead, vigorously condemn the behavior of their rival and defend their own.[15] One cost of resting world order partially upon patterns of control that cannot be acknowledged by their own creators is to cast the entire enterprise of law and order in world affairs into cynical disrepute, except for marginal issues of world security.

I would like to argue, then, that it is important for specialists, at least, to acknowledge Zone II as possessing generally accepted legitimacy within the existing system of world order.[16] Kissinger's formulation is once more germane: "'Legitimacy' as used here should not be confused with justice." Many structures of domination, ranging from colonialism to slavery have enjoyed legitimacy, but few would want to ascribe, at least automatically, justice to each of these arrangements. In international affairs it remains the case that a condition of *de facto* conquest can be converted into a *de jure* expansion of territory by way of a peace treaty that amounts to a *diktat*.[17] The point is that the primary concern of world order is legitimacy, although it can be argued that a legitimate order will be more or less stable to the extent that it accords with the prevailing sense of justice in the relevant portion of the international community.[18] The point here is that the justice or injustice of a legitimacy arrangement is but one of several factors that should be taken into account in assessing its contribution to the maintenance of world order.

It seems appropriate to assess Zone II by reference to a list of principal factors. No effort is made to assess the relative importance of these factors in different situations. The most suitable way to consider these factors is by visualizing a claim by a Zone I actor to assert police (or military) authority in relation to a country situated within its sector of Zone II. More concretely, consider the *type* of assertion of United States authority in the Dominican Republic since 1965 and the type of assertion of Soviet authority in Czechoslovakia since 1968. No effort will be made to discuss the exact circumstances of these two occurrences except to use them as occasions on which the international status of Zone II appears amply demonstrated.[19]

The rest of this essay will attempt to outline the dimensions of legitimacy as they apply to Zone II diplomacy. Legitimacy is not equivalent to the exercise of naked power, nor to compliance with enacted law, nor is it necessarily compatible with prevailing or posited standards of justice. In fact, what is legitimate may be very undesirable in net effect, as it is with Zone II diplomacy which seriously inhibits prospects for social change on a global level and deprives dependent populations of their rights of political self-determination. Instead, the legitimacy of a particular set of actions is a matter of degree, and a consequence of weighting and interrelating a series of factors. The following considerations can be used to assess relative legitimacy and to relate the control of Zone II with other aspects of the present system of world order. These considerations provide a framework for organizing material rather than a calculus enabling a clear conclusion.

1. *Perceived relationship of compatibility or incompatibility with other authoritative norms of behavior.* Zone I claims to act in Zone II depend on threatened and actual uses of military force in violation of the basic postulates of the two dominant explicit normative systems accepted in international society. Zone I claims violate the norms of territorial sovereignty at the base of the Westphalia System and the norm prohibiting non-defensive uses of military force that is at the basis of the Charter System.[20] In this respect, then, Zone I military prerogatives in Zone II appear to be highly "illegitimate," especially when the military force is used overtly, unilaterally, and overcomes violent resistance. The attempts by both the Soviet Union and the United States to collectivize these claims acknowledges, in part, their gross incompatibility with factor 1 in the legitimacy scale. There is also an effort to establish the authority of regional actors to enforce Zone I claims and accord them a greater measure of legitimacy. Such an effort to create counternorms to the Charter at the regional level is both legislative in character and subversive of the role of the United Nations to the degree that it succeeds.

2. *Perceived relationship of compatibility or incompatibility with the*

prevailing regional or global sense of justice. Some claims asserted in violation of factor 1 are not even condemned in global arenas if their assertion satisfies the prevailing sense of justice. The clearest examples may be the use of force by India in 1962 to acquire control of Goa from Portugal or the threatened uses of force by African countries and regional institutions to end the rule of colonial and racist regimes in southern Africa. Zone I claims to uphold justice by military interference in Zone II countries are generally not very widely supported in formal arenas of world opinion nor in the annals of impartial professional commentary on the legal status of such action. There is, however, a sliding scale of perceived injustice depending on the assessment of the circumstances actuating the Zone I claim, the efficiency and effectiveness of its assertion, the stability of its effects, and the time-span over which the violation of Zone II sovereignty is perceived as occurring in some acute sense.

3. *Perceived relationship to the expectations prevailing in the rival Zone I government and in regional and global arenas of diplomatic interaction.* To a certain rhetorical extent, Zone I military assertions in Zone II are always subject to criticism and censure as they violate the professed standards of adherence by Zone I governments with prevailing norms (factor 1) and the prevailing sense of justice (factor 2). However, the rationale for the assertion normally carries with it a more general formula implying claims to act in the future. Both the Soviet military occupation of Czechoslovakia and the American intervention in the Dominican Republic were widely felt to violate expectations about permissible behavior. These violations related to the setting that induced the government of Zone I to assert its military power: in the Dominican case the possibility that a Castroist regime would eventuate, and in the Czech case the pursuit of a set of official policies aiming at domestic liberalization.[21] There are important asymmetries: Czechoslovakia was well administered, the Dominican Republic was in the midst of a struggle for regime-control; Czechoslovakia is bigger, more developed, more closely connected with principal Soviet security and domestic policies,[22] whereas the Dominican Republic is a minor unit in Zone II with no clear course of political leadership. The provisional effect of the Soviet intervention has been to terminate the Czech domestic policies, but not to alter the composition of the administering elite, whereas the American intervention probably converted a rebel victory into a rebel defeat with the consequence that the governing elite is different in personnel and policy orientation.[23] The point is that the relation of the Zone I claim to expectations (factor 3) varies with the kind of setting, and cannot be derived from the structure of the claim. The general stature of the Czech leadership, dignity, discipline, the gallantry of its population, the long struggle of the country for national autonomy, its strategic location in the heart of Europe, and the dampening of prospects for an all-European settlement are among the considerations that appear to make the Soviet acts in Czechoslovakia far more disruptive

of governing expectations than were the American acts in the Dominican Republic.[24]

4. *Reactions of the Zone II victim, of the Zone I adversary, of global and of regional opinion responding to the assertion of the Zone I claim.* One can imagine a spectrum of responses ranging from approval through silent acquiescence over to recourse to counter-violence in the face of an adversary Zone I operation. Hungarian opposition to Soviet military power may well have been partly based on the expectation of or hope for American military support. It is reasonable to speculate that the Czech refusal to use violent means of resistance, no matter what, was based, at least in part, on a learning experience going back to 1956 about the structure of relations within the Soviet sector of Zone II. Similarly, one supposes, the Soviet refusal to become involved in Latin American situations wherein United States military power is being used to thwart the domestic balance of forces has become part of the calculation of prospects being made by various revolutionary groups.[25]

The important conclusion here is that even the most serious exercises of Zone I power (if measured by factors 1–3) in Zone II have not provoked reactions that have represented major dangers to world peace. The major dangers have arisen from contexts such as the smaller divided country settings wherein it was ambiguous as to whether Zone II considerations applied to the maintenance of the jural *status quo,* and wherein Zone I actors have had contradictory perceptions as to the nature of their "commitment" to react with counter-violence.[26] In the setting of an undisputed, unambiguous sector of Zone II, then, world tension might rise, feelings of spontaneous outrage and frustration might mount, but no serious danger of violent confrontation will be present.

Cuba represents a special case in that there was a successful rejection, at least temporarily, of Zone I prerogatives, and a shift of political allegiance to the adversary Zone I actor.[27] American statesmen have had a hard time reconciling their endorsement of the ideology of self-determination with the geopolitics of Soviet–American rivalry.[28] Once the shift of allegiance had taken place, then the Soviet involvement more closely conformed to prevailing rules of competition, for Cuba had apparently escaped from the American sector of Zone II and was no longer unprotectable against former Zone I prerogatives. The Cuban missile crisis, unlike the Bay of Pigs, caused an intense danger to world peace because the United States was maintaining minimal residual Zone I prerogatives in relation to Cuba, namely the insistence on the right to interdict the deployment of nuclear missiles by its Zone I rival on Cuban territory. Would the United States have interdicted missile deployment within the clearly established contours of the Soviet sector of Zone II? It seems doubtful.[29] The relationships of Cuba with both the United States and the Soviet Union since 1959 suggest the tension and potential danger that arises from the sudden erosion of zonal boundaries and affiliations. The problem is accentuated by the absence of any procedure by which to differentiate between action by a Zone I actor to *prevent* disaffiliation and action to *punish* a Zone II actor that has successfully achieved a new affiliation. In the former setting normal deference patterns allow the Zone I actor to assert its control without any adverse reaction stronger than protest, and, possibly, community censure. In the latter setting, the rival Zone I actor is likely to perceive a new *status quo* in which the disaffiliating state is entitled to the option of reaffiliation or, at least, of political autonomy, whereas the former hegemonial actor is less likely to perceive or acknowledge the diminished status of its zonal prerogatives. Changed circumstances are particularly likely to provoke selective perception of critical facts and of their interrelation with norms and community expectations.

5. *Minimization of violence in the execution of the Zone I policy in Zone II.* The relative unacceptability of Zone I policies in Zone II depends to a great degree on the amount of violence used and the amount of bloodshed caused. It also depends on the effort by Zone I to carry out the policy in a minimally provocative way with respect to generating international reactions above certain thresholds (factor 4). In relation to factor 5 the United States policy at the Bay of Pigs and during the missile crisis again provides a useful contrast. In the former instance, violence took place, lives were sacrificed, with no policing effect; there was a certain callousness exhibited by the Zone I claimant that combined with an uneffectual assertion (see factor 6). In the missile crisis, however, maximum precaution was taken to exercise the authority claim without recourse to violence. Part of the precaution consisted of a precise articulation of the claim, another part consisted in bringing to bear such an overwhelming capability as to build a strong deterrent against Soviet miscalculation. The immense size of the Soviet occupation force in Czechoslovakia (over 600,000) may be partly interpreted as an effort to deter Hungarian-type resistance. In any event, the degree of legitimacy attaching to Zone I prerogatives in Zone II is deeply affected by the degree to which violence is minimized. It should be appreciated, of course, that the basic infringement on the autonomy of Zone II actors is sustained by threat, informal structures of influence, and by nonmilitary means of coercion. Only the test case provided by directly challenging or accidently misunderstanding Zone I imperatives provokes military intervention.

An effective system of communication is an important element in the successful administration of Zone II. The Zone I actor can effectively use its overwhelming military superiority and its threat to intervene only if it conveys to the elites of Zone II countries the restrictions placed upon their discretion. It is possible, of course, that radical elites in a Zone II country would welcome under certain circumstances, a confrontation to expose the extent to which a Zone I actor is prepared to use naked force to disrupt the processes of national self-determination that it purports to respect.[30]

Under typical circumstances, however, it is the uncertainty of Zone I parameters of tolerance that induces the major military interventions in Zone II countries. Zone I actors appear to experience difficulty in clearly communicating these parameters because the whole implicit premise of partial hegemony contradicts their general adherence to postulates about the proper basis of world order (factor 1) and their particular postulates about volitional relations with states closely allied with them. It is an ironic reality of recent years that the most brutal suppressions of national autonomy occur in the relations of states that are supposed to be united by bonds of friendship, ideology, interest, and propinquity.

6. *The relative effectiveness of the claim.* Any legal order will eventually work to accommodate a pattern of effective assertion. That which is authoritative reflects considerably under normal conditions that which is effective. Therefore, the success with which Zone I actors pursue their supervisory goals is important both to enable their proper apprehension and to deter defection by members of Zone II. As a principle of order, the capacity to administer authority effectively is obviously of great significance.

The assertion of ineffective Zone I claims by the United States also has the effect of uniting domestic opposition of liberal and conservative persuasion. The absence of any freedom of the press and the punishment of dissent make the Soviet government apparently much less vulnerable to the repercussions that follow from an ineffective and controversial assertion of its authority.[31]

7. *The degree, credibility, and timing of collective participation in the assertion of control by a Zone I actor.* Problems posed by factors 1–3 have led Zone I actors to obscure these issues by acting within a wider framework of decision in policing Zone II. Hegemonial regionalism—where the Zone II members of the sector are more or less compliant with the will of the Zone I leader—are attempts to endow Zone I claims with a certain quality of explicit legitimacy. The decision to enforce the regional will upon an intraregional deviant is alleged to be compatible with Charter norms of collective responsibility. Both the United States and the Soviet Union generally seek to obtain some kind of regional endorsement for uses of force within Zone II. These endorsements may be more or less genuine, and the importance to the Zone I actors of obtaining such endorsements may be more or less influential in moderating its behavior. It is necessary to assess not only the extent to which the supervisory claim acquires additional legitimacy when it has been asserted within a regional, rather than a unilateral framework, but also the extent to which the alleged regionality of the claim is genuine or spurious. Among the relevant considerations are the degree of regional participation in the making and executing of the decision and the degree to which Zone II interests distinct from Zone I interests are visible in the operation. For instance, it is clear that several Zone II members were supportive of, perhaps insistent upon, Zone I initiatives against Czechoslovakia in 1968 and against Cuba in the years since Castro came to power.

There is no question, however, that the normative issues raised by factor 1 are blurred to some extent if some sort of regional consensus can be mobilized in support of Zone I military action in Zone II. The normative traditions underlying both Westphalia and Charter conceptions are based on the rules restraining states in their conduct with one another. The extent to which these norms also constrain action by a regional actor is far less clear, although there is a nominal insistence that regional competence be subordinated to the normative framework of the UN Charter.[32]

8. *Persuasiveness of claim.* The Zone I claimant almost always seeks to *vindicate* with supportive arguments the occasions of its assertions of military control over Zone II. However these arguments may vary from contentions that the welfare and security of the region depend on an ideological solidarity that is threatened by domestic developments in the Zone II target country, to contentions of regional competence to resist extra-regional political and military penetrations. Most efforts at persuasion fall into the following categories: legal arguments, moral arguments, and security arguments. The rhetoric of law, morality, and security is persuasive to the extent that there exists a reasonably close correlation between the control claims advanced and the general appreciation of the facts to which they are supposed to pertain. Occasionally, the standards are themselves controversial, as when the United States and the Soviet Union claim to act on behalf of some regional consensus to uphold certain minimum conditions of ideological solidarity with their respective sectors of Zone II. Why is Marxism-Leninism more incompatible with human welfare if adhered to by Castro's Cuba than by Tito's Yugoslavia? The expulsion of Cuba at Punta del Este from the Interamerican System in 1962 rested on the adherence of the Castro regime to Marxism–Leninism, an ideology alleged in conference resolutions to be incompatible with the ideals of the hemisphere.

There is some connection between this factor and factors 1 and 2. The stress here falls on the pattern of justification invoked by the Zone I actor, rather than upon the perceived relationships between the Zone I claim and legal norms or the prevailing sense of justice. The very willingness to justify Zone I claims in a global forum is itself a significant element of accountability that may over time socialize the elites of Zone I actors toward an acceptance of broader conceptions of international propriety. Therefore, it is of interest, although it is by no means of great significance— after all, Hitler advanced legal, moral, and security arguments for Germany's aggressive moves during the 1930's—to appraise the form and substance of the arguments used by Zone I actors in seeking to support their military interventions in Zone II. Consistency of argument is an element that suggests the strength and sincerity of the Zone I claim. For instance, the original Soviet contention made during the last days of August 1968 to be responding to a Czech invitation, or the original American contention of April 1965 that it had intervened in the Dominican Republic to protect the safety of its nationals, were later abandoned or much muted in favor of slightly more plausible, if even less generally acceptable, arguments of justification. The Soviet argument shifted to an idea of socialist community responsibility to prevent certain kinds of regressive social and political behavior within their sector, and the American argument shifted to the controlling idea of frustrating alleged communist efforts to take advantage of political chaos by seizing control in the Dominican Republic.

9. *The outcome of community review at the global level.* Closely related to, but far from coincident with, the persuasiveness of the claim is the judgment passed upon Zone I action by the political organs of the United Nations. In exercising review functions it seems clear that voting majorities in the United Nations more characteristically reflect political alignment and ideological orientation than an impartial assessment of the merits of a claim by a Zone I actor. The comparatively greater political control of the machinery of the United Nations by the United States, especially during the earlier years of the organization, has meant that Zone II military operations of the United States have fared much better in the United Nations than have Soviet Zone II operations. It is possible to generalize by saying that the Soviet Union would not avoid censure by the United Nations even if its claim to exert control was relatively persuasive as measured by normal criteria, whereas the United States would not, as yet in any event, be subject to censure even if its claim was most unpersuasive. Because of this disparity of political support in the United Nations the conclusions of the Organization with respect to what Zone I actors do in Zone II cannot be taken to represent an impartial determination on the merits of the claim.[33]

It is possible to suggest that there is an inverse relationship for the Soviet Union and the United States with respect to review at the global level and to criticism at the domestic level. The Soviet control over its sector of Zone II is subject to censure in the United Nations and relatively free from opposition pressures at home, whereas the United States is confronted with the opposite situation. The shifting variables of domestic and global settings are significant, however, in assessing the inhibitions upon Zone I discretion in Zone II.

10. *The stability of effect and the general impact of the post-claiming behavior of the Zone I actor.* Recalling factor 6 (effectiveness), it is important to discuss whether the patterns of Zone I claims as asserted and implemented can control the situation for the indefinite future without the reassertion of military power or recourse to violence. After 1956 in Hungary, for instance, there took place a kind of liberalization of domestic policy in Hungary that did not transgress the Soviet conception of what developments were permissible in their sector of Zone II and yet satisfied some of the aspirations of those who were suppressed in 1956. There has been no recurrence of violence and no repetition of military intervention. Soviet troops have left Hungarian soil and there has been no evidence of acute economic exploitation or intimidation by the Zone I actor since 1956,

a set of issues prominent among the original grievances. That is, the Zone I actor can either allow reform to take place in a manner that meets its minimal demands for allegiance in Zone II or it can repress the domestic balance of forces in a variety of ways, either directly or through a client regime.[34] Certainly one of the strongest arguments against the United States role in South Vietnam is that the character of its hegemony has led to such a brutal and pervasive disregard of the welfare of the great majority of the population.[35]

The whole consensus underlying Zone II as a world order arrangement rests on its contribution to the maintenance of a tolerable level of stability essential to survival in the nuclear age. Therefore, the extent to which peace prevails within Zone II is important for an assessment of its impact on international affairs. There are additional considerations, of course, that enter into an appraisal, such as the impact of Zone II status on national self-determination, on minimum human rights for individuals and groups, and on raising standards of living, health, and education among the Zone II population.

11. *The precedential effect of the Zone I claim for the future of Zone II.* In a sense this factor incorporates all other factors. It puts a focus upon what has been claimed by the Zone I actor and upon the extent to which the claim results in a continuing infringement upon the discretion of actors in each sector of Zone II. Changes in the personnel and policy of the Zone I government may lead to the abandonment, moderation, or extension of its controversial claims of the past. World opinion was shocked by the Soviet occupation of Czechoslovakia in 1968 partly because there was a strong international sentiment that the Hungarian precedent of 1956 was no longer operative Soviet policy. Certainly there are significant segments of American public opinion, hopefully including the president elected by the United States in 1968, who would not regard the Dominican precedent of 1965 as a continuing claim for the future.

Nevertheless, the claims of the past are a significant means for communicating to Zone II actors operative restrictions on their discretion. These claims may be more or less significant to the extent that they express abiding lines of policy for the Zone I actor. In this sense, the United States defense of South Korea in 1950 appears to be a far stronger precedent than the United States "defense" of South Vietnam in the period following 1954.[36] The Vietnam claim seems weaker in almost every relevant respect (compare factors 1–10) than does the Korean claim.

12. *The disruption of the normal structure of relations between Zone I and Zone II.* If a Zone I actor began to commit genocide in its sector of Zone II would the rival Zone I actor maintain its response below the level of counterviolence? Such a question raises an issue in relation to the sense of justice (see factor 2) that suggests the potential existence of certain restrictions upon the discretion of Zone I action in its own sector of Zone II.

These restrictions upon Zone I discretion are more readily apparent in its relations to events taking place within the sector of Zone II that belongs to its adversary. The United States response to the Soviet intervention in Czechoslovakia or the Soviet response to the American intervention in the Dominican Republic are good illustrations. The factors governing response are different if the military initiative of a Zone I actor is in a Zone III or Zone IV situation. The fluid character of these restrictions is suggested by the kind of participation by the Soviet Union and the United States in various stages of Congolese strife and in the Nigerian civil war. To react to a Zone II conflict as if it were a Zone III conflict would very likely endanger peace in a most serious way. Similarly, to treat a Zone II conflict as if it were a confrontation between Zone I actors would be to create an almost certain crisis of major magnitude. That is, if the United States reacted to the occupation of Czechoslovakia the way it did to the Berlin blockades the danger to world peace would indeed have been intense. The Berlin blockades could be viewed as a careful test of wills related to the jural *status quo,* whereas a neutralizing intervention on behalf of Dubcek's regime (even assuming, as is unlikely, it had been requested), is a move toward a major revision of the strategic *status quo.* The move may or may not be a good one from the perspective of justice, but it is clearly disruptive of the consensus as to the "legitimacy" (in Kissinger's sense) of Zone I prerogatives in Zone II.

These twelve factors have been advanced to offer a tentative framework for (1) understanding the character of the relationship between Zone I and Zone II, and (2) providing the basis for an assessment of the quality of any particular claim by a Zone I actor to assert its military control over a country situated in its sector of Zone II. The distinctive feature of Zone II dependency is the continuing prospect of military intervention by the Zone I actor in possible defiance of the will of the Zone II government. There are two elements that are present in this dependency relationship: (1) the military dimension of control; and (2) the acceptance of the claim by the only actors capable of challenging it. Therefore, Zone I administration accords with tacit expectations and contradicts the sort of world community values embodied in both positive international law and in the UN Charter.[37] It also restricts the prospect for transition to a world-order system better adapted to the actualities of the nuclear age.

Notes and References

[1] H. & M. Sprout, *The Ecological Perspective on Human Affairs* (Princeton: Princeton University Press, 1965), p. 15.

[2] There are two principal normative principles violated by the imposition of a strong state's will upon a weaker state: (1) the principle of the sovereign equality of states that has been part of the positive law of international society since the Peace of Westphalia in 1648; (2) the prohibition upon the use of force in international relations except in cases of self-defense which has been part of the positive law of international society since the Briand–Kellogg Pact of 1928. It should be understood that the positive law of international society contains contradictory principles of behavior and that the wider framework of world order encompasses normative conceptions that supplement positive international law. See note 3 for further elaboration.

[3] The term "world order" is a difficult term to specify precisely. I use world order to refer to the aggregation of norms, procedures, and institutions that give shape and structure to international society at any given time. There is no implication that a particular system of world order either prohibits recourse to war or is successful as a peace system, although it may do either of these things. There is also no implication that a system of world order is concerned about the promotion of human justice, although it may be. Many systems of world order can be isolated in the history of international relations and many more systems can be projected as alternatives for the future. In essence, what these various systems of world order have in common is a concern with the varying roles of norms in the process by which power is managed in international life. But it should be understood that a rule of positive law is only one kind of norm. Other norms arise from behavioral regularities that are expressed in terms of claims and counter-claims on the part of principal actors.

Likewise, the use of the term "legitimacy" is to identify attitudes toward what is permissible at any given time. These attitudes may be established for formal agreement, as through a treaty, or by more tacit and indirect means, as through Resolutions in the General Assembly of the United Nations. Because the several perspectives bearing on the legitimacy of a specific claim to act may be inconsistent with one another, it is important to regard a particular claim as more or less legitimate rather than either legitimate or illegitimate. Legitimacy is a matter of degree.

[4]Among those books that have influenced my thinking on these issues are the following: John H. Herz, *International Politics in the Atomic Age* (New York: Columbia University Press, 1959); Morton A. Kaplan, *System and Process in International Politics* (New York: John Wiley, 1957); Richard N. Rosecrance, *Action and Reaction in International Politics* (Boston, Little-Brown, 1963); Kenneth E. Boulding, *Conflict and Defense; A Theoretical Statement* (New York: Harper & Row, 1962); E. H. Carr, *Nationalism and After* (London: Macmillan, 1945); Nicholas Spykman, *America's Strategy in World Politics* (New York: Harcourt, Brace, 1942); George Liska, *International Equilibrium* (Cambridge: Harvard University Press, 1957).

An important exception to this observation is Morton A. Kaplan and Nicholas de B. Katzenbach, *The Political Foundations of International Law* (New York: John Wiley, 1961); see also Chapters XI, XX, XXI in Falk, *The Status of Law in International Society* (Princeton: Princeton University Press, 1969).

[5]There is no implication that the Soviet Union and the United States are of equivalent power; there is much force to Liska's analysis of world affairs in light of "the primacy" of the United States. At the same time, Kenneth Waltz's defense of bipolar imagery is persuasive with regard to capability and intention of a projection of national power beyond boundaries. In some subregional settings there are certain relationships that exhibit dependency relationships that have some aspects in common with the relations between Zone I and II: for instance, China and India with small states along their boundary, South Africa with certain states in southern Africa, and France with some former French colonies in west Africa. In none of these instances, except possibly China, is there any pattern of acknowledgment by the community that includes deference to military intervention by the dominant actors.

[6]There are many ways to express the degree of dependency that pertains to a particular country in its relations with other countries. The use of four categories facilitates focus upon one kind of very prominent form of dependency in contemporary world affairs. It may be useful to use scalular measures of relative dependency based on various patterns of behavior: voting behavior in the political organs of the United Nations, trade statistics, cultural exchanges, foreign aid flows, alliance arrangements, and so forth. Gabriel Almond has suggested to me, for instance, that graphic portrayals of dependency relationships might prove more precise and sophisticated than the four categories that I have relied upon.

[7]Charles Tilly suggested the basic form of this diagram. Note that Zone I actors are presented as participants in a pattern of mandatory alignment. Such a designation takes note of a certain measure of latent reciprocity in Zone I–Zone II relationships. Zone II actors can often manipulate Zone I actors despite the power realities of dependency. The Soviet decision to occupy Czechoslovakia in 1968 certainly appears to have been influenced by the pressures of Zone II countries, especially East Germany and Poland. And the United States has been repeatedly manipulated by dependent allies, most spectacularly by Formosa and by the Saigon regime in South Vietnam.

[8]But the category affiliations cannot be clearly established in all cases. China could be either I or IV, Brazil, II or IV, South Africa, I, III, or IV, etc. We are proposing only a framework useful for organizing thought about various sets of relationships in international society. Operating within this framework does not, then, dispense with acts of judgment about the classification of a particular actor, nor with the possibility that reasonable people might disagree about a classificatory choice.

As indicated in Note 5, several of the regional subsystems in international society exhibit superordinate-subordinate relationships. As therein pointed out, China and India each have such patterns of relationships with several of their small contiguous neighbors. These patterns are presently much less centrally related to the management of power in the world today, and do not, at this time, intermesh with the effort to avoid nuclear warfare between the United States and the Soviet Union.

[9]Consider, for instance, the following passage from John Bartlow Martin's long book on the Dominican intervention, bearing the title, *Overtaken by Events* (Garden City, New York: Doubleday, 1966), p. 733:

"Sumner Welles' hope for nonintervention in the Hemisphere seems now to belong with Booth Tarkington and heliotrope and the swish of garden hose at summer dusk. He (Welles) had to deal only with quarreling Dominican *caciques,* Dominican governmental inability, and U.S. and European capitalists' machinations. Today we have to deal with the violent intervention of expert communism. In today's world a more useful doctrine for the Hemisphere would seem to be one of interdependence." Compare Martin's sentiment with the main defense of the Soviet occupation of Czechoslovakia that appeared in *Pravda,* the translated text "Sovereignty and International Duties of Socialist Countries," appearing in the *New York Times,* September 27, 1968. Note, for instance, the following passage: "It has got to be emphasized that when a socialist country seems to adapt a 'nonaffiliated' stand, it retains its national independence, in effect, precisely because of the socialist community, and above all the Soviet Union as a central force, which includes the might of its armed forces. The weakening of any of the links in the world system of socialism directly affects all the socialist countries, which cannot look indifferently upon this." See also C. L. Sulzberger, "Foreign Affairs: The Commonwealth," *New York Times,* November 27, 1968, p. 46.

[10]In this respect, the occurrences within Zone II that result from Zone I's interventions are shielded by a policy of deference not unlike, but more diluted and far less acknowledged, than the deference underlying the idea of "domestic jurisdiction." Perhaps, it might be called "hegemonial jurisdiction"; such deference is related to expectations about the exercise of power in defiance of the will of the regime in the dependent country. Such deference would not shield Zone I intervention from retaliatory response outside Zone II.

[11]The important datum for any social system relates to the quality of consensus among centers of political authority. In the current international system national governments remain the most important centers of political authority. Past systems have had and future systems might have different or additional centers of political authority.

[12]Revisionist pressures and social change within an actor situated totally within one or the other sector of Zone II is characteristically inhibited by Zone I preferences. If these preferences are violated, then the government of the Zone I actor is confronted with the choice between toleration and suppression. It is a challenge to the geopolitical *status quo,* but not one that is likely to upset the basis of global stability.

[13]Henry Kissinger, *A World Restored* (Universal Literary Edition, 1964), p. 1.

[14]These rules function in a dynamic environment and their character is always subject to modification by effective challenge or renunciation. Either Zone I actor can challenge rival claims or renounce his own, or dissolve the consensus pattern that sustains Zone II as a distinct geopolitical category.

[15]Cf. article published in *Pravda* on September 25, 1968 and translated in full under title "Sovereignty and International Duties of Socialist Countries" and republished in the *New York Times,* September 27, 1968, with the arguments used by Secretary of State, Dean Rusk, to explain the American involvement in the Vietnam War by reference to participation in SEATO. See, especially, testimony before the Senate Foreign Relations Committee in February 1966. Also, compare the rejection by the *Pravda* article of what it calls "an abstract, nonclass approach to the question of sovereignty and the rights of nations to self-determination" with the call of the U.S. Legal Adviser Leonard C. Meeker for a rejection of "fundamentalist views about the nature of international law" in the context of the Dominican intervention. Mr. Meeker, in an analysis that parallels the Soviet defense of their Czech intervention, goes on to criticize those "commentators that have been free with the use of categorical imperatives" and to say that "reliance on

absolutes for judging and evaluating the events of our time is artificial." Leonard C. Meeker, "The Dominican Situation in the Perspective of International Law," *Department of State Bulletin,* Vol. LIII (July 12, 1965), pp. 60–65. Each side wants to constrain its opponent within clear normative boundaries and to claim contextual freedom for itself. A world order system, unless imperial in structure, rests upon certain kinds of reciprocal claims and tolerances. Since neither Zone I actor is imperial in relation to the other, there is no prospect for a nonreciprocal structure of world order evolving on a level of behavior as distinct from words. The exertion of Zone I control over sectors of Zone II is an example of reciprocal structures of claim and tolerance on a behavioral level.

[16]To accord legitimacy to a political arrangement is not to confer approval upon it. The word legitimacy has many normative connotations such that it is difficult to avoid the implication that a "legitimate" action is also an appropriate and permissible action. The reason to risk this confusion, despite the disclaimers in the text, is the importance of relating world order to patterns of stable expectation. Legitimacy expresses the compatibility of a pattern of behavior with a system of world order without implying that the pattern is "legal" from the perspective of various hypothetical decision-makers, e.g., the judges of the International Court of Justice.

[17]See e.g., Julius Stone, "The International Law Commission and Imposed Treaties of Peace," *Virginia Journal of International Law,* Vol. 8. (1968), pp. 356–373.

[18]Perceived injustice, at least once some sort of political consciousness takes shape, breeds violence.

[19]For detailed accounts see Richard Lowenthal, "The Sparrow in the Cage—On the Soviet Invasion of Czechoslovakia," *Encounter* (1969); George Lichtheim, "Czechoslovakia 1968," *Commentary,* Vol. XLVI (November 1968), pp. 63–72; Martin, *op. cit.* supra note 14.

[20]One of the main characteristics of the present international legal system is the co-presence of several normative traditions that are in conflict with each other as to the legal basis for permissible uses of force, both in relation to substantive grounds of permissible force and procedural duties of accountability.

[21]For a criticism by a Soviet citizen of the grounds of the Soviet intervention in Czechoslovakia see "the open letter" of Anatoly T. Marchenko, *New York Times,* October 14, 1968, p. 10.

[22]The Soviet Union probably was acting at the time, in part, on the basis of its variant of "the domino theory." In addition, Czech liberalization probably exerted pressures against Soviet domestic controls on political and intellectual activity. It appears likely that the Soviet leadership feared the consequences of "the demonstration effect" of the policies of the Dubcek regime.

[23]See e.g., the account of Richard J. Barnet, *Intervention and Revolution: The United States in the Third World* (New York: World Publishing Co., 1968), pp. 153–180.

[24]The Dominican affair could be decoupled more easily from the main issues of international politics than can the Soviet treatment of Czechoslovakia.

[25]One takes notes, in this connection, of the reports of Che Guevara's disappointment in both Moscow and Peking where he had gone to seek support for staging "wars of national liberation" throughout Latin America. In both capitals he had been told that very little support could be expected.

[26]In this respect, President Johnson's exposition of the United States "commitment" to uphold the Saigon regime is one of the most blatant uses of obligatory rhetoric to describe (and justify) an entirely voluntary (if unpopular) policy.

[27]Cuba, since Castro, has disaffiliated from the United States sector of Zone II, but it has not become part of the Soviet sector of Zone II. There is no reason to think that any internal developments in Cuba adverse to Soviet policies would provoke a Zone I military intervention in defiance of the Havana government. The maximum hostile Soviet response to events in Cuba contrary to its wishes would be to terminate its economic and military support, and possibly, to break off diplomatic relations. In terms of my analysis, then, Cuba has enjoyed a Zone III status since Castro's accession to power. Unless the dependency

relationship includes a conditional claim by the Zone I actor to intervene militarily, there is no basis for according a Zone II status to a dependent or ideologically affiliated state.

[28]Consider, for instance, the responses of McGeorge Bundy and Dean Rusk to a question by a news correspondent (Harry Reasoner) suggesting that the Dominican intervention violated the principle of self-determination:

"Mr. Bundy: . . . Our action there—first, to save lives, then to prevent a particular kind of Communist hazard—has developed into an action designed precisely to give a reasonable opportunity for the people of the Dominican Republic to make their own choice about the kind of government and the kind of society they want to have. . . .

"Mr. Rusk: Mr. Reasoner, there is a very deep commitment of the American people to the simple notion that governments derive their just powers from the consent of the governed, and we have not seen a government—a Communist government—brought to power by the free election of its own people."

"Vietnam: Winning the Peace," *Department of State Bulletin,* Vol. LIII, (September 13, 1965), pp. 431–444, at 438.

[29]The deployment of nuclear missiles in Zone III countries would also be outside rules of competition and might provoke a global confrontation. Many contextual factors would probably determine the nature and resolution of such a confrontation.

[30]The tactics of confrontation consciously used in a domestic context to expose the brutal apparatus of the state in Chicago during the demonstration against the 1968 Democratic Convention is an instance. The rationality of such tactics presupposes a meaningful capacity for change and opposition.

[31]Even the Soviet attentive public may not "know" about ineffective claims exerted by its government. The Soviet press, for instance, presented the Cuban Missile Crisis as a routine, tactical victory for Soviet diplomacy, whereby a pledge by the United States not to invade Cuba was extracted in exchange for Soviet willingness not to deploy missiles in Cuba's defense.

There was no suggestion in the public Soviet accounts that the effort at missile deployment brought the world to the brink of World War III.

[32]For legal arguments that rely mainly upon the regional basis of the claim see Abram Chayes, "The Legal Case for U.S. Action on Cuba," *U.S. State Department Bulletin,* Vol. XLVIII (Nov. 19, 1962), pp. 763–65; Leonard C. Meeker, "Defensive Quarantine and the Law," *American Journal of International Law,* Vol. 57 (1963), p. 515.

[33]This conclusion is not meant to deprecate the role of review by the United Nations, but to put this role in realistic perspective. It is not merely the disparity in political following, but the strong tendency of states to vote in accordance with their overall political allies.

[34]As the Soviet intervention of 1956 in Hungary and the U.S. intervention of 1965 in the Dominican Republic both suggest it is possible for the Zone I actor to repress, first, and then allow, even encourage, liberalizing reforms to take place in the target country. There is a choice of tactics at different phases of the policy process unfolding in the Zone I government. Decisions may be revised and may reflect a compromise between opposed preferences between Zone I factions contending for influence. An important factor will be an assessment of trends in the Zone II country, especially attitudes toward future challenges directed at Zone I supremacy.

[35]There have been many different kinds of effects of the American presence on life in South Vietnam since 1954. These effects range from the building of the war for control of the government to a very large-scale and sustained conflict, the displacement of people from their homes, casualties, disease, inflation, corruption, and the support of reactionary elements in positions of control.

[36]This argument is made in some detail in Falk, *The Status of Law in International Society* (Princeton: Princeton University Press, 1969), Chapter XXI.

[37]For a general discussion of the relevance of regionalist tendencies to the character of world order, see Ronald J. Yalem, *Regionalism and World Order* (Washington, D.C.: Public Affairs Press, 1965).

PART THREE

Empirical Concerns

DINA A. ZINNES

Some Evidence Relevant to the Man–Milieu Hypothesis*

One of the central themes in the works of Harold and Margret Sprout is the relationship between the environment, the perceptions of the decision-making heads of state, and the resulting actions taken by those individuals. This relationship is the principal thesis of their *Man-Milieu Relationship Hypotheses in the Context of International Politics* (1956) and their more recent *The Ecological Perspective on Human Affairs* (1965). Reacting against writers who implicitly theorize that the environment determines national policies, the Sprouts argue that the environment can only affect national policies in two ways: (1) in so far as it is perceived or misperceived and therefore considered in the calculations of decision-makers, and (2) in so far as it is a limitation or controlling factor on the outcome of those decisions. As they expressly put their contention:

So far as we can determine, environmental factors (both nonhuman and social) can affect human activities in only two ways. Such factors can be perceived, reacted to, and taken into account by the human individual or individuals under consideration. In this way, *and in this way only* ... environmental factors can be said to 'influence,' or to 'condition,' or otherwise to 'affect' human values and preferences, moods, and attitudes, choices and decisions. On the other hand, the relation of environmental factors to performance and accomplishment (that is, to the operational outcomes of results of decisions and under-takings) may present an additional

* I would like to express my thanks to the Editors, Maurice East, James N. Rosenau and Vincent Davis, and to Ole Holsti and John Gillespie for their very helpful comments on an earlier draft of this paper.

Notes and References for this selection will be found on pages 248–251.

dimension. In the latter context environmental factors may be conceived as a sort of matrix or encompassing channel, metaphorically speaking, which limits the execution of undertakings. Such limitations on performance, accomplishment, outcome, or operational result may not—often do not—derive from or depend upon the environed individual's perception or other psychological behavior (Sprout and Sprout, 1965, p. 11).

The relationship between environment, perceptions, actions, and outcomes might be diagrammed as shown in Fig. 1. Thus the environment affects the perceptions of the decision-makers and the outcomes of their decisions, and the outcomes are a function of both the environment and the behavioral acts of the decision-maker.

Figure 1. Diagramatic Representation of the Man—Milieu Hypothesis.

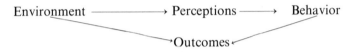

While the Sprouts proposed this model more than ten years ago their thesis has yet to be directly tested. There have, however, been a series of studies that implicitly address themselves to this thesis: the content analytic work done with the 1914 crisis, Richardson's compilation and analysis of certain statistics of deadly quarrels, and some of the aggregate cross-national data analyses all carry with them results relevant to the Sprouts' contention. Consequently, the purpose of the present essay is to survey these works—making no claim to an exhaustive or even systematic consideration of all possible works that are relevant—in an effort to present and evaluate what evidence can be gleaned for or against the Sprout model.

The Sprout Model

Before examining the relevant studies, it is necessary to consider in greater detail the meaning and implications of the model proposed by the Sprouts. First, it must be recognized that this is a decision-making model. While the Sprouts are concerned with the environment and the consequences of decisions, their interest in these two facets is completely subsidiary to their primary focus on the decision-maker. The Sprouts wish to understand the acts of those individuals who hold top level decision-making positions in government, i.e., they wish to explain the decisions of individuals who have the power to commit whole populations to various courses of actions. This decision-making focus should become obvious as we examine the parts of the model diagrammed above.

The components of Figure 1 were labeled using somewhat general terminology, and so must now be redefined from the Sprouts' point of reference. The term "environment" should be the first to be redefined, since it is this concept that most disturbs the Sprouts. Indeed, because of the confusion surrounding the concept "environment" the Sprouts have opted for another which they feel more precisely captures their meaning: *Milieu*. As they put it:

Because of the tendency . . . to restrict the term environment to nonhuman factors . . . we have deliberately introduced the French term *milieu*. Henceforth we shall use milieu instead of environment when the reference is general: that is, to denote the whole spectrum of environing factors; human as well as nonhuman, intangible as well as tangible. (Sprout and Sprout, 1965, p. 27)

Thus the milieu is the totality of factors that surrounds a given unit. But the Sprouts go on to identify three milieu. First, there is the *total milieu*, or "the milieu as it actually is (or as it would be known to an omniscient observer, if one existed, as of course, is not the case)" (Sprout and Sprout, 1965, p. 28). Second, since only a portion of the total milieu is ever relevant to an individual making a particular decision and, because an omniscient observer does not exist, there is the *operational milieu*. The operational milieu is defined by "any outside observer (that is, an observer other than the individual whose achievements are being investigated)" (Sprout and Sprout, 1965, p. 30) and specifies which facets of the environment are specifically relevant to the individual in a specific decision situation. Finally, there is the *psychomilieu*: "the milieu as it is perceived and reacted to by a particular individual." (Sprout and Sprout, 1965, p. 28).

Thus a reconsideration of Figure 1 shows that what was labeled "environment" is for the Sprouts either the total milieu or the operational milieu. Which of the two is relevant will depend on the particular proposition being examined. "Perceptions" in Figure 1 are then equivalent to the psychomilieu. The third component of Figure 1, "behavior," denotes for the Sprouts a broad class of human activity, one part of which they designate as "actions." "Action" is a subcategory of behavior, "it is behavior which is consciously purposeful." "Decisions" are then identified as a further subclass of actions and are specifically "defined as purposeful *choice* of ends or means or both" (underlining mine). It is this last category, "decisions," which is of principal concern to the Sprouts. Thus the more general concept "behavior" of Figure 1 must be relabeled as "decisions." The last element of Figure 1, "outcomes," is not explicitly considered by the Sprouts and their discussion seems to indicate that the label given in Figure 1 is adequate. The new definitions produce the revised model shown in Figure 2.

Strictly speaking, Figure 2 is incomplete. It appears to show that the operational environment is the sole determinant of the psychomilieu. Obviously this is not the meaning of the Sprouts. The operational environment is one, perhaps very significant, facet in shaping the psychomilieu, but other elements (like the personality of the decision-makers) also contribute. Consequently Figure 2 should show other arrows affecting the psychomilieu. For simplicity they are omitted here.

Figure 2. Diagramatic Representation of Man–Milieu Hypothesis Using Sprout and Sprout Terminology.

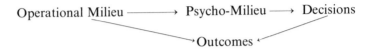

With the redefined model before us we can now consider the hypotheses which are derived from it. The Sprouts have three principal contentions. First, they argue that the operational environment taken by itself is inadequate to explain decisions. They wish to counter such assertions as "the general character of England's foreign policy is determined by the immutable conditions of her geographical situation," (quoted by the Sprouts, 1965, p. 2) or "the great wars of history are the outcomes of the uneven distribution of fertility and strategical opportunity upon the face of the globe," (quoted by Sprouts, 1965, p. 4). The Sprouts do not feel that past events can be explained or future trends predicted "by reference to some set of environmental factors," (Sprout and Sprout, 1965, p. 5).

The second contention proposed by the Sprouts is that while the operational environment is inadequate to explain decisions, the decisions *can* be understood with reference to the perceptions of the decision-makers, or their psychomilieu. Decision-makers act with reference to and in terms of their perception of the environment. These two arguments—that the environment does not determine decisions but that perceptions do—underlie most of the discussion that the Sprouts devote to their model. There is, however, some consideration given to a third aspect. Their third argument is that the decision plus the operational (perhaps even total) environment together determine the payoffs or outcomes of any given decision.

Since the first two contentions form the main foundation for the theory, the focus in the remaining pages will be primarily on research relevant to these two aspects. For the first two arguements to hold, the following must be shown. First, it must be shown that, in general, *decisions are not a function of the operational environment* in which the decision-makers of states reside. In other words, it must be the case that the decision-makers of states having such similar environmental conditions as length of oceanic boundaries, mountain ranges, geographical size, types of government and economic systems, etc., *do not* make similar decisions. For example, there must be *no* relationship between decisions to go to war, and, let us say, the geographical size of a country. Or, similarly, the same state, over time, (assuming that the environmental factors remain constant), should change its decision-making behavior, e.g., it should be very warlike at one time, but very pacific at another.[1]

The second point that must be shown is that the *decisions being made are a function of the psychomilieu*, that decision-makers with the same perceptions react similarly. Thus, all decision-makers who *perceive* that their country is surrounded by enemies must react with similar decisions.

Assuming that the first and second factors have been demonstrated, it is then necessary to control for interactions between the environment and perceptions. It must be shown that the psychomilieu determines decisions regardless of, or controlling for, the environment (operational). Thus it must be shown that states having the same environment, but in which the psychomilieu of the decision-makers differs, produce different decisions. Conversely, it must be shown that given different environments but similar decision-maker psychomilieu, the decisions must be similar. All this is to say that it must be the case that the psychomilieu and the environment are not directly related. If there were a direct correspondence between the two the Sprout contention would not be of much value. If the environment completely and predictably determines the perceptions, and the perceptions in turn influence the decisions, then it would be the case that the environment, through the medium of the perceptions, affected the decisions. In that case the environment and the psychomilieu would be interchangeable variables for predicting decisions, and statements about the environment being the principal determinant in decisions would be perfectly in order.

The studies to be considered address themselves to each of the above three issues. The first argument—that the operational environment is not related to the actions of states—comes into focus in the many recent cross-national, aggregate data analyses, and in some of the studies initiated by Richardson. The second and third arguments—that decisions are determined by perceptions and that perceptions are not totally a function of the environment—are found in the various content analytic studies which principally analyze the 1914 crisis.

Aggregate Data Studies: The Relationship Between Operational Milieu and Decisions

A series of studies have now been completed in which environmental factors are examined against state behavior. By and large these studies fall in a classification frequently referred to as "aggregate data studies." These analyses have primarily been conducted using correlation, regression and factor analysis and they most typically involve the examination of a very large number of variables across a considerable number of states, usually for rather short periods of time. These studies provide us with a wealth of material relevant to the Sprout model.

Before exploring these results, however, it is necessary to arrive at working definition of "operational milieu" and "decision" that are meaningful within the context of these studies. For the purpose of this initial examination of the data, the reader is asked to accept a rather broad definition of "operational milieu", but one which seems clearly implicit in the writings of the Sprouts. Accordingly, "operational milieu" denotes not just the physical characteristics of a state such as its geography, but includes *the total internal condition of a state at any given time.* Thus it would include such factors as a state's economic development, its general level of education and health, the type of government it contains, the resources it has available, the composition of its population, the extent of internal disturbances (riots, revolutions, etc.) and similar characteristics.

The concept of "decision" is somewhat more ambiguous in the writings of the Sprouts. The model which the Sprouts present is completely general in form. It can be seen from the quotes given above, that the model is applicable to any "decision" emanating from heads of state. However, it is clear from the context of the Sprout discussions that they are not concerned with decision making in general, but rather with the specific application of their model to *foreign policy decision-making.* Indeed, at certain points they imply that domestic policy decisions are part of the operational milieu *for* the foreign policy decisions. Consequently the focus here will be on *foreign policy decisions.* A foreign policy decision is then very loosely defined as any act taken by a state which is a reaction to, or involves, other states. Defense budgets, trade, aid, membership in international organizations are all examples of foreign policy acts.

Using these definitions of "operational milieu" and "decision" we find that all of the articles to be discussed here share one common trait. In each case the attempt is to predict the decision on the basis of the operational milieu, i.e., "decisions" are the dependent variable and the operational milieu is the independent variable. With this in mind it is possible to classify the articles along two dimensions following a suggestion made by Rummel (1966). Rummel suggests that the activities of states—or in our terms, the decisions made by states—can be classified into (1) decisions to *engage in conflicts* with other states, i.e., conflictful behavior, and (2) all other foreign policy decisions. The various relationships explored in the studies under consideration clearly fall into one of these two categories. However, Rummel's suggestion can be extended along a second dimension. Operational milieu, or the independent variable in these studies, can similarly be divided into two corresponding classes: (1) environmental or operational milieu attributes which reflect the *internal disturbances* (internal conflicts) of a state, and (2) *other* environmental factors. Again, the hypotheses tested in these studies examine either one or the other type of independent variable. These two dimensions, then, representing the dependent and independent variables, together produce a fourfold table as shown in Figure 3. Figure 3 shows which articles test what relationships between the dependent and independent variables. Since several of the studies examine more than one of the four types of relationships, these articles appear in several cells. This classification highlights the emphasis of most of the research today: most of the analyses have been devoted to understanding conflict behavior. It is also interesting to discover that there have been no studies directed at understanding the effects on internal disruption of nonconflict behavior at the international level.

The Relationship between Internal Disruption and External Conflict Behavior—We will summarize the principal findings of the studies in each cell of Figure 3 and then consider their implications for the Sprout model. The first four studies listed in the left-hand corner of Figure 3 have the same conceptual focus; studies two through four are in fact based on, and represent a further development of the first study, Rummel (1963). It is therefore appropriate to summarize the findings of these four studies first. In the original article, Rummel (1963) collected data on twenty-two measures of what he termed "foreign and domestic conflict behavior" (9 measures of domestic conflict, thirteen measures of foreign conflict) for 77 states for the years 1955 through 1957. The 77 states represented all entities in the international system during those three years which met certain minimal requirements.[2] Through three successive factor analyses of (1) the indicators of domestic conflict behavior, (2) the measures of foreign conflict behavior, and (3) all twenty-two measures together, Rummel drew three conclusions. First, he found considerable interrelationship between the domestic conflict measures; second, he discovered that the foreign conflict measures had high intercorrelations; and finally, and for our purposes most importantly, he found that there appeared to be little interrelationship between the domestic conflict measures and the foreign conflict measures. The three domestic and three foreign conflict dimensions are shown with their labels along with the conflict variables most highly associated with them in Tables 1 and 2. This result was tested further by regressing the three domestic conflict factors on to each foreign conflict factor. None of these multiple correlations were significant. Thus, this initial study suggested that there was

Figure 3. Classification of Crossnational Studies Relevant to the Man-Mileu Hypothesis

"Operational Milieu": Internal Conditions	"Decisions": External Behavior			
	Conflict		Nonconflict	
Conflict	Rummel	(1963)		
	Tanter	(1966)		
	Rummel	(1964)		
	Wilkenfeld	(1968)		
	Haas	(1968)		
Nonconflict	Rummel	(1964)	Rummel	(1966)
	Richardson	(1960)		
	Rummel	(1968)		
	Haas	(1965)		
	Rummel	(1966)		

no relationship between the internal conflict of a state and its external conflict behavior.

Table 1—Factor Analysis of Domestic Conflict Measures for 77 States for 1955–1957*

Measures	FACTOR MATRIX[a]			ORTHOGONALLY ROTATED FACTOR MATRIX[a]			h^2
					Revolu-	Sub-	
	D_1	D_2	D_3	Turmoil	tionary[b]	versive[b]	
1. Assassinations	(.62)	.17	(.61)	(.59)	−.03	(.66)	.78
2. General Strikes	(.75)	.05	−.24	(.52)	(.60)	.05	.63
3. Guerrilla Warfare	.48	(−.57)	(.59)	−.04	.28	(.90)	.90
4. Major Government Crisis	(.52)	.35	−.10	(.60)	.21	−.04	.41
5. Purges	(.67)	−.14	−.34	.32	(.71)	.03	.60
6. Riots	(.76)	.38	−.03	(.79)	.31	.09	.73
7. Revolutions	(.66)	−.43	−.36	.09	(.85)	.13	.75
8. Anti-Government Demonstrations	(.74)	.46	.14	(.85)	.17	.19	.79
9. Domestic Number Killed	(.80)	−.40	−.05	.23	(.75)	.42	.79
% Common Variance	65.0	18.0	16.0	39.0	37.6	23.4	100.0
% Total Variance	45.8	13.3	11.7	27.7	26.7	16.6	70.8

* Taken from R.J. Rummel. "Dimensions of Conflict Behavior Within and Between Nations," *General Systems Yearbook*, VIII, 1963, 12.
[a] Parentheses indicate loadings ≥ .50.
[b] Signs reversed.

Tanter's (1966) analysis is a replication of the Rummel study. Collecting data on 83 states for 1958 through 1960, Tanter produced the same three factor analyses of (1) domestic conflict variables, (2) foreign conflict measures, and (3) all twenty-two conflict measures simultaneously. With some slight variation in the factors obtained for the analysis of the domestic conflict measures, Tanter's results and conclusions closely followed those of Rummel. Essentially, Tanter argued, there was a relationship between the various domestic measures and amongst the various foreign conflict measures, but not between domestic and foreign conflict variables. As in Rummel's study, these results were further supported by a regression analysis. Again, the multiple correlation between the domestic conflict factors, and each of the three foreign conflict factors was not significant.[3] Tanter, however, was able to go one step beyond Rummel's analysis. Tanter regressed Rummel's 1955–1957 domestic factors on to his 1958–1960 foreign conflict variables. Here the multiple correlations between the three domestic factors, on the one hand, and (1) the "protest" foreign conflict factor is .42, and

(2) "severance of diplomatic relations" is .40. Both of the correlations are significant. This would seem to indicate that a time lag begins to pick up some relationship which across the board correlations might be obscuring.

Table 2—Factor Analysis of Foreign Conflict Measures for 77 States for 1955–1957*

Measures	FACTOR MATRIX[1]			ORTHOGONALLY ROTATED FACTOR MATRIX[1]			h^2
	$F_1{}^2$	F_2	F_3	War	Diplo-macy	Bellig-erency	
1. Anti-Foreign Demonstrations	(.59)	.14	.48	.13	.42	(−.63)	.60
2. Negative Sanctions	(.65)	.11	.44	.20	.41	(−.64)	.62
3. Protests	(.78)	.22	−.13	(.62)	.49	.22	.67
4. Severance of Diplo-matic Relations	.45	−.46	(.54)	.13	−.17	(.82)	.71
5. Expulsions or Recalls—Ambassadors	.10	(.67)	.12	−.16	(.66)	−.08	.47
6. Expulsions or Recalls—Lesser Officials	(.53)	.44	−.06	.33	(.60)	.08	.48
7. Threats	(.91)	.07	.05	(.65)	.43	.48	.84
8. Military Action	(.73)	−.48	.04	(.65)	−.14	(.57)	.77
9. Wars	(.65)	−.04	(−.57)	(.85)	.15	−.10	.75
10. Troop Movements	(.73)	.33	.01	.47	(.59)	.28	.64
11. Mobilizations	(.61)	−.34	−.10	(.60)	−.08	.35	.49
12. Accusations	(.89)	.01	−.05	(.70)	.35	.41	.79
13. Number Killed—Foreign	(.80)	−.19	−.36	(.87)	.10	.19	.80
% Common Variance	69.2	16.6	14.2	46.2	24.6	29.1	100.0
% Total Variance	46.0	11.0	9.4	30.7	16.3	19.3	66.4

* Taken from R.J. Rummel. "Dimensions of Conflict Behavior Within and Between Nations," *General Systems Year-book,* VIII, 1963, 12.

[1] Parentheses indicate loadings, ≥ .50.

[2] Sign reversed.

The third study (Rummel, 1964), as can be seen from the chart in Figure 3, falls into both the upper left and bottom left cells. In fact, the bulk of this study was designed to examine non-conflict determinants of state behavior. Thus the summary presented here only concerns that part of the study relevant to the upper left-hand cell. The relevant results are found in a portion of one of the tables presented by Rummel. Specifically, this table relates the correlation and the partial correlation coefficients between the three domestic conflict factors on the one hand and each of the thirteen foreign conflict variables, for Rummel's original 77 states for 1955–1957. These results are presented here in Table 3. The partial correlations represent correlations between a given domestic conflict dimension and a particular foreign conflict measure, holding constant the effects of the other two dimensions along with several other nonconflict factors to be discussed below. Thus −.35 is the correlation between the subversive dimension and

Table 3—Correlation of 1955–1957 Foreign Conflict Data and Domestic Conflict Behavior Dimensions*

Dependent Variable	INDEPENDENT VARIABLES					
	DOMESTIC CONFLICT DIMENSIONS					
	TURMOIL		REVOLUTIONARY		SUBVERSION	
Foreign Conflict Behavior Measures	r	r_p	r	r_p	r	r_p
1. Accusations	.02	−.03	−.04	−.04	−.34[b]	−.32[a]
2. Protests	−.11	−.10	−.20	−.21	−.30[b]	−.25[a]
3. Antiforeign Demonstrations	.03	.08	−.01	.00	−.38[b]	−.35[b]
4. Threats	−.04	−.07	−.06	−.07	−.28[a]	−.27[a]
5. Negative Sanctions	−.12	−.10	.05	.03	−.34[b]	−.34[b]
6. Expelled/Recalled lesser officials, etc.	.06	.14	−.16	−.10	−.15	−.09
7. Expelled/Recalled Ambassador, etc.	.12	.10	.16	.16	−.14	−.19
8. Severed Diplomatic Relations	.09	−.02	−.19	−.24[a]	−.23	−.27[a]
9. Mobilizations	−.18	−.20	.03	−.01	−.24[a]	−.28[a]
10. Troop Movements	.07	−.01	−.07	−.04	−.10	−.04
11. Military Action	.08	.01	−.08	−.16	−.16	−.20
12. War	−.07	−.01	−.01	−.03	−.28[a]	−.27[a]
13. Foreign killed, International Conflict	.14	.13	−.01	−.06	−.20	−.21

* Taken from R.J. Rummel. "Testing Some Possible Predictors of Conflict Behavior Within and Between Nations," *Peace Research Society* (International), Vol. I (1964) p. 97.
[a] Would be significant at .05 (dependent variable has nonnormal distribution).
[b] Would be significant at .01 (dependent variable has nonnormal distribution).
[c] r_p = partial correlation coefficient based on both the Domestic Conflict Dimensions and Berry's factors. See text for discussion.

anti-foreign demonstrations holding the other two factors of turmoil and revolution (plus additional variables discussed below) constant.[4]

The turmoil and revolutionary dimensions have clearly very little relationship with the thirteen foreign conflict variables as can be seen by the fact that only one coefficient in the first four columns is starred. The striking feature of this table is found in the last two columns for the third domestic conflict dimension: subversion. Here we find a majority (eight out of thirteen) of the correlations are significant and this significance is not lost when other factors are held constant, as evidenced by the still significant partial correlations. The other interesting feature of this table is that the correlations are negative. To interpret these results we need to recall that the subversion factor is principally composed of two variables: assassinations and guerrilla warfare. These significant negative correlations, then, indicate that the greater the number of assassinations and guerrilla warfare experienced by a state the *less* it will engage in foreign conflict behaviors, such as protests, threats, negative sanctions, etc.

The fourth study utilized the data from both the original Rummel study and the subsequent replication performed by Tanter. Wilkenfeld (1968) was concerned that the Rummel and Tanter analyses might have obscured a potential internal to external conflict relationship by not discriminating between the various types of states in the international system. Using the Gregg and Banks factor analysis (1965) of a variety of political variables across all states in the contemporary international system, Wilkenfeld grouped states into three categories: personalist (primarily the Latin-American countries), centrist (communist governments plus many Middle-Eastern states), and polyarchic (the European and democratic governments, principally). Using both factor scores and a derived composite measure based on the original raw data taken from both the Rummel and Tanter data (i.e., from 1955–1960), Wilkenfeld correlated each of the domestic conflict factors with each of the foreign conflict factors *within the three-state groupings*. This analysis was performed using no lags and one and two year lags. The results for the composite index based on the raw data are summarized in Table 4.

As can be seen in Table 4 a number of significant correlations do appear within each of the groupings. Furthermore, a consideration of the no-lag condition suggests a pattern across the three state groupings. Within the personalist group one finds that all three of the foreign conflict factors (i.e., the war, diplomatic and belligerency factors) are significantly related to the subversive dimension, and the relationship is *positive*. Thus, for the personalist states (mainly Latin American countries) the greater the number of assassinations and guerrilla warfare (subversive dimension) the more these countries engage in foreign conflict behaviors of all varieties. Note the contrast between this result and that found by Rummel. Rummel found that over *all* states a significant *negative* relationship exists between the subversive factor and foreign conflict dimensions. [5]

Within the centrist grouping it appears that the principal factor affecting foreign conflict is the revolutionary dimension. Here, however, the revolutionary factor only significantly correlates with two foreign conflict factors, belligerency and war. Thus general strikes, purges, revolutions, and number of domestic killed—the variables which defined the revolutionary dimension—within the communist and Middle-Eastern countries appear to affect their involvement in certain military (wars, military action, mobilizations, accusations and threats) and belligerent (anti-foreign demonstrations, negative sanctions) activities.

The pattern within the polyarchic grouping is more pronounced. Here

Table 4—Correlations Between Indices Derived from Rummel's 1955–1957 and Tanter's 1957–1960 Factor Analyses*

	Personalist States			Centrist States			Polyarchic States		
	lag = 0[f]	lag = +1[c]	lag = +2[d]	lag = 0[i]	lag = +1[h]	lag = +2[g]	lag = 0[l]	lag = +1[k]	lag = +2[j]
TUR—WAR	.14	-.05	.01	.10	.13	.10	.36[c]	.26[c]	.42[c]
TUR—DIP	.29[b]	.22	.16	.13	.19[a]	.08	.23[c]	.10	.10
TUR—BEL	.20	.21	.40[c]	.26[c]	.18[a]	.06	.30[c]	.19[a]	.20[a]
REV—WAR	.13	-.05	-.16	.21[b]	.21[a]	.34[c]	.03	.00	.04
REV—DIP	.29[b]	.23[a]	.22	.07	.20[a]	.13	-.01	-.04	-.06
REV—BEL	.14	.18	.31[a]	.24[c]	.24[b]	.30[c]	.16[a]	.06	.13
SUB—WAR	.24[a]	.14	-.01	-.04	.01	.05	.12	.17[a]	.14
SUB—DIP	.49[c]	.11	-.04	-.07	.02	.02	.05	.00	.01
SUB—BEL	.34[c]	.31[b]	.40[c]	.10	.08	.25[b]	.16[a]	.09	-.01

* Taken from Jonathan Wilkenfeld. "Domestic and Foreign Conflict Behavior of Nations." *Journal of Peace Research.*
l (1968), 63, 64, & 66.

[a] p < .05   [b] p < .01   [c] p < .005   [d] N = 60   [e] N = 75
[f] N = 90   [g] N = 104   [h] N = 130   [i] N = 156   [j] N = 132
[k] N = 165   [l] N = 198

the turmoil dimension (riots, antigovernment demonstrations, major government crises, etc.) correlates with all foreign conflict factors. Thus within the European democratic-type countries the "turmoil" variables influence the foreign conflict behavior.

The fifth study in this grouping was concerned with a different facet of internal disruption, namely societal stresses and strains. Haas (1968) examined the effects of unemployment, industrialization, suicides, homicides and deaths due to alcoholism, as indicators of the stress and strain experienced by a state, on the military expenditures, frequency of war, and war aggressiveness of a state. Considering ten states (Australia, Finland, France, Germany, Great Britain, Japan, Norway, Spain, Switzerland and the United States) from 1900 to 1960 he found, as shown in Table 5, almost no relationship as determined by Pearson Product and rho correlations

Table 5—Correlations Between Stress and Strain Societal Indicators and Military Behavior[†]

	1	2	3	4	5	6	7	8
STRESS								
1. Unemployment						−.02 (18)	.33 (16)	−.64 (9)
2. Industrialization						.17 (20)	−.32 (20)	.51 (10)
STRAIN								
3. Suicide						.18 (27)	.02 (27)	.47[a] (14)
4. Homicide						.05 (24)	−.11 (24)	.08 (12)
5. Alcoholism Deaths						.51[a] (25)	.14 (26)	.03 (12)
MILITARY BEHAVIOR								
6. Expenditures	−.08 (20)	.17 (20)	.29 (29)	−.20 (24)	−.08 (25)			
7. War Frequency								
8. War Aggressiveness								

† Median of all Pearsonian correlations to left of diagonal; rho correlations to right; *N* in parentheses.
a p ≦ .10
b p ≦ .01

between stress and strain factors and the various indicators of foreign conflict behavior.

How do these five studies bear on the Sprout model? As defined at the outset, the conflict variables along with the indicators of societal stress and strain are equivalent in the Sprout model to the "operational milieu." The foreign conflict behavior represents the "decisions" or actions taken by the states. The results of the five studies, then, do not present consistent findings with respect to the Sprout hypothesis. On the one hand, Rummel (1963), Tanter (1966), and Haas (1968) all provide evidence in favor of the Sprout model, namely that there is no relationship between internal disruptive factors and external foreign conflict. On the other hand, Rummel (1964), Wilkenfeld (1968), and two of the multiple regressions done by Tanter (1966) suggest that a relationship does exist between internal and external conflict behavior provided that certain additional conditions are present. Let us examine this contradictatory evidence in more depth.

These conflicting results are highlighted by some additional results provided by both Rummel (1963) and Tanter (1966). In both articles, as a byproduct of the factor analyses, correlation matrices are given which report the Pearson product moment correlation coefficients between all pairs of domestic and foreign conflict variables. These correlations are reproduced in Table 6. Rummel's correlations are reported in the first half of each cell and cover, it will be recalled, the period from 1955–1957; Tanter's correlations appear in the second half of each cell and are for 1958–1960. Rummel's correlations are based on 77 states, while Tanter's are computed over 83 states; roughly with $N = 77$ any correlation equal to or greater than .26 is significant at the .01 level, and when $N = 83$ correlations equal to or greater than .25 are significant at the .01 level. All significant correlations are indicated.[6]

Table 6 provides further evidence in support of the Sprout model and consistent with Rummel (1963), Tanter (1966) and Haas (1968). First, Table 6 contains $9 \times 13 = 117$ possible correlations. Of these correlations, in Rummel's 1955–57 data only $17/117 = 14$ per cent are significant and in Tanter's 1958–1960 data only $15/117 = 13$ per cent are significant. In general, then, over all the indicators there are very few internal-external conflict relationships. Second, the largest correlation in Rummel's study is .38 (between antigovernment demonstrations and antiforeign demonstrations) while the largest in Tanter's study is .40 (between riots and troop movements). Thus the strongest relationship in each study still shows that one variable predicts only 16 per cent or less of the variation in the other.

The third interesting feature of Table 6 concerns the gradation between the various foreign conflict measures. If the variable "number of foreign killed" is omitted on the grounds that it is not parallel with the other twelve measures, then the remaining foreign conflict measures can be scaled along a dimension indicating greater and greater overt foreign conflict: accusa-

Table 6—Correlations Between Foreign and Domestic Conflict Variables from Rummel's 1955–1957 and Tanter's 1957–1960 Studies*

Foreign Conflict Variables

	Domestic Conflict Variables								
	Assassinations	General Strikes	Guerrilla Warfare	Major Government Crisis	Purges	Riots	Revolutions	Anti-government Demons	Domestic Number Killed
Accusations	.20 / .18	.07 / -.07	-.09 / .17	.11 / .07	.27ᵃ / .32ᵃ	.21 / .19	.04 / .16	.35ᵃ / .18	.12 / .12
Protests	.01 / .04	-.01 / .15	-.23 / .05	.10 / -.01	.08 / .07	.19 / .29ᵃ	-.11 / -.01	.29ᵃ / .24	.00 / .04
Anti-foreign Demonstrations	.23 / .29ᵃ	.20 / .28ᵃ	.00 / .27ᵃ	.21 / .12	.24 / .17	.36ᵃ / .38ᵃ	.05 / .26ᵃ	.38ᵃ / .22	.16 / .31ᵃ
Threats	.15 / .10	-.04 / .01	-.10 / .07	.09 / -.08	.26ᵃ / .06	.15 / .20	-.04 / -.05	.36ᵃ / .18	.05 / .07
Negative Sanctions	.28ᵃ / .23	-.01 / .00	-.00 / .20	.29ᵃ / .14	.13 / .20	.16 / .17	-.04 / .10	.26ᵃ / .13	-.04 / .13
Expelled Lesser Officials	-.09 / .27ᵃ	.07 / .11	-.11 / .10	.05 / .08	.24 / .11	.08 / .17	-.11 / -.01	.28ᵃ / .15	.16 / .04
Expelled Ambassadors	.16 / .05	.13 / .27ᵃ	.17 / .08	-.01 / .10	.18 / -.03	.26ᵃ / .16	.12 / -.13	.26ᵃ / .18	.25 / -.08
Severance Diplomatic Relations	.03 / .08	.14 / .19	-.08 / .27ᵃ	.28ᵃ / .28ᵃ	.32ᵃ / .05	.18 / .23	.03 / .19	.14 / .21	-.03 / .11
Mobilizations	.28ᵃ / .00	-.09 / .04	-.11 / .07	.05 / .00	.13 / .31ᵃ	.02 / .05	-.12 / .04	.21 / .03	-.06 / .14
Troop Movements	.06 / .14	-.10 / .01	-.11 / .01	-.05 / -.07	.24 / .19	.13 / .40ᵃ	.07 / .02	.23 / .24	.14 / .11
Military Action	.15 / .05	.01 / .03	-.10 / .05	.11 / .06	.30ᵃ / .19	.08 / .12	.12 / .06	.16 / .10	.02 / .12
War	.19 / .00	-.06 / -.01	-.05 / -.10	.09 / .01	.17 / .03	.12 / .01	-.04 / -.02	.20 / .02	.07 / .07
Killed	.18 / .34ᵃ	.04 / .16	-.04 / .30ᵃ	.13 / .21	.34ᵃ / .25	.19 / .24	.12 / .23	.21 / .15	.22 / .27ᵃ

* Note: Rummel's correlations appear in top half of each cell and are based on *N* = 77. Tanter's correlations are in bottom half of each cell and are based on *N* = 83.

ᵃ $P \leq .05$

tions, protests, antiforeign demonstrations, threats, negative sanctions, the recall of lesser officials, the recall of ambassadors, severance of diplomatic relations, mobilizations, troop movements, military actions, and finally war.[7] On the basis of this scale, both studies show that the more extreme measures of foreign conflict behavior, from mobilizations through wars, have no, or only one, significant correlation with a domestic conflict variable. "War", for example, does not significantly correlate with *any* domestic conflict variable in either study.

However, while the above results coincide with the Sprout model, Table 6 appears to also provide evidence against the Sprout model. There are a number of correlations in Table 6 that *are* significant, indicating that under certain conditions some relationship does exist between domestic conflict and foreign conflict behavior. A careful perusal of Table 6, however, shows that in most instances these relationships are not stable over the two studies.[8] Only three correlations are significant in *both* studies. This would seem to suggest that a three-year period is too short to detect these relationships. We will confine our attention then to the three significant correlations that occur in both studies.

The three significant correlations are between (1) purges and accusations, (2) governmental crises and the severance of diplomatic relations, and (3) riots and antiforeign demonstrations. It is questionable whether the third relationship can be considered as evidence against the Sprout model. Riots are operationally defined as clashes between large groups of people and governmental police forces. Antiforeign demonstrations are essentially riots focused against foreign governments. Thus the cooccurence of these two phenomena does not seem to indicate that a relationship exists between environmental factors and external conflict behavior, but rather more simply that riots beget more riots.

The second relationship, between governmental crises and the severence of diplomatic relations, may also be questioned. Major government crises represent "Any rapidly developing situation which threatens to bring the immediate downfall of the present government . . . evidenced by the declaration of military law, a state of seige or the suspension or abrogation of the constitution." A vote of no confidence by a parliamentary majority, or the forced resignation or impeachment of top officials are also considered major government crises (Rummel, 1963, p. 25). While this category does not include coup d'états (placed in the revolution category), major governmental crises, by definition, do frequently involve the replacement of top level decision-makers. When this is the case, the cooccurence of government crises and the severance of diplomatic relations could reflect something quite different from a relationship between internal conditions and external behavior. It could reflect the fact that a change in government is often accompanied by a reluctance on the part of other states in the system to immediately recognize the new government. The severance of diplomatic relations is mutual; if a state refuses to recognize the newly constituted government the "new" state is forced to sever relations. Thus the significant correlation between governmental crises and the severance of diplomatic relations may represent the effect of governmental crises *on the actions of other states in the system* towards the particular state in question. Thus it seems dubious whether this second significant correlation provides evidence against the Sprout model.

The correlation of particular interest that is significant over both studies occurs between purges and accusations. A purge is "The systematic elimination by the political elite either of opposition within their ranks or of opposition within the country by jailing or execution" (Rummel, 1963, p. 25), while accusations represent "Any official diplomatic or governmental statement by the executive leaders of a country which makes a charge or allegation against another country" (Rummel, 1963, p. 27). The interpretation of this correlation is not altogether clear. It could be taken as evidence in support of the contention that internal conflict does affect foreign conflict behavior, that decision makers do attempt to turn the attention of their population away from internal problems by engaging in external foreign conflict activities. But the nature of the domestic conflict variable here makes me suspicious of this interpretation. The often discussed relationship posited between internal conditions and external conflict behavior is usually based on the assumption that the redirection of attention is occasioned by the fact that *the government cannot control* the internal problems of its population. Thus support for this proposition should involve a significant correlation between: (1) acts perpetrated by the population, and (2) foreign conflict behavior by the government. But "purges" are not acts taken by the populace against its government. Rather, they are acts perpetrated *by* the government *against its people* who, by virture of this act are very much in the control of the government. Consequently, there would seem to be little reason to use foreign conflict behavior as a diversionary tactic.

This significant correlation, however, could be given another interpretation positing a different relationship between internal and external conflict behavior. It could be argued that both factors, purges, and accusations, demonstrate a kind of paranoia on the part of the decision makers. The paranoia internally manifests itself against the populace and externally shows itself in the form of accusations against the rest of the world. The importance of this interpretation within the present context is that the correlation would then support, rather than refute, the Sprout argument. It would indicate, as the Sprouts contend, that certain perceptual or personality factors in the makeup of decision makers determine their actions, internally or externally. Thus this interpretation of the relationship, instead of contradicting the Sprout model, indirectly lends it support.

Consider now other apparent evidence against the Sprout model. Rummel's (1964) discovery of a significant negative relationship between his subversive dimension (assassinations and guerilla warfare) and a variety of the foreign conflict variables offers rather strange findings in respect to the

Sprout model. In its extreme form it means that a state that has no assassinations and no guerilla warfare will engage in considerable foreign conflict. The absence of these internal factors, then, provides the conditions for foreign conflict behavior and this appears to be true even when a variety of other factors (as indicated by the partial correlations) are held constant. As assassinations and guerilla warfare increase the foreign conflict activity of the state drops off. Thus, while a relationship has been found, the nature of that relationship supports the original Rummel-Tanter hypothesis, i.e., *the existence of internal difficulties does not enhance a state's foreign conflict activity.* Consequently these results also support the Sprout model. The Sprouts are arguing against writers who propose that factor X (e.g., mountain ranges) determines a state's activities. The Sprouts are arguing, along with Rummel and Tanter, that environmental factors do not determine a state's activities. This finding, then, futher supports their contention.

Tanter's (1966) lagged multiple correlations and Wilkenfeld's (1968) findings are the most serious pieces of evidence against the Sprout model. It would appear that the determinants of conflict behavior probably do involve certain dislocations within states *when these dislocations are considered together with other structural factors,* like the type of government, and *when looked at over certain time periods.* This constitutes the first set of results that refute the Sprout model.

The Relationship between Other Environmental Factors and Foreign Conflict Behavior—Thus far we have only considered internal conflict and its effect on external conflict. We turn now to a consideration of other structural factors that might have a bearing on a state's foreign conflict behavior. These studies are found in the lower left-hand cell of Figure 3. Here the evidence is more mixed and conflicting. Two studies suggest that various environmental factors *do* affect foreign conflict behavior; a third study concludes that these factors are not major determinants, but the results presented could be interpreted conversely; and four studies give evidence against the proposition of environmental determinism. We will consider first the two studies that do not support the Sprout model.

The first study that shows some relationship between various internal factors of states and their foreign conflict behavior is the Rummel (1964) study partially discussed earlier. In this study Rummel combined the results of his factor analysis of the 77 states for 1955–1957 with a factor analysis done by Brian Berry of 43 variables of the internal conditions of 25 states. Berry discerned four basic patterns: (1) *technology* (high loading variables were transportation, trade, external relations, industrialization, urbanization, national product); (2) *demography* (high loading variables were population, birth and death rates, infant mortality, population growth rates, population densities); (3) *contrast in income and external relations* (defining variables: total national product, total energy consumption, intensity of freight movement on railroads, per capital foreign trade, per capita international mail flows); and (4) *size* (large versus small). These four patterns along with Rummel's three domestic conflict factors were regressed on to each of the 13 foreign conflict variables described earlier; the results are shown in Table 7.

We have already noted the high relationship between the subversion dimension and the various foreign conflict factors, and the essential lack of relationship between any of the other conflict dimensions. Berry's factor "income and external relations" produces the greatest number of significant relationships, but none of these relationships remain after the effects of the other variables are held constant (see the partial correlation coefficients in contrast to the correlation for this factor). Furthermore, since this factor appears to contain two different types of variables, the interpretation of the significant correlations is not obvious. Some of the variables could be considered environmental factors, e.g., national product and total energy consumption, but other variables seem to measure state actions, or decisions, e.g., foreign trade and mail flows. Consequently, it is difficult to determine whether the results indicate a relationship between two types of foreign policy decisions (trade and foreign conflict behavior) or whether they show a relationship between environmental factors like energy consumption and foreign conflict behavior.

Table 7 does, however, provide a surprising number of significant multiple correlations between the four Berry factors along with the three Rummel domestic factors, and the 13 foreign conflict variables: seven of the 13 multiple correlations are significant. As can be seen in the first column, the data of Table 7 have been ordered on the basis of the degree of hostility scale discussed earlier. Unlike the results found earlier, however no pattern emerges here. Thus we find that war and military actions *are* significantly correlated with the various environmental factors. With the exception of Berry's income and external relations factor, which contains the conceptual problem noted above, the other six significant multiple correlation factors do index a variety of internal or environmental factors of states. Consequently these significant multiple correlation results show that certain environmental factors, *when considered together* (note that they are *not*, when taken separately) are important in determining foreign conflict behavior.

The second study that refutes the Sprout model was done by Louis Fry Richardson and is found in his *Statistics of Deadly Quarrel* (1960). Richardson's concern with finding the causes of war leads him at one juncture to consider the effects of frontiers on the decision to engage in a war (Richardson, 1960, p. 176). His principal assumption is that borders are frequently the source of interstate conflict. Thus his hypothesis is that the more borders a state has in common with other states the more conflicts that state will become a party to and consequently the greater the likelihood that state will engage in wars. Considering all states that met certain minimal population, sovereignty, and permanence requirements during the years between 1820 and 1945, Richardson computed a correlation between the number of

Table 7—Regression of 1955–1957 Foreign Conflict Behavior Data Upon Berry's Basic Pattern and 1955–1957 Domestic Conflict Behavior Dimensions—Multiple (R), Simple (r) and Partial (r_p) Correlation Coefficients*

Dependent Variable	Independent Variables[1]														
	MULT R	BERRY'S BASIC PATTERNS								DOMESTIC CONFLICT DIMENSIONS					
		TECHNOLOGY[2]		DEMO-GRAPHY[3]		SIZE[4]		INCOME-EXTERNAL[2]		TURMOIL		REVOLU-TIONARY		SUBVER-SION	
Foreign Conflict Behavior Measures		r	r_p	r	r_p	r	r_p	r	r_p	r	r_p	r	r_p	r	r_p
1. Accusations	.44[b]	-.03	-.08	-.13	-.16	-.03	.05	-.28[a]	-.14	.02	-.03	-.04	-.04	-.34[a]	-.32[a]
2. Protests	.49[b]	-.23[a]	-.13	.07	-.11	.03	.08	-.38[b]	-.19	-.11	-.10	-.20	-.21	-.30[b]	-.25[a]
3. Anti-foreign Demonstrations	.44[a]	-.12	-.03	.03	.01	.09	.13	-.27[a]	-.14	.03	.08	-.01	.00	-.38[b]	-.35[b]
4. Threats	.33[a]	-.07	-.11	-.04	-.15	-.05	-.01	-.11	.02	-.04	-.07	-.06	-.07	-.28[a]	-.27[a]
5. Negative Sanctions	.39[a]	-.12	-.13	.05	-.11	.05	.09	-.08	.08	-.12	-.10	.05	.03	-.34[b]	-.34[b]
6. Expelled/Recalled lesser official, etc.	.40[a]	-.27[a]	-.02	.20	.11	-.19	-.13	-.23[a]	-.16	.06	.14	-.16	-.10	-.15	-.09
7. Expelled/Recalled Ambassador, etc.	.34[a]	.08	.03	-.03	.04	-.12	-.11	.19	.15	.12	.10	.16	.16	-.14	-.19
8. Severed Diplomatic Relations	.43[a]	.22	.03	-.26[a]	-.14	.09	.09	-.03	.02	.09	-.02	-.19	-.24[a]	-.23[a]	-.27[a]
9. Mobilizations	.37[a]	.03	-.05	-.02	-.10	.14	.14	.06	.13	-.18	-.20	.03	-.01	-.24[a]	-.28[a]
10. Troop Movements	.36[a]	-.06	-.05	-.11	-.12	-.17	-.17	-.27[a]	-.20	.07	-.01	-.07	-.04	-.10	-.04
11. Military Action	.40[a]	.16	-.17	-.24[a]	-.26[a]	.19	.24[a]	.01	.16	.08	.01	-.08	-.16	-.16	-.20
12. War	.40[a]	-.23[a]	-.25[a]	.10	-.17	.05	.16	-.13	.10	-.07	-.01	-.01	-.03	-.28[a]	-.27[a]
13. Foreign Killed, Int'l Conflict	.38[a]	-.01	-.24[a]	-.15	-.25[a]	.12	.21	-.12	.09	.14	.13	-.01	-.06	-.20	-.21
% total variance ($\sum r^2/13$)	16.0	2.3	1.6	1.8	2.2	1.3	1.9	3.9	1.8	1.0	0.9	1.1	1.3	6.5	6.4

* Taken from R.J. Rummel. "Testing Some Possible Predictors of Conflict Behavior Within and Between Nations," *Peace Research Society (International),* Vol. I (1964), p. 97.
[1] N = 69.   [2] Developed nations generally have lower values.   [3] Developed nations generally have higher values.   [4] Larger countries generally have lower values.
[a] Would be significant at .05 (dependent variable has nonnormal distribution).   [b] Would be significant at .01 (dependent variable has nonnormal distribution).

frontiers shared by states and the frequency of wars. The correlation was .77 which with $N = 33$ is significant beyond the .001 level. Again, a relationship has been found between an environmental factor and the acts of states.

The study which has two possible interpretations was done by Rummel (1968). Apparently using the original 1955–1957 data for conflict (this is not specified in the study) Rummel added a large range of other variables which index what he terms "situations." The foreign conflict variables have been correlated with these 235 situational variables to test hypotheses concerning relationships between foreign conflict on the one hand and

1. The level of economic or technological development of a nation.
2. The level of international communications or transactions of a nation.
3. The amount of cooperation of a nation with others.
4. The totalitarianism of a nation's government.
5. The power of a nation.
6. The instability of a nation.
7. The military capabilities of a nation.
8. The psychological motivations of a nation's people.
9. The values of a nation.
10. The number of borders of a nation.
11. The interaction of combinations of the above characteristics. . . . (Rummel, 1968, p. 203)

While for our purposes hypotheses 2 and 3 are not relevant, Rummel finds that the correlations do not support *any* of the hypotheses. He arrives at this conclusion by operationalizing each of the above ten variables in terms of a set of indicators from his 235 variables. For example, totalitarianism in hypothesis 4 is defined by "freedom of opposition," "the voting system," and "press censorship." Since none of these three variables produce correlations with any of the 13 foreign conflict variables greater than the absolute value of .30 (i.e., with or without the negative sign), he concludes that hypothesis 4 above is not supported.[9] Thus, in so far as the above variables index the operational milieu, these results support the Sprout model.

On the other hand, a perusal of the correlation matrix does show a number of significant findings. They are not brought out in the study principally because these significant findings are not related to the specific hypotheses being tested. For our purposes, however, they provide further information relevant to the Sprout model. The correlation table, which covers 11 pages in the original article, cannot, for obvious reasons be reproduced here. Instead, certain relevant sections have been abstracted and appear here as Table 8. I have selected those variables which seem to be environmental factors and which have at least one significant correlation with foreign conflict behavior.

It was argued above that twelve of Rummel's foreign conflict variables

Table 8—Correlations Between Environmental Variables and Foreign Conflict Behavior*

Environmental Variables	Accusations	Protests	Anti-Foreign Demons.	Threats	Negative Sanctions	Expelled Lesser Officials	Expelled Ambassadors	Severance Diplomatic	Mobilization	Troop Movement	Military Action	War
Development Variables												
Agr. Pop./Pop.						-30(63)						-30(63)
Rate of Pop. increase							31(72)				31(72)	
Population		38(77)	31(77)	32(77)						49(77)		
GNP		42(72)		30(72)		37(72)				43(72)		
Calories Consumed—Cal. Req'd/Cal. Req'd						40(34)		-46(34)				
Total Energy Poten. Avail.	32(72)	32(72)		34(72)						43(72)		
Sci: Book titles/Book titles		38(58)				46(58)						
Total energy consumed		35(74)				39(74)				33(74)		
Electricity Generation		32(74)				33(74)						
Steel Prod.		39(50)				33(50)				38(50)		
Other Variables												
National Area										38(77)		
Arable Nat'l Land		30(75)		31(75)		32(75)						
Age of Country			-33(77)									
Political Centralization	36(36)a	41(36)	32(36)b			38(36)a				37(36)a		
Religious Groups ≧ 1% Population	33(63)											
Language Groups ≧ 1% Population											33(65)	
Protestant Pop./Pop.						33(72)						
Mohammedan Pop./Pop.	42(70)			40(70)				47(70)			38(70)	
Achievement Desire	36(37)a		37(37)a				42(37)					
Nations Contiguous	32(77)									31(77)		
Immigrants			31(51)	36(51)	48(51)		30(51)a					

* This table has been completed based on Rummel's Table 1 in "The Relationship Between National Attributes and Foreign Conflict Behavior," reprinted from *Quantitative International Politics*, ed J. David Singer, New York: The Free Press, 1968, pp. 187–214. Note: All correlations *not* footnoted p ≦ .01. Brackets (N) indicate sample size.

a .01 ≦ p ≦ .05. b Not significant at .05.

could be placed on a scale representing the magnitude or severity of conflict behavior. Table 8, like the earlier tables, has been rearranged to reflect this scale. Thus the columns of Table 8 move from the less severe forms of foreign conflict behavior to the more severe aspects. If we consider this scale in three parts, an interesting pattern emerges, not unlike the one discussed earlier. The twelve variables can be divided into three groups of four variables each, groups which make intuitive sense. The first group of four—accusations, protests, antiforeign demonstrations, and threats—might be considered to be the initial sparring that takes place before the participants engage one another in overt conflict. The second set of four variables—negative sanctions, expulsion of lesser diplomatic personnel, expulsion of ambassadors, and the severance of diplomatic relations—represent the first stage of actions taken in a conflict. The last four variables—mobilizations, troop movements, military activities, and war—reflect the final stages of actions taken in conflict situations. If the classification is granted, then a pattern emerges as we move from the initial stages of a conflict to the more severe acts: the first group of four foreign conflict variables contains 25 significant relationships with the various environmental factors, the second set of four conflict indicators has 16 significant correlations with the environmental variables, and the last set of foreign conflict indicators produces only 13 significant correlations. There appears to be a general trend comparable to our earlier finding: the less severe forms of foreign conflict behavior are more likely to have determinants amongst the environmental factors. Note again that there is only one significant correlation involving war.

Table 8 can also be viewed from another perspecive. The Table has been constructed so as to distinguish between two types of environmental variables. The top half of the table gives those variables that principally index the level of development or underdevelopment of a state, e.g., GNP, rate of population increase, the number of calories consumed in relation to the number required, steel production, electricity generated. The bottom half of the tables gives other more general types of variables. More than half of the significant correlations occur in the upper half of the table, and of these 28 only three are negative. The 25 positive correlations would seem to indicate that the more developed countries, as indexed by these variables, evidence more foreign conflict behavior. Furthermore, these developed states tend to primarily engage in three forms of conflict behavior: protests, the expulsion of lesser diplomatic personnel, and troop movements. Comparable to the Wilkenfeld (1968) study then, these results suggest that a relationship does exist between certain types of states (developed vs. less developed) and their foreign conflict behavior patterns. Furthermore, it indicates that the operational milieux of these states does somehow influence their decision patterns, contrary to the Sprouts.

Consider now the three studies that support the Sprout model. The first was done by Lewis Fry Richardson (1960). Richardson wished to test an underlying assumption of the establishment of the United Nations, namely that membership "should be open to all peace-loving states." Richardson comments: this ". . . proposal would be satisfactory if . . . peace-lovingness were a permanent characteristic of most . . ." states (Richardson, 1960, p. 169). This proposition is examined by considering all fatal quarrels (not just of states) greater than a specified magnitude that occurred between 1820 and 1945. This period was divided into six equal blocks of 21 years and "for each block a note was made of those belligerents which have not appeared in any previous block. . . . The purpose of the investigation was to notice whether the number of new belligerents dwindled towards zero as the background increased for successive blocks" (Richardson, 1960, p. 170). If the same states were perpetually the wrong-doers throughout history then the number of new belligerents per block of 21 years should go to zero. Surprisingly, the number of new belligerents in each block remained within the same range, from 18 to 26, with 26 new belligerents actually occurring in the last block, from 1924–1945. Clearly the number of new belligerents did not dwindle towards zero. Thus it must be said that conflicts resulting in violence between 1820 and 1945 were not principally the result of the activities of a few. In other words, there are no consistently "bad" states; the same states are not consistently the cause of wars. The states represented in Richardson's analysis covered many different environmental conditions. By finding that there is no special class of states that cause all wars, Richardson has given additional evidence in favor of the Sprout argument that environmental factors do not determine decisions—at least not the decision for war.

For our purposes, however, there are certain difficulties with this analysis. Principally, Richardson does not distinguish between groups of people and actual states (e.g., the massacre of the Janissaries is classified as a violent conflict along with the Russo-Turkish War). Thus Richardson's second analysis is more directly relevant to the Sprout model. The second analysis considers whether there existed any state—and here Richardson *does* confine his attention to bonafide states—between 1820 and 1945 that did not engage in belligerent activities. Through a process of elimination Richardson finds that "only Sweden had no war at all during the interval A.D. 1820–1939" (Richardson, 1960, p. 173). Thus the decision *not* to engage in war (if this is a decision) may be a function of the operational milieu— since Sweden consistently chose this course of action. However, the decision *to* engage in war cannot be said to be a function of the operational milieu; all other states were involved in wars. Since there are considerable environmental differences between these states, this finding also provides evidence in favor of the Sprout contention.

While supportive of the Sprout model these two Richardson analyses contain a hidden problem. Namely, the decision to go to war is not always comparable across states. Principally, there is a difference between the decision to *initiate* a war and the decision to *defend* when attacked. Unfortunately, in the above analyses Richardson did not distinguish between these two situations. All states which engaged in wars, however initiated, were considered together. For our purposes, the distinction could be critical. While there may be no relationship between all states which participate in wars and environmental factors, it is still conceivable that states which *initiate wars* share common environmental factors. Thus the Richardson findings are only suggestive with respect to the Sprout model.

There are two studies which provide substantial support for the Sprout model. The first was done by Haas (1965). While Haas did not draw these conclusions himself, the results of his analyses clearly indicate that there is no relationship between a variety of environmental variables and foreign conflict behavior. Using data from Banks and Textor (1964), Rummel (1963), and Tanter (1966), Haas computes chi squares between the environmental factors: type of regime (constitutional, authoritarian, totalitarian), economic development status (from very underdeveloped to developed), urbanization, and density of population, on the one hand, and the extent of foreign conflict (significant, moderate, limited, and negligible) on the other. None of the relationships are statistically significant.

The second study which supports the Sprout model was done by Rummel (1966). The methodology of this study is comparable to the other Rummel articles: "the design consisted of collecting data on 94 foreign behavior variables . . . assessing the correlations . . . (and) factoring. . . ." (Rummel, 1966, p. 202)[10] The 94 "foreign behavior variables" are not, strictly speaking, all "behavioral" variables. There are essentially three types of variables to be found in Rummel's list of 94 variables. First, the list includes the original 13 conflict behavior variables. Second, most of the remaining variables on the list index other forms of international behavior, such as trade or involvement in international organizations. Third, however, the list also includes a number of variables that reflect environmental characteristics of states, such as economic aid received, possesion of colonies, air distance to U.S., or percentage of immigrants to the total population. The factor analysis of these three types of variables produces two intriguing conclusions, one of which is relevant in the present context, the other of which will be reported below in the discussion of nonconflict behavior. Rummel finds that all but one of the foreign conflict behavior variables have a high loading on one and the same factor. Furthermore, this factor does not contain any high loading variables from either of the other two sets of variables, the nonconflict behavior set, or the environmental set. Thus, once again, Rummel concludes that foreign conflict behavior is unrelated to the various environmental variables. Furthermore, since the nonconflict behavior variables did not produce high loadings on this foreign conflict factor he also concludes that foreign conflict behavior is a different species of behavior.

These last two studies raise some serious and puzzling questions. Thus far we have found four studies which clearly provide evidence against the Sprout model with respect to foreign conflict behavior: Wilkenfeld (1968), Rummel (1964), Richardson (1960), and Rummel (1968). The results from all but the Richardson study are contradicted by the analyses performed by both Haas (1968) and Rummel (1966). Wilkenfeld found a relationship between internal conflict conditions and external conflict behavior when types of government were held constant, implying that the form of government has some effect on foreign conflict behavior. Haas, however, finds no relationship between types of regimes and the amount of conflict in which a state engages. The Rummel (1964) and Rummel (1968) studies both show a large number of relationships between a variety of development indicators and various foreign conflict behaviors. Both Haas (1968) and Rummel (1966) find no relationship between economic development and the extent of foreign conflict. Furthermore, the Rummel (1964, 1968) studies show relationships between urbanization and density of population and certain foreign conflict behaviors. Haas finds no relationship.

These differences in results could be attributed to one or more of three sources: (1) differences in data used, (2) differences in operationalization of concepts like "development" or "extent of foreign conflict," or (3) differences in research design and statistical tests, ie., one study uses factor analysis, another chi square. Although the studies are not based on precisely the same data, the differences in this regard are not extensive. All the studies are based on Rummel's original 1955–1957 data; Wilkenfeld adds the Tanter (1966) data, Rummel (1964) adds the Berry data. Haas adds both the Tanter and Banks and Textor data, and Rummel (1966) adds additional variables. The data added to the original Rummel data is primarily of the same quality and comes from the same general historical period. Consequently, the differences in results are probably due less to data sources than to the other two factors.

A comparison of operational measures and statistical analyses would carry us far beyond the scope of the present enterprise. What is disturbing and must be emphasized here is that the results of these studies appear not to be invariant over such factors as measurement techniques and statistical tests. This is unfortunate; the goal is to find similar results using different analyses and operational measures. The four studies suggest instead that some or perhaps all of the results are artifacts of the research techniques.

The Relationship between Other Environmental Factors and Nonconflict Behavior

While the results for foreign conflict behavior are contradictory and confusing, the corresponding findings for international *nonconflict behavior* seem completely unambiguous. Perhaps this is because to date only one study has been directed towards this issue: Rummel (1966). The methodology of this study was just described above, along with the first major conclusion drawn from the study. The second major finding of the study was that the other factors extracted from the factor analysis of the 94 variables contained high loading variables from two of the three sets: the international nonconflict behavior set *and* the environmental set. This result led Rummel to conclude: ". . . participation in the international system is internally derived behavior. Participation is a resultant of the properties of the nation. Specifically, the level of involvement in the system depends on the economic development of a nation and its power capability. . . ." (Rummel, 1966, p. 212). Thus we have evidence which directly contradicts the Sprout model. The important limitation on this result is, as Rummel himself points out, that it must be confined to the specific operationalization of the variables given within the study; factor analysis is unique to the particular set of data. Nevertheless, the results are indicative and cannot be discarded.

The Content Analytic Studies

The second set of studies analyzes two facets in the Sprout model: the relationship between the perceptions of decision-makers and their subsequent behavior, and the relationship between the environment and the perceptions of decision-makers. These are all content analytic studies which have attempted to test hypotheses by collecting data from the written documents of decision-makers. All but two of the studies share a common data source: the 1914 crisis.

Holsti, North, and Brody (1968) present a type of stimulus-response learning model which underlies the analyses done in their other two studies and can be found implicit in all of the other articles. Since this model directly parallels the Sprout model, it is a useful organizing device for presenting the various findings. The Holsti, North, and Brody (1968) model is shown in Figure 4.

"S" represents the incoming stimulus to a particulur state, "r" indicates the state's evaluation or perception of the incoming stimulus, "s" are the states's expressed intentions as a function of its perceptions, and "R" represents the state's actions. These writers have captured two of the significant facets that concerned the Sprouts. The relationship between S and r describes the relationship in the Sprout context between the operational milieu and the perceptions of the decision-makers, while the relationship between r and either s or R provides information on how the perceptions of decision-makers affect their decisions and actions. The tests of the relationships posited in the Holsti, North, and Brody model should therefore produce results of considerable significance for our present purposes. Table 9 summarizes the relevant findings within the context of the model given in Figure 4.

The first two studies as shown in Table 9 (Zinnes, North, and Koch, 1961; Holsti and North, 1965) examine the relationship between: (1) two types of perceptions, perceptions of relative power and perceptions of

Figure 4. The Interaction Model.

	State A				State B	
	r	s			r	s
S	Perception of B's Attitude and Behavior Toward A	Statement of A's Plans and Intentions Toward B	Behavior Output R	S	Perception of A's Attitude and Behavior Toward B	Statement of B's Plans and Intentions Toward A	R
			Behavior Output			

(Taken from Holsti, North, and Brody. "Perception and Action in the 1914 Crisis," in *Quantitative International Politics,* ed. J. David Singer, New York: The Free Press, 1968, 133.)

injury, and (2) the decision to go to war; in the above model this is the relationship between "r" and "s" (or "R" depending on how the decision to go to war is expressed). The argument of these two initial studies is presented in the form of two contrasting hypotheses. It contends that under certain conditions perceptions of relative power, or capability, are superseded by feelings of injury in the decision to go to war. The theory was stated to contradict the usual conception of deterrence, namely, that the perception of superior power prevents war. Under deterrence theory, wars should only be initiated by superior powers, or by states having gross misperceptions of capabilities. The theory presented by these two studies is that inferior powers will *also* initiate wars under certain contingencies: when feelings of injury are particularly acute. Thus the purpose of the two studies was to disprove the first hypothesis but substantiate the second:

Hypothesis 1: A state will not go to war . . . if it perceives its power . . . as 'significantly' less than that of the enemy at the time that such a decision must be made. Hypothesis 2: If a state's perception of injury . . . to itself is 'sufficiently' great, this perception will effect perceptions of insufficient capability, making the perception of capability much less important a factor in a decision to go to war (Zinnes, North and Koch, 1961, p. 470).

It is important to note the requirements for a test of the two hypotheses. Both hypotheses are only concerned with the decision for an offensive war, i.e., they are not predicting the behavior of states against which aggression has been committed or war already declared. Obviously in these latter instances the target state has no option but to fight, regardless of the status of its power or its feelings of injury. The 1914 case presents a rather ambiguous situation as even historians find it difficult to determine who was in fact the initiator state or side. Let us assume, then, that all five of the states, Great Britain, France, Russia, Austria and Germany (clearly Serbia was attacked and therefore not in this category), simultaneously made the decision to go to war. To disprove the first hypothesis it must be shown that at least one of the five states perceived itself to be inferior in power to its potential enemies, i.e., it went to war even though it perceived itself inferior in power. The second hypothesis is then relevant only to those

Table 9—Correlation Results from Content Analytic Studies Shown Within the Context of the Stimulus–Response Model

Study	S–r	r : s	s–R	S–R
1. Zinnes, North, Koch (1961)		Relationship examined but not really tested		
2. Holsti, North (1965)		Relationship holds for Germany		
3. North, Brody, Holsti (1964)	.63^b		.53^b	
Triple Entente		Frequency .86^b Intensity .87^b		
Dual Alliance		Frequency .78^b Intensity .33		
4. Zinnes (1968)[1]	Frequency / Intensity	Frequency / Intensity		Frequency / Intensity
All Statements	.04 / −.19^a	.56^b / −.14		−.16 / −.50^b
Threat Statements	−.16 / −.49^b	.32^b / −.35^b		−.27 / −.72^b
Action Statements	−.01 / −.19	.30^a / .07		−.21 / −.33
5. Brody (1963)	Intensity	Intensity		Intensity
Threat Statements	.43^b	.34^b		.73^a
Action Statements	.49^b	.49^b		
6. Zinnes (1966)	Intensity	Intensity		Intensity
Threat Statements	.70^b	.74^b		.51^b
Action Statements	.73^b	.73^b		
7. Zinnes, Zinnes, McClure (in press)[2]	Yes	Yes		
8. Holsti, Brody, North (1965)[3]	−.93^b			.89^b
	−.82^b			

^{a} $P \leq .1$. ^{b} $P \leq .05$.

[1] Many lags and models were used in the initial study. Some of these analyses contained problems. Consequently the results reported here are only for the most viable set of analyses.

[2] Yes means that the relation was tested and in general found to hold.

[3] There were many other correlations reported in the study, only the significant ones are given here.

states which were cases against the first hypothesis. Thus, the second hypothesis argues that those states that perceive themselves inferior in power will still opt for war *if their feelings of injury are sufficiently great.*

The principal difficulty with the first study (Zinnes, North, and Koch, 1961) is that we were not fully cognizant of what constituted a test of the hypotheses. Consequently, the hypotheses were not in fact tested.[11] The logical flaws of the first study are cleared away in the second (Holsti and North, 1965) as the writers begin their analysis with an appraisal of the implications of a test of the second hypothesis:

> . . .knowledge of inferior forces must be ascribed to one of the parties. The pilot study of the 1914 crisis showed that top German decision-makers were fully cognizant of Germany's inability successfully to wage a general European war in 1914 (Zinnes, North and Koch, 1961). Finally it must be shown that the same leaders perceived themselves to be the victims of injury during the course of the crisis which led to the outbreak of war.

Thus the focus of the study is principally Germany and the purpose of the analysis is to demonstrate that German decision-makers felt themselves to be "victims of injury." To this end an index of injury is constructed based on the intensities of perception and expressions of hostility and friendship.[12] The index can vary from zero to plus infinity, the range of one to plus infinity indicating the extent of injury.[13] Germany's index of injury is found to be 2.73. Thus, since Germany was one of the initiators of the war, and since it was previously shown that she perceived herself inferior in power with respect to her potential enemies, this index of injury demonstrates that with respect to Germany the hypothesis is supported.

There are, however, two additional sets of results reported in the article which, while not directly relevant to the argument being presented there, provide further information for the Sprout model. The first set of results shows that the indices of injury for all five of the states range between 1.80 and 2.73 implying that *all* the states felt themselves to be "persecuted" and "rejected." Since it was argued above that all of the states might be considered to be the simultaneous initiators of the war, it would appear that regardless of whether they perceived themselves to be superior or inferior in power (it has not been shown how the others perceived their power position) the decision-makers all perceived themselves "injured." Without a "control" group for comparison (the perceptions of states who don't begin wars) these results can only be taken as indicative, but from the point of view of the Sprout model it does suggest that perceptions, particularly of injury, are probably an important factor in decisions, thus supporting one of the Sprout hypotheses.

There are, however, some problems in the measurement techniques used in this study which, while not negating the results, indicate that the results must be considered within this context. Every theme coded was scaled and assigned an intensity value. This means that the variables can be measured in three ways: (1) through a simple frequency count of the number of themes representing that variable (e.g., the number of themes in which state *X* perceived itself the target of hostility); (2) by adding all the intensity values for all the themes representing the variable (e.g., by adding the intensity values for all the themes in which *X* perceived itself the target of hostility); and (3) by computing the mean intensity by dividing (2) by (1) for each variable. Good arguments can be made for the use of either (2) or (3). The use of (2) means that one wishes to exphasize the frequency with which statements are made, while the use of (3) indicates a desire to control for frequency and examine the average intensity of the statements. Holsti and North chose (2) and the above results are based on this choice. If the index of injury is recomputed using (3), the mean intensity values, different results are obtained as shown in Table 10 in column two. The first column of Table 10 gives the results of the Holsti and North study for comparison purposes. Using mean intensities, the index values are close to unity, thus wiping out some conclusions about feelings of injury, and Germany's index is no longer the largest of the five. Furthermore, two of the indices now lie in the zero to one range indicating "negative" injury. This does not mean that the results of the study are wrong. It does mean, however, that the findings are not invariant over measurement techniques.

The second set of results given by the authors reports how the countries viewed each other with respect to the index of injury. For example, they report the index which shows Germany's perception of Austria's index of injury. The five states are divided into the two opposing alliances and each state is perceived by the members of his own alliance and the opposing alliance. Significantly, these values are, in all cases, *less* than the index of injury as originally computed for each state. Thus Austria-Hungary considered itself to be more injured than it was perceived to be injured by *either* its partner Germany or the opposing Triple Entente. These results are also reported in Table 10 in columns three and four. Note that all but two of the indices are in the "negative" range, between zero and one.

The results of columns three and four in Table 10 have been further summarized in column five. A comparison of column three, which reports the perceptions of allies, with four, which reports the perceptions of enemies, shows the not surprising fact that in most cases (Britain is the exception) allies tended to see one another as more injured than did the enemies. By taking an average of the two perceptions, as reported in column five, we might get some feeling for "reality" or the "environment." The averaged values are all less than or equal to 1.02. A comparison of column five with column one, then, suggests that a discrepancy does exist between the environment, or in this case the operational environment as defined by the other states, and the perceptions of the states themselves—a result consistent with the Sprout model.

While the first two articles concentrate on the "*r*" to "*s*" link in the Hol-

Table 10—A Comparison of Different Indices of Injury*

	Holsti-North Index[a]	Mean Index of Injury[b]	Percep-tions by Enemy	Percep-tions by Ally	"Objective" Index: Enemy + Ally / 2
Austria-Hungary	2.21	1.01	.30	.86	.68
Germany	2.73	1.11	.49	1.33	.91
Great Britain	2.07	1.23	.98	.40	.69
France	2.70	.88	.27	1.77	1.02
Russia	1.80	.86	.45	.91	.68

* Based on data given in Ole Holsti's and Robert North's "The History of Human Conflict," in *Nature of Human Conflict*, ed. Elton B. McNeil, New Jersey: Prentice-Hall, 1965, pp. 155–172.

[a] Holsti's index used the sum of the intensities of friendship and hostility statements in the formula:

$$\frac{\text{units of hostility as target} + \text{units of friendship as agent}}{\text{units of hostility as agent} + \text{units of friendship as target}}$$

[b] This index uses Holsti's formula given above in (1) but uses mean intensity values rather than totals, i.e., this index controls for the number of statements made.

sti, North, Brody model the third article, North, Brody, and Holsti (1964), as shown in Table 9, considers three stages of the model. They do this on the one hand through the use of hostility themes, and on the other, through the use of mobilization data obtained from military histories. The duration of the crisis, from June 27 through August 4, is divided into twelve periods such that each period contains approximately the same number of hostility themes.[14] The five states in the crisis are then divided into the two historical alliances: the Dual Alliance (Germany and Austria-Hungary) and the Triple Entente (Great Britain, France, and Russia). Thus the system under consideration contains two units opposing one another.

Hostility themes are pooled within each alliance and in a like manner the mobilization statistics are added within each alliance. The variables of the model are operationalized from these data. "S", or the stimulus for one alliance, is the mobilization effected by the other alliance. Thus if Germany mobilizes 1,000 men this becomes a stimulus for the Triple Entente. The second variable in the model, "r", is operationalized by those hostility themes in which states perceive themselves as targets of hostility. A correlation between S and r then represents a correlation between the mobilizations of one alliance and the perceptions by the other alliance that it is the target of hostility. The correlation as reported in Table 10 is .63 and significant at the .01 level.

This relationship is of particular relevance to the Sprout model. The positive significant correlation would seem to belie the argument that decision-makers do not correctly perceive their environment. Contrary to the Sprout contention, decision-makers appear to perceive hostility when threatening actions occur in the system. As discussed earlier, if a one-to-one relationship existed between the environment and the perceptions of decision-makers, then the Sprout argument would be meaningless.

The third variable in the model, "*s*" is operationalized by the expressions of hostility on the part of either alliance towards the members of the other alliance. The relationship between "*r*" and "*s*" then describes the extent to which when one alliance perceives itself the target of the other alliance it then expresses hostility to the other alliance. In this instance the correlations are reported separately for each alliance and for frequency as well as intensity values. For the frequency condition the results are .86 and .78 for the Triple Entente and Dual Alliance respectively; both values are statistically significant. When intensities are used, however, only the results for the Triple Entente are significant (.87).

The final variable in the model is "*R*" and is operationalized again with the mobilization data. Now, however, Germany's mobilization of 1,000 men represents "*R*" for the Dual Alliance. Thus the computation of a correlation between "*s*" and "*R*" indicates the extent to which expressions of hostility are followed by acts of overt hostility, namely mobilizations. The correlation here is .53 (over both alliances) and is significant at the .01 level.

The last two stages of the model, from "*r*" to "*s*" to "*R*" are again important to the Sprout model. In this context "*r*" represents the perceptions of decision-makers while "*s*" and "*R*" become the "decisions." In support of the Sprout model the results show that perceptions *are* a factor in the decision process.

The fourth article shown in Table 9 (Zinnes, 1968) considered almost the same relationships explored by North, Brody, and Holsti:

1. the expressions of hostility by one state against another and the perceptions of those expressions by the target state (the relationship between "*S*" and "*r*"),
2. the relationship between perceptions of self as target and the expression of hostility at the offending state (the relationship between "*r*" and "*s*"),
3. and the relationship between state *X*'s expression of hostility to *Y* and *Y*'s expression of hostility back to *X* (the relationship between "*S*" and "*R*").[15]

An important difference exists between the two studies with respect to the operationalization of "*R*." In the first study "*R*" consisted of mobilizations by the alliance. Here "*R*" is measured simply by the expressions of hostility by the alliance. In effect, the model has been shortened, for the expressions of hostility also serve as the actions of the state:

$$S; r \text{——} s = R$$

In a later study Holsti, North, and Brody (1968) argue that there is a distinction between "*s*" and "*R*"; "*s*" represents an expression of intent while "*R*" represents the actual decisions taken. Strictly speaking, however, within the context of the 1914 data this is not correct. Many of the statements that were coded as expressions of hostility were essentially *reports* of hostile actions *that had been taken.* For example, "Today we bombed X," would have been coded as an expression of hostility against X by the decision-maker writing the statement. Actual statements coded from the 1914 documents include the following as expressions of hostility: "military action against Serbia has been decided; an order for mobilization against Austria was given in Serbia; Austria declared war on Serbia." To some extent the difference between these report-type statements and other more emotive or threatening forms of expression was captured in the Zinnes (1968) analysis by the use of a classification scheme. All hostility statements were categorized into "Threats," a statement made in the future tense, and "Actions," statements made in the present or past tense. The "Action" category would contain the report statements. Unfortunately, it also contains other types of hostile expressions so that it is not equivalent to "R" in the North-Holsti-Brody model. However, results obtained using only action statements have been computed and are reported in Table 9.

The study tested the three relationships under various combinations of conditions. First, as was described in the context of the Holsti and North (1965) study, the variables were measured both by simple frequency counts and by intensity measures obtained from scaling the hostility themes. Second, as mentioned above, all hostility themes were classified into threats or actions. Consequently, combining the two measuring techniques with the classification dimension, there are six conditions under which the analyses could be done (frequency, intensity; all statements, threats, actions). A third condition consisted of a variety of data compilation procedures labeled models. These models involved various techniques for aggregating the data and the use of time lags in computing the correlations. Each of the six conditions were analyzed for each model. Since completing this study, I have come to regard some of these models as dubious, as the data compilation procedures made the data interdependent and thus violated a critical assumption in the use of the correlation coefficient. The results reported in Table 9 are therefore taken from the models which do not contain this defect.

Table 9 reports the results obtained in the study that are relevant to the North, Holsti, and Brody model. While the "S" to "r" results are given, the principal findings of the study concern the relationship between "r" and "s". The "S" to "r" relationships produced negative correlations which posed curious interpretations. A further investigation of these negative relationships, as described in detail in the original study, seemed to suggest that they were an artifact of the data compilation procedures. Consequently, the main result is that a significant relationship exists between the perception of hostility, "r", and the expression of hostility, "s". However, this relationship is significant only when the frequency measure is used. Thus for all pairs of countries there appears to be a significant relationship between the *number* of hostility themes perceived and the *number* expressed. Note that the relationship is significant for *both* threats and actions.

Brody's (1963) study was primarily concerned with the effects of the spread of nuclear weapons on a tight bipolar world and to this end various hypotheses were tested using the Inter-Nation Simulation developed by Gvetzkow and his associates at Northwestern. One of the variables investigated was hostility, and as a byproduct of his exploration of this system he tested the three relationships lited above. As shown in Table 9 the correlations are positive and significant for all three parts of the model, "*S*" to "*r*", "*r*" to "*s*", and "*S*" to "*R*".

The purpose of the fifth study, Zinnes (1966), was to compare results for the 1914 data with Brody's (1963) simulation. The same three (among others) hypotheses described above were analyzed, but with several differences in research design. [16] As can be seen from Table 9 the results are all significant, positive, and large, supporting both the Sprout model and the earlier contention that the strange negative results of the Zinnes (1968) study were artifacts.

The Zinnes, Zinnes, and McClure (in press) study, listed as the seventh study in Table 9, was an attempt to construct a somewhat more complicated model than was implicit in the simple correlations originally computed. Here it was suggested that perceptions of hostility were not only a function of incoming hostile messages (i.e., the stimulus or *S*) but also a product of the frame of mind which the decision-maker brought to bear on his reading of an incoming message. Thus the decision-maker's previous perception *as well as* the incoming messages determine a decsion-maker's subsequent perceptions. In a like manner, it was argued that the expression of hostility is a function not only of perceptions but of the previously stated expressions.

This model was tested using the same 1914 data but with several modifications. [17] The results of the analyses are difficult to cast in the framework of Table 9. All other studies in this table are based on correlations, while this model was tested through chi-square analyses of the transition probabilities for each of the three main variables: reception, perception, and expression of hostility. [18] With one exception, all the relationships posited in the model were found to hold. Thus both perceptions and receptions affect subsequent perceptions, and expressions and perceptions affect subsequent expressions. Table 9, then, simply reports that the relationships generally hold.

The last study reported in Table 9 (Holsti, Brody, and North, 1965) considered the stimulus-response model within the context of the Cuban missile crisis. Using the General Inquirer computer content analysis program, 15 United States, 10 Soviet, and 10 Chinese documents were content analyzed for the period from October 22, 1962 through October 31, 1962. "*S*" and "*R*" were obtained by scaling "action data." This is not fully described in the text, but apparently involved the rank ordering of each of the ten days of the crisis for each state in terms of how much hostility it evidenced. Thus on October 24 the United States exhibited the greatest amount of hostility, while on October 29 it showed the least amount. In contrast, October 23 was the most hostile day for the USSR and October 31 its least hostile day. The perception and expression variables, "*r*" and "*s*", respectively, came from the content analysis. While not described in detail here, one must surmise from the tables that all four variables were classified into the categories: positive affect, negative affect, strong, weak, active and passive. Thus actions ("*S*" or "*R*") or hostility statements ("*r*" or "*s*") contained either positive affect or negative affect, reflected strong or weak evaluations, and (or?) were active or passive. Unfortunately the details of the coding procedure for these six categories are left to an appendix that was not published with the article. Consequently, interpretations of results based on these data are somewhat difficult.

A number of the analyses presented in the paper are not immediately relevant to our present purpose and so we will consider only those results which bear on the stimulus-response, and consequently the Sprout, model. The first analysis involves a Spearman rank-order correlation between the scaling of the ten days for the two countries. Since the hostile acts of one country can be considered the stimulus, "*S*", for the other country, while the actions of the recipient country can be considered its response, "*R*", a correlation between the scaling of the days for the two countries gives evidence for the *S-R* relationship. This correlation is .89 and significant at the .01 level, as shown in Table 9.

The remaining relevant analyses consist of the computation of Spearman rank order correlations within each of the categories (positive or negative affect, etc.) between "*S*" and "*R*" on the one hand and "*s*" and "*r*" on the other. No explanation is given for why the "*r*" and "*s*" relationship is not also examined. Of the computed correlations only those between "*S*" and "*r*" and "*s*" and "*R*" are relevant to this discussion. The size of the samples are very small since, of the ten days of the crisis over which the correlations are being computed, only seven days show any perceptions or expressions of hostility for the United States and only six show values for "*s*" and "*r*" for the Soviet Union. Thus the *N* for the United States is seven and for the Soviet Union six. For the Soviet Union the *S-r* and *s-R* relationships are not significant for any of the six types of themes. For the United States the only significant correlations are found between *S-r*, as shown in Table 9. Here only two of the correlations are significant.

Having looked at each of the eight articles reported in Table 9 it is now constructive to view the Table more generally. The most surprisng feature of Table 9 is that the stimulus response model appears to be generally supported. This would appear to be particularly significant since these studies use three different sets of data—the 1914 data, a simulation run of a bipolarized world, and the Cuban missile crisis—and use a wide variety of statistical tests. It is clearly reasonable to conclude that the perceptions of decision-makers are an important factor in the decisions to express hostility whether by verbal reports or by overt actions. This is seen in the significant results for "*r*" and "*s*", "*S*" and "*R*", and "*S*" and "*s*". Thus these data and analyses support the Sprout model concerning the significance of the perceptual factor in the decision-making process.

On the other hand, Table 9 provides information on the relationship between a decision-maker's perceptions and the environment. If we assume that "*S*" or the incoming stimulus is a reasonable measure of the external environment, then the correlations between "*S*" and "*r*", where "*r*" represents the perceptions of the decision-makers, gives some evidence of whether the decision-makers match their perceptions to external stimuli. Except for the questionable results in the Zinnes (1968) study, which were probably a consequence of inappropriate analysis, the correlations seem to imply that a relationship does exist: the perceptions of decision-makers do correspond to environmental conditions. Thus this contention of the Sprout model is not supported by these data.

Summary and Conclusions

There were three facets of the Sprout model that we originally set out to explore. First, to what extent can the decisions of states be predicted simply on the basis of environmental factors. According to the Sprouts, the relationship here should be almost nonexistent: they maintain that environmental factors are not the determinants of state decisions. A variety of crossnational studies were examined to determine the viability of this argument. It was suggested that "environment" within the context of these studies could refer to (1) internal conflict problems or (2) other factors like socioeconomic factors. Similarly, foreign policy decisions were classified into two types: (1) decisions which eventuate in foreign conflict activity and (2) other foreign policy decisions. Given these breakdowns, the literature showed that when other factors were *not* held constant there was no relationship between internal conflict problems and external foreign conflict behavior—a result which supports the Sprout model. However, it was also found that if internal conflict problems are considered along with another environmental factor, namely the type of government, foreign conflict behavior can be predicted on the basis of domestic conflict difficulties—a result that contradicts the Sprout argument.

When "environment" is operationalized using nonconflict variables the evidence is ambiguous: some studies show that nonconflict environmental variables predict foreign conflict behavior, while other studies refute this proposition. The only other relationship explored thus far in the literature concerns the relationship between nonconflict variables as definitions of the environment and nonconflict foreign policy decisions. The one study that has examined this question seems to suggest that the Sprout contention is not warranted within this context: that there is a relationship between the environment so defined and foreign policy decisions. But as pointed out above, the study is limited in scope and so can only be used here as suggestive.

Consequently, it would appear that considerably more evidence is required before any conclusions can be drawn with regard to this facet of the Sprout model. At least three lines of development are suggested by the studies examined here. First, these studies all point to the need for an examination of the relationship between internal conflict and foreign conflict behavior when other factors are held constant. Wilkenfeld's (1968) study strongly suggests that domestic conflict may be relevant to external conflict when combined and considered in conjunction with other environmental factors. The second obvious extension is a further consideration of the various indicators of the environment and their impact on foreign conflict behavior, to clarify the contradictory evidence seen earlier. Finally, more attention should be devoted to the determinants of other state decisions. As this review has shown, all but one of the studies focuses on foreign conflict behavior, ignoring the fact that most of the decisions made by states are of a peaceful nature. We now need studies which will further examine, following Rummel's (1966) lead, the determinants of peaceful state activities.

The second aspect of the Sprout model explored in these pages was the relationship between the perceptions held by decision-makers and their actions. If "actions" are interpreted very broadly, then the overwhelming evidence from the studies reviewed here is in favor of the Sprout contention. While I cannot claim to have considered every relevant study, it is noteworthy that the studies reviewed for this aspect of the Sprout model did cover three different data sources and a variety of different analytical approaches. In contrast to the contradictory results just seen in the cross-national researches, where the data were very similar, we find that the perception-decision relationship even over disparate data sources (1914, simulation, Cuban missile crisis) generally supports the Sprout model. While further research is always warranted, these results are probably the most impressive of all.

The third facet of the Sprout model explored was the relationship between the environment and the perceptions of the decision-makers. The Sprouts, to maintain their first objection (that the environment does not determine state decisions), have to contend that there is a discrepancy between perceptions and the environment. Here most of the evidence has shown that this is not true. Except for the small evidence gleaned from the Holsti and North (1965) study all the analyses indicate that decision-makers do perceive their environment reasonably correctly.

However, these last results need not be taken as a complete refutation of the Sprout contention. Perhaps the logic of the preceding pages has been overly severe. The Sprout argument does not require that a discrepancy *always* exist between the perceptions of decision-makers and the environment. Indeed, the examples cited by the Sprouts (Pearl Harbor) would suggest that they considered the absence of a relationship to be a function of *particular contingencies*. Thus it could be the case that decision-makers correctly perceive their environment *except* under conditions *A*, *B*, or *C*. If these particular contingencies can be specified and it can be shown that the studies reviewed here do not meet these specifications, then the ground has been cleared for further study. It would then be necessary to uncover cases which do meet the *A*, *B*, *C* requirements and determine whether the perception-environment relationship does not hold.

Notes and References

[1] Geography probably will remain constant unless territory is gained or lost, but since the Sprouts mean by environment such things as governmental structures, etc., these facets would also have to be checked.

[2] A State had to have two characteristics:

[1] Sovereign statehood for at least two years, as evidenced by diplomatic relations with other countries and the existence of a foreign ministry or its equivalent.

[2] A minimum population of 800,000 which eliminates aberrations within the nation-state system like Monaco and Liechtenstein.

[3] It should be pointed out that these multiple correlations and regressions can be done in two ways, depending on whether one uses the factor scores or the values of the variable having the highest loading on each factor. For example, one of the factors Rummel obtained was termed "war and the highest loading variable was 'war.'" One of the factors obtained from the domestic conflict analysis was termed "turmoil" and the highest loading variable here was "antigovernment demonstrations." Thus a correlation between the war dimensions and the turmoil dimension could be computed by simply correlating the values for the two variables "war" and "anti-government demonstrations." This was the option chosen by Tanter. The alternative is to retain the factor which reflects a variety of inter-correlations and obtain "factor scores" for all the states on both the "war" and "turmoil" factors and then correlate these factor scores. Both of Rummel's studies have used this approach.

[4] Rummel's original table starred those coefficients that were significant, but there appears to have been some error in the reproduction of the table. Since the table specifies that all the correlations are based on the same number of cases ($N = 69$) there appear to be a number of significant correlations that were not starred. I have taken the liberty to add these stars.

[5] It should be pointed out that Wilkenfeld's study was not conducted in a fashion parallel to Rummel's. First, analysis is here based on six years, Rummel's on three. Second, Wilkenfeld uses the raw data rather than factor scores. Third, Wilkenfeld did his analysis year-by-year, while Rummel's appears to have been done by compiling the results for the entire three-year period. Whether these differences are sufficient to account for the different findings is not clear.

[6] I recognize that a number of writers, including Rummel, do not consider significance tests appropriate. Suffice it to say, at this juncture, that there are two principal ways one can evaluate a correla-

tion coefficient: (1) by determining whether or not it is significantly different from zero and can therefore be inferred as indicating that some relationship exists between the two variables, and (2) by squaring the correlation and finding the amount of variance that one variable can explain in another. My only argument at this point is that both techniques of evaluation ought to be utilized.

[7]The number of foreign killed has been omitted since it is not a measure parallel with the remaining measures; whereas all the other measures represent the frequency of action specified by the variable taken *by* a given state, foreign killed represents the *total* number of deaths *for all* parties participating in a conflict.

[8]Tanter finds a similarity between the two sets of correlations in that both sets appear to be generally positive. This is, however, a somewhat weak comparison. In addition to the fact that only three correlations are significant in both studies, Table 6 shows that the pattern of the correlations in both studies is not the same. In the Rummel study more of the significant correlations are found between purges and anti-foreign demonstrations and the foreign conflict variables. The correlations in the Tanter study do not group around any one or two variables but are spread over most of the domestic variables.

[9]Rummel's criterion for reporting correlations in his table is the .30 value and only correlations that exceed this absolute value are given. While Rummel does not report significance tests, a correlation of .30 is only significant at the .05 level when $N = 50$ or more. Most of the N's appear to range between 77 and 30. Consequently, one can reasonably assume that the values not reported are also not significant.

[10]Since some of these variables remain constant over long periods of time (e.g., air distance to U.S.) the period over which the data was collected varied. The years included in the study are given in Rummel's variable list and appear to cover from 1954 through 1960.

[11]A more detailed discussion of these problems will appear in D.A. Zinnes, "A Review of the Decision-Making Literature in International Politics," *Peace Research Reviews*, forthcoming.

[12]They define four variables:

1. "... hostility... which the decision-makers of State *A* express toward State *B* (State *A* as the agent of hostility) ...

2. (hostility) which the leaders of State *A* perceive themselves to be the recipient (State *A* as the *target* of hostility) ...

3. Friendship may similarly be divided into the decision-maker's perceptions of his nation as the *agent* of friendship

4. and the *target* of friendship," (Holsti and North, 1965, p. 161).

And on the basis of these four variables three indices are constructed:

$$\frac{\text{index of}}{\text{persecution}} = \frac{\text{Units of hostility as target}}{\text{Units of hostility as agent}}$$

$$\frac{\text{index of}}{\text{rejection}} = \frac{\text{Units of friendship as agent}}{\text{Units of friendship as target}}$$

index of injury = index of persecution × index of rejection.

[13]Assuming that the denominators are never zero, the indices given in footnote 12 range from zero to any positive value. The labels, index of persecution and index of rejection indicate that certain interpretations are being placed on specific values of the ratios. In particular, when the first two indices are approximately one the authors would probably argue that the perceiving decision-makers have a well balanced perception of the world: they are perceiving and expressing in equal amounts. Thus the extent to which either fraction exceeds unity is the measure of the state's feelings of persecution and rejection. Contrariwise, the range between zero and one indicates the extent to which there is a kind of negative imbalance, where in the case of hostility the state expresses more hostility than it perceives itself to be the target of, and in the case of friendship, becomes the target of more friendship than it initiates. Note that the construction of these indices overemphasizes persecution and rejection, and underemphasizes the zero to one range. Thus, the range

between zero and one is conceptually equivalent to the range between one and plus infinity. This makes comparisons between the ranges difficult if not impossible. A value of .60 has considerably greater significance than does a value of 2.70.

[14]The purpose of this unequal division for the subsequent analyses is not entirely clear.

[15]There are three principal differences between this study and the previous one, North, Brody, and Holsti (1964). The previous study acquired intensity values using Q-sort scaling techniques; here a simple absolute scale was used against which each statement received an intensity value. The previous study pooled the data into two alliances; here the analyses were done for each individual state to test the first hypothesis, and over all possible pairs of states for the second and third hypotheses. In the first study the correlations were computed over twelve time periods; in this study the correlations were computed over all 38 days of the crisis.

[16]The hypotheses in Zinnes (1966) were tested only with intensity measures. In addition, the data were combined over the 38 days for each state. Thus the correlations were computed over all possible pairs of six states, for the combined 38-day period. A third difference between Zinnes (1968) and Zinnes (1966) is that the first study used Pearson Product Moment correlations,

while the second study, in an attempt to be comparable to Brody's analysis, used the Spearman rank order correlation.

[17]As in the North, Brody, and Holsti (1965) study, alliances were used and the data was pooled within the alliances. An expression of hostility by Germany now became an expression of hostility for the Dual Alliance, and when Great Britain received a hostile message it was assumed that the message was received by the entire Triple Entente. However, unlike an earlier study (Zinnes, 1966), all 38 days for each of the participating states, was used in the analysis. The other principle modification was that this study used only "dichotomized" data. For each day of the thirty-eight days of the crisis we determined only *whether or not* a state expressed or perceived hostility. Thus Austria on June 28 either had a positive value (it perceived hostility) or a zero value (it did not perceive hostility) for that day. In analyses currently being pursued the positive values are further broken down into two levels of hostility.

[18]Transition probabilities were obtained by determining the number of times the members of an alliance made a transition from one level of hostility to another on the following day. Thus we counted the number of instances in which a zero day was followed by a zero day. Dividing this number by the possible number of transitions, produced transition probabilities.

References

A. Banks and R. Textor, *A Cross Polity Survey* (Cambridge: M.I.T. Press, 1963).

Richard A. Brody, "Some Systemic Effects of the Spread of Nuclear Weapons Technology: A Study through Simulation of a Multi-nuclear Future," *Journal of Conflict Resolution,* Vol. VII (December 1963), pp. 663–753.

P. Gregg and A. Banks, "Dimensions of Political Systems: Factor Analysis of a Cross-Polity Survey," *American Political Science Review,* Vol. LIX (September 1965), pp. 602–615.

Michael Haas, "Social Change and National Aggressiveness, 1900–1960," in *Quantitative International Politics,* ed. J. David

Singer (New York: The Free Press, 1968), pp. 215–247.

———, "Societal Approaches to the Study of War," *Journal of Peace Research,* Vol. IV (1965), pp. 307–324.

Ole Holsti and Robert North, "History of Human Conflict," in *Nature of Human Conflict,* ed. Elton B. McNeil (New Jersey: Prentice-Hall, 1965), pp. 155–172.

Ole Holsti, R. Brody, and R. North, "Measuring Affect and Action in International Reaction Models: Empirical Materials from the 1962 Cuban Crisis," *Peace Research Society (International),* Vol. II (1965), pp. 170–190.

Ole Holsti, R. North, and R. Brody, "Perception and Action in the 1914 Crisis," in *Quantitative International Politics*, ed. J. David Singer (New York: The Free Press, 1968), pp. 123–159.

R. North, R. Brody, and O. Holsti, "Some Empirical Data on the Conflict Spiral," *Peace Research Society (International)*, Vol. I (1964), pp. 1–15.

Lewis F. Richardson, *Statistics of Deadly Quarrels* (Pittsburgh: Boxwood Press and Chicago: Quadrangle, 1960), p. 373.

R. J. Rummel, "Dimensions of Conflict Behavior Within and Between Nations," *General Systems Yearbook*, Vol. VIII (1963), pp. 1–50.

———, "Testing Some Possible Predictors of Conflict Behavior Within and Between Nations," *Peace Research Society (International)*, Vol. I (1964), p. 97.

———, "Some Dimensions in the Foreign Behavior of Nations," *Journal of Peace Research*, Vol. III (1966), pp. 201–224.

———, "The Relationship Between National Attributes and Foreign Conflict Behavior," reprinted from *Quantitative International Politics*, ed. J. David Singer (New York: The Free Press, 1968), pp. 187–214.

Harold Sprout and Margaret Sprout, *Man-Milieu Relationship Hypotheses in the Context of International Politics* (New Jersey: Center of International Studies, Princeton University, 1956), p. 101.

———, *Ecological Perspective on Human Affairs* (New Jersey: Princeton University Press, 1965), p. 236.

———, *Foundations of International Politics* (Princeton, New Jersey: D. Van Nostrand, 1962), p. 734.

Raymond Tanter, "Dimensions of Conflict Behavior Within and Between Nations, 1958–60," *Journal of Conflict Resolution*, Vol. X (March 1966), pp. 41–65.

Jonathan Wilkenfeld, "Domestic and Foreign Conflict Behavior of Nations," *Journal of Peace Research*, Vol. I (1968), pp. 57–68.

Dina A. Zinnes, "A Comparison of Hostile Behavior of Decision-Makers in Simulate and Historical Data," *World Politics*, Vol. XVIII (April 1966), pp. 474–501.

———, "Expression and Perception of Hostility in Prewar Crisis: 1914," in *Quantitative International Politics*, ed. J. David Singer (New York: The Free Press, 1968), pp. 85–123.

D. Zinnes, R. North, and H. Koch, Jr., "Capability, Threat, and the Outbreak of War," in *International Politics and Foreign Policy*, ed. James Rosenau (New York: The Free Press of Glencoe, 1961), pp. 469–483.

D. Zinnes, J. Zinnes, and R. McClure, "Markovian Analyses of Hostile Communications in the 1914 Crisis," in *Crisis in International Politis*, ed. C. Hermann (in press).

MICHAEL HAAS

Sources of International Conflict

I. The Analysis of Violent Conflict

Conflict may be defined as norm-oriented behavior that seeks to preserve or change the structure of a system through direct representation of demands by adversaries. International conflict, hence, may pave the way for constructive change when it has been resolved in a manner that leads to an improvement in the harmony or capabilities of a system. The means for expressing conflict, however, can vary from institutionalized discussion, through activist protestations, to violent and physical acts that infringe upon the well-being of a party to a dispute. In international affairs, diplomacy constitutes the most nonviolent form of conflict, war the most violent. Why violent means are preferred to nonviolent means has been one of the age-old questions of international relations. In the discussion to follow, findings on correlates of the violent expression of international conflict are surveyed.[1]

To facilitate our survey of the sources of international conflict, the essay is divided into three main parts, each dealing with a distinct level of analysis. At the level of *interpersonal* factors, we shall seek to uncover background factors associated with violent choices by individuals; some types of persons are closer to a peaceful, dovish position on foreign policy issues, others tend to be more hawkish. Countries, too, differ in their propensities to participate in wars; the *societal* level of analysis will be examined to discover which kinds of polities opt for violent more than nonviolent

Notes and References for this selection will be found on pages 274–277.

responses to conflict situation. The *systemic* level will be considered, thirdly, in order to find how power distribution and other characteristics of groups of states may affect the probabilities that war will arise. Within each of these three levels of analysis there are a number of approaches and analytical strategies for determining the relationships between relevant variables, as we shall now see.

II. Interpersonal Factors

The view that "war begins in the minds of men" is central to those focusing on interpersonal correlates of dove and hawk foreign policy preferences. *Dualistic* theorists, such as Plato and Aristotle, believe that man's reason is engaged in a constant battle for supremacy over his passions, with neither reason nor emotions ever emerging as the victor, and both leading to warlike acts. *Augustinian* analysis stresses that passions prevail and account for the woeful yet inexorable presence of war in the City of Man. *Perfectibility* theorists, notably Kant and Dewey, seek to restructure human affairs in such a manner that reason can prevail over irrational tendencies. The desire among perfectibility theorists for more self-awareness by man of forces driving him to err has encouraged research on the interpersonal level by many modern social scientists. Two approaches have been attempted so far: *public opinion* analysts poll samples of persons and report on factors correlated with warlike and peaceful attitudes; *decision-making* analysts seek to link aspects of a problem-solving situation with choices by decision-makers to use violence.

Public Opinion Approach—The studies surveyed for this section of the chapter are based on several types of samples—representative cross-sections of a country[2] or a community,[3] and selective samples of college students[4] and faculty,[5] political leaders[6] and various adult groups or individuals.[7] Our summary of findings is broken into three parts: social characteristics, personality characteristics, and political preferences.

Turning first of all to *social characteristics* associated with attitudes favorable to war and unfavorable to peace, we find an almost universal tendency for women to be reluctant to select belligerent options in foreign policy. In the Putney-Middleton study, however, females who see themselves as nonconformists are more willing to accept war. Consistent with this finding, persons with prior military experience, whether war veterans or college ROTC students, are more often warminded.

Age correlates are more difficult to handle theoretically, for if respondents of a particular age in general accept war, the underlying factor could be either a stage in an individual's life cycle or the fact that an ideological perspective is shared among members of his cohort, or age group. The fact that earlier studies show older persons most favorable to war, and more recent studies report just the opposite, prompt Bobrow and Cutler to employ an analysis of age groups (cohorts) in order to determine which of the two factors is most salient. They find that persons who were in the 20–30 age group during World War I today reject both military and nonmilitary foreign policies. The depression cohort, which was between 20 and 30 years of age in the 1930s, prefers nonmilitary to military means of coping with international affairs. The third age group studied by Bobrow and Cutler consists of persons reaching their twenties after 1945 but before American entry into Vietnam, and this current nuclear era cohort favors both the military and nonmilitary tools of statecraft. They also note that support for war on the part of younger persons, who were born in the nuclear era, has lessened as they have grown older. Gergen and Back argue that older persons are short-term oriented and thus favor total peace or total war, whereas younger persons have more long-range perspectives and hold moderate views on public questions. In a similar manner, Armor and associates, find that tenured professors are more likely to oppose American policy in Vietnam, while nontenured professors are more likely to be uncommitted on the subject. Schuman and Laumann find more doves among full professors, hawks among assistant professors, and ostriches among associate professors.

Jews have been the most unwilling to endorse war among the major religious denominations, except for a study that Katzoff and Gilliland conducted when Hitler was ravaging Europe, but before the United States entered World War II. Blau, controlling for extent of church attendance, finds that Protestants who are regular churchgoers tend to be less ready to approve the use of military strategies in international politics, which is consistent with a finding of McClosky's that there is a positive relation between Calvinism scale scores and a preference for foreign aid as opposed to defense spending. Jews and Catholics who stay away from religious services are also less militaristic than their more devout counterparts. Laulicht, however, finds that regular churchgoers are more inclined to oppose coexistence policies; M. Rosenberg reports a positive relation between religiosity and opposition to coexistence policies, but Scott (1960) finds the opposite.

Cities, ironically the most likely target area for nuclear attack, are more prone to contain proponents of the arms race, undoubtedly because defense industries cluster around large urban centers. With respect to regions of the United States, Putney and Middleton find that more pacifists are in the West, fewer are in the Midwest, with the South and Northeast in between. M.J. Rosenberg also finds that Midwest students are more supportive of an aggressive foreign policy.

In the Verba study, often referred to as the Stanford Poll, even when level of political information is held constant, Negroes are more consistently opposed to American policy in Vietnam than Caucasians. Laulicht finds no such significant ethnicity correlate when comparing English Canadians and French Canadians.

The rise in income among members of the lower socioeconomic status groups within welfare states appears to have resulted in a lack of correlation between income levels and war-mindedness. Income, however, may be used to purchase a better education for the next generation, or a family could spend its resources in other ways. For those persons fortunate enough to complete high school or attend college, there is a tendency to be peaceminded. The impact of college education has been the subject of a number of studies, and an attempt to unravel determining conditions has not produced conclusive results. Carlson, Corey, Droba (1931), Farnsworth, Jones, and Putney and Middleton find that pacifistic views are more common among upperclassmen as opposed to freshmen, but Dudycha and Pilhblad encounter no such difference. However, these latter two studies were conducted at small private colleges. Armor and associates locate more opponents of American Vietnam policy in a large public university; private universities, smaller and Catholic institutions were centers of support for American policy in Vietnam. Since more intelligent persons are likely to attend college in the first place, a high IQ level might account for peacemindedness; Corey and Jones do report such a relation, but Droba does not find that a higher IQ is a predictor of peacemindedness.

The nature of subjects learned and taught at colleges does have a relation to warmindedness and thus reflects an occupational correlate. English and humanities students and professors are more peaceminded in general in the Armor, Jones, Putney-Middleton, and Schuman-Laumann studies. Social scientists are doves at the faculty level, but hawks abound among such students surveyed by Putney and Middleton. In the Jones study, history and geography majors, however, are more warminded than economists and sociologists. The professional schools are havens for hawks by and large, though Day and Quackenbush find that law majors are much more favorable to war than medical students. Natural scientists are hawk-oriented only among the faculty; male students in the natural sciences are among the moderately pacifist group in the Putney-Middleton study, females are militaristic, while both sexes together are on the fence in Jones' investigation. Such student and faculty attitudinal preferences are mirrored outside of academia, where professionals are among the peaceminded, businessmen favor a more power-oriented policy; and in M. J. Rosenberg's study, sons of businessmen are more hardline, sons of professionals take a less militaristic view toward foreign affairs. Laborers are not consistent from study to study. It is reassuring to find that political leaders are among those least favorable to war. Even among French leaders Gorden and Lerner note a switch between 1959 and 1961 from deterence to disarmament as a preferred objective.

In reviewing *personality correlates* of warmindedness, there is more consistency within the fewer number of studies. Persons high on authoritarianism, ethnocentrism, dogmatism, status concern, cynicism, anomie, and pessimism measures are likely to support war; a high degree of intellectualism is characteristic of an individual who is reluctant to advocate war.

Authoritarians in Lane's study, for example, supported either complete withdrawal or the bombing of China in the Korean War; nonauthoritarians favored a negotiated settlement. Such correlates of authoritarianism as ethnocentrism and dogmatism are also related to warmindedness. In Crown's investigation toughmindedness and Antisemitism are positively correlated. The relationship persists when education is held constant in Farris' survey and even after the United States entered World War II in the study by Stagner published in 1944.

Status concern and neuroticism are commonly found among persons disposed to favor warlike politics. Blau, however, notes that strivers who do not attain A grades in college are more likely to be power-oriented than those with high grade point averages, for the latter do not need an ideology rendering a gap between achievement and aspiration less dissonant. Kuroda, similarly, finds that high scorers on Machiavellism scale questions are more warminded. Stagner's 1944 study reports a tendency among persons approving of force as a general policy to be highly supportive of war, both in peacetime and wartime.

Political cynicism evidently differs from a more generalized cynical view of life, for Kuroda finds that in Japan the former is related to peace, while McClosky and Laulicht link the latter with jingoism. Anomie and alienation, which according to Marx are concomitants of capitalism, are highly related to preferences for war.

Optimism and high personal morale characterize persons opposing war, though Stagner computes low correlations that disagree in sign in his 1944 publication. Persons sociable in Japan oppose war, according to Kuroda; a high value on social skills correlates positively with coexistence and pacifist views in Scott's 1960 study.

McClosky, Scott, and Stagner present much more detailed findings on personality correlates but fail to replicate each other. McClosky, for example, finds that persons with high need inviolacy, hostility, obsessiveness, paranoid tendencies, and intolerance of ambiguity endorse defense preparations more than foreign aid. Scott in 1960 reports that pacifist and coexistence policies are supported by persons valuing self-control, kindness, and interpersonal loyalty. Stagner attempts to develop a theory that war advocacy is related to the psychological mechanism of sublimation in his 1944 study, pointing out that those favoring war enjoy strenuous games, prefer to have others subordinate, enjoy public speaking, but neither express annoyance openly nor relish the sight of blood. Stagner notes that displacement may also play a role: subjects preferring their mothers to their fathers or liking both equally are much less warlike than those identifying with their fathers or rejecting their parents. Students recalling their childhood as satisfying are more likely to be warminded than children feeling dissatisfied with their upbringing. Similarly, Scott (1960) reports that those British who favored the bombing of Germany in the early days of World War II tended to blame the German people for the war, not just German political leaders. Opponents of an American invasion of Cuba saw the United States as partly responsible for poor U.S.-Cuba relations, perceived that Cubans preferred Castro to Batista, and thought that the United Nations had been assisting in the improvement of such relations, according to Ekman and associates.

Students reporting the least satisfactory relationships with parents, however, are active radicals; liberal students reported some disatisfaction as well, but subjects with better family morale tended to be more conservative in Stagner's study of Dartmouth men. It might, therefore, seem appropriate to study *political orientations* directly as indicative of the propensity to favor warlike foreign policy options. Political-economic conservatism, for example, is definitely related to warmindedness, whether expressed as a general ideology or transmuted into a superpatriotic nationalism.

The relationship between political party preferences and advocacy of war is less clear, however, and seems to be a function of which party is in power at the time a policy position relevant to war and peace is being evaluated. Democrats favored war in Jones' survey just prior to American entry into World War II, and Republicans are more warminded in two studies, conducted when the international environment was less threatening, by Droba and Ekman and associates. But the prevailing finding, that political party identification is unrelated to preferences for war as opposed to peace, is decomposed when actual votes or political activity are taken into account. Goldwater voters, for example, favor escalation in Vietnam much more in the investigation by Verba and associates than Johnson voters.

Political participation is generally high among peace-conscious individuals, both in the Japanese community study by Kuroda and among university and college faculty surveyed by Armor and his coauthors and in the Schuman-Laumann questionnaire. In Verba's team investigation, however, no correlation is found between pro- or antiescalatory policies concerning Vietnam and the frequency of letter writing to Congressmen (or others) in order to express such views.

Extent of general political interest and level of political information are not consistently related to peacemindedness. Persons for whom war and peace issues are most salient, are for deescalation in the study by Verba and associates and are peaceminded in Kuroda's sample, but those who think a great deal about the possibility of war regard war as more acceptable in the Putney and Middleton student survey. According to Verba and associates the relation between information and peacemindedness washes out when race and sex are held constant, which might account for the split on war policy among Canadians polled by Laulicht as well as college and university teachers in Armor's team investigation. More intense newspaper reading characterizes Japanese pacifists interviewed by Kuroda, but Putney and Middleton discover that students well informed on the technology of nuclear weapons have no particular revulsion toward their use.

The correlation between warmindedness and knowledge of the destructiveness of war may be a function of high versus low expectations of war. Kuroda and Putney and Middleton report that those who anticipate war within a decade are inclined to accept what they feel is inevitable; those who regard peace as possible are in favor of policies of coexistence, deescalation, or pacifism. However, Deutsch and Merritt report that, in the Cuban missiles crisis, interviewees anticipating full-scale war with the USSR in response to a possible United States invasion were least in favor of such an interventionist stand. An expectation that an individual will survive nuclear war or that his country will win in a conventional war is clearly related to war advocacy in studies by Ekman and associates, Putney and Middleton, and Scott (1965). Military supporters were quite willing to pay the costs of escalation in Verba's Stanford poll and prepared to enlist in the army in Stagner's 1942 study.

Among findings concerning the interrelationships between specific attitudes on political issue-areas, McClosky finds that scores on his isolationist scale correlate only $+.46$ with scores on a jingoism scale. We may therefore assume that the isolationist-internationalist and hawk-dove dimensions of foreign policy opinion are empirically quite separable, since this means that only 21 per cènt of the variance ($.46 \times .46 = .21$) in one scale is predicted by the other. Duffy and Stagner (1944) report an equally moderate correlation between warmindedness and support for capital punishment. Peacemindedness is related to desires for world cultural development, support for a world peace conference, and humanitarianism, according to Scott (1960). Ekman and associates find that warmindedness seems to entail a preference for federal funds to build fallout shelters, but no willingness to encourage efforts at disarmament.

Decision-Making Approach—Two major research strategies are employed in analyzing interpersonal factors that dispose decision-makers to choose violent rather than nonviolent alternatives. *Experimental* methods are used by some scholars so that initial inputs can be controlled, observational data collected accurately, and replication can be made more possible. In simulated experimental settings, foreign affairs problems are given to experimental subjects, so we will report the results from these studies as more pertinent than abstract games. *Case studies* are a second source of hypotheses, having been undertaken comparatively by a number of students of historically documented decisions.

There are about eight relevant *simulation* studies. Richard Brody and Michael Driver start with an initial bipolar international system in the Northwestern Inter-Nation Simulation, with the country heading each of the two blocs in possession of thermonuclear weapons, and they study consequences of the spread of nuclear weapons to other countries.[8] Marc Pilisuk and associates conduct both abstract and simulated games dealing with armament-disarmament decision options.[9] Wayman Crown and John Raser determine the effects of the presence of one country in an international system with the capacity to delay responses.[10] Roger Sisson and Russell Ackoff find conditions that may predict the occurrence of military escalation and deescalation.[11] Otomar Bartos correlates variables accounting for concession making in bargaining at simulated international conferences.[12] And Kenneth Terhune, finally, employs the Princeton Internation Game to trace the impact of motivational variables on conflictual and cooperative decisions.[13] All of the findings to be codified below are based on comparisons among a series of simulation runs.

Bartos' study, conducted at the University of Hawaii, is the only one to treat *social background characteristics*. In one half of the experiments the subjects are informed in advance concerning hawkish or dovish characteristics of their opponents, under the code words "tough" and "soft," and in the other half the subjects were not so informed. In all conditions hawks are younger in age, and hawkish behavior most often appears when a subject's opponent is female or younger than himself. Subjects uninformed of the type of opponets faced were hawkish when non-Caucasian and when facing Caucasian opponents; subjects told about their opponents were hawkish if Caucasians or playing against non-Caucasians. This curious ethnic difference, that Caucasians are more hawkish only when cued that toughness-softness might be present within the experimental setting, suggests that Caucasians are hawkish only when self-conscious about toughness, but that Orientals are inclined to be less hawkish only when they are alerted that their opponents might be either tough or soft. Similarly, Crow and Raser find that Mexican subjects are less inclined to go to war than Americans, and they attribute the difference to the tendency for Mexicans to be more passive than Americans.

Personality characteristics are handled by several investigators. Comparing hawks, doves, and mugwumps on five scales, Pilisuk and associates find no strong relation between any of the personality characteristics and levels of cooperative behavior. Hawks score somewhat higher than doves on self-acceptance, internationalism, and on monetary and social risk preferences; doves have a higher tolerance for ambiguity; but mugwumps exhibit no consistent pattern. Bartos uses the California Personality Inventory to determine degrees of adjustment, discovering that well-adjusted subjects are hawks when told that their opponents are either doves or hawks, especially if the opponents are poorly adjusted, whereas well adjusted subjects in experiments without such information are doves. Bartos also finds that once a subject starts to play a tough role, he continues to do so, particularly if the opponent has previously displayed weakness in an experiment where subjects have not been informed of the toughness or weakness of one another. Terhune classifies subjects with high needs for achievement, power, or for affiliation. Those with needs for affiliation value cooperativeness for its own sake; other subjects see cooperation as a means toward more desired ends. Nevertheless, subjects with high needs for achievement initiate more cooperative than conflictual acts and have lower military efforts; high needs for power entails more initiation of conflictual acts and military efforts; an equal number of conflictual and cooperative acts are initiated by subjects having high needs for affiliation, and their over-all military efforts are midway between the two other groups. Driver demonstrates a positive relation between authoritarianism and the tendency for aggression, but the frequency of wars and number of unprovoked arms increases are unrelated to authoritarianism. Ideologism was positively related to wars among major powers but unrelated to the seriousness of aggression and to unprovoked armaments buildups. Liberalism-conservatism was unrelated to all measures of hawkness-doveness.

Driver also introduces variables concerning *cognitive and informational aspects* of the decision-making task. War was associated with indicators of perceptual complexity, cognitive simplicity (conceiving of concrete matters rather than abstract elements), and high levels of tension, the latter a composite of low trust, low communications and high hostility. Unprovoked arms increases and serious (as opposed to minor) acts of aggression were positively related to cognitive simplicity. Sisson and Ackoff, similarly, report that cooperativeness and deescalation are likely to increase when communication among participants is frequent and open. Pilisuk and Rapoport compare results from a short and a long disarmament game, the former an experiment in which there is feedback on each move of the game, the latter situation referring to a game wherein feedback is withheld until the final move. The propensity to cooperate is higher in the longer game, in contrast with the Sisson-Ackoff finding on openness of communication. Varying the disarmament game so that subjects can play both games, in either the long-short or short-long order, Pilisuk and Rapoport encounter hawks more often in the short-long combination, which evidently socializes players to a move-countermove scenario wherein subjects are tempted to behave noncooperatively.

Systematic data concerning *historical decisions* has been unusually skimpy, in contradistinction to the simulation approach. The reason for the handful of studies employing this latter approach seems to be that the necessary time and energy required are out of proportion to the research payoff or to the methodological skills of those interested in exhaustively mining historical situations. Lloyd Jensen has collected data on Soviet-American disarmament negotiations between the years 1947 and 1963.[14] Glenn Paige compares the American decision in 1950 to enter the Korean War with American decision making in the Cuban missiles crisis of 1962.[15] Robert North, Ole Holsti, and associates at Stanford University compare the same 1962 decision with decision making in 1914 on the part of the Triple Entente and Dual Alliance powers.[16] Bruce Russett derives hypotheses from a number of cases of successful and unsuccessful deterrence, notably 1914 and the Pearl Harbor decision of 1941.[17] Quincy Wright reviews 45 international conflicts between 1921 and 1965 to ascertain why some escalate and others fail to do so.[18]

Message flow and other *informational* variables are treated by North and Holsti, and also by Paige. The Stanford group reports that aggressors tend to experience message overload much earlier than decision makers who must eventually respond to an aggressor. Fewer messages are sent to future adversaries than to future allies; the aggressor closes off communication channels first. Direct communication between the heads of state increases as war seems increasingly imminent. The principal targets of hostile messages sent by decision-makers who embark upon war are members of the opposing bloc, rather than alliance partners. Aggressors, thus, articulate in an inflammatory manner while seeking to obtain support from close allies. Within the decision-making body itself, Paige finds that the American decision on Cuba (nonwar) differed from the Korean (war) decision insofar as the former was characterized by more discussion and even contention over alternatives; consultation with experts and allies was more extensive; more accurate, comprehensive, and documentary information was available; the adversary was better informed on possible contigencies; more information was kept secret from the public, from the early Soviet forewarnings in 1962 (which had been absent in 1950) to the conclusion of the decision-making situation.

The variables examined in the case studies differ significantly in scope from the simulation approach. Social, personality and political background characteristics of the decision-makers are not covered at all. Instead, the perceptual, cognitive, informational and international aspects are analyzed.

North and Holsti focus largely on *perceptions,* and most of their findings have been replicated in the Brody-Driver simulation. Perceptions of hostility, for example, show a considerable rise in frequency and in intensity among decision-makers prior to military moves and especially within states initiating war. Aggressive decision-makers decode events as implying consequences harmful or antagonistic to their own state's interests. Perceptions of hostility exceed perceptions of capability, suggesting that the main concern within decision-makers initiating war is in pinpointing friends and enemies rather than making calculations concerning the relative power that the contending forces will muster on the battlefield. Aggressors, moreover, are likely to overperceive the actions of their adversaries, erroneously regarding their level of violence as high and provocative, whereupon the aggressor will overrespond by escalating its response toward higher levels of violence.

As aggressive decision-makers perceive that other states are behaving in a distressing or hostile manner, they tend to use language containing a hostile tone. The preoccupation with threats is associated with a mood in which verbal behavior departs from elegance and refinement and instead describes the situation as a stereotypic black-and-white contest between the forces of good and evil. Accordingly, aggressive decision-makers increasingly perceive that their states are rejected by others before war. If one state seems particularly menacing, hostility is generalized or projected onto many other states, and a feeling of persecution develops. As war approaches, aggressive decision-makers believe that their own states have fewer policy alternatives than do their adversaries, and that the alternatives of the latter expand. Perceiving fewer ways of handling the crisis, the most primitive method of dealing with the other country seems attractive. The possible magnitude of the war is deemed more important by decision-makers who eventually avoid war than by those who opt for war. Attention to the extent of destruction that would result from a possible war is diverted to a moralistic concern with how much the adversary's misdeeds need to be redressed. Although time is perceived of greater importance by the aggressor than the target of aggression, a decision-maker in a country initiating aggression will be more concerned with the immediate present than with the long-range trends and consequences of his actions. Decision-makers staying out of war perceive actions of their opponents in a neutral, rather than a hostile, manner. Rational discussion of goals decreases among decision-makers going to war. If a leader perceives that other states constitute potential threats, he will respond by making even more menacing counterthreats. Statements of aggressive decision-makers lack logical linkage and tend to express an affective mood, notably hostility and unfriendliness. Bloc membership results in an inflated estimate of the degree of threat and unfriendliness on the part of decision-makers in opposing blocs. Leaders of neutral countries are unlikely to be drawn into the spiraling of misperceptions and fears of malevolent plots.

The decision to go to war or to avoid war involves the cognitive task of weighing utilities and disutilities of various goals vis-à-vis probabilities that certain events will occur. A longer decision time is recommended by Russett in order to facilitate some experimentation with techniques for resolving disputes short of war. According to Paige, the Cuba decision was deliberated over a longer period of time than the Korea decision, which may account for a number of further peculiarities: the organizational roles were more heterogeneous and the organizational structure more informal; an elaborate set of contingency plans was developed for many possible Soviet moves; the Cuba decision was regarded as without precedent, whereas in the Korea case decision-makers relied on Munich as a source of intellectual capital on which to draw in making a response that would profit from socalled lessons of history. Despite the apparent overdramatic equation of Korea in 1950 with Munich in 1938, the former situation was much less in the forefront of debate than was Cuba in 1962; vital interests were believed to be much more affected while war was avoided in 1962, though Wright argues that escalation is more likely when both sides consider vital interests at stake in a dispute. Initially, however, the duplicity of Soviet actions leading up to the supplying of missiles to Cuba was related to an early preference in Washington for military reprisals; in 1950 no such duplicity was present, and diplomatic efforts were advocated at first. Evidently in the intervening twelve years American decision-makers were more aware of the principle that the most severe among various alternatives being considered should be presented immediately in order to prevent misunderstanding by the adversary on how the situation might eventually be resolved if not tempered. Despite the existence of prior military plans for coping with Cuba, which had been lacking in the Korean case, a peaceful outcome resulted as the values thought to be threatened and symbols used to legitimize American actions shifted to a more concrete level; many decision-makers changed their original positions and others who disagreed found themselves withdrawing from the discussions. In 1950 President Truman revealed more intolerance of ambiguity, legitimating values remained constant, original positions hardened, and when diplomatic methods appeared to be failing war was declared. Russett's analysis indicates that deterrence fails to operate: (a) when the utility of war greatly exceeds the utility of peace; (b) when the opponent is vulnerable to an attack; even though (c) the subjective probability of ultimate victory might be slim. Yet in 1962 American decision-makers were aware of a risk of much stronger counteraction by the Soviet Union than would have been the case in 1950 following entry of the United States into war, and Wright claims that escalation will be avoided if too costly for the aggressor.

III. Societal Factors

Types of political and economic systems and various kinds of social characteristics of nation states have been postulated as factors disposing some states to enter more wars than others. *Classical* theorists, especially Plato, regarded democracies as far too warlike; countries with moderate amounts of wealth and considerable internal cohesion were observed to have avoided war successfully. *Enlightenment* thinkers, such as Kant, Bentham, and Paine, urged democracy as an antidote to the hypertrophy of dynastic war, while *capitalistic* spokesmen launched economies on the road to higher levels of economic development with the expectation that greater wealth and fewer governmental restrictions would bring peace. *Utopian socialists* rejected mass society, preferring the peace of small self-contained communities built around light industries wherein citizens would not need elites to govern themselves. *Marxist* theory looked toward the eventual abolition of wars by abolishing states, national and class identifications while retaining an industrial society, yet linked together in a vast communication network with self-government at the local level. *Leninists,* however, observed capitalists engaging in imperial struggles as the viability of capitalism was declining, and sparked militants to seize power so that the working class, having no interest in war, would be able to rebuild society along more humane lines.

In contrast with the clarion appeals to end war by restructuring the nature of political, social, and economic systems, there is little support for any of the above theories, either pro or con. In correlating variables indicating warlike behavior of states with some 200 societal characteristics, very few of the correlation coefficients have exceeded the level of +.40. Nevertheless, the higher and more statistically significant findings do reveal a pattern.[19]

Nondiplomatic, but nonviolent *foreign conflict* is highly related to resort to international aggression. The use of military mobilizations, troop movements, high levels of military expenditures per GNP, threats, and severances of diplomatic relations are most closely associated with such indicators as numbers of wars, persons killed in wars, and violent military actions short of full fledged wars.

Participation in foreign affairs per se seems to make a country more likely to become involved in war. Bloc prominence, for example, is associated with all types of foreign violence. High levels in receiving *or* contributing to foreign aid also are correlated with warlike behavior. Countries with many representatives at the United Nations find themselves involved in wars most frequently.

Types of political systems have been linked by Jonathan Wilkenfeld to foreign violence. Centrist or totalitarian countries engage in war following revolutionary disturbances. Democratic countries have internal turmoil and subversion before, during, and after wars. Authoritarian or personalist countries tend to have internal subversion a year or two after entering foreign wars.

Although nearly all types of *domestic violent conflict* behavior are positively related to high levels of national aggression, few of the correlations are above the +.40 level. An exception is rioting, however, which is related to foreign violence to a much greater degree. Political apathy at home seems to guarantee international tranquility for a state.

Economic underdevelopment indicators are more in line with Plato's recommendation for a spartan economy. Aggressiveness is lower among countries with higher increments in per capita electricity production and with more economic equality. High unemployment makes for more aggressiveness, and high density in the use of railroads (rail freight/rail length) is associated with a lower incidence of war.

Social unrest manifests itself in three main causes of death: suicides, homicides, and alcoholism. Using time-lagged longitudinal correlations, Michael Haas discovers that countries with high rates of suicides and fatal alcoholism are much more likely to be participants in arms races. Countries with rising rates of homicides, on the conrary, decrease their financing of military efforts.

The *heterogeneity* in composition of a population is consistently associated with the frequency of wars, military actions, and foreign conflict casualties. Countries with many different ethnic groups, language communities, nationality groups, religious, and racial groups enter wars more often than homogeneous polities.

There are some negative findings at the societal level as well. Violent foreign conflict is not related to the side that countries take in the East-West cold war, as reflected in their United Nations voting. Migration and receipt of much foreign mail, foreign trade, many foreign visitors and students are not related to the incidence of war. Geographic proximity to the United States, rather than to the Soviet Union, is also unrelated to a country's resort to violent means for settling disputes.

IV. Systemic Factors

The structure of groups of countries which together constitute international systems and subsystems has been suggested as the root cause of warfare by two types of theorists. *Unipolar* theorists, from Augustine to Dante, believed that the best guarantee of peace would be an all-powerful single state based upon a single common culture shared by all peoples in the same system. *Multistate* theorists living in post-reformation Europe argued that a loose arrangement of many states, no one of which would assume hegemony, might bring war from time to time but would be the most likely to preserve an equilibrium in the long run. Whether articulated by Hobbes, Grotius, de Sully, Kant, Rousseau, or Hume, the preference for multipolarity was based upon the apotheosis of individualism.

Two analytical approaches to systemic influences on war and peace have appeared. The *community* approach focuses on factors accounting for harmonized goal seeking and the success of permanent supranational structural arrangements between states. *The stratification* approach looks upon war as a concomitant of types of power distributions and alliance configurations.

Community Approach—Karl Deutsch, Amitai Etzioni, and Ernst Haas are the main researchers of community building at the international level. Deutsch was rapporteur for a team investigation of successes and failures at pluralistic and amalgamated security communities in the North Atlantic area.[20] Etzioni compares the success of the European "Common Market" and the Nordic Council with the failures of the West Indies Federation and United Arab Republic.[21] Haas comments on the European Coal and Steel Community as well as on the Common Market.[22] Deutsch comments that either the pluralistic or amalgamated paths may lead to a decline in the use of military means to resolve disputes among constituent parts of an integrated subsystem. He states that most cases of successful amalgamation have occurred in the premodern era. Etzioni, on the other hand, asserts that conditions are ripest in modern times for the formation of transnational structures, inasmuch as a higher level of political and administrative skill is attainable through modern education and social scientific research; a mass-based loyalty to an integrative structure is only possible where literacy and educational levels permit the spread of information about such integrating structures, and more international business is transacted by the most developed political and economic systems. Data assembled by Deutsch, however, clearly reveal that developed countries have a high volume of traffic with other countries but proportionately fewer international preoccupations, since internal transactions skyrocket in later stages of economic and political development. According to Deutsch, the pluralistic form of integration seems to be a more feasible choice wherever domestic problems begin to overload administrative capabilities of national governments. Moreover, Bruce Russett has found that civil violence within states is historically more prevalent than interstate warfare,[23] an observation consistent with the preference for pluralistic integration as a pathway to peace. Parts of existing states with only a rudimentary sense of community can settle disputes most parsimoniously by secession. Differences between members of highly integrated structures often seem to be most effectively resolvable through the application of coercive measures, such as through revolution or by attempting mass arrests of dissenters.

Consonance in major values seems to be the most essential precondition to integration. The politically relevant strata of successfully integrated polities would be unable to agree upon specific goals and means without a high level of cultural compatibility. An understanding to depoliticize questions on which the units will continue to differ is a corollary. Beyond the mere verbal attachment to a similar intellectual position, a "we-feeling" seems to be necessary in order to assure a mutual perception of needs and responsiveness in political decision-making, as local foci for loyalties gradually come into competition with a higher level structure. The tendency for peoples of an integrated framework to perceive potential war as almost unthinkably fratricidal is perhaps a special case of this development of a cultural distinctiveness. Indeed the data of L. F. Richardson demonstrate that former alliance partnership reduces the likelihood of war between countries, though the effect wears off in time.[24]

Political amalgamation requires leadership by partcular elite units, who are located in a "core area." The elites generally possess a more advanced political system. If political and administrative economic capabilities are steadily rising within the core, each nonelite unit is assured that the capacity to act decisively is present. An alternation in majority and minority roles by units of the integrated structure seems to assist in overcoming localism and the solidification of strong or privileged positions, which may resist the course of social change. A recent broadening of the strata from which the political or social elites emerge enables the integration effort to appear mass-based, thereby attracting support from all strata. Extension of suffrage after unification can be a disintegrative factor, for previously politically passive strata might well see that their self-interest is promoted by secession, and closure in the established political elite might encourage the rise of revolutionary counterelites. If other conditions favorable to integration are present, an outside military threat may serve to trigger structural mergers between countries, but pragmatic prewar alliances are notoriously shortlived once the threat has passed.

Politically relevant strata must perceive that integration will lead to increased economic gain or to an expansion in political and social rights and liberties. Economic stagnation or excessive military burdens, contrariwise, may suggest the utility of secession by the most secure units. A delay in the granting of political reforms may provide time for a revolutionary spirit to rise. If there is superior economic development on the part of the core units, an expectation of economic gain is enhanced, provided that each unit is able to cash in on the benefits of integration. Previous strong economic linkages between members of an integrating subsystem are indicative of success in future efforts to achieve international cooperation, but if other essential conditions are present such a prior experience is not an indispensible element in integration.

To insure that integration is felt evenly across a subsystem there should be unbroken horizontal and vertical communication networks, that is, both geographically between territories and socially between the political relevant strata of each country. Increasing linguistic or ethnic diversity may result in barriers to communication that will militate toward a schism in political attitudes. Channels of communication must not only be open but also used frequently, an observation that negates Rousseau's disdain for international communications. A high volume of mail, cultural, and educational exchange, scientific integration, trade, intermarriage, and tourism is essential for political amalgamation.

In a critique of the North Atlantic study, Ernst Haas points out that the findings should be qualified, inasmuch as nearly all of the cases under analysis antedate nuclear weapons systems, cold war bipolarity, the industrial revolution, mass democracy, mass society, and totalitarianism. The six conditions bound entirely different eras, he feels. Haas then proceeds to check Deutsch's conclusions by referring to the period just prior to the establishment of the European Coal and Steel Community in 1950. While in the ECSC case there was a consonance in the goal to form a supranational economic institution (pluralistic integration), not much mutual responsiveness actually existed among the Europeans supporting integration. Compatibility of values was present but not mutual responsiveness, which flatly contradicts Deutsch's assertion of the necessity of both conditions for pluralistic integration. Despite the use of Pan-European symbols, no new way of life was emerging in any form; indeed, decision makers in the six countries seem to have entered ECSC in order to preserve an old way of life—a strong Europe of proud national states.

Most of the remaining conditions are able to stand up under the Coal Steel Community case. A core area was distinctly present: France formed the bulwark of momentum for the Community, and French economic progress was just beginning to accelerate. Some broadening of the elite strata occurred, for many postwar European states extended the suffrage to women, and trade union leaders were at last assuming positions of political power. In 1950 the cold war was undergoing a blizzard, with the Soviet Union as a powerful military adversary goading the North Koreans and Communist Chinese to battle. Consistent with one of Haas' six boundary conditions, the industrial revolution brought a wide range of economic ties among the six members of the European Coal and Steel Community. Partly as a result of the use of Marshall Plan funds, Europe was soaring in political, administrative, and economic capabilities, with the prospect that economic integration would strengthen its position vis-à-vis both the Soviet Union and the United States.

Wide social communication patterns, on the other hand, were not established until after the Schuman Plan assumed an institutional form, with its elaborate framework for transnational participation; a higher mobility of persons and wider ranges of transactions followed the formation of the Coal and Steel Community, rather than being antecedent conditions. The presence of these conditions to a higher degree after 1950 no doubt explains in part the early establishment of the far-reaching European Economic Community in 1958. Ethnic and linguistic assimilation is a long way off. Nevertheless, had the four communication factors been entirely absent, Deutsch's hypotheses would not be challenged by the ECSC case.

The major import of the ECSC case, in short, is to demote the variable mutual responsiveness to the level of a nonessential though helpful factor in pluralistic integration. The existence of a common intergovernmental framework within ECSC greatly assisted in bringing many conditions to higher levels through a spillover process. As one substantive issue opened up for cooperation, ramifications flowed into other problems areas, and ECSC's effects were felt by increasing numbers of groups and persons throughout Europe. The fulfillment of most of Deutsch's predictions in the case of the European Common Market in 1958 was possible only because of steps taken by the Coal and Steel Community in steering its own course despite an initial lesser fulfillment of Deutsch's background condition.

Etzioni echoes Deutsch's hypothesis that the most significant harbinger of integration is a common positive ideology, rather than merely an anti-ideology. Charisma is of dubious value. Especially when integration is already in existence, adequate representation of constituent units is a precondition for responsiveness by elites operating the common structures to fulfill needs and demands of all the members.

In treating the concept of "core area," Etzioni suggests many useful refinements. Three types of elites are delineated. *Member elites* are units with the majority of coercive power qua actors in world politics; *system elites* are persons or units administering transnational integrated structures; *external elites* consist of any actors giving impetus to integration without actually joining the resulting structure. Success is assured more fully when external elites apply power in accordance with the member-elite constellation, rather than trying to break down the power of member elites in order to vest power in system elites. Nevertheless, successful integration is always associated with the rise of system elites, and the decline in coercive influence of member elites. When an external elite finally departs from the scene, the timing should coincide with a transfer in power from system elites to member elites that is accepted fully by all relevant parties. Political unions are more successful and accelerate faster as the system elite grows in strength relative to member-elite and external-elite countries. Etzioni also distinguishes between the number of elite units. Contrary to Deutsch, he finds that the absence of a dominant elite element, can be just as successful as monoelite integration. If two elites are in coalition, the effect is similar to monoelite unification, but otherwise unions with fewer elites have endured longer than those with more. Egalitarian unions generate higher commitments than unions with elites, although a core area insures more decisiveness. The use of coercive assets often serves to prolong unification. A weak union may decay from lack of enforcement of norms, making the structure seem to be purely a formalistic anachronism. Too much exercise of naked power, however, will also jeopardize success, so the application of force should be within some optimal range.

Utilitarian aspects of unification are deemed somewhat less crucial for Etzioni. The elite unit usually gains nonmonetarily through greater international prestige, for it must be prepared to invest utilitarian resources in order to assume a leadership role. The promise of economic gain is most salient for nonelite units, and there should not be grossly uneven economic rewards among the various units or the enterprise will be abandoned. Definite utilitarian gains should be registered before reallocations are contemplated.

Although Etzioni credits effective communication patterns with some of the eventual success of unions, he tends to relegate communication variables to a more peripheral role. Cultural similarity is believed to be helpful but certainly does not make integration inevitable. Effective upward and downward communication channels are judged to be success-breeding. Formal and informal horizontal communication among the various units is helpful but cannot carry as much information as integrated structures with their own decision-making centers; spillover potential is highest when hierarchy exists in a structure. Similarly, identity in language and religion between a pair of states has a low correlation with the frequency of international aggression between the pair, according to Richardson's data.

In sum, Etzioni suggests the possibility of egalitarian integration, and the necessity for occasional applications of force vis-à-vis dissenting units of persons. The existence of a core area becomes only a helpful, rather than an essential, condition for political amalgamation, whereas rising capabilities of system elites are hypothesized to be essential for increases in scope. The discussion on egalitarian, monoelite, and bipolar leadership ties into much of the current debate among advocates of the stratification approach, as descussed below.

Stratification Approach—The most systematic efforts to relate power structure in international systems with the extent of international violence have been undertaken by Richard Rosecrance, J. David Singer and Melvin Small, and Michael Haas.[25]

Guided by some elementary notions of general systems theory, Rosecrance establishes time boundaries for nine historical "international systems" between 1740 and 1960, each defined in terms of power stratification. After delineating a number of qualitative categories for describing an international system, he supplies codings for each of the nine systems. In a manner similar to the community theorists, Rosecrance conducts a necessary and sufficient condition analysis of preconditions to "stability," which he defines as the ability of a regulator to cope with disturbances threatening to undermine an existing power distribution. With respect to power distribution, the lone unipolar system in his sample is fairly stable, but multipolarity is clearly more stable than bipolarity. Considering "resources" either as areas ripe for colonial and imperial expansion or as new states that may be targets for ideological or political proselytization, Rosecrance's codings reveal that the availability of unappropriated resources makes for stability; scarcity, for instability. The existence in a system of contending or nonstatus quo ideologies means that conflict will be intense, but a divergency in elites' ethos is neither a necessary nor a sufficient condition for instability, thus confirming the suspicions of many scholars concerning the insignificance of ideological aspects of the contemporary bipolar world. Insecurity of elites' tenure at home is always associated with instability abroad. But in contrast with the community theorists the drawing of boundaries such that allegiances are now more nationalist than dynastic has not resulted in a more benign international arena; in fact, unstable systems have been encountered more frequently since the rise of nationalism and the use of citizen forces. Increasing world levels in economic development, as Organski has hypothesized, are more useful for disturbers than in buttressing the power of regulators of international systems. And no single regulator, whether balance of power, concert of great powers, alliance system, or international organization, has been able to maintain stability in all of the cases. The record of the concert of Europe is better, but the breakdowns of 1848 and 1914 were too extraordinary for an informal practice of summit conferences to avert or to resolve; whenever the disturbance level is high, regulators have been inadequate.

Singer and Small pay closer attention to alliance configuration patterns. Starting with the hypothesis that the onset of war is associated with an increase in alliance commitments between countries, they assemble an impressive array of data on wars and alliances in order to test balance-of-power theory empirically. For the year between 1815 and 1945 they collect statistical indicators for each member of the family of nations. Singer and Small slice international systems in a manner somewhat similar to Rosecrance, for they analyze four subsamples of international systems—a "central system" composed mostly of European countries for two eras, 1815–1899 and 1900–1945, and a "total system" of central and peripheral countries for the same two eras. Although intercorrelations between the independent and dependent variables are mostly positive when data are aggregated across all years for the total and central systems, when results for the nineteenth century are compared with twentieth-century findings, the two eras exhibit opposite patterns. For the 1900–1945 period most correlations are positive, demonstrating that wars have been preceded by the formation of many alliances; between 1815 and 1899, in contrast, correlations are moderately negative, revealing that alliance involvement must have served as a deterrent to the expression of international conflict by military means.

Michael Haas, carving out 21 international subsystems in Europe, Aisa, and Hawaii, intercorrelates 68 variables, half of which pertain to international stratification, and the other half of which index international violence. Among the 21 subsystems, unipolar power distributions are the most peaceful; most members of these systems prefer to engage in war outside their home region, if at all. Bipolarity is associated consistently with longer wars, and countries seeking to upset an existing distribution of resources are most successful in bipolar systems. Major powers in bipolar systems must be content to accept infrequent, localized yet prolonged conflicts during cold wars in which there is nibbling at the few ambiguous peripheries of superbloc domains. Tripolarity and bipolarity contain the highest rates in incidence of war, and most countries in such systems dispatch troops to battlefields.

V. Conclusion

In our quest to determine sources of international violence at various levels of analysis, three scenarios emerge. The prototypic dove decision-maker is seen as a middle-aged Jewish Negress who has received a college education to attain the status of a physician or college professor, who resides outside a big city but not too far from the nation's capital; she is non-authoritarian, nonethnocentric, flexible, achievement-oriented, uncynical, nonalienated, optimistic, and an intellectual with much tolerance of ambiguity; her political views are neither conservative nor nationalist; she participates politically, does not anticipate war, does not expect her country to survive or be victorious in war, and takes few risks. Her decisions are peaceful when the information inputs are neither perceptually complex nor cognitively simple, and made when mutual trust, friendliness, and communications are maintained at high levels (though short of communications overload). Peace is more likely to emerge if the prototypic decision-maker is in possession of accurate information, adivsers are in disagreement over alternatives, while stereotypic decoding of inputs and provocative encoding of outputs is absent; there is concern for long-range implications and longer time for making a decision and drawing up contigency plans.

In scenario two we observe that the most peaceful states are minor powers, which seldom participate in foreign affairs; which engage only in foreign conflict that is diplomatic; which have little domestic violence and are economically underdeveloped. Countries with homogeneous populations, and with more homicides than either suicides or alcoholics, are less often on the battlefield.

Unipolar and bipolar international arenas are more peaceful than those with tripolarity and multipolarity. States are more likely to settle their differences peacefully if they share compatibility in main values, a distinctive way of life, mutual responsiveness, a joint core area with rising capabilities, expect economic growth, have an unbroken social communication network with a wide range of transactions.

Research on international conflict, as the above inventory of findings suggests, has focused largely on interpersonal factors. But even at this level of analysis (scenario one) there are occasional ambiguities and contradictory findings, since each study employs a different sample, data point, and defines its relevant variables in the absence of an over-all integrative theory. If results of research at the societal and systemic levels (scenarios two and three) lack breadth, it is largely because scholars have turned to these latter two foci only in very recent years, though they have been guided by meta-theoretical concerns, such as communication, field, and equilibrium theories, and have employed multivariate research strategies to great advantage.

The next step in research on international conflict might well be that of allowing an accumulation of individual studies to appear and, several years hence, of attempting another delineation of findings. This will doubtless be the stance of the consumer of conflict research, but those undertaking current reviews of the literature see a manyfold task ahead. One of the main problems is that of conceptual integration. Within each of the three levels of analysis and scenarios each investigator has felt free to define his concepts and variables without adequte reference to prior re-search or the theoretical import of the study for a macrotheory of inter-national conflict. But, perhaps more importantly from the standpoint of achieving unity in the scientific enterprise, we lack multilanguage dic-tionaries that enable us to translate the concepts of one theoretical lan-guage into those of another. As a result the assumption that the interpersonal, societal, and systemic levels of analysis are separable empirically remains untestable: if we had either a broad metaconceptual language (à la Esperanto) or a set of dictionaries that translated communication theory jargon into field theory jargon, across various levels of analysis, we could move more in the direction of theoretical integration of empirical findings.

A second problem is to develop parsimonious causal models from the mass of empirical correlations which are likely to grow exponentially in the years ahead. Such techniques as causal modeling and computer simu-lation are currently under development to handle this task.

The conceptual and empirical problems of international conflict re-search are, of course, similar to those within many other areas of international politics. So long as theory and research is conducted in tandem, the current lack of pyramided knowledge of international conflict—its origins, processes, and consequences—will be short in duration. By focusing directly on a distillation of current research findings this essay aims to telescope the problem of locating linkages and agendas for more integrative research in the years ahead.

Notes and References

[1] This paper is based upon Michael Haas, *International Conflict* (Indianapolis: Bobbs-Merrill, in press.

[2] Kurt W. Back and Kenneth J. Gergen, "Apocalyptic and Serial Time Orientations and the Structure of Opinions," *Public Opinion Quarterly*, Vol. XXVII (Fall 1963), pp. 427–42; Davis B. Bobrow and Neal E. Cutler, "Time-Oriented Explanations of National Security Beliefs: Cohort, Life-stage and Situation," *Peace Research Society, Papers*, Vol. VIII (1967), pp. 31–58; Bobrow and Allen R. Wilcos, "Dimensions of Defense Opinion in the American Public," *ibid.*, Vol. VI (1966), pp. 101–142. Morris Davis and Sidney Verba, "Party Affiliation and International Opinions in Britain and France, 1947–1956," *Public Opinion Quarterly*, Vol. XXIV (Winter 1960), pp. 590–604; Karl W. Deutsch and Richard L. Merritt, "Effects of Events on National and International Images," *Internaional Behavior*, ed. Herbert C. Kelman, (New York: Holt, Rinehart, Winston, 1965), pp. 130–87; Johan Galtung, "Social Position, Party Identification and Foreign Policy Orientation: A Norwegian Case Study," *Domestic Sources of Foreign Policy*, ed. James N. Rosenau (New York: Free Press, 1967), pp. 161–93; Galtung, "Foreign Policy Opinion as a Function of Social Position," *Journal Of Peace Research*, Vol. I, 1 (1966), pp. 206–31; Gergen and Back, "Aging, Time Perspective, and Preferred Solutions to International Conflicts," *Journal of Conflict Resolution*, Vol. IX (June 1965), pp. 177–86; Nils H. Halle, *Journal of Peace Research*, Vol. III (# 1, 1966), pp. 46–74; Robert E. Lane, "Political Personality and Electoral Choice," *American Political Science Review*, Vol. XVIX (March 1955), pp. 173–90; Jerome Laulicht, "Public Opinion and Foreign Policy Decisions," *Journal of Peace Research*, Vol. II (# 2, 1965), pp. 147–60; Jerome Laulicht, "An Analysis of Canadian Foreign Policy Attitudes," *Peace Research Society, Papers*, Vol. III (1965), pp. 121–36; Herbert McClosky, "Personality and Attitude Correlates of Foreign Policy Orientation," *Domestic Source of Foreign Policy*, ed. Rosenau, *op. cit.*, pp. 51–110; William A. Scott, "Psychological and Social Correlates of International Images," *International Behavior*, ed. Kelman, *op. cit.*, pp. 70–103; Ross Stagner *et al.*, "A Survey of Public Opinion on the Prevention of War," *Journal of Social Psychology*, Vol. XVI (SPSSI Bulletin, 1942), pp. 109–30; Sidney Verba *et al.*, "Public Opinion and the War in Vietnam," *American Political Science Review*, Vol. LXI (June 1967), pp. 317–33.

[3] Charles D. Farris, "Selected Attitudes on Foreign Affairs As Correlates of Authoritarianism and Political Anomie," *Journal of Politics*, Vol. XXII (February 1960), pp. 50–67; Yasumasa Kuroda," Peace-War Orientation in a Japanese Community," *Journal of Peace Research*, Vol. III, (# 4, 1966), pp. 380–88.

[4] Peter M. Blau, "Orientation of College Students Toward International Relations," *American Journal of Sociology*, Vol. LIX (November 1953), pp. 205–24; Hilding B. Carlson, "Attitudes of Undergraduate Students," *Journal of Social Psychology*, Vol. V (May 1934), pp. 202–12; Mark Chesler and Richard Schmuck, "Student Reactions to the Cuban Crisis and Public Dissent," *Public Opinion Quarterly*, Vol. XXVIII (Fall 1964), pp. 467–82; Stephen M. Corey, "Changes in the Opinions of Female Students After One Year at a University," *Journal of Social Psychology*, Vol. XI (May 1940), pp. 341–51; Sidney Crown, "Some Personality Correlates of War-Mindedness and Anti-Semitism," *ibid.*, Vol. XXXI (February 1950), pp. 131–43; Daniel Droba Day and O. F. Quackenbush, "Attitudes Toward Defensive, Cooperative, and Aggressive War," *ibid.*, Vol. XVI (August 1942), pp. 11–20; D. D. Droba, "A Scale of Militarism-Pacifism," *Journal of Educational Psychology*, Vol. XXII (January 1931), pp. 96–111; Droba, "Political Parties and War Attitudes," *Journal of Abnormal and Social Psychology*, Vol. XXVIII (January 1934), pp. 468–72; George J. Dudycha, "The Attitude of College Students Toward War," *Journal of Social Psychology*, Vol. XV (February 1942), pp. 75–89; Elizabeth Duffy, "Attitudes of Parents and Daughters Toward War and Toward the Treatment of Criminals," *Psychological Record*, Vol. IV (June 1941), pp. 366–72; Stanford C. Ericksen, "A Skeptical Note on the Use of Attitude Scales Toward War," *Journal of Social Psychology*, Vol. XVI (November 1942), pp. 229–42; Vol. XX (August 1944), pp. 31–38; Maurice L. Farber, "The Armageddon Complex: Dynamics of Opinion," *Public Opinion Quarterly*, Vol. XV (Summer 1951), pp. 217–24; Paul R. Farnsworth, "Changes in 'Attitude Toward War' During the College Years," *Journal of Social Psy-chology*, Vol. VIII (May 1937), pp. 274–279; Harry A. Grace and Jack Olin Neuhaus, "Information and Social Distance as Predictors of Hostility Toward Nations," *Journal of Abnormal and Social Psychology*, Vol. XLVII (April 1952), pp. 540–45; Vernon Jones, "Attitudes of College Students and the Changes in Such Attitudes During Four Years in College," *Journal of Educational Psychology*, Vol. XXIX (January 1938), pp. 14–25; (February 1938), pp. 114–34; E. T. Katzoff and A. R. Gilliland, "Student Attitudes Toward Participation in the War," *Sociometry*, Vol. VI (May 1943), pp. 149–55; C. Terrence Pihlblad, "Students Attitudes Toward War," *Sociology and Sociological Research*, Vol. XX (January–February 1936), pp. 248–54; Snell Putney and Russell Middleton, "Some Factors Associated with Student Acceptance or Rejection of War," *American Sociological Review*, Vol. XXVII (October 1962), pp. 655–66; A. C. Rosander, "Age and Sex Patterns of Social Attitudes," *Journal of Educational Psychology*, Vol. XXX (October 1939), pp. 481–96; Milton J. Rosenberg, "Images in Relation to the Policy Process: American Public Opinion on Cold-War Issues," *International Behavior*, ed. Kelman, *op. cit.*, pp. 277–34; Morris Rosenberg, "Misanthropy and Attitudes Toward International Affairs," *Journal of Conflict Resolution*, Vol. I (December 1957), pp. 340–45; Bert R. Sappenfeld, "The Attitudes and Attitude Estimates of Catholic, Protestant, and Jewish Students," *Journal of Social Psychology*, Vol. XVI (November 1942), pp. 173–97; William A. Scott, "International Ideology and Interpersonal Ideology," *Public Opinion Quarterly*, Vol. XXIV (Fall 1960), pp. 419–35; John Jeffrey Smith, "What One College Thinks Concerning War and Peace," *Journal of Applied Psychology*, Vol. XVII (# 1, 1933), pp. 17–28; Ross Stagner, "Some Factors Related to Attitude Toward War," *Journal of Social Psychology*, Vol. XVI (SPSSI Bulletin, 1942), pp. 131–42; Stagner, "Studies of Aggressive Social Attitudes," *ibid.*, Vol. XX (August 1944), pp. 109–20; 121–28; 129–40.

[5] David J. Armor *et al.*, "Professors' Attitudes Toward the Vietnam War," *Public*

Opinion Quarterly, Vol. XXXI (Summer 1967), pp. 160–75; Howard Schuman and Edward O. Laumann, "Do Most Professors Support the War," *Trans-Action*, Vol. V (November 1967), pp. 32–35; Smith, *op. cit.*

[6] Paul Ekman *et al.*, "Coping with Cuba: Divergent Policy Preferences of State Political Leaders," *Journal of Conflict Resolution*, Vol. X (June 1966), pp. 180–97; Morton Gorden and Daniel Lerner, "The Setting for European Arms Controls: Political and Strategic Choices of European Elites," *ibid.*, Vol. IX (December 1965), pp. 419–33; Laulicht, *loc. cit.*; Laulicht, "Public Opinion and Foreign Policy Decisions," *op. cit.*; McClosky, *loc. cit.*

[7] Laulicht's sample in both studies cited above in n. 2 consists also of labor leaders, business leaders, and various financial contributors to the Canadian Peace Research Institute. See also: Warren C. Middleton and Paul J. Fay, "Attitudes of Delinquent and Non-Delinquent Girls Toward Sunday Observance, the Bible, and War," *Journal of Educational Psychology*, Vol. XXXII (October 1941), pp. 555–58; Middleton and Fay, "A Comparison of Delinquent and Non-Delinquent Boys with Respect to Certain Attitudes," *Journal of Social Psychology*, Vol. XVIII (August 1943), pp. 155–58. Delinquency is not itself related to warmindedness.

[8] Richard A. Brody, "Some Systemic Effects of the Spread of Nuclear Weapons Technology: A Study Through Simulation of a Multi-Nuclear Future," *Journal of Conflict Resolution*, Vol. VII (December 1963), pp. 663–753; Michael J. Driver, "A Structural Analysis of Aggression, Stress, and Personality in an Inter-Nation Simulation" (Lafayette: Purdue University, multilith, August, 1965).

[9] Marc Pilisuk *et al.*, "War Hawks and Peace Doves: Alternate Resolutions of Experimental Conflicts," *Journal of Conflict Resolution*, Vol. IX (December 1965), pp. 491–508. Pilisuk and Anatol Rapoport, "Stepwise Disarmament and Sudden Destruction in a Two-Person Game," *ibid.*, Vol. VIII (March 1964), pp. 36–49.

[10] John R. Raser and Wayman J. Crow, "A Simulation Study of Deterrence Theories," *Proceedings of the International Peace Research Association Inaugural Conference*

(Assen: Van Gorcum, 1966), pp. 146–65.

[11] Roger L. Sisson and Russell L. Ackoff, "Toward a Theory of the Dynamics of Conflict," *Peace Research Society, Papers*, Vol. V (1966), pp. 183–98.

[12] Otomar J. Bartos, "How Predictable Are Negotiations?" *Journal of Conflict Resolution*, Vol. XI (December 1967), pp. 481–98.

[13] Kenneth W. Terhune, "Studies of Motives, Cooperation and Conflict Within Laboratory Microcosms," *Buffalo Studies*, Vol. IV (April 1968), pp. 29–58, esp. pp. 42ff.

[14] Lloyd Jensen, "Military Capabilities and Bargaining Behavior," *Journal of Conflict Resolution*, Vol. IX (June 1965), pp. 155–63; Jensen, "Approach-Avoidance Bargaining in the Test Ban Negotiations," *International Studies Quarterly*, Vol. XII (June, 1968), pp. 152–60.

[15] Glenn D. Paige, "Comparative Case Analysis of Crisis Decisions: Korea and Cuba," *International Crises*, ed. Charles F. Hermann (Indianapolis: Bobbs-Merrill, forthcoming). See also his *The Korean Decision* (New York: Free Press, 1968). In using codings of the two decisions as correlates of war and nonwar outcomes of decision-making situations I am going beyond the inferences suggested by Paige.

[16] Dina A. Zinnes, Robert C. North, and Howard E. Koch, Jr., "Capability, Threat and the Outbreak of War," *International Politics and Foreign Policy*, ed. James N. Rosenau (1st ed.; New York: Free Press, 1961), pp. 468–82; Ole R. Hosti, Richard A. Brody, and Robert C. North, "Affect and Action in International Reaction Models," *Journal of Peace Research*, Vol. I (3–4, 1964), pp. 170–90; North, Brody, Holsti, "Some Empirical Data on the Conflict Spiral," *Peace Research Society, Papers*, Vol. I (1964), pp. 1–14; Holsti, "Perceptions of Time and Alternatives As Factors in Crisis Decision-Making," *ibid.*, Vol. III (1965), pp. 79–120; Holsti and North, "The History of Human Conflict," *The Nature of Human Conflict*, ed. Elton B. McNeil (Englewood Cliffs: Prentice-Hall, 1965), pp. 155–71; Holsti "The 1914 Case," *American Political Science Review*, Vol. LIX (June 1965), pp. 365–78; Zinnes, *op. cit.*; Zinnes, "Hostility in International Decision-Making," *Journal of Conflict Resolution*, Vol. VI (September 1962), pp. 236–43; Zinnes, "The Expression and Per-

ception of Hostility in Prewar Crisis: 1914," *Quantitative International Politics,* ed. J. David Singer (New York: Free Press, 1968), pp. 85–119. See also: Charles F. Hermann and Margaret G. Hermann, "An Attempt to Simulate the Outbreak of World War I," *American Politcal Science Review,* Vol. LXI (June 1967), pp. 400–16; Zinnes, "A Comparison of Hostile Behavior of Decision-Makers in Simulate and Historical Data," *World Politics,* Vol. XVIII (April 1966), pp. 474–502.

[17]Bruce M. Russett, "Cause, Surprise, and No Escape," *Journal of Politics,* Vol. XXIV (February 1962), pp. 3–22; Russett, "The Calculus of Deterrence," *Journal of Conflict Resolution,* Vol. VII (June 1963), pp. 97–109; Russett, "Pearl Harbor: Deterrence Theory and Decision Theory," *Journal of Peace Research,* Vol. IV (# 2, 1967), pp. 89–106.

[18]Quincy Wright, "The Escalation of International Conflicts," *Journal of Conflict Resolutions,* Vol. IX (December 1965), pp. 434–49.

[19]Most of the findings in this section are based upon Haas, *op. cit.,* Part III. See also: Haas, "Social Change and National Aggressiveness, 1900–1960," *Quantitative International Politics,* ed. Singer, *op. cit.,* pp. 215–44; Haas, "Toward the Study of Biopolitics: A Cross-Sectional Analysis of Mortality Rates," *Behavioral Science,* Vol. XIV (July, 1969), pp. 257–80; Jonathan Wilkenfeld, "Domestic and Foreign Conflict Behavior of Nations," *Journal of Peace Research,* Vol. V (# 1, 1968), pp. 56–69. See also Rudolph J.

Rummel, "The Relationship Between National Attributes and Foreign Conflict Behavior," *Quantitative International Politics,* ed. Singer, *op. cit.,* pp. 187–214; Rummel, "Some Dimensions in the Foreign Behavior of Nations," *Journal of Peace Research,* Vol. III (# 3, 1966), pp. 201–24.

[20]Karl W. Deutsch *et al., Political Community and the North Atlantic Area* (Princeton: Princeton University Press, 1957). See also his *Nationalism and Social Communication* (New York: Wiley, 1953); Deutsch and Alexander Eckstein, "National Industrialization and the Declining Share of the International Economic Sector, 1890–1959," *World Politics,* Vol. XIII (January 1961), pp. 267–99.

[21]Amitai Etzioni, *Political Unification* (New York: Holt, Rinehart, Winston, 1965).

[22]Ernst B. Haas, "The Challenge of Regionalism," *International Organization,* Vol. XII (Autumn 1958), pp. 440–58.

[23]Bruce M. Russett, *Trends in World Politics* (New York: Macmillan, 1965), p. 56.

[24]Lewis F. Richardson, *Statistics on Deadly Quarrels* (Chicago: Quadrangle, 1960), pp. 194, 197.

[25]Richard N. Rosecrance, *Action and Reaction in World Politics* (Boston: Little, Brown, 1963); J. David Singer and Melvin Small, "Alliance Aggregation and the Onset of War, 1815–1945," *Quantitative International Politics,* ed. Singer, *op. cit.,* pp. 247–86; Michael Haas, "International Subsystems: Stability and Polarity," *American Political Science Review,* Vol. LXIX (March 1970), pp. 98–123.

CHADWICK F. ALGER

Negotiation, Regional Groups, Interaction, and Public Debate in the Development of Consensus in the United Nations General Assembly*

Introduction
As is the case with all represent-
ative assemblies, decisions taken by United Nations bodies are shaped
only partially by public debate. The public sessions admit questions to the
agenda of an organization and thereby insure the attention of members to
certain problems. They also offer agreed criteria for making a group decision. But the nature of the public debate and of the decisions agreed upon
in the public arena are determined largely by a multitude of more private
discussions. Particularly in large bodies with heterogeneous membership,
the development of sufficient consensus to make a decision requires considerable activity outside the public arena.

This paper will examine how members of one main committee of the
United Nations General Assembly, the 111 nation Administrative and
Budgetary Committee, worked for eight weeks on problems presented by
disagreement on the financing of the United Nations Emergency Force
in Suez (UNEF) and the United Nations Force in the Congo (ONUC). The
disagreement was based partly on the claim of some nations, primarily
France, and the Soviet group, that these operations violated the Charter.
There was dispute also over the appropriate method for apportioning
expenses among members. The main purpose of this paper will be to show
how negotiations and regional group meetings outside the public arena were
combined with private discussion, public debate, and voting in the public

* This is a revised version of a paper presented to the Working Group on Sociology of
International Organizations, Sixth World Congress of Sociology, International Sociological
Association. Evian, France, September 1966. Mrs. Lucille Mayer provided valuable assistance
in the preparation of this paper, particularly in the preparation of data in the tables.

Notes and References for this selection will be found on page 298.

arena in order to generate resolutions supported by most of the committee.

This study builds on two earlier efforts to discern the potential usefulness of data acquired through observation of the Fifth Committee of the General Assembly. The first study was largely an exploratory effort to discern possible relationships between observed private conversations during public sessions and (1) characteristics of individual participants (noncommittee roles and reputation for being capable and informed), (2) characteristics of nations (a variety of measures of United Nations participation as well as population, GNP, etc.), and (3) regional alignments.[1] A second study compared some of the results of this study (based on the 1962 regular session) with data collected on an additional session of the Fifth Committee (the 1963 Special Session).[2] This comparison revealed changes in the participation of national delegations in private conversations as these delegations (and their individual members) assumed key roles in negotiations taking place outside the committee and revealed rather conclusively that private conversations are not just random behavior, as some participants had asserted. The patterns of delegate participation in private conversations have strong relationships to negotiations outside the chamber and are remarkably different than patterns of participation in public debate.

These findings led to the present study in which the decision-making of the Fifth Committee in the Fourth Special Session is analyzed in terms of four kinds of behavior—behind the scenes negotiation, regional group meetings, public debate, and private conversation carried out concurrent with this debate. The study not only demonstrates how these four kinds of behavior were intertwined as the Fifth Committee attempted to develop a consensus on peacekeeping finance. It also demonstrates how a battery of methods for collecting data (documentary analysis, observation, and interview) were required in order to obtain information on the different arenas of committee activity.

In order to acquire information reported in this paper the writer attended all twenty-two sessions of the committee during the Special Session, May 14 to June 27, 1963. Through systematic observation, data were obtained on participation in public debate and on delegate interaction that takes place concurrent with public debate.[3] All seventy sessions of the previous session of the Fifth Committee, from September to December 1962, had been attended also. On the basis of contact made with members of the committee in the earlier session, it was possible to obtain information on committee activity outside the public arena. This was achieved through conversations with delegates in the committee room (before, during, and after meetings) and in the lounges, corridors, and dining rooms of the United Nations, and occasionally at locations outside the U.N. In addition to more casual conversation with participants during the Special Session, after the session was over ten of the most active participants in the negotiations were interviewed.

The Special Session of the General Assembly, devoted entirely to

U.N. financial problems,[4] was called by the Seventeenth Regular Session in December 1962 in the face of arrears for UNEF and ONUC totaling $105,000,000 and in light of the fact that no assessments had been made on members for peace-keeping expenditures for the period commencing July 1962. Many nations deemed it vital that means be found for getting more nations to pay for UNEF and ONUC. It was believed that a Special Session devoted to the financing of peacekeeping would isolate the problem and encourage wider interest and competence of the United Nations diplomatic community in UN financial problems. The Special Session produced seven resolutions which all received between 79 and 95 affirmative votes. These resolutions: (1) provided general principles to serve as guidelines for the sharing of the costs of future peacekeeping operations involving heavy expenditures, (2) and (3) authorized the Secretary General to spend $6,580,000 monthly for the ONUC and UNEF between July 1 and Decmber 31, 1963, and apportioned the costs among members, (4) appealed to members to pay their arrears for UNEF and ONUC, (5) extended the period in which United Nations Bonds could be sold to December 31, 1963, (6) asked the Secretary-General to investigate the feasibility of establishing a voluntary peace fund, and (7) continued a 21 nation working group devoted to developing more long-range solutions to the organization's financial problems. Before proceeding to a more analytic treatment of committee activity, the reader will be given a short chronological account of events leading up to the Special Session and an overview of negotiations during the Special Session.

Preparation for the Special Session

When the General Assembly called for a Special Session in the spring of 1963, it also established a working group of representatives from 21 nations that was instructed to consider the U.N.'s financial problems and make recommendations to the Special Session of the Assembly. This working group was the successor to a fifteen-nation group established in April 1961, which had been unable to develop a broad consensus on peacekeeping finance.[5] The Working Group of Twenty-one held eighteen meetings between January 29 and March 29. It became apparent early that the hoped for, but not expected, consensus on the apportionment of peacekeeping expenses was not to be achieved by the Group as it became clear that the three members from the Soviet group—USSR, Bulgaria, and Mongolia—and also France, had no intention of shifting their positions. There was hope, however, that the remainder of the membership could agree on a single position. If all members of the United Nations but the Soviet group and France, and perhaps only two or three others, could agree on financing arrangements, it was believed that over the long run the few isolated nations would desire to reach some sort of compromise with the rest of the membership. Therefore, many of the members of the Working Group of Twenty-one hoped that the two financial interest groups represented could reach some sort of agreement: i.e., the so-called developed countries (Australia, Canada, Italy, Japan, Netherlands, Sweden, U.K., and U.S.) and the so-called lesser developed countries (Argentina, Brazil, Cameroon, India, Mexico, Nigeria, Pakistan and Unite Arab Republic).

The Working Group of Twenty-one was not able to provide the Special Session of the General Assembly, to whom it reported, with a solution to the financial problem, but it did educate its members on the political and financial problems to be faced in the Special Session of the General Assembly and developed an embryonic negotiation organization that would handle most of the negotiations during the session. Although the Special Session was not to begin until May 14, the political process was well under way before the session opened. The participants in these negotiations, largely because of their ability to get negotiating mandates from large groups of nations, were to have great influence on subsequent events in the General Assembly. With the Soviet group not able to negotiate because of its stand that all peacekeeping expenses not authorized by the Security Council are illegal, the field was left largely to the developed and lesser developed groupings that had participated in the Working Group of Twenty-one, with the latter composed of two sub-groups, the Afro-Asians and the Latin Americans.

At the end of April representatives of Australia, Canada, United Kingdom, and the United States gathered in New York to discuss drafts of resolutions that would provide financing for UNEF and ONUC for the relevant period. Then on May 3 the eight developed nations who had worked together in the Working Group of Twenty-one gathered to consider these resolutions. On May 10 these eight (Australia, Canada, Italy, Japan, Netherlands, U.K., U.S.) were joined by Austria, Belgium, Finland, France, Iceland, Ireland, Luxembourg, and Norway. Although Belgian and French delegates contributed almost nothing to these sessions because their governments were unwilling to pay for ONUC, they kept in contact with the negotiations through attending sessions of the developed nation group. Therefore, they were informed fully of developments at each stage of the negotiation.

At the May 3 and May 10 meetings a broad consensus was developed on a formula for ONUC and UNEF financing and a proposal that a few delegations be designated to carry on negotiations with the lesser developed nations was accepted. Canada, Netherlands, Sweden, the United Kingdom, and the United States were appointed and given a mandate to negotiate for the entire group. The Canadian representative, who had played a leading role in moving Western consultation along and in obtaining the participation of the lesser developed nations in the proposed negotiations, became the natural chairman of the negotiating team. This was due also to the fact that Canada had played a leading role in U.N. financial questions for some years and played a major role in steering acceptance of the advisory opinion of the International Court on peacekeeping financing through the General Assembly in December 1962.[6]

Meanwhile, the Latin American group, that had had a subcommittee on financing for several years, met four times on financing before the opening of the Special Session, on April 14 and 25 and on May 6 and 13. The Latin Americans were the most unified of the three groups (Latin American, Afro-Asian, and developed) to be involved in the approaching negotiations. Although an advisory opinion of the International Court of Justice had caused them to change their former assertion that peacekeeping expenses are not the responsiblity of all U.N. members, they maintained a unified stand that peacekeeping financing is mainly the responsibility of the developed nations. The group gave a clear mandate to the delegations of Brazil and Argentina to negotiate with members of other groups.

The Afro–Asian group, consisting of 56 nations that include such widely scattered interests as those of Guinea, Indonesia, and Jamaica did not have the degree of consensus on U.N. financing that was evident in Latin America. Afro–Asia not only encompasses a wider range of cultures and political viewpoints, but in this area are to be found nations involved directly in the conflicts that created the need for peacekeeping operations, as well as the main contributors of troops to these operations. The Afro–Asian group designated India, Nigeria, and Pakistan to represent them in the negotiations. The group, as a whole, had not, however, given the financial question the degree of consideration that it had been given by the Latin Americans and the developed nations. This, in addition to the more heterogeneous nature of the group, was to make the task of representing the interests of their group more difficult for the Afro-Asian negotiators.

Negotiations During the Special Session

The ten-nation negotiating group began its deliberations on May 10 four days before the first meeting of the Fifth Committee, under the chairmanship of the Counsellor of the Canadian Mission. None of the participants would have predicted that their deliberations would not conclude until June 17 and that their work would require 18 sessions. Nor did they realize that the negotiation organization that they were creating would schedule over 70 meetings in addition to the 22 public meetings of the Fifth Committee, and two plenary meetings of the General Assembly (see Table 1).

The organization that developed to handle the negotiations did not consist only of meetings of the ten-nation negotiation group. It also included separate sessions of the two five-nation components of the negotiating group and included sessions between negotiators and the regional groups of nations that they represented. The two negotiating teams came to be designated the LDC (lesser developed countries: Argentina, Brazil, India, Nigeria, Pakistan), and the DC (developed countries: Canada, Netherlands, Sweden, United Kingdom, United States). The DC held at least 12 separate sessions and the LDC, chaired by Argentina, at least six. The five DC were responsible to the sixteen-nation developed nation group

Table 1—Number of Meetings of Negotiators, Regional Groups, and Entire Fifth Committee in Special Session

Negotiators		No.
Developed Countries (DC)		12
Lesser Developed Countries (LDC)		6
DC and LDC		18
		—
	Total	36
		—

Regional Groups		No.
Developed (W. Europe, Australia, Canada, Japan, New Zealand, U.S.)		8
Latin America		6
Afro-Asia		15
Afro-Asia subgroup (LDC + Cameroon, Japan, United Arab Republic)		3
Commonwealth		2
Arab		4
		—
	Total	38
		—

Entire Fifth Committee	No.
Public Meetings of the Fifth Committee	22
	—

with whom they met eight times after the negotiations had begun. The Latin American negotiators met with their 19-nation group six times during this period. The three Afro-Asian negotiators met with the fifty-six nation Afro-Asian caucus 15 times. The Afro-Asian negotiators also met several times with the other Afro-Asian members of the Working Group of Twenty-one—Cameroon, Japan, and the United Arab Republic. This meant that Japan, a developed Afro-Asian nation, had some contact with both negotiating teams. It also provided an additional link to the United Arab Republic, whose views on UNEF were important but caused it to refuse to participate in the Afro-Asian negotiating team because of the likelihood that it could not support the UNEF financing resolution that was to be drafted. There were also two Commonwealth meetings, on May 10 and 17. These occasions provided an opportunity for five of the negotiators (Canada, India, Nigeria, Pakistan, and United Kingdom) to discuss financial issues in a different context and to appeal to other Commonwealth nations for support of their point of view. Finally, the Arab nations, a subgroup of the Afro-Asian group, had four or five meetings on financial questions.

In the negotiating sessions between DC and LDC most work was carried on by individuals who might be called "working level" members of permanent missions who represented their nations in the Fifth Committee of the General Assembly. Therefore, most had spent the months of September to December 1962, together during the last regular General Assembly session. Then, most of those who were involved in the negotiations had worked together in the Working Group of Twenty-one from January 29 to March 29. In most cases one man handled most of the negotiations for his nation, this being true for Argentina, Brazil, India, Netherlands, Pakistan, and Sweden. With the Canadian negotiator chairing the DC, DC-LDC, and Western meetings, he made considerable use of an aide. Because the Nigerian Ambassador had been the chairman of the Working Group of Twenty-one, he still continued to serve as a monitor of progress in the negotiations and occasionally entered the proceedings, though one of his aides usually represented Nigeria. Both the United States and the United Kingdom sent their Deputy Permanent Representatives to the negotiations, an Ambassador and a Minister respectively, and both had three other officials rather prominently involved in the negotiations. Two of the United Kingdom delegates came from the Treasury, one permanently posted at the U.N. One of the United States delegates was from the State Department.

The negotiations can be divided into two phases. In the first phase, from May 10 to May 31, the negotiators produced four resolutions for approval by the nations that they represented: two authorized expenditures for UNEF and ONUC for the second half of 1963 and apportioned these expenses among members, the third provided a set of general principles to guide the apportionment of expenses for future peacekeeping operations and the fourth dealt with the collection of arrears in the payment of peacekeeping expenses. The second phase of negotiations, from June 1 to June 19, was required because the Afro-Asian group rejected the results of the first phase. The major difficulty arose over a clause in the general principles resolution that attempted to respond to the insistence of Arab nations that victims of aggression should receive special consideration when assessments are made for peacekeeping operations. Negotiations had removed the words "victim" and "aggressor" in favor of vaguer terminology. The Afro-Asian group demonstrated its displeasure with its negotiators by adding five nations to its negotiating team before the second phase of negotiations began: Cameroon, Guinea, Malaya, Philippines, and Uganda. It took the Afro-Asian group six meetings to reach a formulation of the "victim and aggressor" clause acceptable to the entire group and to the DC negotiators. The agreement put "victim" back in but accepted a substitute phrase for "aggressor" which read: "Member States . . . responsible for acts which led to a peacekeeping operation."

After negotiations were completed the Fifth Committee completed its work between June 20 and 26. The four resolutions produced by the negotiations were accepted. In addition, three less controversial resolutions not handled in the negotiations were introduced in the committee and approved. One continued the Working Group of Twenty-one, another asked the Secretary-General to investigate the feasibility of a voluntary peace fund, and a third extended the period in which the U.N. bonds could be sold to December 31, 1963. On June 27 work of the committee was approved by a single General Assembly plenary session. The seven resolutions received between 79 and 95 supporting votes, with two to 17 nations abstaining. The Soviet group, including Cuba, cast 12 negative votes for each resolution. The only other negative votes came from France which voted against all but two of the resolutions.

Public and Private Meetings

As Table 1 has indicated, with 36 meetings of negotiators and 33 meetings of regional groups, the meetings outside the public arena far exceed the 22 meetings of the Fifth Committee. Table 2 shows how meetings are distributed across the eight weeks. Notable is the extent of regional group and negotiation group activity before the Fifth Committee began its sessions. In the first two weeks there were nine regional group meetings and six negotiator meetings but only one session of the Fifth Committee, its first session on May 15.

Table 3 provides the same information collapsed into four time periods: Phase I of the negotiations, Phase II of the negotiations, and the period before and after negotiations between LDC and DC. Activity of negotiators and regional groups is most concentrated before or during Phase I of negotiations (70 per cent of the negotiation meetings and 60 per cent of the regional meetings). The distribution of the meetings of the Afro-Asian group, however, runs counter to the general pattern, with five meetings during Phase I and ten meetings during Phase II. This pattern reflects the group's refusal to accept the settlement made by their negotiators during Phase I of the negotiations. Even after they had increased their negotiating team from five to eight, thereby indicating a lack of confidence in their original negotiators, it took the group many meetings to reach an agreement among themselves.

Table 3 also indicates that the activities of the negotiating and regional groups were concluded before the last week of the meetings of the Fifth Committee, the week of most concentrated activity in the public arena. During this week the Fifth Committee convened one-third of the meetings held during its six-week session. In addition Table 3 reveals that there were more speakers in the Fifth Committee during this week than in the other five weeks of the session.

Table 4 provides a more vivid picture of the relationship between negotiation progress and participation in the public debate of the Fifth Committee. During Phase I of the negotiations the public debate got under way slowly, with only one meeting and one speaker during the first three days. For the remainder of Phase I there was a public meeting approximately every other day, with an average of five speakers per session.

In the first session of the Fifth Committee after the negotiated settle-

Table 2—Meetings of Negotiators, Regional Groups and Fifth Committee (Weekly Totals)

WEEK OF	Negotiators			Regional Groups						Public Meetings	
	DEV. COUNTRIES[1] (DC)	LESS DEV. COUNTRIES[2] (LDC)	DC AND LDC	DEVELOPED[3]	LATIN AMERICAN	AFRO-ASIAN	AFRO-ASIAN MEMBERS OF COMM. OF 21[4]	COMMON-WEALTH		FIFTH COMMITTEE OF GA[5]	TOTAL
5/6	—	—	1	1	1	1	—	—	—	—	4
5/13	2	—	3	1	1	1	2	1	—	1	12
5/20	5	2	4	2	2	2	—	—	—	3	20
5/27	3	1	4	2	—	1	1	1	—	3	16
6/3	—	1	2	1	1	3	—	—	1	5	14
6/10	2	1	3	1	—	5	—	—	—	3	15
6/17	—	1	1	—	1	2	—	—	—	3	8
6/24	—	—	—	—	—	—	—	—	—	4	4
TOTAL	12	6	18	8	6	15	3	2	4 (est.)	22	96[6]

[1] Canada, Netherlands, Sweden, US, UK.

[2] Argentina, Brazil, India, Nigeria, Pakistan.

[3] Scandinavian, 3 Benelux, Canada, US, UK, Austria, Japan, Australia, NZ, Italy.

[4] LDC plus Cameroon, Japan, Mexico

[5] Total UN Membership.

[6] Two plenary meetings of the General Assembly were also held.

Table 3—Meetings of Negotiators, Regional Groups and Fifth Committee (Phase Totals)

DATE	Negotiators			Regional Groups						Public Meetings	TOTAL
	DC	LDC	DC AND LDC	DEVELOPED	LATIN AMERICAN	AFRO-ASIAN	AFRO-ASIAN MEMBERS OF COMM. OF 21	COMMON-WEALTH	ARAB	FIFTH COMMITTEE OF GA	
May 6–10	—	—	—	2	3	1	—	—	—	—	6
Negotiation Phase I											
May 10–31	10	3	12	5	3	4	3	2	—	7 (30 speeches)	49
Negotiation Phase II											
June 1–19	2	3	6	2	2	10	—	—	1	8 (27 speeches)	34
June 20–26	—	—	—	—	—	—	—	—	—	7 (63 speeches)	7
Total	12	6	18	9	8	15	3	2	4 (est.)	22	96

Table 4—Number of Speakers in Fifth Committee for Each
Working Day (Monday to Friday)

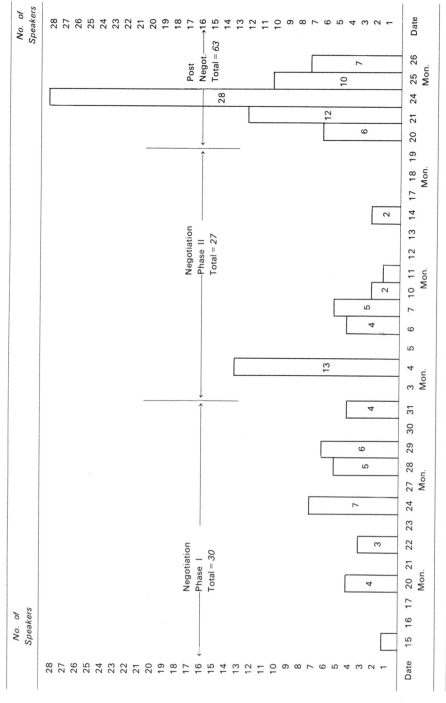

ment of Phase I thirteeen delegates spoke. But after it became clear that a new settlement would have to be negotiated, the committee returned to an average of five speakers for the next two sessions, the same as during Phase I. Then, as negotiations stalled over the inability of the Afro-Asian group to come to an agreement, Table 4 reveals that the public debate almost ceased. During the last six working days of Phase II, there was only one meeting of the Fifth Committee with only two speakers. Despite continual requests for speakers by the committee chairman, members of the committee refused to participate further in the debate until the negotiating teams had brought forth new draft resolutions. After negotiations had concluded, 63 delegates spoke in five days, more than had spoken in the preceding month.

Private Conversation in Public Meetings

An observer of large public bodies, and the U.N. is no exception, soon becomes aware that two kinds of activity are taking place simultaneously before his eyes. There is a continuous flow of *public* debate heard by all in the room, and there are frequent *private* conversations heard only by those delegates involved. In a General Assembly committee delegates are seated at two long horseshoe desks, one placed inside the other. Conversations may be carried on by delegates seated next to each other. Delegates also move around the chamber, sometimes sitting down behind another delegate to talk and at other times standing and talking with others who are circulating.

During the first 18 of the 22 sessions of the Fifth Committee an observer recorded in a notebook each private conversation (interaction) between delegates in the committee. During the meetings of the Fifth Committee in the Fourth Special Session, 1192 interactions between delegates were recorded.[7] For all nations in the committee there is a .72 correlation between rank in time consumed in public speaking and rank in number of interactions. This rather high correlation could lead to the conclusion that interaction data provide little more than public debate records concerning nation participation in committee activity. But examination of lists of the highest ranked nations in both public speaking and interaction indicate a closer relationship between high interaction and negotiation participation than is the relationship between high participation in public speaking and negotiation. Table 5 lists the first 20 nations in order of their participation in both public speaking and interaction. The table indicates that only four negotiators were among the first 20 in public speaking. On the other hand, all ten negotiators appear in the list of the 20 highest interactors. Particularly impressive is the fact that negotiators hold the first seven ranks in interaction.

Table 6 provides another perspective on the highest interactors by listing the 20 highest interacting pairs. Once again the strong relationship

Table 5—Highest Ranked Nations in Interaction and Public Speaking

Interactions		Total Length of Speeches (in minutes)	
[a]Canada	315	[b]USSR	126
[a]US	149	[b]Ukraine	71
[a]India	140	[a]Pakistan	61
[a]Brazil	120	[b]Bulgaria	56
[a]Netherlands	96	Indonesia	47
[a]UK	93	[b]Hungary	45
[a]Pakistan	91	Cameroon	43
New Zealand	86	Fed. of Malaya	43
Ireland	75	[a]Nigeria	43
[a]Nigeria	70	[b]Poland	43
Bulgaria	69	Cyprus	41
[a]Argentina	68	[b]Czechoslovakia	41
Norway	63	[a]Argentina	39
Australia	60	Ceylon	38
Italy	60	Jamaica	36
[b]USSR	46	Tunisia	36
Yugoslavia	39	Iran	35
[a]Sweden	39	Ghana	34
[b]Hungary	33	[b]Byelorussia	33
Israel	30	[a]Canada	33
		[b]France	33

[a] Negotiator   [b] Dissenter

between the negotiating organization outside the committee chamber and interaction in the chamber is revealed, with pairs of negotiators taking the first five ranks and at least one negotiator participating in 16 of the 20 pairs.

Particularly notable in Table 6 is the fact that Canada is a member of ten of the first 12 ranked pairs. Canada's central role in the interaction network is portrayed more dramatically in Table 7, a diagram of the 20 highest interacting pairs. Examination of the diagram reveals that 11 nations are linked to Canada, with no other nation having more than four links. Canada's position as highest ranked in number of interactions and in number of links to other high interactors is intriguing in the light of the knowledge that a Canadian delegate served as chairman of the DC negotiating group and as chairman of the negotiation sessions between the DC and LDC. Despite the very prominent role of Canada in the negotiations, Canada ranked only 19 in participation in public debate.

Table 5 also raises interesting questions about the character of high participants in public debate. The Soviet Union, a nation that voted against all of the seven resolutions passed by the committee, ranks first in participation in public speaking. Only two of the 11 dissenters appear in the list of

Table 6—Highest Interacting Nation Pairs[a]

Nonseatmates[b]	
Canada/US	48
Canada/Netherlands	31
Canada/India	27
Canada/UK	24
Canada/Brazil	21
Canada/Ireland	19 ⎫
Canada/New Zealand	19 ⎭
Canada/Pakistan	17
Canada/Australia	14 ⎫
Canada/Italy	14 ⎪
India/New Zealand	14 ⎪
Ireland/New Zealand	14 ⎭
Argentina/Brazil	13 ⎫
Bulgaria/Byelorussia	13 ⎬
India/US	13 ⎭
Brazil/India	12 ⎫
Bulgaria/USSR	12 ⎬
Nigeria/Pakistan	12 ⎭
Bulgaria/Hungary	11 ⎫
Canada/Sweden	11 ⎭

[a] Total interactions for all interacting pairs of nations were compiled by using NUCROS, a general cross-classification program. Kenneth Janda, *Data Processing: Applications to Political Research.* (Evanston: Northwestern University Press, 1965), Chapter 6, describes this program. On pp. 40—42 he describes how it was used for this study.

[b] Underlining indicates negotiator.

high interactors, the USSR (ranked 16) and Hungary (ranked nine). But eight dissenters appear in the list of high participants in public debate. Thus the pattern for dissenters tends to be opposite of that for negotiators, as is summarized briefly in Table 8.

Further insight on the performance of negotiators and dissenters can be obtained by plotting the total length of each nation's speeches and their number of interactions on a scatter diagram. Table 9 provides a plot

Table 8—Negotiator and Dissenter Participation in Interaction and in Debate

	High Interaction Participation	High Debate Participation
Negotiators	10	4
Dissenters	2	8

Table 7—Diagram of interaction between first twenty ranked nonseatmate pairs, Special Session.

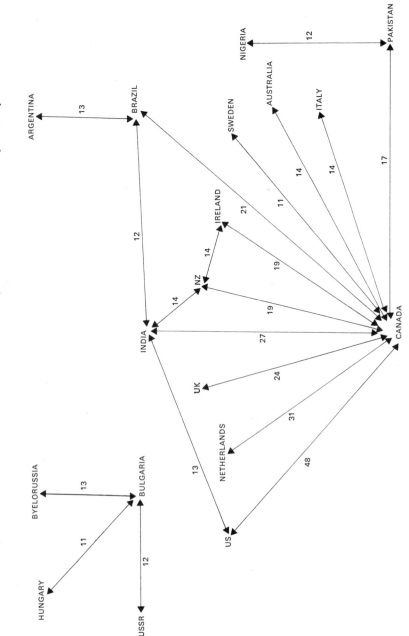

Table 9—Length of Speeches and Number of Interactions of Negotiators and Dissenters (Negotiators are underlined.)

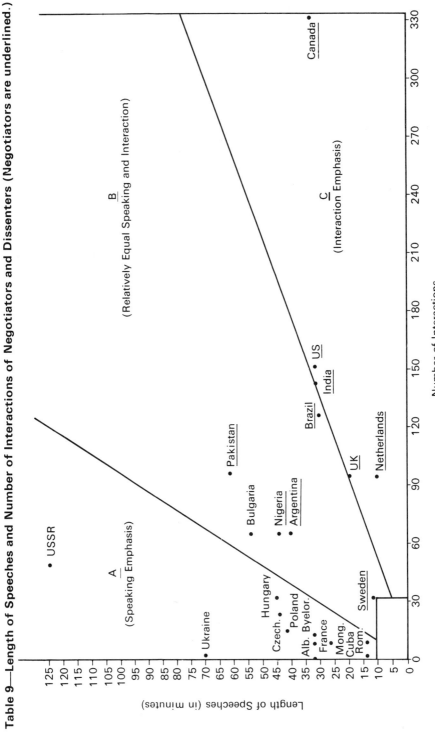

for each dissenting and negotiating nation. The diagram has been divided arbitrarily into three sectors. In Sector A, to the upper left, are found nations who emphasize speaking and in Sector C, to the lower right, are found nations who emphasize interaction. Between these two is Sector B, where nations are found who emphasize neither interaction nor speaking. It is obvious that dissenters cluster toward the upper left of the diagram and negotiators cluster toward the lower right. Table 10 gives a brief overview of the distribution of dissenters and negotiators in the scatter diagram. Eleven of the 12 dissenters are located in Sector A (speaking emphasis) and none

Table 10—Recapitulation of Sector Location of Negotiators and Dissenters

Sector	Negotiators	Dissenters
Sector *A* (Speaking Emphasis)	0	11
Sector *B*	5	1
Sector *C* (Interaction Emphasis)	5	0

in Sector C (interaction emphasis). The ten negotiators are split equally between Sectors C (interaction emphasis) and B (emphasis on neither), but none are in Sector A (speaking emphasis).

Overview of Pace of Negotiation, Regional Meetings, Interaction, and Public Speaking

In the preceding discussion some indication has been given of the comparative pace of the various activities of members of the Fifth Committee. Table 11 provides a graphic overview that facilitates a summary of earlier comments and also offers new insight. Negotiation meetings, regional meetings, Fifth Committee speeches, and Fifth Committee interactions are plotted for the six-week period that began two weeks before the first session of the Fifth Committee and ended with the last session of the committee. For each week the graph indicates the percentage of activity for the entire session that took place during that week.

Table 11 shows definite peaks of negotiation, interaction, and speaking, but regional meetings maintained a steady pace for five weeks and then dropped off. Negotiation activity peaked in the week of May 20–26, as public sessions of the Fifth Committee got under way. Twelve per cent of negotiator meetings were held during this week. Interaction in the Fifth Committee reached a peak two weeks later, in the week of June 3 to 9.

Table 11—Distribution of Activity by Week

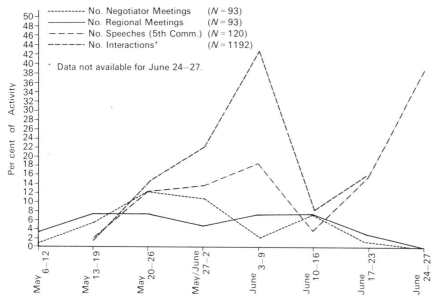

Thirty-nine per cent of interaction took place during this week. Public speaking did not reach a peak until three more weeks had elapsed, from June 24 to June 27. During this four day period 38 per cent of the speeches in the public debate were made. This sequence of peaks suggests a process in the development of consensus that moves from negotiation outside the committee to an extension of consensus through interaction that extends into the committee chamber and then to public statements.

The fact that the negotiations in this session went through two phases may explain the secondary peaks which account for 16 to 18 per cent of both the interaction (June 17–23) and public speaking (June 3–9) activities and eight per cent of the negotiation activity (June 10 to 16). If the three primary and three secondary peaks are numbered in sequence, there are two sequences, one for each negotiation stage, both of which peak in the same order: negotiation, interaction, speeches. Had the results of Phase I negotiations been accepted by the Afro-Asians it would be likely that the secondary peak in speaking (June 3–9) would have matured into the concluding phase of the committee's work. Instead it may be conjectured that the developing peak in speaking subsided as committee members became aware that negotiations were not concluded yet.

Summary and Conclusion

Analysis of information on a number of kinds of activity of delegates of the Fifth Committee of the U.N. General Assembly has revealed that regional groups and designated negotiating teams played important roles in the development of wide consensus for seven resolutions accepted by the committee. The picture obtained in this committee agrees with Hadwen and Kaufmann's assertion that public debate in U.N. bodies is like the small portion of an iceberg that appears above the surface.[8] The extensive discussion and negotiation system outside the pubic debate were vital for the achievement of high consensus (with the exception of the Soviet group and France) in resolutions dealing with very controversial issues. It is reasonable to conclude that the high consensus achieved would not have been attained if the negotiations had not been well under way before the public debate commenced. Because negotiations were in progress many delegates were restrained in committee debate so as not to put negotiations in jeopardy and in order to avoid taking positions that would inhibit working in the context of agreements reached in negotiations.

On the other hand, the public forum was found to be more than a public debate. Patterns of interactions that occur simultaneously with public debate suggest that the negotiating system carries over into the public arena. High rank in interaction is a useful indicator of who is involved in negotiation and patterns of interaction seem to offer leads on special roles in the negotiating system. It appears that public sessions could be useful in keeping negotiators in contact at times when negotiations have reached an impasse. It also is the case (revealed in discussions with participants) that fear of what could happen in public sessions stimulates negotiators to reach agreements. As negotiations bogged down in the Fifth Committee session under study, delegates frequently voiced the concern that some nations would become exasperated with the negotiations and directly introduce their own resolutions in the Fifth Committee.

Although high participation in public debate is a much less useful indicator of who is participating in negotiation than is participation in interaction, participation in public debate is a more reliable indicator of dissent. Although the dissenters did not participate in negotiation and relatively little (compared to negotiators) in interaction, they ranked high in public debate.

While noting the importance of negotiating teams and regional groups to the development of consensus, the significance of individual roles in these activities should not be overlooked. Although the most talented negotiator, the chairman of a negotiation session, or the chairman of a regional group, cannot generate a consensus under all conditions, it is apparent that variation in the capabilities of individuals in these roles makes a difference. In interviews some delegates gave the Canadian chairman of the negotiating sessions considerable credit for the successful conclusion of the negotiations. Some delegates asserted that the Afro-Asian group needed many sessions to reach a consensus partially because they had an inexperienced chairman. Thus, the outcomes of "parliamentary diplomacy" depend not only on speaking in the public arena, but probably depend much more on the presence of diplomats able and willing to play the variety of roles that mold divergent national policies into resolutions supportable by many nations.

Finally, this investigation has implications for the research methodologies of the scholar interested in understanding the political process in international organizations. Documentary analysis, observation, interview, and patient development of contact with participants were all used in the collection of information. The contribution of each of these data collection methods suggests that the international organization scholar can employ fruitfully a variety of social science research techniques. Furthermore, the way in which information obtained from different kinds of data collection techniques complement each other illustrates the advantage of research strategies that combine several data collection techniques.

Notes and References

[1]Chadwick F. Alger, "Interaction in a Committee of the United Nations General Assembly," in J. David Singer (ed.), *Quantitative International Politics: Insights and Evidence* (New York: The Free Press, 1968), pp. 51–84.

[2]Chadwick F. Alger, "Interaction and Negotiation in a Committee of the United Nations General Assembly," in James N. Rosenau (ed.), *International Politics and Foreign Policy: A Reader in Research and Theory* (New York: The Free Press, revised ed., 1969), pp. 483–497.

[3]Robert Weiner, now Chairman, Political Science Division, State College at Boston, Massachusetts, assisted in the collection of interaction data.

[4]With the exception of the speedy admission of Kuwait to membership.

[5]*Report of the Working Group of Fifteen on Examination of the Administrative Procedures of the United Nations,* A/4971, 1961. This group was composed of representatives of Brazil, Bulgaria, Canada, China, France, India, Italy, Japan, Mexico, Nigeria, Sweden, USSR, United Arab Republic, and United States. The enlarged group, officially named the Working Group on the Examination of the Administrative and Budgetary Procedures of the United Nations, also included Argentina, Australia, Cameroon, Mongolia, Netherlands, and Pakistan.

[6]The Advisory Opinion, published in *ICJ Reports,* 1962, pp. 151–181, declared that all members of the U.N. are obligated to pay assessments levied against them to cover expenses for ONUC and UNEF.

[7]Only nonseatmate interactions are included on the assumption that a delegate who leaves his seat to talk to another delegate more often is working on Committee business than a delegate who makes a comment to his seatmate. Therefore, 560 seatmate interactions are not included in this analysis. See C. F. Alger (*op. cit.*) for further discussion of this issue and for analysis of interaction in the 1962 regular session of the Fifth Committee. Also see Garland C. Routt, "Interpersonal Relationships and the Legislative Process," *American Academy of Political and Social Science Annals,* Vol. 195 (January 1938), pp. 129–136, for an exploratory effort to analyze observed interaction in the Illinois Senate.

[8]John Hadwen and Johan Kaufmann, *How United Nations Decisions are Made* (Leyden: A. W. Sythoff, 1960), p. 55.

MAURICE A. EAST

Status Discrepancy and Violence in the International System: An Empirical Analysis*

This analysis employs an international systems perspective to explain certain aspects of the inter-nation behavior of states. Underlying the use of the concept of the international system is the assumption that this global system has a *social* component, i.e., there is a global society. It is the characteristics of the stratification of this assumed world society that will be the focus of this article.

According to Melvin Tumin, social stratification can be defined as

... the arrangement of any social group or society into a hierarchy of positions that are unequal with regard to power, property, social evaluation and/or psychic gratification.[1]

Tumin goes on to argue that not only does a stratification system have a hierarchy of unequal positions, but that one's position in the stratification system makes an important difference in one's behavior.[2] In the area of international politics, this would mean that the position of a state in the stratification system of world society has important consequences for that state's behavior in a wide range of important activities. While this seems intuitively to be the case, it is in fact an empirical question which will be investigated in some depth here.[3]

* The research presented in this article is directly and significantly influenced by the questions asked and points raised by Harold Sprout during the three years the author worked under him as a graduate student at Princeton. Harold's acute concern for the empirical and theoretical payoffs of the systems approach to the study of international politics had led me to initiate a series of studies along these lines. While it is likely that not all the findings and conclusions of my research will be agreed to by the Sprouts, nevertheless their intellectual and personal support underlines to a very large degree the efforts represented here.

Notes and References for this selection will be found on pages 317–319.

This concern for the stratification system of the world society is not unique. For example, Gustavo Lagos uses a similar approach to examine the behavior of nations.

In this study, we shall assume that the nations of the world can be considered a great social system composed of different groups interacting and that these national groups occupy various positions within the social system. These positions can be ranked in terms of economic stature, power and prestige, and they constitute the status of a nation.[4]

Another scholar who has done much work in the general area is the Norwegian sociologist, Johan Galtung.[5] He and his students have carried out a number of studies using the general idea of stratification in the international system.

While our study has been influenced by the theoretical concerns of both Galtung and Lagos, there are several ways in which it goes beyond their work. First, this analysis concentrates most heavily on the *systemic* consequences of stratification, whereas both Galtung and Lagos are more concerned with these consequences for *individual* nation-states in the system. Second, data to be used in testing hypotheses have been collected on a world wide scale for a twenty year period. This is in contrast to much of the work done, e.g., by Galtung and Lagos, which has focused on only a single geographical area (primarily Latin America) and usually one limited time period. The present study attempts to apply a three-dimensional stratification system model to the entire international system during the post-1945 period.

Our basic approach to the international stratification system is based on Weber's classic three-dimensional model using class, status, and power. For our purposes, it will be more illuminating to refer to these dimensions as economic position, prestige, and politico-military force potential. Specifically, our emphasis here is on status discrepancy and its relationship to international conflict. Status discrepancy can be considered a structural attribute in the sense that when one says something about status discrepancy in a social system, he is saying something about the way the units making up the system are related, i.e., about the way the system is structured. In the case of an international system, the units are most likely to be nation-states. Most studies attempting to explain the occurrence of violence have failed to pay sufficient attention to such structural attributes. Criticizing several popular theories of aggression, Galtung states that

The difficulty with these theories . . . is that they are nonstructural; they do not take the social context sufficiently into consideration. . . . Granted the importance of individual characteristics, it is at least as unlikely that the chance of aggression for a given individual (unit) is independent of social position as it is that all individuals in the same position should display exactly the same tendency towards aggression.[6]

In a similar vein, we want to raise the same question with reference to the study of international violence solely in terms of the individual attributes of the units involved, i.e., the nation-states. Several empirical studies have been done which focus upon the nation-state level when seeking the causes of international conflict behavior. Michael Haas has explored the societal factors which relate to fluctuations of war and peace.[7] Rudolph Rummel has used factor analytic techniques to examine the dimensions of conflict between nations in terms of the relationship between variables characterizing nation-states and the conflict behavior of these states. Although the technique of factor analysis may tend to blur the fact, it is still essentially a means of discovering relationships between attributes of individual units and a certain type of behavior by the units.[8] The question raised here is whether the relationships found in these studies at the nation-state level may not be profoundly influenced by the over-all structure of the international system of which they are all a part. Can variations in the patterns of war and peace in the international system be accounted for in terms of systemic variables as well as in terms of nation-state level variables?[9]

However, most of these studies of international conflict done at the nation-state level have been synchronic in nature and do not allow for the time element which in turn allows for the systemic variation necessary to test the impact of systemic structural differences on relationships. Our strategy here will be to bypass the nation-state level and concentrate primarily on the relationship between system structure—more specifically, its stratification—and international conflict. Although our empirical research will be carried out in the above manner, in no way should this be interpreted as an argument for excluding nation-state (or even individual personality) variables from a more comprehensive analysis. If our chosen strategy shows the structural variables to be at all useful for explaining and accounting for some of the more important variations in international behavior, then the next step must be to undertake a more sophisticated multivariate analysis adding intervening variables from both the nation-state and individual levels.

The Hypothesis: Status Discrepancy and Violence

The central relationship to be explored is that between status discrepancy in the system and international violence exhibited by the system. The hypothesis is that the greater the amount of status discrepancy in the system, the more international violence in the system. The general thrust of this hypothesis is structural in nature, positing that a certain type of behavior in the system is correlated with a given structural characteristic of that system.

It is important to note that the hypothesis does not attempt to identify the units of the system where violence is likely to occur; rather the relationship merely claims an association between the structure of the system and the amount of violence. This type of hypothesis differs from those most generally identified with status discrepancy. The most frequently encountered hypotheses predict certain types of behavior based upon the degree of status discrepancy (or incongruence) found in the individual, e.g., "the greater the incongruence of simultaneously perceived status factors of the given individual, the more insecure is his status."[10]

At the nation-state level, there is a very good example of this same attempt to use the degree of status discrepancy (in this instance, the author talks about rank-disequilibrium) in a nation-state as a predictor of its behavior. Galtung, after discussing a multidimensional stratification system for nation-states and distinguishing between various status profiles for nations on the various dimensions, argues that it is extremely unlikely that aggression is randomly distributed among nation-states regardless of their social position. "The theoretical problem is now: *where in the system (and) for what social types is aggression most likely to accumulate and express itself?*"[11] He talks about three possible answers to the problem—aggression will emanate primarily from (1) the topdogs, (2) the underdogs, or (3) from those exhibiting status discrepancy. Using a five-dimensional stratification system, the profiles of these three respectively would be (1) T T T T T, (2) U U U U U, or (3) any combination of T's and U's, e.g., T T U U T or T U T U T or U T U T U (all such combinations would be status discrepant situations). After examining each of the three possible answers, Galtung argues that those social positions in rank-disequilibrium, i.e., those manifesting status discrepancy, are the most likely sources of aggression.

But as mentioned above, we do not claim this ability to pinpoint likely sources of aggression within a system. Our interest is solely in the likelihood of a system having certain structural attributes to experience violence. Our reason for rejecting the more specific type of theory is based on a questioning, if not a rejection, of some of its underlying assumptions. For example, much of the theory rests on psychologcal propositions involving concepts such as intra-personal strain, frustration, and achievement. While such concepts are meaningful at the individual level, there is strong reason to doubt their applicability to entities such as nation-states or international systems. To quote from the Sprouts,

... all such (psychological) theories are derived from, and purport to explain or predict, the behavior of biological organisms. Serious difficulties arise the moment such theories are wrenched from their human-biological context and applied to abstract entities such as the state or the international system. Difficulties arise, to be more specific, because perception and cognition, stimulus and response, and other phenomena from which psychological theories are derived have no close counterparts in entities that lack the anatomical structures and physiological mechanisms and processes of biological organisms.[12]

This type of doubt or rejection of the validity of such psychological concepts when applied to nations or the international system calls into question the ability of any such theories to predict exactly which entities are going to "experience" the psychological states (frustration, anger, etc.) which might cause violence.

On the other hand, we do not have such doubts or reservations about using a more structural or sociological approach to the problem of status discrepancy. The general argument here is that in any system with multi-dimensional stratification, there will be less violence if the various dimensions of stratification are congruent for the large portion of units in the system. Such congruence makes for less ambiguous behavior, more clearly defined roles and role-expectations, and less incentive for social change. For example, behavior will be less ambiguous in systems where the large proportion of units are either topdogs on all dimensions or underdogs on all dimensions. Similarly, role-definition will be more unambiguous if there are fewer situations where leaders in one context are followers in another. Also where there is relatively high congruence, there will be little motivation for change for two reasons: (1) those who have the top positions will have little desire to change the system which has awarded them privileged position, and (2) those with underdog status have neither the material resources nor the ideas and inspiration to better themselves. It is only in the system with status discrepancy where the resources necessary for initiating social change are in the hands of those with the motivation and skill to better themselves.

> . . . the underdog is deprived of the resources that make revolutions possible: ideas, visions, acquaintances, weapons, social experience, empathy, courage necessary to imagine oneself as a ruler, etc. What the underdog does not have he can get, but he gets it, we believe, precisely by changing one of his (underdog) statuses into a (topdog) status. . . .[13]

When such an underdog status on one dimension becomes a topdog status, status discrepancy increases, and hence our hypothesis predicts an increased level of international violence.

This general approach underlying our hypothesis relies more on sociological concepts of role and social change and less upon psychological concepts such as frustration, anger, etc. It should also be evident that while our theory appears to be relatively independent of any psychological theory of violence, it may in fact be compatible with several of them. The point is, however, that we believe international violence can be accounted for at the level of social structure without necessarily going to the level of psychological investigations.[14]

With the foregoing as background information, we can now focus upon the hypothesis itself in the context of international politics. What we are saying, for example, is that an international system in which high prestige is allocated to the more powerful and more economically developed nation-states is less likely to exhibit international violence than is a system where prestige is withheld from these nations. To bring this closer to our data, we can say that the closer the rankings of most of the nations on the prestige measure are to their rankings on the economic power dimension, the less violence we would expect in the system. The degree of closeness of the two rankings is our indicator of status discrepancy, which is in turn our independent variable. The dependent variable is the amount of violence in the system. Having collected data on the stratification dimensions over several years, it is possible to determine the degree of association between status discrepancy and amount of international violence in the international system over time.

The Data

Given our general hypothesis referring to a three-dimensional model, it is necessary to operationalize all three dimensions—economic position, prestige, and politico-military potential ("power"). *Economic position* is measured by total gross national product of a country.[15] The *"power" dimension* is operationalized using total defense expenditures by the central government in a given year.[16] Both of these concepts are quite complex, and an argument could easily be made for using some sort of composite measure. However, given the fact that data were being gathered for some 120 nations over a 20-year period and given the limitations of time and resources, it was necessary to employ relatively simple measures. More specifically, total gross national product is utilized because international economic potential is a function of the total amount of economic resources available to be allocated to various sectors. This concept differs significantly from the more frequently used measures of economic development where G.N.P. is discounted for population size. As for the use of total defense expenditures, the same general argument applies. By using a measure of the total amount available to the military domain for allocation between human and material resources, one is able to assess to some degree the "power" potential of a country.

Although every effort has been made to gather reliable data on these two variables for all countries during the years 1948–1964, we claim no particularly high degree of reliability for our figures. In many cases we simply do not have any standard by which the reliability of our figures can be estimated. While it is possible to find what can be assumed to be highly reliable data for a vast majority of the countries of the world *for a given year*, it is quite another task to find this type of data for more than two or three isolated years.

Even though the above "disclaimer" has been made, working with the data has convinced us that the data are in general very accurate in depicting relative position among the countries for a given year, and this is in fact the way the data will be used in this study. We will not be trying to analyze one country's defense expenditures over time, but rather our interest is in the relative position of countries on these dimensions for a given year.

Also the statistical analysis employed relies heavily on nonparametric procedures and ordinal measures which require only that the rank ordering of countries be accurate. Having examined the data at some length, we feel that at this level of measurement the data are reliable and accurate.

The third measure, which operationalizes the concept of *prestige*, is the number of embassies (or embassies plus legations) in the capital city of a country. The general idea for this measure comes from a study by Singer and Small, where they use a weighted frequency count of diplomatic missions in a capital city as a measure of prestige in the international system for the period from 1815 to 1945.[17] In that study, the authors argue that this particular weighting system is not appropriate after the Second World War due to the tremendous increase in the diplomatic relations between states. While agreeing that the Singer and Small method of weighting is not valid after 1945, we do contend that using the *absolute number* of embassies (or embassies and legations) in the capital city is valid.[18]

The general theory underlying this indicator of prestige closely parallels that of the reputational school of social position.[19] The process which is assumed to underly the establishment of an embassy in a foreign capital is the result of the consideration of a large number of factors. The question posed is this: Given limited resources and a choice between several capital cities, where should an embassy be established in order to gain the greatest benefits? The answers to this question can be many. We need an embassy in this country in order to facilitate the successful establishment of trade agreements. We need an embassy here in order to work for a mutual assistance pact involving military supplies. We need an embassy here to handle more efficiently the problems created by our large merchant marine fleet. We need an embassy here just to keep an eye on other nations' diplomats and what they are doing, i.e., for informational and intelligence purposes. All of these are legitimate and valid reasons for establishing an embassy. Our contention is that the sum total of embassies in a nation's capital city is an indicator of the degree to which other nations consider the country important along any number of dimensions. In this sense, our measure is tapping the concept of ascribed influence. By placing an embassy in a given country, you are ascribing influence and power to it. You are in effect indicating that this nation can be influential for your country, because placing an embassy there will be more of an advantage to your country than placing it elsewhere. Prestige can be defined as the sum of this ascribed influence. Hence, the index is the total number of embassies.[20]

The dependent variable in our hypothesis is the amount of international violence in the international system. Two different measures of violence are used to test our hypothesis. One is the international war data collected and coded by Singer and Small. These data are described more fully elsewhere,[21] but a brief overview will be presented here. The wars are limited to those involving at least one independent nation which is a member of the system and has a population of over 500,000; another criterion they used is that the best estimate of battle deaths must be over 1,000.[22] These data have been used to provide an over-all, aggregate measure of the amount of violence in the international system at a given time. Three separate measures have been devised on the basis of their raw data.

1. A measure of the amount of conflict based on a frequency count of the number of separate conflicts which began or were going on in a given year, coded only once in a single year.
2. A measure based on a frequency count of the number of separate conflicts which began or were underway in each quarter of a given year. For example, a war which lasted from February until August would be counted three times, once for each quarter of the year during which it ran.
3. A measure based on a frequency count of the number of separate conflicts which began or were under way in each month of a given year. For example, a war which lasted from February until August would be counted seven times, once for each month during which it ran.

Included in the Singer data are the 12 interstate conflicts listed below:

Palestine	May 15, 1948 to July 18, 1948 and October 22, 1948 to January 7, 1949
Korean	June 24, 1950 to July 27, 1953
Sinai	October 31, 1956 to November 7, 1956
Russo-Hungarian	October 23, 1956 to November 14, 1956
Sino-Indian	October 20, 1962 to November 22, 1962
Second Kashmir	August 4, 1965 to September 23, 1965
First Kashmir	October 26, 1947 to January 1, 1949
Indonesian	November 10, 1945 to October 15, 1946
Indochinese	December 1, 1945 to June 1, 1954
Madagascan	March 29, 1947 to December 1, 1948
Algerian	November 1, 1954 to March 17, 1962
Tibetan	March 1, 1956 to March 22, 1959

The second set of data used to measure international violence in the system comes from an Office of Naval Research Study conducted in 1965. The original study produced data on 381 conflict events occurring from 1945 to 1964.[23] Our analysis will be based on a subset of those conflicts including only those coded as inter-state as opposed to internal conflicts. The subset has an N of 58 cases. Information for these international conflicts was taken from *Keesings Contemporary Archives*, *The New York Times*, and *Facts on File*.

Using the Office of Naval Research data, several measures of inter-state violence for the international system have been devised:

1. A measure of the amount of conflict based on a frequency count of the number of separate conflicts which began or were going on in a given year, coded only once in a single year.
2. A measure derived from a frequency count of the number of separate conflicts which began or were underway in each quarter of a given year.

3. A third measure based on a frequency count of the number of separate conflicts which began or were underway in each month of a given year.

The Analysis

We have employed the Spearman rank-order correlation coefficient as the statistic used to indicate the degree of status discrepancy between prestige and power and economic wealth. This statistic measures the "agreement" between the ranks on these variables, i.e., the tendency of two rank orderings to be similar. Its range is from plus 1.00 to minus 1.00, with a large positive value indicating a large amount of agreement or association between the rank orders.[24] Thus, the larger the value of a positive Spearman correlation (frequently called the Spearman rho and noted as $r\hat{s}$), the less the amount of status discrepancy between the variables. Our hypothesis predicts, therefore, that increasing amounts of international violence will be correlated with decreasing values of the Spearman rho and, conversely, decreasing amounts of violence will be correlated with increasing values of rho.

Theoretically, our hypothesis calls for a measure of status discrepancy which aggregates the amount of disagreement found between all pairs of variables in the stratification system, i.e., between prestige and power, prestige and wealth, and wealth and power. However, the correlations between our indices of power (total defense expenditures by central government) and wealth (total gross national product) are so high that no appreciable difference occurs in status discrepancy when using the aggregate measure as compared to the simple Spearman correlation between prestige and either one of the other two measures. (Table 1 shows the Pearsonian correlation coefficients for the data on GNP and defense expenditures.) Therefore in presenting our findings, relationships involving status discrepancy based on prestige and economic position, on the one hand, and prestige and power, on the other, will be reported. This means that Spearman rho values will be reported on rank orderings of (1) embassies and total G.N.P., (2) embassies plus legations and total G.N.P., (3) embassies and total defense expenditures, and, (4) embassies plus legations and total defense expenditures.

By way of summary, we have two separate sets of data on violence in the international system—the Singer and Small data and the Office of Naval Research data. For both of these sets, three different measures of inter-state violence have been generated from the raw data, giving a total of six measures of inter-state violence. Four sets of status discrepancy measures, i.e., Spearman rho values, are presented: Embassies and total G.N.P., embassies plus legations and total G.N.P., embassies and total defense expenditures, embassies plus legations and total defense expenditures. Thus it is possible to examine the relationship between various measures of status discrepancy and various measures of international violence over time.

First, let us examine the relationship using the Singer-Small data.

Table 1—Total Gross National Product and Total Defense Expenditures: Pearson Correlation Coefficients by Year, 1948–1964

Year	r
1948[a]	.702
1949[a]	.665
1950	.662
1951	.817
1952	.948
1953	.958
1954	.960
1955	.935
1956	.955
1957	.965
1958	.972
1959	.980
1960	.976
1961	.964
1962	.966
1963	.958
1964	.966

[a] Due to lack of data for total GNP in these years, the correlation is computed using GNP data for 1950 and the 1948 and 1949 Defense expenditure data.

The general tendency exhibited by this set of data is a slight (but non-monotonic) decrease in the amount of violence over time. This can be seen in Figure 1, which is a graph of three indices of the amount of inter-state violence in the system from 1946 through 1965. If our hypothesis is correct, the general tendency of the status discrepancy measure, our Spearman rho, should be slightly increasing. This is in fact the case as is demonstrated by the graph of rho values over time shown in Figure 2.

Having seen the general form of the relationship between status discrepancy and international violence using the Singer-Small data, it is now possible to get some idea of the direction and the magnitude of this relationship by using a Pearson correlation coefficient. The correlation values are set forth at the top of the next page.

An examination of Table 2 shows that in every instance the relationship is a negative one as predicted by the hypothesis. As the Spearman rho values increase (indicating a *decrease* in the actual amount of status discrepancy), the amount of violence in the system tends to decrease. Furthermore, the magnitudes of all the correlations are in the same general range. The fact that there are *no* relationships contrary to the hypothesized direction is relatively unusual in this type of research where many correlations are reported, all bearing on the validity of the hypothesis. Also unusual for

Table 2—Interstate Conflict and Status Discrepancy.[a]
(Based on Singer-Small Data for 1949–1964, N = 16)

Inter-state[c] Conflict	Status Status Discrepancy[b]			
	$r_s(1)$	$r_s(2)$	$r_s(3)$	$r_s(4)$
S-S(1)	−.482	−.363	−.464	−.361
S-S(2)	−.441	−.433	−.303	−.335
S-S(3)	−.470	−.487	−.305	−.328

[a] This table reports Pearson product moment correlations calculated for values for each pair of variables over time.
[b] The status discrepancy variables are represented in the table as follows:
  $r_s(1)$—Spearman rho for status discrepancy on embassies and GNP,
  $r_s(2)$—Spearman rho for status discrepancy on embassies plus legations and GNP,
  $r_s(3)$—Spearman rho for status discrepancy on embassies and defense,
  $r_s(4)$—Spearman rho for status discrepancy on embassies plus legations and defense.
[c] The interstate conflict variables are generated from the Singer-Small data and are represented in the table as follows:
  S-S(1)—Amount of international violence based on the number of conflict events beginning in each year,
  S-S(2)—Amount of international violence based on number of conflict events in each quarter and summed for the year,
  S·S(3)—Amount of international violence based on number of conflict events in each month and summed for the year.

this type of research is the similarity of magnitudes of the relationships. This consistency of direction and magnitude adds support to the substantive significance of our findings.[25]

It is now necessary to look at the same relationship for the Office of Naval Research (O.N.R.) data on international violence. Do we get the same general pattern of relationships using these data? The predictions from our general hypothesis remain the same—that there should be a negative correlation between the amount of violence in the system and the measures of status discrepancy.

When one inspects a graph of the three measures of international violence based on the O.N.R. data, the general relationship that emerges is in the form of an inverted U-shape with its modal point occurring in the year 1955. Another way of interpreting these data is that there was an increasing amount of international violence up to 1955 with a decrease in violence since that time. These relationships are seen in Figure 3.

As will be recalled, the general tendency of our Spearman rho values was a slightly increasing one. This can be interpreted as meaning that for years after 1955 our hypothesis holds to a very high degree, but for the years prior to 1955 the hypothesis is less accurate. The over-all correlation coefficients in Table 3 represent the cumulated relationship for the entire period. Thus we would expect these correlations to be slightly lower than those in Table 2.

There are several very obvious aspects of Table 3 that have to be examined. First, it is true that the magnitudes of the relationships in the table

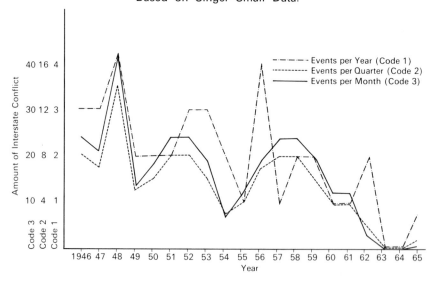

Figure 1. Fluctuations of Interstate Conflict, 1946–1965, Based on Singer–Small Data.

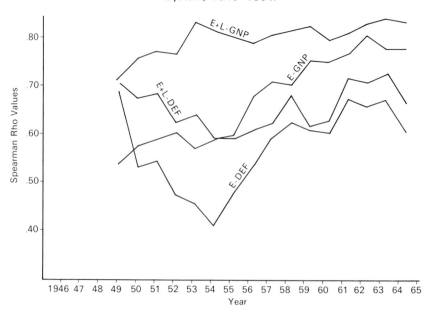

Figure 2. Four Indices of Status Discrepancy in the International System, 1949–1964.

are smaller than those found when using the Singer-Small data (see Table 2). Second, there is a distinct difference in the relationship between the status) discrepancy measures using G.N.P. and those using defense expenditures.

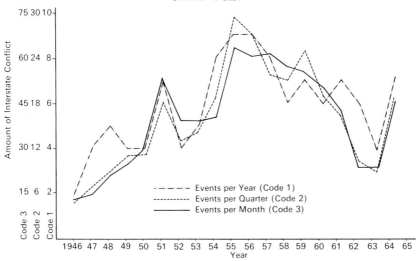

Figure 3. Fluctuations of Interstate Conflict, 1946–1964, Based on O.N.R. Data.

The latter have negative correlations, and, in one instance (using embassies plus legations and defense), the relationship is quite large.

Table 3—Interstate Conflict and Status Discrepancy.[a]
(Based on O.N.R. Data for 1946–1964, $N = 16$)

| | Status Discrepancy[b] | | | |
Inter-state[c] Conflict	$r_s(1)$	$r_s(2)$	$r_s(3)$	$r_s(4)$
O.N.R.(1)	.163	.299	−.250	−.548
O.N.R.(2)	.042	.162	−.294	−.703
O.N.R.(3)	.045	.139	−.279	−.629

[a] This table reports Pearson product moment correlations calculated for values for each pair of variables over time.
[b] The status discrepancy variables are represented in the table as follows:
   $r_s(1)$—Spearman rho for rank orderings of embassies and G.N.P.,
   $r_s(2)$—Spearman rho for rank orderings of embassies plus legations and G.N.P.
   $r_s(3)$—Spearman rho for status discrepancy on embassies and defense,
   $r_s(4)$—Spearman rho for status discrepancy on embassies plus legations and defense.
[c] The interstate conflict variables are generated from the O.N.R. data and represented in the table as follows:
   O.N.R.(1)—Amount of international violence based on number of conflict events beginning in each year,
   O.N.R.(2)—Amount of international violence based on number of conflict events in each quarter and summed for the year,
   O.N.R.(3)—Amount of international violence based on number of conflict events in each month and summed for the year.

An examination of the *shape* of the distributions of the four status discrepancy measures (as seen in Figure 1) can help to explain this difference to some degree. It can be seen that the two status discrepancy values representing the defense expenditure components have more of a U-shape to them. Given the general inverted U-shape of the international violence data from the O.N.R. data, this would make for a relatively strong negative correlation between the two variables—over time, a downward change in status discrepancy is correlated by and large with an upward change in amount of violence and vice-versa. This then accounts for the negative relationship found in two of the rho values, $r\hat{s}(3)$ and $r\hat{s}(4)$. The greater magnitude of the $r\hat{s}(4)$ values is accounted for by the more pronounced U-shaped form of the distribution.

As for "explaining away" the positive correlations for the other two rho values, all that can be said is that while the hypothesized relationship seems to hold for the years after 1955, the correlation coefficient shows an overall positive correlation because of the predominant effect of evidence contrary to our hypothesis in the years before 1955.

Although one of the most satisfying and least difficult intellectual operations (and perhaps one of the most misleading) is coming up with theoretical reasons to justify empirical results already arrived at, we can nevertheless mention several lines of reasoning which would tend to be compatible with our findings. The first is that during the middle 1950's, there was a period of mutual deterrence balance brought about by the relatively swift and unexpected development of the Soviet nuclear delivery capability which tended to offset the United States lead in the development of nuclear warheads.[26] This period of relative equality of military might brought decision-makers in capitals all over the world to make a more realistic assessment of the world power balance. The "true worth" of states became an important factor in international politics. It became increasingly difficult (especially for the smaller states) to maintain one's status in the world on the basis of friendship or alliance with the assumed preponderant world power, because it was no longer clear which was preponderant. The over-all effect was that nation-states had to reassess their commitments, and this accounts for the decreasing amount of status discrepancy in the international system after 1955. This decrease is indicated by the increasing Spearman rho values for all four indices after 1955.

Another possible explanation for the relationship found in the O.N.R. data is that the effects of status discrepancy in the system were temporarily nullified during the post-1955 period. Because of an expansion and increase in the size of the international system at this time, there was a period when the topdog–underdog discrepancy was not very salient. As newer members entered the system, e.g., the entry of sixteen new members into the United Nations in 1955 and the independence granted to former colonial territories in the late 1950's and early 1960's, their newly acquired status made them forget momentarily about their relative position in the world. On the other hand, the expansion of the system meant that former underdogs now became at least middle dogs, being replaced at the bottom by the newer members. The topdogs felt even more content in that they were even farther out in front relative to the new underdogs. Thus everybody existed in a state of euphoria for a time. Under such conditions objective indices of status discrepancy would have little relevance and international violence would tend to decrease.

It is also interesting to note that both the Singer-Small data and the O.N.R. data give evidence that as of 1964, this euphoria began to wane as we see a slight increase in the amount of international violence occurring. (See Figures 1 and 3.)

However, it must be mentioned again that the two possible explanations offered immediately above were arrived at after inspecting the data. There is no claim whatsoever made to their validity. Independent empirical investigation would have to be carried out in order to shed any further light on their usefulness in accounting for international behavior.

Status Discrepancy and International Violence with One- and Two-Year Lags

Because of the time element as a factor in all causal type relationships, an examination of the relationship between status discrepancy and international violence ought to include some time lag. The reasoning here is that any of the sociological conditions which are generated by status discrepancy in a system do not immediately become factors affecting the behavior of the component units of the system. It may be the case that status discrepancy in the international system will be responsible for international violence and conflict in the system a year hence, or perhaps two years hence. In order to test for the possibility of such a relationship, we have performed the same type of analysis as above lagging the international violence data one and two years. This means, for example that status discrepancy for

Table 4—Interstate Conflict and Status Discrepancy.[a]
(Data on Conflict are Lagged One Year)

Inter-state[b] *Conflict*	*Status Discrepancy*[b]			
	$r_s(1)$	$r_s(2)$	$r_s(3)$	$r^s(4)$
S-S(1)	−.632	−.465	−.424	−.287
S-S(2)	−.561	−.633	−.356	−.434
S-S(3)	−.591	−.634	−.383	−.451
O.N.R.(1)	−.127	.390	−.554	−.589
O.N.R.(2)	−.209	.298	−.561	−.666
O.N.R.(3)	−.214	.135	−.542	−.710

[a] This table reports Pearson product moment correlations calculated for values for each pair of variables over time.
[b] The variables are represented in this table in the same manner as they are in Tables 2 and 3.

1950 is correlated with international violence data for 1951 in the case of the one year lag, and with international violence data for 1952 for a two year lag. The results of these two analyses are clearly presented in Tables 4 and 5.[27]

What difference, if any, does the result of lagging the data make in our interpretation of the hypothesis? Generally speaking, the correlations are higher when the data is lagged. This is true of both sets of data for both the one-year and the two-year lag, as can be seen by taking the arithmetic mean of the absolute values of the correlation coefficients for each of the lagged years separately and comparing this value with the arithmetic mean of the coefficients of the nonlagged data. These mean values are as follows:

Nonlagged data using *S-S*	.385
S-S data lagged one year:	.460
S-S data lagged two years:	.422
Nonlagged data using O.N.R.	.296
O.N.R. data lagged one year:	.416
O.N.R. data lagged two years:	.482

These findings would tend to confirm the idea that the effects of status discrepancy are stronger when time is taken into consideration. The relationship between status discrepancy and international violence is stronger if one assumes a one- or two-year time lag between the measure of discrepancy and its effects.

Table 5—Interstate Conflict and Status Discrepancy.[a]
(Data on Conflict are Lagged Two Years)

Inter-state Conflict[b]	Status Discrepancy[b]			
	$r_s(1)$	$r_s(2)$	$r_s(3)$	$r_s(4)$
S-S(1)	−.682	−.671	−.305	−.172
S-S(2)	−.723	−.680	−.140	−.102
S-S(3)	−.742	−.706	−.162	−.129
O.N.R.(1)	−.157	.439	−.654	−.665
O.N.R.(2)	−.179	.503	−.677	−.603
O.N.R.(3)	−.209	.442	−.676	−.589

[a] This table reports Pearson product moment correlations calculated for values for each pair of variables over time.
[b] The variables are represented in this table in the same manner as they are in Tables 2 and 3.

In both cases the direction of the relationship in the lagged data is at least as favorable to our hypothesis as it is in the nonlagged data. And in the case of the O.N.R. data, the relationship using $r\hat{s}$ (1), which is based on embassies and G.N.P., is in the predicted direction of the lagged data when it was not in the nonlagged data. In this example, lagging the data makes for a larger proportion of favorable correlations given our major hypothesis, i.e., an inverse correlation between Spearman rho values and amount of international violence.

More specifically, when the Singer-Small data are examined, it can be seen that the magnitude of the relationships between violence and the status discrepancy values based on G.N.P. figures [$r\hat{s}(1)$ and $r\hat{s}(2)$] increases as you move from nonlagged to one-year lag to two-year lag. The magnitudes using $r\hat{s}(3)$ and $r\hat{s}(4)$ based on defense expenditures tend to decrease.

A closer examination of the values for the O.N.R. data shows that there is no clear-cut pattern beyond the monotonic increase in the over-all means as you move from nonlagged to one-year lag to two-year lag. The values for $r\hat{s}(2)$ and $r\hat{s}(3)$ increase monotonically also, but the other two values show no such pattern.

As for our interpretation of these data, the major conclusion seems to be that lagging the data, which assumes a time factor for the effect of status discrepancy on the international system, does bring about stronger relationships in the predicted direction in the overwhelming number of cases. As far as having to choose between the values arrived at using the one-year lag over the two-year, the evidence is far from clear. For example, in the case of the O.N.R. data, the mean value of the one-year lag coefficients is less than that for the two-year lag, while the opposite is true for the Singer-Small data, with the mean value for the one-year lag being larger than that for the two-year lag.

Thus, there seems to be no compelling factors in the data that would lead us to use one set of figures over the other. Generally speaking, both sets of figures serve equally well to verify our major hypothesis relating status discrepancy to interstate conflict in the international system.

Summary

We have hypothesized that there is a general relationship between the amount of interstate conflict in the world system and certain characteristics of that system. More specifically, we have stated that the amount of violence occurring in the international system is directly related to the degree of status discrepancy in the system. Using the general three-dimensional model of stratification offered by Weber, the following concepts have been operationalized for the majority of nation-states in the international system for the years 1946–1964: economic position, prestige, and politico-military potential. Two different sets of data have been used to measure the amount of interstate conflict in the system during the chosen time period.

The evidence indicates a general and consistent pattern supporting our hypothesis. This pattern holds across a relatively large number of alternative measures used in operationalizing the variables represented in the hypothesis. The analysis also supports the hypothesis when the conflict data are lagged one and two years in order to take a time factor into account for causal relationships. Given the weight of our evidence supporting the relationship between stratification and interstate conflict, we feel that there is a need to research further the influence of other systemic characteristics on international political behavior.

The evidence presented here is also relevant, if only indirectly, for a competing hypothesis—the cross-cutting cleavages hypothesis. According to this competing argument, it is the presence in the system of units which are status discrepant that tends to alleviate or moderate conflict. These units can act as mediators between topdogs and underdogs, to use Galtung's terminology again, because being status discrepant means that they represent elements of both statuses.[28] Although the evidence presented here cannot serve as any sort of critical test for these two competing hypotheses, it seriously challenges certain aspects of the cross-cutting cleavages hypothesis. The questions raised are again an invitation to further research.

Insofar as our findings relating status discrepancy and interstate conflict are valid, there are several implications for foreign policy. In general, the most peaceful international system will be the one with the least amount of status discrepancy. Therefore, the foreign policies of nation-states should be aimed at reducing status discrepancy in the system by coping with at least the more obvious cases. One prime example of such status discrepancy may be Communist China, whose population, resources, and nuclear force give her a "power" status far above the prestige status she now has in the system. A similar case may also be East Germany. On the other hand, nation-states such as India and the U.A.R. may be cases where the prestige status is greater than the "power" status.

Finally, the general position of the "have-not" states in the world is a troublesome one, assuming the validity of our hypothesis. In an international system with low status discrepancy, the "have-not" states would be denied high status on any and all relevant dimensions of stratification, i.e., there would be a high degree of cumulative inequality in the system. It should be pointed out, however, that our hypothesis says nothing about how large the gap must be between topdog and underdog status. It would be possible for a future international system to have cumulative inequality (as the consequence of a low level of status discrepancy) but with a much narrower gap between the top and bottom. Under such conditions, which do not seem likely in the near future, the cumulative inequalities brought about as a result of low status discrepancy may be less destabilizing given the narrowing distance between rich and poor.

Notes and References

[1] Melvin M. Tumin, *Social Stratification* (New York: Prentice-Hall 1967), p. 12.

[2] *Ibid.*, p. 18.

[3] One good example of the consequentiality of stratification in international politics is found in the Concert of Europe where the position held by a state was extremely important in determining its rights and obligations. Great powers possessed certain rights to act that were denied to lesser powers. See Robert L. Rothstein, *Alliances and Small Powers* (New York: Columbia University Press, 1968), pp. 12–16.

[4] Gustavo Lagos, *International Stratification and Underdeveloped Countries* (Chapel Hill: University of North Carolina Press, 1963), pp. 6–8.

[5] A listing of articles by Galtung and his students in this area of concern:

Johan Galtung, "A Structural Theory of Agression," *Journal of Peace Research*, No. 2, (1964), pp. 95–119.

———, "East-West Interaction Patterns," *Journal of Peace Research*, Number 2 (1966), pp. 146–177.

———, "International Relations and Internation Conflicts: A Sociological Approach," *Transaction of the Sixth World Congress of Sociology*, Vol. I (September 1966), pp. 121–161.

Simon Schwartzman, "International Development and International Feudalism: The Latin American Case," *Proceedings of the International Peace Research Association Conference*, Groningen, Netherlands (July 3–5, 1965), pp. 52–77.

———, and Manuel Mora y Araujo, "The Images of International Stratification in in Latin America," *Journal of Peace Research*, Number 3 (1966), pp. 225–243.

Per Olav Reinton, "International Structure and International Integration: The Case of Latin America," *Journal of Peace Research*, Number 4 (1967), pp. 334–365.

Johan Galtung, "Rank and Social Integration: A Multidimensional Approach," in Berger, Zelditch, and Anderson, *Sociological Theories in Progress* (Boston: Houghton-Mifflin, 1966), pp. 145–198.

Nils Petter Gleditsch, "Trends in World Airline Patterns," *Journal of Peace Research*, Number 4 (1967), pp. 366–408.

[6] Galtung, "Structural Theory of Aggression," p. 96.

[7] Michael Haas, "Societal Approaches to the Study of War," *Journal of Peace Research*, Number 4 (1965), pp. 307–323.

[8] Rudolph J. Rummel, "Dimensions of Conflict Behavior Within and Between Nations," *General Systems*, Vol. 8 (1963), pp. 1–50.

[9] It is interesting to note that Raymond Tanter replicated Rummel's 1955–1957

study using the data collected for the years 1958–1960. Assuming that these two sets of data are from international systems having different systemic attributes, it should be possible to investigate the impact of differential systemic effects on relationships between societal variables and international conflict. Although we do not propose to undertake such an analysis at the present time, pointing out the possibility of such a study does much to make the point at hand. See Raymond Tanter, "Dimensions of Conflict Behavior Within and Between Nations, 1958–1960," Ph.D. dissertation, Indiana University, 1964.

[10] This hypothesis is taken from Andrzej Malewski, "The Degree of Status Incongruence and Its Effects," in Bendix and Lipset (eds.), *Class, Status and Power* (New York: 2nd ed., Free Press, 1966), p. 305. This entire article deals with the behavioral characteristics of individuals with status discrepancy.

[11] Galtung, "Structural Theory of Aggression," p. 97. The emphasis is found in the original article.

[12] Harold and Margaret Sprout, *The Ecological Perspective on Human Affairs* (Princeton: Princeton University Press, 1965), p. 28.

[13] Galtung, "Structural Theory of Aggression," p. 98.

[14] While it is readily admitted that the line between social and psychological phenomena is a fine one, and while it may be argued that much of what we have been talking about herein is within the realm of social psychology, nevertheless we still maintain the general thrust of our argument: behavior can be accounted for, in large part, in terms of the pattern of relationships between and among actors without delving into the individual units *per se*.

[15] The bulk of the data for this measure comes from an Agency for International Development publication, *GNP Growth Rates and Trend Data* (Statistics and Reports Division, June 15, 1966). The G.N.P. is given in millions of U.S. dollars at constant 1962 prices. Where this AID publication was missing data, every attempt was made to find comparable information elsewhere; other sources used included the United Nations' National

Statistical Yearbook, Moody's Municipal and Government Manual, and individual reference works for such countries as the People's Republic of China, the Soviet Union, and Eastern Europe.

[16] Data for this measure were gathered primarily from the United Nations Statistical Yearbook. However, reporting here was quite spotty for Communist countries and for some Latin American countries. Other sources used included Moody's Manual of Investments: American and Foreign Governments and Municipalities, United Nations reports for the Economic Commission for Europe, *Europa Yearbook, Stateman's Yearbook*, and Institute for Strategic Studies estimates. There was one set of highly complete data on defense expenditures for 1964 which was frequently used as a benchmark for this measure. These 1964 data are found in a report by William Sprecher, *World-Wide Defense Expenditures and Selected Economic Data* (Arms Control and Disarmament Agency, Research Report 66-1), January 1966.

[17] See J. David Singer and Melvin Small, "The Composition and Status Ordering of the International System: 1815–1940," *World Politics*, Vol. XVIII, No. 2 (January 1966), pp. 236–282.

[18] Data have been collected for both embassies and embassies plus legations, and in reporting our research we will include measures of status discrepancy using both sets of data on diplomatic missions.

[19] For a discussion of the reputation vs. event analysis, see William Spinrad, "Power in Local Communities," in Bendix and Lipset, *op. cit.*, pp. 218–231.

[20] Two types of validity tests were performed on our "prestige" data. In one we compared our earliest rank-ordering of the system (1949) with Singer's most recent rank ordering (1940). The Spearman rho was a .436 for 54 cases where data were available in both measures. This is significant at the .005 level in a one-tailed test. The second test compared the ability of our measure to rank order nations in the Latin American subsystem to the orderings arrived at by another researcher, namely Schwartzman (cited above in note 4). The Spearman rho value between our 1964 data and Schwartzman's was .79. Unfortunately, we have not been able to

find similar data for other geographic subsystems to further verify our data.

[21]See J. David Singer and Melvin Small, "National Alliance Commitments and War Involvement, 1815–1945," *Peace Research Society (International)*, Vol. V (1966), pp. 109–140; also by Singer and Small, "Alliance Aggregation and the Onset of War, 1815–1945," in J. D. Singer (ed.), *Quantitive International Politics* (New York: Free Press, 1968), pp. 247–286.

[22]It should be noted here that the Singer-Small articles referred to here do not include nor discuss data for the 1945–1964 period. These data were generously supplied to me by Singer. Their publication appears to be forthcoming; see Singer and Small, *International War, 1815–1965; a Statiscal Handbook* (New York: Wiley, 1971).

[23]A deck containing portions of the data from the Office of Naval Research study was supplied very graciously by a former colleague, Richard Perle. Complete responsiblity for all analysis and conclusions based on this set of data rest with the author.

[24]For interesting discussions of this rank order statistic, see William L. Hays, *Statistics for Psychologists* (New York: Holt, Rinehart and Winston, 1963), pp. 641–652; and Sidney Siegel, *Nonparametric Statistics for the Behavioral Sciences* (New York: McGraw-Hill, 1956), pp. 202–213.

[25]Given the value of correlations reported in this article, the reader may very well raise the question of significance. Our position is that significance tests are not entirely appropriate for these values. In the first place, no sampling has taken place, and thus the problem of inferring from a sample to some universe does not arise. Secondly, the variables used in computing these statistics are obviously not independent of one another from year to year, and this is an important condition to be met when using significance tests. For similar views on this probelm, see David Gold, "Some Problems in Generalizing Aggregate Associations," *American Behavioral Scientist*, Vol. VII (December 1964), pp. 16–18; Michael Haas, "Com-

parative Analysis," *Western Political Quarterly*, Vol. XV (1962), pp. 294–303; and Seymour Martin Lipset, Martin Trow, and James Coleman, *Union Democracy* (Garden City: Doubleday, 1962), pp. 480–485.

In summary, while our tables do not show statistical significance to any high degree, we are still impressed by the consistency of the general tendencies apparent in the data. These tendencies appear many times using different sets of data, and this substantive significance may be the more important factor in this study.

[26]This general view of the mid-1950's is shared by Peter Calvocoressi, *International Politics Since 1945* (New York: Praeger, 1968). He writes:

In the fifties both sides exploded a thermonuclear or hydrogen bomb, the Americans in November 1952 and the Russians (who had exploded their first atom bomb in 1949) nine months later. Despite the Russian advances the Americans retained their supremacy until about 1953 owing to their superior capacity to deliver... The Russians, however, rapidly developed their means of delivery so that *a mutual deterrence ruled the mid-fifties.* . . . (p. 27, emphasis added).

[27]For other examples of lagging data in the area of international relations, see Michael Haas, "Social Change and National Aggressiveness, 1900–1960," in J. D. Singer (ed.), *Quantitative International Politics,* pp. 215–244 and especially p. 266; also Singer and Small, "Alliance Aggregation and the Onset of War, 1815–1945," *ibid.,* pp. 247–286.

[28]See Galtung, "Structural Theory of Aggression," pp. 98–99. For another study using the cross-cutting cleavages hypothesis, see Karl W. Deutsch and J. David Singer, "Multipolar Power Systems and International Stability," *World Politics,* Vol. XVI, No. 3 (April 1964), pp. 390–406. An excellent critique of the Deutsch-Singer piece is found in Dina Zinnes, "An Analytical Study of the Balance of Power Theories," *Journal of Peace Research,* No. 3, (1967), pp. 270–288.

BURTON M. SAPIN

The Politico-Military Approach to American Foreign Policy*

The last 25 years have been marked by the dominant role of the United States in international politics. An accompanying characteristic of almost equal significance has been the importance of military factors, military forces, military doctrines, and military organizations and personnel in the business of defining American purposes and defending and pursuing American policies in the international arena. It might be added that while nuclear weapons and missile delivery systems have contributed to this state of affairs, they by no means provide its full explanation.

It seems clear that the international role of the United States over the next 25 years, or even the next decade, will be more limited. This is to be explained in good part by major changes in the international system, including the renewed strength and vitality of nations badly damaged in World War Two and the emergence of new centers of national power or, at least, independence. An apparent slowness of American response and accommodation to some of these changes has been accelerated in the past

---

* It should be noted that this essay was prepared in the waning days of the Johnson administration and the early weeks of President Nixon's. While there have been the inevitable modifications in organizational arrangements and responsibilities since then, nothing has happened that would require significant change in the analysis and point of view of this essay. A number of books, some polemical and some more dispassionately analytical, have recently appeared that attempt to explore the "impacts" of the military establishment on American politics and society. However, the politico-military dimension of American foreign policy continues to get rather scanty scholarly attention.

Notes and References for this selection will be found on pages 342–344.

few years by the pressure of urgent domestic problems and the painful experience of the Vietnam war.[1]

It is not the purpose of this paper, however, to debate the limits or the arrogance, past or present, of American foreign policy. Its premise is that military factors and forces will continue to play a most important role in the making and carrying out of American foreign policy no matter what the grand strategy, or the specific policy directions, of the next decade or two. If this assumption is a reasonable one (and we are talking about what is quite probable rather than what might be desirable in someone's elaborate scheme for world order), are there conclusions to be drawn, lessons to be learned, from the experience of the past 25 years? Has the involvement of "the military" in American foreign policy been the source of many or most of our troubles, as a few critics argue? Has it been just moderately harmful, or can it even be demonstrated to have contributed net benefits to the interests of the nation? Perhaps the military establishment and the career military services are not the heart of the matter at all but rather their civilian colleagues in government.

Confident statement of all these positions can be found somewhere in the public prints, but I will argue in this paper that we have neither the well-defined criteria nor the necessary empirical data to make such judgments with confidence. Before doing so, it may be useful to sketch the organizational arrangements and the personnel training programs through which the United States has attempted to harness its military and foreign policy establishments in the pursuit of American objectives abroad.

I. Politico-Military Organizational Arrangements and Personnel Training

It is precisely the implication of the term, "politico-military," that foreign policy problems and responsibilities and those of the military establishment are closely related and must therefore be viewed and dealt with in terms of one another. The nature of the interrelationship and, therefore, the degree of coordinated or integrated effort required will vary from problem to problem. My own assumption is that the need for such an approach by contemporary American policy makers is deep and fundamental.

These are familiar formulations, particularly to the relatively narrow band of practitioners and academics who have interested themselves in these matters. They are also stated so abstractly as to be essentially meaningless in terms of specific guidance for dealing with substantive policy problems or the related questions of organization and personnel. Regarding the latter, it seems fair to say that the United States has gone through a substantial learning process in the postwar period, gradually becoming more sophisticated about the requirements and implications of a politico-military approach to the nation's security problems.[2]

Perhaps the basic point of departure was that the postwar international environment, as it unfolded, presented the same fundamental problem to the defense establishment and the foreign policy organization—the security of the nation—and presented it with a clarity, directness, and urgency unparalleled in American historical experience. The defense and foreign policy establishments, of course, had subsidiary interests and activities not clearly related to the national security, and each brought to common problems its own special responsibilities, skills, and professional preoccupations. There was nevertheless a notable area of overlap and a shared, overriding concern—the safety and security of the nation vis-à-vis the world outside its boundaries. No doubt this explains the great popularity of the term "national security" as applied to organizational arrangements, policy goals, and related, new curricula in the universities.

As I have suggested, awareness and self-consciousness in this field did not emerge full-blown. In the conduct of the war itself, broader national policy considerations, including those related to our foreign relations, were supplied by President Franklin Roosevelt and his entourage of civilian and military advisors with little assistance from the obvious institutional embodiment of the foreign policy perspective, the Department of State. Nevertheless, as practical problems such as the occupation and governing of the defeated nations began to emerge, a mechanism to bring together the responsible agencies also appeared, the State-War-Navy Coordinating Committee (S.W.N.C.C., or "Swink" to those who worked with it). It was established in 1944, at the Assistant Secretary level, and operated until 1949, concerning itself primarily with problems of the occupied nations. A much more important step came, of course, with the passage of the National Security Act of 1947, undoubtedly the most important piece of postwar legislation in the field of national security organization.[3]

This Act provided the statutory basis for a unified military establishment under a single Secretary of Defense and a Joint Chiefs of Staff and an integrated national intelligence mechanism under a newly established Central Intelligence Agency. At the same time, it brought into being a National Security Council (N.S.C.) chaired by and advisory to the President, on which the Secretaries of State and Defense (also Army, Navy, and Air Force in the original legislation) sat as members, and the chairman of the Joint Chiefs of Staff and the Director, Central Intelligence, as statutory advisors.[4] The Council was charged with providing, at the highest level of the government, an overview of the nation's security problems from the relevant departmental and professional perspectives.

Historians of the N.S.C. tell us that the strong thrust for its establishment came from the military services and from civilians, like James Forrestal and Ferdinand Eberstadt, who had been associated with one of the military departments during the War. Nevertheless, the Council from its inception dealt with foreign policy as well as military policy problems and, indeed, primarily the former. After all, it was in the international political arena that the shocks and surprises came in the years immediately after World War II. Militarily, there seemed little question of American superiority.

It is also true that the N.S.C. has been used, and organized, differently by the various Presidents who have had it available to them. This should come as no surprise to students of the American Presidency. But whether the N.S.C. has been convened for regular, weekly meetings or on an occasional basis, been elaborately organized or operated more informally, or even been superseded by other governmental forums for decision, its underlying raison d'être seems to have won general acceptance in the U.S. Government, namely, that major foreign policy and, to a somewhat lesser extent, military policy decisions need to be considered at the top from a variety of governmental perspectives, including at a minimum representatives of the State and Defense Departments, the Joint Chiefs of Staff, and the Central Intelligence Agency. This premise is in fact so much taken for granted at present that stating it appears a ponderous effort at the obvious.

There has been continuing debate and discussion as to other agencies or perspectives that should be represented at the seats of the mighty. Given the significance of international and domestic financial and economic considerations, the Secretary of the Treasury has been an increasingly frequent participant in national security decision-making at the highest levels. The Council of Economic Advisers has had a voice much less frequently. The informational and foreign-aid arms of the foreign policy establishment are other obvious candiates. But the necessity, somehow, to get this kind of perspective on national security problems close to or at the very apex of the government is no longer questioned.

If the military establishment is to deal directly and on a large scale with foreign governments (as in military occupation of defeated nations, military assistance programs, and international military commands like NATO), if other activities and responsibilities bring it into direct contact with foreign governments and their nationals (stationing of American forces abroad, for example), its civilian and military leaders obviously need foreign policy guidance, and on a detailed, continuing basis. Perhaps there is some ideal bureaucratic world where this requirement could be met by provision of detailed policy guidelines from the State Department directly to the responsible military policy and program officers without the need for any intervening mechanism.

In matter of fact, Secretaries of Defense needed their own, "in-house" source of foreign policy advice for a number of reasons. First of all, since military establishment responsibilities and activities were involved, there might be military desiderata that would argue for handling a foreign policy problem somewhat differently. For a variety of reasons, perhaps nonmilitary as well as military (and these categories are not always easily differentiated, which compounds the problem under discussion), different foreign policy conclusions might be reached. In addition to looking "out," to the State Department and the White House, the Secretary of Defense had to look "down," to the three military services placed under his general direction and, increasingly, under his detailed control. An in-house foreign policy staff could interpret and transmit foreign policy guidance to the many military elements affected by it, no mean task in itself.[5]

In December 1950, the position of Special Assistant to the Secretary of Defense for International Security Affairs was established; in 1953, the unit was converted to an office and its head became an Assistant Secretary of Defense. The Office of International Security Affairs (known as I.S.A.) has been in continuing existence since then and is today one of the major component units of the Office of the Secretary of Defense (O.S.D.), the substantial organizational mechanism through which the Secretary of Defense attempts to control and direct the military establishment.

Given their command relationship to operational forces and field commanders, the Joint Chiefs of Staff have their own requirements for foreign policy advice and analysis which are met by action officers of their Joint Staff working closely with ISA and the State Department. Special staffs have been developed within the Joint Staff as needs have arisen in such broad national security fields as arms control and disarmament and counterinsurgency.

In spite of the increasing importance of the Secretary of Defense and the Joint Chiefs of Staff in the direction of the military establishment, the three military services still retain considerable power in certain policy and action areas. Thus, it is not surprising to find that each service has an international security affairs staff of its own. Clearly, the organizational arrangements of the contemporary American defense establishment, even briefly summarized, suggest a very substantial capability for dealing with the foreign policy dimensions of the problems it faces. The same can be said with regard to the training and development of personnel in this field, as will be seen below.

How does this picture look from the State Department perspective? The generally accepted view is that the Department of State, and the foreign policy organization more generally (I have in mind here particularly the information and foreign-aid agencies), have lagged far behind the military establishment in terms of both politico-military organization and personnel. As one example, while ISA dates its organizational birth from 1950, the equivalent State Department unit, the Politico-Military Affairs staff (G/PM), was first established in 1961. In the personnel training field, a similar lag can be noted.

While there is little doubt that the military establishment has led the way in the politico-military field, State Department efforts before 1961 cannot be dismissed out of hand. The now oft-told story of NSC-68, the policy paper developed in the months before the outbreak of the Korean War that urged a considerable expansion in U.S. conventional military capabilities in the light of Soviet development of the atomic bomb, is a case in point.[6] Leadership in developing this paper came from the State Department, notably from Paul Nitze, then head of the State Department's Policy Planning Staff and later to be Assistant Secretary of Defense for International Security Affairs, Secretary of the Navy, and Deputy Secretary of Defense in the Kennedy-Johnson Administrations. From its inception in 1946, the National War College had both State Department faculty and students; the first Deputy Commandant for Foreign Affairs was George F. Kennan.

In the heyday of the National Security Council structure under President Eisenhower, the Policy Planning Staff played a major role in developing State Department views on NSC problems, including those with a considerable military element. The Policy Planning Staff (now Council) has had a longstanding relationship with elements of the military establishment, including the Joint Chiefs of Staff. There was also a small cadre of State Department officers with continuing experience in the arms control and disarmament negotiations of the 1950's.

The Deputy Under Secretary of State for Political Affairs, to whom the new Politico-Military Affairs staff was attached, had politico-military responsibilities that predated the arrival of this new unit. The five geographical bureaus of the Department had long had units or individual officers with responsibilities for the politico-military activities (military assistance agreements, base rights, military overflights, status of forces agreements, visits of military personnel or ships) relevant to their areas. Thus, while the establishment of the Politico-Military Affairs staff may be regarded as representing a substantial and, in the view of most observers, badly needed increment to the politico-military orientation and capabilities of the Department of State, it would not be accurate to view it as a completely new departure.[7]

Just what does the politico-military perspective mean as applied to the responsibilities and problems of the State Department? Obviously, the military instrument of foreign policy, as any other, should operate within established foreign policy guidelines and be fully responsive to national policy objectives. As painful as this premise has sometimes proved to be to the military establishment, particularly when it is asked to commit some of its forces to combat, there can really be no argument with it. Military forces are employed to accomplish national policy objectives, not as ends in themselves, and must respond accordingly. (Clearly, interdepartmental debate about the appropriateness of the policy objectives and their translation into specific actions and programs is possible, even desirable, and in any event inevitable.)

Difficulties are bound to arise in the organizational and operational implementation of the underlying premise. Presumably, the military establishment expects from the foreign policy structure clearly defined, timely, and relevant policy guidance. It should also be able to feel some confidence in the foreign policy organization's understanding of the military business and of the problems that the foreign policy parameters may raise for the military effectiveness of what is being done or contemplated. If major defense policy as well as foreign policy objectives are involved in a particular situation (for example, in the establishment or maintenance of overseas bases or the equipping of friendly foreign military forces), the process of weighing and balancing the relevant considerations may have to take place at the highest decision-making levels of the government.

From their perspective, the foreign policy-makers presumably hope for a considerable military sensitivity and sophistication regarding the foreign relations implications of military activities located in (or directed to) the external environment. Furthermore, it helps if "the word" has gotten well down the line organizationally speaking so that the desired understanding at the higher levels, or in Washington, is not undercut by lack of understanding or awareness of foreign policy implications at working or field levels.

Effective and appropriate use of the military establishment in the carrying out of foreign policy is, as with other desirable human situations, much easier to endorse in principle than to implement in practice. These difficulties aside, it became increasingly evident to thoughtful foreign policy officials as well as outside observers that the military as foreign policy instrument represented only one part of a broader politico-military picture. The detailed capabilities and vulnerabilities of American military forces, their positioning at home and overseas, and the development of strategy and doctrine for their employment were clearly matters that affected the foreign policy behavior of other nations and their relations with the United States. Just as the significant consequences of foreign policy decisions for military establishment responsibilities brought military officials into the processes of foreign policy-making, it was increasingly argued that the foreign policy implications of major military policy decisions required some participation of foreign policy officials in the making of those decisions. Thus, the increasing politico-military capabilities made available to the State Department with the establishment of the Politico-Military Affairs staff in the spring of 1961 were soon reflected in the beginnings of formal State Department involvement in Defense Department decision-making.

This is an important development which has received quite limited attention outside the immediate governmental milieu in which it took place. (This comment applies more generally to the politico-military arrangements under discussion.) Nevertheless, the Secretary of Defense began in 1961 to submit a draft of his Five Year Force Structure and Budget statement to the Secretary of State for review and comment before it went to the President. In the relatively short time available, these annual military-budget documents were analyzed and critiqued from a foreign policy perspective and were usually the subject of a conversation or other exchange of views between the Secretaries of State and Defense.

Since there is little hard data available on this matter, one is left with impressions. It would probably be fair to say that during the first few years of this arrangement, the fact of its existence, of formal acknowledgment by the Secretary of Defense that the State Department had a legitimate interest in the major military concepts and decisions reflected in the military budget, was more significant than the substantive impact of State Department views. Having had no personal contact with this particular State-Defense relationship in the last few years, it is difficult for me to assess where it now stands.

The outgrowth of what began as an annual exercise was the development of working relations on a continuing, year-round basis between the State Department's politico-military people and the systems analysis staff centrally involved in the preparation of the military budget. At this writing, in the early months of the Nixon administration, it is not clear how these relationships vis-à-vis the military budget will develop either organizationally or substantively. However, one indicator that the State Department's participation in major military policy-making is still regarded as legitimate is its substantial involvement in the review of the American security posture initiated by President Nixon and headed by Deputy Defense Secretary Packard.

Beyond the military budget *per se*, there have been related developments designed to link the two departments more closely in a number of other primarily military activities. Examples would include contingency planning, the review and potential veto from a foreign relations perspective of overseas research supported by military funds,[8] State Department participation in some major military research studies and planning exercises, and closer, continuing contact with new developments in military technology.

It can probably still be argued that the State Department has a long way to go in terms of availability of appropriately skilled personnel in this field and in effective impact on the substance of military policies. What can be noted with some assurance is that the need for State Department involvement in these matters has been recognized within that department and, apparently, acknowledged and even encouraged by the Defense Department.[9]

This survey of the development of politico-military organizational arrangements in the U.S. government since World War Two has focused on the Presidency, the State Department, and the military establishment. The selection was deliberate, for the President is the central figure in all of these matters, and the State and Defense Departments are his principal instruments for dealing with them. For the sake of a more balanced if not complete picture, some additional elements should be noted.

In its intelligence collection and analysis efforts as well as its covert operational activities, the Central Intelligence Agency has a variety of interests and responsibilities that fall in the politico-military area. It is linked in many ways to both the State and Defense Departments. The expanding role and responsibilities of the U.S. Arms Control and Disarmament Agency (A.C.D.A.), again, fall between those of State and Defense, with the Atomic Energy Commission thrown in for good measure. A.C.D.A. not only has its own staff of politico-military and politico-scientific officials but also draws on the military establishment and the State Department for additional personnel.

During most of the Kennedy-Johnson period, the Secretary of State delegated to the Agency for International Development (A.I.D.) foreign policy control and coordination responsibilities with regard to the military assistance program. Beyond this, A.I.D.'s own public safety (i.e., assistance to foreign police forces) programs, its participatory role in military civic action programs, and the broader interrelations between economic and military aid, bring with them organizational-apparatus and personnel requirements in the politico-military field. However, the need to integrate military assistance programs with broader foreign policy objectives pre-dates the establishment of A.I.D. (in 1961) by many years. It arose with the start of substantial military aid to western Europe in 1950 and has expressed itself through a variety of organizational mechanisms and mandates ranging from a White House-based Director of Mutual Security to a powerful Under Secretary of State. I would guess that systematic empirical inves-tigation of those civilian career officials in the foreign policy organization who regard themselves as politico-military affairs specialists would reveal a substantial number who began to learn the trade in some aspect of the foreign aid program.

The Atomic Energy Commission has also spawned some talent in this field; this is not surprising in the light of its strong interests in the military applications of atomic energy, peaceful as well as military uses of the atom as an element in our foreign relations, and the significant nuclear aspects of arms control and disarmament concerns. A recent avenue for U.S. In-formation Agency entrance into this field has been its involvement in governmental counterinsurgency programs. For example, a U.S.I.A. offi-cer has been assigned for the last few years to the staff of the U.S. Army Special Warfare Center at Fort Bragg, North Carolina. Furthermore, beginning in 1965, responsibility for policy direction and coordination of all U.S. psychological action programs in Vietnam, including those of the military, was given to U.S.I.A., operating through a Joint United States Public Affairs Office (J.U.S.P.A.O.) in Saigon.

This is still not a complete cataloguing of the politico-military units and specialists now at work within the government, but it should suffice for present purposes. What salient characteristics emerge? First of all, to say the least, the relevant organizational arrangements and relationships are neither tidy nor well-defined. They rest on an implicit if not explicit assump-tion that the major participating agencies need specialized politico-military units, both to deal with their opposite numbers in the other agencies and to mediate the requests and problems of the other agency in their own. Thus, we have the Office of International Security Affairs in the Pentagon and the Politico-Military Affairs staff in the State Department, both relatively large staff units (by the lights of their respective agencies). However, while the mandate of I.S.A. as the foreign office of the Defense Department is much more clearly and exclusively defined than that of G/PM, neither has the politico-military field to itself within its own agency, and both have a number of roughly similar units to deal with in other agencies.

The untidiness of these arrangements is also reflected in the active, continuing contact between the State and Defense Departments at many levels from desk officer to Secretary. In spite of the formal mandate as exclusive channel granted to I.S.A., there continues to be considerable direct contact between State Department officials and officers of the Joint Staff and the three service staffs.

The mixture and interspersion of organizations and their professional personnel are further reinforced by other phenomena. Senior State Department Foreign Service Officers are assigned as Political Advisers (or PolAds) to certain major military commanders, primarily, the so-called unified commands with broad, overseas responsibilities (for example, in Europe, the Far East, and Latin America). When so assigned, these officers are not in the State Department chain of command or formal communications system. They are conceived of as senior members of the military commander's staff; the commander, indeed, prepares their annual efficiency reports. While they can and do draw on the Department of State for policy information and studies and presumably can get informal policy advice, they are successful to the extent that they can develop a good working relationship with the military commander and be of service to him. Such an arrangement, it should be pointed out, assumes that these major military commanders will benefit significantly from having a seasoned foreign policy adviser at their side, over and above the foreign policy guidance that is reaching them through normal military channels. Perhaps the volume and urgency of the matters they must deal with that have significant foreign policy dimensions justify this arrangement. The assumption is nevertheless worth noting.

There are also interesting patterns and relationships in United States embassies and overseas missions. In many foreign countries, there are at least two major military elements attached or related to the American ambassador and his mission—the military attachés and a military assistance group. In the past five or six years, the State Department has begun to establish embassy positions as politico-military affairs specialists, to be filled by Foreign Service Officers, so that the ambassador can have on his own diplomatic staff a relatively senior official to advise him on military matters and help him deal with the military elements assigned to his country (which may also include U.S. military field forces).

A number of personnel programs contribute to the pattern of interpenetration and intermixture. They seem to rest on two basic (and not very startling) assumptions: first, that those who are going to work in this field should have some formal educational experience that will help sensitize them to its special problems and to relevant factors which lie outside their normal professional competence and work-experiences; and, second, that the more effective harnessing of foreign policy and military policy will be assisted by the assignment of professionals from the one area to working positions in the other.

On the formal educational side, there is no doubt that the military services have led the way within the government. It may be argued that one service has done better than the others or that the detailed curricula of the senior military colleges sometimes are less impressive than the general conceptions or goals that motivate them.[10] Nevertheless, if one accepts the premise that the horizons of the professional military officer need considerable broadening if he is to perform usefully in the national security arena and that this can be accomplished at least in part by a formal educational experience, the military services have since World War II moved effectively and vigorously, and in some cases with considerable imagination, in this direction. The curricula of the five senior service colleges (Army, Navy, Air Force, and two joint ones—National War College and Industrial College of the Armed Forces) reflect a broad approach to the external problems of the nation, stressing the political, diplomatic, economic, and social factors that control and limit in many ways the uses of the military instruments of statecraft. If imitation, even of a very high quality, is the highest form of compliment, the Department of State's establishment of a course for its senior officers (called the Senior Seminar) in 1958 suggests its belated recognition of the need for broadened professional horizons.

The politico-military theme is underscored in all of these courses by the presence of a mixed, military-civilian student body and faculty. For example, the student spaces at the National War College are divided equally among the three services and, as a fourth component, civilians representing a number of government agencies but with the largest representation from the Department of State. While the three individual service colleges and the State Department Senior Seminar are designed primarily for the training of officers of those services, the other services and civilian national security and foreign policy agencies are represented at all of them.

It is impossible in this paper to list, no less evaluate critically, all the relevant personnel training programs of the military and foreign policy agencies. In addition to the various in-house training institutions, it has become increasingly common to send military officers and Foreign Service personnel to universities for periods ranging up to three years, for graduate study in such fields (relevant to the concerns of this paper) as political science, international relations, area studies, economics, management, and public administration.

The broadening of horizons through formal education has, as noted above, been supplemented by personnel assignment policies. The assignment of Foreign Service Officer PolAds to major military commanders has already been mentioned. Military officers have been assigned to international military headquarters, notably the N.A.T.O. headquarters of Supreme Allied Commander, Europe (S.A.C.E.U.R.), itself a highly important politico-military assignment held from the start by American officers. Military officers have also served in a variety of United States joint staffs and joint commands.

The most significant effort to mix military and foreign policy personnel is the State-Defense Exchange Program, agreed to at the close of the Eisenhower Administration and actually instituted early in the Kennedy Administration. It has involved the continuing assignment of twelve to fifteen Foreign Service Officers for two-year tours in various working positions in the Office of the Secretary of Defense, the Joint Staff, and the staffs of the three services, and equivalent assignments in the State Department for an equal number of military and civilian officers from the Department of Defense. In addition, there is an exchange of personnel on the same basis between the key command posts and communications centers for the two agencies, the National Military Command Center and the State Department's Operations Center.

While I have had no personal contact with the program since 1965, up to that point it was generally adjudged to have been quite successful. Because of the personal and organizational contacts that the exchange officers leave behind in their parent agency, it can be assumed that this program reinforces the characteristic of intermixed organizations, people, perspectives, and responsibilities already noted.[11] I have occasionally suggested to those interested in communications networks that it would be a fascinating as well as challenging enterprise to "map" the totality of connections between and among the various elements of the State Department and the military establishment, in the field as well as at home.

It should probably be noted in passing that some of the characteristics of the politico-military field referred to—for example, the increasing interest in interdepartmental training and exchange of personnel, the interpenetration of various agencies, and the seeming duplication of effort and redundancy of staff units—represent broader patterns and problems of the federal government. It still remains to attempt to evaluate their consequences for the foreign policy performance of the United States.

II. Critical Evaluation

The problem of evaluation is one sorely neglected by contemporary political scientists. It may be argued that scientific empirical research, directed to political phenomena presumably regarded as significant and flowing from some larger body of theory or set of hypotheses, is all that the political scientist, *qua* scientist, is required to do. This is an acceptable position, but it also seems to be the case that most political scientists, in their work, do apply values to political phenomena or problems, do make judgments, or draw inferences relevant to public policy questions. It seems to me essential that they bring to these intellectual operations the same self-consciousness, logic, and scientific rigor that they apply to their empirical research.

With regard to the study of foreign policy, it is almost impossible to avoid the position that evaluation is an important part of the scholarly enterprise. For one thing, so much of the writing in this field, academic as well as more popular, has been and continues to be highly judgmental. Furthermore, the very fact that an academic field of study of some respectability has developed around an area of *public policy* would suggest that a good part of the interest has been, and should be, the critical evaluation and the practical improvement of that which is being studied.

It is much easier to justify an effort at evaluation than to carry it out with any degree of rigor or precision. What criteria are relevant to the politico-military activities sketched above? At least one fundamental concern should be to link what we know about civilian and military approaches to foreign policy to the actual foreign policy performance of the United States. Here we face two fundamental handicaps: it is difficult to find the elements of successful foreign policy performance, by the United States or any other nation, adequately spelled out anywhere in the literature; and, second, if progress could be made in developing such benchmarks, there would still be the extremely difficult problem of locating United States performance somewhere along such a scale or, more likely, what would turn out to be a number of scales.

One point of departure for developing criteria for American foreign policy performance would be the external environment. We could specify a desirable set of characteristics for the international system (e.g., levels of international and intra-national violence, world trade patterns and levels, international cultural and educational exchange), from the perspective of American interests or some broader point of view, and evaluate American policy in terms of the gap between the desirable and the actual. One basic assumption underlying such an approach would be that the role of the United States in contemporary international affairs is powerful enough to warrant it being blamed or credited in good part for these states of affairs.

Perhaps it makes more sense to look at actual American relationships with the world outside and make one's judgments from this somewhat narrower perspective. We might examine gross amounts, or percentages, of G.N.P. devoted over time to the pursuit of national security and foreign policy objectives. Are we to infer that rising absolute costs, or rising proportions of G.N.P., indicate that all is not well? If it depends on what we are getting for the money spent, we have come full circle to the need to measure those items, like national security, most difficult to treat in quantitative terms.

We could examine trends in the actual military involvements of the United States since World War II, including military casualty figures. At the same time, we might want to look at the American stewardship of nuclear weapons since the two bombs were dropped on Japan at the end of the Second World War. To take another tack, are there discernible trends in the development of regimes hostile or friendly to the United States, or of more or less democratically oriented political systems? What is our batting average in the development of Communist regimes—does one measure this in terms of numbers of people now governed by such regimes, percentages of Communist movements that have actually been successful in taking power, or relative Communist success in the light of assumed worldwide vulnerabilities to their political programs and techniques?

If observable international conditions or American inputs and involvements in the international arena are to be the measures of success, how does one weigh their importance and how does one develop acceptable indices of success and failure within each category? Are there other critical categories that need to be added?

Perhaps we will do better if we get closer to our original point of departure. Can we make certain assumptions as to those characteristics of a political system, governmental structure, or of personnel staffing likely to produce effective foreign policy performance? If we did, we could examine the American political and governmental system to see how closely it approximated or deviated from the model posited. Perhaps one could focus on the governmental structure or the personnel system or a subsystem thereof, and evaluate them in terms of some model of organizational efficiency borrowed from the sociologists of bureaucracy or the students of public administration.

At all these levels of analysis and evaluation it seems to me that we are in poor shape. Whether one's point of departure is the state of the international system and the relationship of the United States to it, the foreign policy actions, decisions, and programs of the United States and the style and manner of their performance, the functioning of the American political system broadly defined or its governmental machinery more narrowly defined, one must face the fact that there are neither adequate models, guidelines, or criteria for the purposes of evaluation, nor a sufficient base of agreed-upon matters of fact and interpretation to which to apply the criteria if they could be developed.

Given these larger uncertainties, it is most difficult to specify those organizational arrangements, as among State, Defense and the White House, and those personnel training and assignment programs that would produce the most desirable results for the actual conduct of American foreign policy. Given all the other factors which affect the latter, it might even be hypothesized that the influence of politico-military organization and staffing is quite marginal, looming as important to those directly involved as practitioners or deeply interested as outside observers but making very little difference in ultimate foreign policy consequences for the United States.

This viewpoint is not one that can be easily dismissed. After one has taken into account the significant factors in the external environment that lie largely beyond the power of the United States to influence, the equally potent and largely uncontrollable trends in the social and political life of the United States itself, plus the central and always uncertain role of the President in the American governmental structure, the possible impact of specific organizational and personnel arrangements is clearly quite limited at best. Indeed, those who periodically try to strengthen or reform the Presidency, the State Department, the military establishment, or the Foreign Service do well to be reminded of these powerful limitations on what they can reasonably hope to accomplish. It is great fun to examine the American political system or national governmental structure in microscopic detail and enjoy its many subtle, intriguing and ironic features, but it is a mistake to attempt to tune them like a fine musical instrument.

Given the great difficulties that stand in the way of meaningful evaluation, are there any other options available aside from faith or intuition (which are probably the same thing in this case)? Are there any specific questions we can ask, or tests that we can apply, that will provide some basis for assessing what has happened in the politico-military field and whether, in net balance, it has made a difference in the foreign policy performance of the United States?

Are we prepared to accept the assumption that the foreign policy and military policy realms should be organizationally linked and intertwined at many levels in the government hierarchy, in the making of policy and the carrying out of programs, at home and abroad? It seems to me that they impinge on one another in so many ways, in so many places, in a great variety of modest or routine situations as well as the mighty ones, that it is not practically possible to opt for the simpler, neater solution of separate structures linked by coordinating mechanisms close to the top of government and guided in their overlapping activities by clearly written and consistently informative policy and program guidelines. There is a place for the latter, but I would argue that the practical requirements of contemporary international politics necessitate the continuance of the more confused and complicated arrangements described above, or some rough equivalent to them.

The same reasoning applies in the personnel field. Those actively involved in one or another major aspect of the foreign policy-national security business should have some awareness of the ways in which other agencies, other personnel competences, and other bureaucratic responsibilities may limit and, upon occasion, even facilitate their own work. In at least some cases, this awareness should be quite keen and substantial.

All of this adds up to saying that what the United States has developed in this field since World War II is essentially desirable. Are more refined or illuminating judgments possible; are there any caveats that ought to be entered? One critical question that can be asked is whether the military dimension has been kept in proper balance with the other relevant foreign policy dimensions. What this rather general concern usually boils down to is whether military force, and those who represent it in the councils of government, have had too powerful a voice in the making of decisions. Again, we are faced with terms—"proper balance," "too powerful"—that cry for careful definition and measurement, though not necessarily quantitative. Presumably, evidence lies in the instances of actual resort to military force by the United States and, even more so, in indications that those considerations relating to the use of force have tended more often than not to override other relevant considerations in decision-making situations.

Some will protest that, in the light of our experiences in Vietnam over the past five years, the answer is clear, and if the author does not see it clearly, he is either stupid or playing analytical games for his own amusement. In my view, it is by no means clear. In many parts of the world, the presence of United States military forces and the provision of U.S. military assistance have not led to international violence and, indeed, may have prevented it. N.A.T.O. and Western Europe represent the most obvious example; the United States role in the Mediterranean, the Near and Middle East, and Africa has been, on the whole, judicious and restraining. Even in Asia, the picture is a mixed one.

In the case of Korea, the original attack represented North Korean aggression, presumably with the cognizance if not the active support of the Soviet Union. The United States paid the price for some poor policy analysis (perhaps it might be called wishful policy thinking) after the initial victory against the North Koreans and the subsequent decisions to move toward the Yalu; it also paid the price for putting in field command a military prima donna who was not responsive to Washington policy direction but had too much domestic political support, it was thought, to be relieved. The country paid a heavy political and military price for this first major experience with the uncertainties and ambiguities of limited war, but it should be remembered that the war was, indeed, kept limited and the general was finally relieved (with the approval of the senior military officers then in the government). It does not seem reasonable to lay the errors and problems of the Korean War at the doorstep of excessive military influence, however defined.

The Vietnam experience has underscored a number of rough generalizations about the relationship between domestic politics and foreign policy in the United States, particularly in the circumstances of large-scale hostilities. At least two are worth noting here: first, once major military forces are committed, it is difficult for an American president to refuse what seem reasonable requests by the American military field commander for the support and protection of his forces (particularly when they include large numbers of draftees?); and, second, as in the case of the Korean War, the American public has only a limited tolerance for the uncertainties, ambiguities, and constraints that may be essential or inevitable in this kind of military engagement.

A number of salient characteristics of the Vietnam situation should be pointed out. First, President Johnson was not at his best in the foreign policy field. He apparently defined the situation in overly simple terms and made a basic decision and commitment that proved in the end to be much too open-ended. He was not prepared to let South Vietnam fall into the hands of the Viet Cong (and/or Communist North Vietnam) and was willing to use American forces to help bring the situation back into balance. At the same time, he felt other, contravening domestic and international pressures so that he was prepared to go only so far in his responsiveness to requests and advice from his senior military advisers and the field commander. He, too, kept tight limits and tight control on the fighting of the war. Once again, the nation has paid a very heavy price for a series of what now, with hindsight wisdom, seem like errors in policy analysis and policy judgment.

It should also be pointed out that in this situation, there was not really available, aside from Under Secretary of State George Ball, a strong voice in high policy councils arguing for a perspective less oriented to the use of force (by the United States, on an increasing scale) in the situation. Both the Secretary of State, Mr. Rusk, and the senior White House foreign policy adviser, Mr. Rostow, were strong advocates of what was being done. President Johnson seemed increasingly to be boxing himself in, even in the choice of those immediately around him. Those officials identified with somewhat differing views on the war, Under Secretary Ball and, finally, Secretary of Defense McNamara, eventually departed the Johnson Administration.

The Vietnam war seems to me to demonstrate less the dominance of the professional military and of narrow military considerations in the making of national security policy than the character and style of the Presidential incumbent and the particular way he responded to the pressures and logic of the military situation itself as viewed in the perspective of the American political system. Without stopping to discuss the point, I would say that this comment about the President also applies to his handling of the Dominican situation in 1965.

These brief and sketchy comments can do no more than emphasize that the question of "military influence" on American foreign policy, however defined, is an open one. We are certainly far from having *prima facie* evidence for the view that the military establishment and military desiderata have been too influential, with unfortunate policy consequences. It is interesting to note that few academic observers have seriously raised the question of insufficient military influence, or the possibility of desirable consequences emerging from military involvement in foreign policy-making.

There are two other crude benchmarks that are often applied to the national security machinery of the United States. One can be expressed briefly as the expeditious handling of policy problems. The concern is with speed and efficiency of process and procedure. The other concern is more substantive: it is directed to the analytical keenness, imagination, innovation, sensitivity to short-term problems and limitations, and longer-term perspective that are being applied to policy problems. It tends to be rather commonly assumed that the machinery is cumbersome, that there are too many interested bureaucratic parties, too many organizational levels, and too many required procedures involved in every problem, large or small. The net result, supposedly, is both slowness and dullness of response. In other words, the extreme complexity and apparent redundancy of much of the organization not only slow down policy and program reaction-time but also, in part for the sake of getting on with the job, result in a poorer quality of analysis and problem-solving.

My own view is that the lack of expeditious response has been considerably exaggerated; while the structure and processes are certainly not esthetically appealing, their negative policy consequences are far less dire than appearance would suggest. Obviously, there are problems of policy analysis; in the U.S. Government as in any large organization we are far from perfect in our wisdom, particularly before the event. Even here, as I will suggest below, the remedies are by no means as simple and sure-fire as some critics have implied, and the intrinsic difficulties of policy may still prove to be more reasonably explained by the intractability and novelty of the international problems the United States faces than the inadequacy of the intellectual and organizational tools it has applied to their solution.

III. Research Directions for the Future

If we have not gotten very far in defining the elements of successful foreign policy performance, and what political and governmental characteristics contribute thereto, we have done almost as poorly in developing a solid empirical basis for discussing these matters. In part, we have not been asking the right questions. Scholars, journalists, and practitioners alike seem to prefer debate and discussion about specific policy problems to analysis of why the system works as it does and what the consequences seem to be for American foreign policy. Even where foreign policy-making or military policy-making have been studied in their various dimensions, the organizations, institutions, or political realms under consideration have usually been studied in isolation, in their own terms, rather than in relation to the larger political and governmental system and the international setting in which the latter in turn is enmeshed.[12] Finally, the politico-military area with which we have been concerned in this paper has been, surprisingly, very largely ignored by students of American government and foreign policy.

As we have already indicated, the development and refinement of relevant criteria is in itself an urgent task for students in this field. Beyond that, a number of interesting substantive research problems beckon. For those concerned about the impact of the military on foreign policy-making, why not attempt to reconstruct on the basis of the available data the development of policy in 20 or 25 major cases since the end of World War II. A number of relevant studies already exist. It will, of course, be difficult in some cases to infer the nature and extent of the impact of military establishment advice and views, and to differentiate the views of civilian leaders and advisors from those of the professional officers.[13] These are no more than the normal hazards of such research.

We should also be able to do far better than we have in the analysis of policy substance. Given the great quantity of writing about American foreign policy, it is depressing to note the poor intellectual quality of most of it. The outside observer or scholar should be able to dissect and lay bare the assumptions, values, perceptions, and hypotheses that underlie most major policies, while at the same time recognizing that the policy process cannot be approached as a completely rational one, given the deep uncertainties embedded in the problems themselves as well as the other considerations and pressures that inevitably affect decisions reached. The effort at systematic analysis is nevertheless an essential one, particularly for the outsider free of the operator's pressures to do and decide. It should prove instructive to the scholar and those he teaches. If persistently pursued over time, it may even prove helpful to the practitioner.[14]

Another noteworthy point about the study of foreign policy in the United States is that psychologists and sociologists have for the most part stayed away from it. Some of those who have become interested might well have stayed away. As others have noted, the occasional sallies of social psychologists on behalf of their deep concerns with war and peace have been, to say the least, simplistic.[15]

On the other hand, the organization of the Department of State and the arrangements by which State, Defense and the other national security agencies are and have been linked—S.I.G. (Senior Interdepartmental Group), I.R.G.'s (Interdepartmental Regional Groups), N.S.C. (National Security Council), O.C.B. (Operations Coordinating Board), and all the rest—would seem to be fertile fields of investigation for the sociological student of complex organizations.

There are problems of security-classification and, more generally, of access to relevant people and documentation in doing decision-making case studies. There are other difficulties of a more academic nature. I would therefore argue that a more fruitful and economical way of understanding the State Department, the Foreign Service or the politico-military arena, and how they affect foreign policy, may be through the study of the attitudes, values, and frames of reference of those actually involved in them.

An obvious assumption underlying such research would be that the latter do indeed have consequences for foreign policy performance. If so, research directed to large numbers of those involved in foreign policy-making—through mail questionnaires, interviews, analysis of available socioeconomic and educational background data, and of related published materials like memoirs and the specialized journals directed to, for example, military men and diplomats—should provide highly useful data which is more likely to avoid the pitfalls of classified or highly sensitive information than the decision-making case study and at the same time have more general relevance than one or a handful of case studies.

The field is wide open. The Foreign Service has only recently begun to get this kind of attention, notably in a study by John Harr.[16] Morris Janowitz directed a very ambitious effort toward *The Professional Soldier*,[17] but the research reflected in that study is more than ten years old; as far as I know, it has not been systematically developed, expanded, or updated in a major way by Janowitz or anyone else.

There are many possible payoffs in this kind of research. First, it would give us extensive data on the intellectual equipment that American officials bring to their analysis of policy problems. If several of these projects were carried out, we would have some basis for comparison of different major career (and noncareer) groups and, perhaps, of subcareer specialties. We might be able to make more refined judgments about the impact of war college training on career military officers. More generally, we might be able to reach some conclusions about the consequences of interdepartmental training and work experience for the horizons of those involved.

In the case of the Foreign Service, it should give us a much improved information base for efforts to strengthen the organization of the State Department and its personnel policies and programs. Harr concludes his study of the Foreign Service with a proposed "managerial strategy for the future" for the State Department and the Foreign Service. While it is possible to raise questions, even serious ones, about any such proposal, Harr's recommendations certainly are the more persuasive for the substantial empirical research base which represents one of their points of departure.[18]

IV. Conclusions

Even as we emphasize the relevance and interest of such research, we must return to our earlier comments on the limits of its significance. A program of sustained research directed to the Foreign Service of the United States should make for better understanding and teaching about the subject and might eventually contribute to the development of more rational personnel programs in the Department of State. These are not results to be sneered at. However, they may not produce any noteworthy improvements in American foreign policy performance, and if they do, it will probably take so long and be so difficult to demonstrate as not to be worth arguing about on those grounds.

Similarly, if the State Department or State-Defense relations are so fortunate as to come under the extended scrutiny of students of complex organizational behavior during the next decade, the taxpayer may eventually benefit and there may even be a greater tidiness in how we carry on our business in these fields, but we should be somewhat cautious in leaping to the conclusion that United States foreign policy or military policy performance will thereby be greatly enhanced.

Unfortunately for our sense of symmetry, apparent organizational shortcomings sometimes have positive consequences or side-effects. For example, multiplicity or redundancy of staffs may give senior officials a greater variety of views to choose from or, perhaps, the ability to bring the energy and intellectual resources of one staff into play when they are dissatisfied with the performance of another—even if the latter is formally responsible for the matter under consideration. On the other hand, superb staff talent may exist but be ignored by those above, who in some cases may not even be aware that this competence is available to them. The interpenetration of the private and governmental sectors which is so salient a characteristic of the contemporary American scene means that outside talent and ideas can easily be tapped if this is viewed as desirable.

None of these options is available cost-free to those at the top; some of them may prove a tremendous drain on the energies of those involved. Outward appearances may be messy. The point is that the policy or program consequences may bear little relationship to this appearance. Poor decisions or programs may emerge from a neat, efficiently run operation, and, equally, first-rate performance may be the net result of a rough-and-tumble, free-wheeling operation. It has often been remarked of the two major American political parties that the Democratic party, which seems to enjoy public brawls and fracases among its adherents, has at the same time been by far the more imaginative and innovative in contributing to the solution of public policy problems in mid-twentieth century America. Similarly, Kenneth Waltz argues rather persuasively in his recent study that while the functioning of the U.S. Congress, and its relations with the executive, are noisy, messy and often most unattractive, the net foreign policy consequences over the past twenty-five years have unquestionably been positive.[19]

The same caveat needs to be applied to efforts to improve the analysis of policies and programs. I am a great admirer of Mr. McNamara and regard his contribution to the more efficient running of the military establishment and the rationalizing of its decision-making processes as a major one. It nevertheless seems to be the case that the analytical procedures he employed, and imposed upon the military services, were sometimes used to justify decisions made on other grounds (which may, in themselves, have been appropriate—that is not the point) and that they may, on occasion, have induced or supported a confidence in the rightness of certain decisions which proved illusory. I would put in the latter category the F-111 program which, it now seems clear, must be regarded as one of Mr. McNamara's failures.

I am not suggesting that sophisticated analytical techniques not be applied to policy problems. Rather, as with other potent medicines, they should be used with care and with as much intellectual honesty and rigor as possible. In a word, elegant schemes for intellectual analysis may upon occasion, like their earlier, cruder antecedents, produce poor policy results. Indeed, as in Mr. McNamara's case, the fall may be the harder for the very pretentions and ambition of the analytical schemes employed.

The same point is applicable to the various proposals for the improved measurement and comparison of United States foreign policy activities and programs abroad, both within single countries and between and among countries. I favor efforts to experiment with and introduce such methods. Over time they may give us a more precise picture of what we are getting for our various categories of expenditure, identify unnecessary overlaps of effort within particular countries, and thereby indicate ways of getting improved program results for the same outlay of money.[20] We should at the same time remind ourselves that such efficiency may not necessarily improve the overall relationship of the United States with particular countries; it may be outweighed, for example, by the burden of justifying U.S. efforts elsewhere, as in Vietnam or the Dominican Republic, or simply by the fact that the local government has grown tired of the American presence. An increasingly efficient American effort and a better U.S. relationship with the local government may be overturned by a coup d'état and the emergence of a new and ideologically unfriendly government. The deepseated indigenous obstacles to development in many of the less-developed countries may severely limit the impact of even the most impressive American assistance efforts. In other words, the more efficient and economical carrying out of American foreign policy is undoubtedly desirable, but it should by no means be regarded as equivalent to successful American policy abroad.

Does one really grow wiser as one grows older, or—more likely—are the views reflected in these pages rather those of increasing conservatism and, perhaps, overexposure to the practitioners in the field? The message of this paper is, in any event, a mixed one: the intellectual apparatus that we now bring to the study of American foreign policy is woefully inadequate; in politico-military affairs, as elsewhere, there is a lopsided allocation of research resources with a consequently slender empirical basis for our views. We need to do much more in both these areas, but as we pursue our studies, we should enjoy them for their own sake and for what they will add to the richness and excitement of our teaching, holding out only modest hopes, if any, for startling improvements in the way the United States responds to the problems of the external world.

Notes and References

[1]Hopefully, the pain and frustrations of this transitional period will not erase from memory the very substantial contribution made by American power and diplomacy to international peace and stability, the revival of the world economy, and the opportunity for nation-states, new and old, to build and rebuild in a relatively free and protected environment during the first two decades after the Second World War.

[2]There are a number of ambiguities that arise from use of the short-hand term, "politico-military." First of all, if "politico" or "political" is meant to cover all the nonmilitary considerations that enter into foreign policy choices, it includes a whole host of matters usually labeled economic, social, cultural, scientific, and so on. It should also be recognized that "military" itself represents a very broad category.

The whole point of the term, of course, is that these factors are interdependent; often, it will be most difficult to separate out the various elements involved. How important each will be will also vary from problem to problem. The term does not imply that military factors stand on an equal footing with all the rest.

Finally, it should be pointed out that in the making of important national policy decisions, not only will foreign relations and military defense considerations be taken into account but also a broad range of domestic policies and problems that are sometimes labeled "political." In the sense that all of these factors must be weighed and balanced before important choices are made, the latter are inevitably "political" decisions.

For purposes of the present analysis, the term "politico-military" refers to the broad policy area where considerations of foreign relations and military security must both be weighed, and seen in relationship to one another, before policies can be decided upon and implementing programs and actions carried on. The weight given to these factors will vary from situation to situation. Where the foreign relations dimensions are paramount, military considerations must presumably be approached accordingly. The reverse is also true.

[3]Public Law 253, 61 Stat. 500.

[4]There is a fifth statutory member, the director of the Office of Emergency Preparedness, a Presidential staff unit. In the original legislation, this seat on the N.S.C. was assigned to the head of the National Security Resources Board. Through a variety of organizational changes, the official charged with civilian emergency planning has continued, somewhat in-

appropriately in my view, to retain it. From time to time in this essay, I will cite my own *The Making of United States Foreign Policy* (Washington, D.C.: The Brookings Institution, 1966) for a more detailed discussion of the matter under consideration. In this case, see Sapin, pp. 76–90 and 147–149.

[5]For a more detailed discussion of the Secretary of Defense's requirement for foreign policy advice and staffing, and the organizational responses thereto, see *ibid.*, pp. 156–180.

[6]See the detailed case study by Paul Y. Hammond, "NSC-68: Prologue to Re-armament," in W. Schilling. P. Y. Hammond, and G. Snyder, *Strategy, Politics and Defense Budgets* (New York: Columbia University Press, 1962), pp. 271–378.

[7]It should probably be pointed out that the author served on the Politico-Military Affairs staff from June 1962 to June 1965 in the course of an almost four-year stint in the Department of State.

[8]For a brief indication of the background of this function, see Sapin, *op. cit.*, p. 317, n. 17.

[9]For a more detailed presentation and analysis, see *ibid.*, pp. 122–125 and Appendix B, "Memorandum on the Department of State's Politico-Military Organization and Staffing." The latter document was originally submitted by the Department of State in 1963 to the Subcommittee on National Security Staffing and Operations (the so-called Jackson committee) of the Senate Government Operations Committee.

[10]Although a dozen years have passed since its publication, the most useful description and most thoughtful evaluation of the senior military colleges are probably still to be found in John W. Masland and Laurence I. Radway, *Soldiers and Scholars: Military Education and National Policy* (Princeton: Princeton University Press, 1957), pp. 319–440. For some briefer but more recent comments, see Gene M. Lyons and Louis Morton, *Schools for Strategy: Education and Research in National Security Affairs* (New York: Frederick A. Praeger, 1965), pp. 226–230. The latter, very useful study is primarily concerned with the contribution of civilian universities and other institutions to the study of national security problems and the preparation of civilians to deal with them.

[11]See Sapin, *op. cit.*, pp. 363–366 and Appendix B.

[12]For an extended, first-rate critique of the foreign policy literature, see James N. Rosenau, "Pre-theories and Theories of Foriegn Policy," in R. Barry Farrell (ed.), *Approaches to Comparative and International Politics* (Evanston: Northwestern University Press, 1966), pp. 27–92.

[13]One ambitious effort to study military influence on foreign policy systematically and comparatively, using historical case materials from Germany, France, Britain and Japan as well as the United States, is reflected in Lewis J. Edinger, "Military Leaders and Foreign Policy-Making," *American Political Science Review*, Vol. 57 (June 1963), pp. 392–405, and Roger W. Benjamin, *Military Influence in Foreign Policy-Making*, unpublished doctoral dissertation, Washington University, St. Louis, 1967.

[14]One recent foreign policy study that makes a commendable effort in this direction is Seyom Brown, *The Faces of Power: Constancy and Change in United States Foreign Policy from Truman to Johnson* (New York: Columbia University Press, 1968).

[15]See, for example, the critical review article by James N. Rosenau, "Behavioral Science, Behavioral Scientists, and the Study of International Phenomena: A Review," *Journal of Conflict Resolution*, Vol. IX (December 1965), pp. 509–520. More thoughtful, responsible research efforts by psychologists are reflected in Joseph H. de Rivera, *The Psychological Dimension of Foreign Policy* (Columbus: Charles E. Merrill, 1968) and Dean G. Pruitt, *Problem Solving in the Department of State* (Denver: University of Denver, Social Science Foundation and Department of International Relations Monograph Series in World Affairs, 1964–65, No. 2).

[16]For a considerable first step in the needed direction, see John Ensor Harr, *The Professional Diplomat* (Princeton: Princeton University Press, 1969). Harr does not grapple at length with the question of how the attitudes, norms, and behavior patterns he identifies affect Foreign Service Officer performance and foreign policy outcomes. He does offer them as an ex-

planation for what are widely regarded as major inadequacies in the State Department and Foreign Service response to problems of governmental leadership and coordination in the foreign policy field.

A study that received considerable attention and provoked widespread debate within the Foreign Service several years ago was *Some Causes of Organizational Ineffectiveness within the Department of State*, prepared for the Department of State by Professor Chris Argyris of Yale. Argyris focused on what he called the "living system," the norms and values, of the State Department and the Foreign Service and their consequences, mostly unfortunate, for the functioning of the organization. In my view, Argyris' analysis, while quite challenging, suffered from too narrow a data base and a somewhat suspect methodology. His report is summarized in the *Foreign Service Journal*, Vol. 44 (January 1967), pp. 21–26; further discussion of it is to be found in the March, April and May 1967 issues of the same journal.

Several monographs prepared for the Committee on Foreign Affairs Personnel (the Herter Committee) provide relevant data and analysis. See, for example, Regis Walther, *Orientations and Behavioral Styles of Foreign Service Officers*, and two stu-

dies by John E. Harr, *The Development of Careers in the Foreign Service* and *The Anatomy of the Foreign Service: A Statistical Profile* (Carnegie Endowment for International Peace, 1965). For further comments and references to the relevant literature, see Sapin, *op. cit.*, pp. 329 and 346–349.

[17] *The Professional Soldier: A Social and Political Portrait* (Glencoe: The Free Press, 1960).

[18] See Harr, *The Professional Diplomat*, Chapter 9.

[19] See Kenneth Waltz, *Foreign Policy and Democratic Politics* (Boston: Little, Brown, 1967), *passim*.

[20] The most recent governmental effort along these lines, the Planning-Programming-Budgeting System (PPBS), has been the subject of considerable attention by the Subcommittee on National Security and International Operations, chaired by Senator Jackson (D., Washington), of the Senate Government Operations Committee. Hearings were conducted and documentation prepared in the first and second sessions of the 90th Congress, 1967 and 1968. Among the items of particular interest to students of foreign policy is a memorandum prepared for the Subcommittee by Professor Thomas Schelling, "P.P.B.S. and Foreign Affairs."

VINCENT DAVIS

The Office of the Secretary of Defense and the U.S. Department of Defense*

Introduction

In the late 1930s Harold and Margaret Sprout led the way among modern political scientists in the realization that the scholarly study of international relations required a systematic analysis of the military dimensions of statecraft. At that time any American scholar coming to this realization probably would have thought it appropriate to look first at the role of military force in American foreign affairs, and that conclusion in turn probably would have led initially to an examination of one or more of the separately organized U.S. armed services. The Army and the Navy from the American Revolutionary War until after World War II were the primary visible forms of institutionalized American military force. Accordingly, the first two major books produced by the Sprouts dealt with the U.S. Navy, which was the favored military instrument of American statecraft for most of the half-century preceding the entry of the United States into World War II.[1]

In the late 1960s and early 1970s, some thirty years after the Sprouts' two pioneering books on the Navy, any scholar continuing to believe in the importance of systematic analytical study of the military dimensions of American statecraft probably would not have seen the separate U.S. armed services as constituting the most significant visible component of American military force. A seed of an idea was planted in the American political soil around 1900 and began to grow slowly—so slowly, in fact,

---

* This chapter was largely written in the fall of 1968, with minor revisions in early 1969. Therefore, the footnote references for this chapter do not include any citations to the voluminous pertinent literature on the subject emerging in 1969, 1970, and early 1971.

Notes and References for this selection will be found on pages 368–370.

that it was not noticed as late as the 1930s by the Sprouts and the very few other political scientists then beginning to write about military force and organized forces. But World War II substantially enriched the soil in which this seed was embedded—an idea most often referred to as "unification of the armed forces." In 1947 the idea bore statutory fruit in basic legislation called the National Security Act, which created the Office of the Secretary of Defense (O.S.D.). In 1949 important amendments to the basic law created the U.S. Department of Defense (D.O.D.) over which the Secretary presided.[2] Subsequent developments over the next two decades so greatly enhanced the roles, structural scope, authority and responsibilities of O.S.D. and D.O.D. that any scholar by the late 1960s probably would have agreed that O.S.D./D.O.D. rather than the separate armed services had become the most important visible component of American organized military force.[3]

Accordingly, this essay will be an introductory commentary on the evolution of the Department of Defense, with special reference to the Office of the Secretary of Defense, and with a primary emphasis on the 1960s during the tenure of Secretary Robert S. McNamara. This kind of exercise, however, must be highly tentative for several reasons. First, the two-plus decades following World War II still constitute very recent history, and personal biases derived from the emotional politics of the period are evident in almost all of the pertinent scholarly literature no matter how much authors (including this one) may have tried to divest themselves of such perspectives. Second, the basic descriptive literature on the organizational structures, functions and processes of American governmental institutions in the over-all field of foreign and military policy following World War II is sketchy and uneven. The behavioral science literature attempting to apply theoretical perspectives to, or to derive theoretical conclusions from, a study of these structures, functions and processes is all but nonexistent. Therefore, neither the descriptive empirical base nor the theoretical foundations, in quantity or in quality, provide a reassuring point of departure for the kind of generalized survey essay intended here.

Nevertheless, the Department of Defense had existed for twenty years as of 1969, and the Secretary of Defense had been a primary Cabinet officer for two years longer. Some tentative comments consequently appear warranted, if for no other reason than to emphasize how much more research is needed on that agency of the U.S. Government which has accounted for approximately half of the annual federal budget for most of D.O.D.'s existence and which has a literally devastating potential impact on the lives of Americans and all other peoples around the world. At least some basic descriptive research has been performed which can serve as the basis for this essay, and the remarks here will hopefully point the way toward more research.[4]

The Several Roles of the Defense Secretary

The one most important trend in the organization and direction of American armed forces after World War II was the steady growth in the authority and responsibilities of the two centralized Pentagon agencies—the Office of the Secretary of Defense (O.S.D.) on the civilian side, and the Office of the Joint Chiefs of Staff (O.J.C.S.) on the uniformed side—at the expense of all agencies and components at lower D.O.D. levels. However, the growth patterns on the O.S.D. and O.J.C.S. sides were not in all respects even and parallel. "Civilian control" was never really the problem. There was automatically civilian control in the fact that the President is a civilian, and this control was substantially enhanced by the relatively greater growth of O.S.D. powers in contrast to the slower development of O.J.C.S. while the traditionally separate armed services were losing powers to both O.S.D. and O.J.C.S. The real problem was efficient control producing desired outcomes, which required an organization allowing for the complex mixture of policy inputs and policy implementation based on the special qualifications of both the civilians and the professional military men.

Leaders on both the civilian and the military sides of the Pentagon notwithstanding abundant talent and good will often appeared to be in some sort of conflict with each other, or at least to harbor serious misgivings, when the root of the trouble was a failure to appreciate the role requirements of and the necessary contributions from colleagues on the opposite side. Moreover, the men themselves were not always solely at fault in these misunderstandings, because both statutes and directives frequently failed to be precise about many of these critical questions concerning roles and relationships.

The Secretary of Defense must perform in several distinguishable roles within the Executive Branch context, as well as in other roles based on external relationships. In the jargon of the times, he "wears many hats," and those who work with and for him as well as occasionally the Secretary himself can become confused as to which hat he is wearing at any particular moment and further confused by the idiosyncratic requirements of any one hat. Needless to add, the several roles or hats are only part of the story, because much will depend on the personalities of key individuals—especially the President and the Secretary—and the nature of the personal relationships emerging between them. Nevertheless, at least three critical roles can be identified for the Secretary and except in rare circumstances (such as the Eisenhower Administration, to be noted later) any Secretary must to some extent try to play all three roles regardless of personalities.[5]

The first of the Secretary's roles is that of foremost military *adviser* to the President. He is "the President's man," the President's choice to lead and direct the Department of Defense, a member of the Cabinet, and indeed during the 1960s one of the closest members of the inner circle within the President's official family. The Secretary in principle ought to be the most knowledgeable man in the Government concerning everything that pertains to the nature and use of military force. Any President, depending on his personal needs and style, will reach out for a variety of advice on most questions including national security issues, but he will undoubtedly turn first and most often to the Secretary on national security measures if the Secretary has gained any reasonable measure of the President's confidence.

The second of the Secretary's roles is more formal and structured than the first. The Defense Reorganization Act of 1958 specified that the Secretary would be the first in the chain of command directly under the Commander in Chief, meaning that the second role which can be identified for the Secretary is that of the traditional *military commander*. The Secretary therefore became the Deputy Commander in Chief, or the second-in-command of the armed services. Although the Vice President was not formally incorporated in this command chain, certain Vice Presidents have played important roles in making defense policy, and the 1958 legislation strongly suggested that the Deputy Secretary of Defense would ordinarily be the third in the chain of command directly under the Secretary.[6] Therefore, at least two (the President and the Secretary) and in some interpretations more than two civilians constituted the top levels in the leadership structure of the U.S. armed forces. They are civilians, but in this sense and in this role they are traditional military commanders. These facts, including the fact that a professional military officer is not ordinarily encountered before reaching approximately the fourth level in the command chain, have not always been understood and appreciated by concerned civilian and military officials as well as by some Congressmen and by the general public.

The third of the Secretary's roles is that of *manager* or chief administrative officer of the Department of Defense. While it is misleading to push too far an analogy between a large industrial corporation and a big governmental agency such as D.O.D., there are obvious parallels: the receipt and disbursement of money, the maintenance of plant and equipment, procurement of goods and services, and probably most important—the leadership and management of personnel, all within a geographically dispersed operation. D.O.D. in all of these respects is larger and far more complex than any other governmental agency or private corporation. Hence, the Secretary as the "big boss" of this enterprise has enormous managerial responsibilities. If the President is chief executive officer and chairman of the board, then the Secretary is clearly the general manager of that part of the over-all governmental corporation which is the Defense Department.[7] That Presidents have attached great weight to this third or managerial role of the Secretary is underscored by the fact that they have most often turned to men with backgrounds in large corporate businesses or investment banking when choosing their Defense Secretaries. However, these backgrounds are not necessarily ideal preparation for the Secretary's other two roles, and a failure on the part of some Secretaries to understand this as well as to understand the crucial differences between D.O.D. and a large industrial corporation have led to a number of the problems experienced by more than a few Defense Secretaries.

The "McNamara Revolution"

Robert S. McNamara's tenure as Defense Secretary from early 1961 to early 1968 was often referred to as the "McNamara Revolution" in the Pentagon because of his firm, vigorous, and innovative leadership techniques. On the other hand, one could argue that his work was more accurately a continuation of an evolutionary centralization process initiated by the 1947 and 1949 defense reorganization legislation of the Truman Administration and the 1953 and 1958 reorganizations of the Eisenhower Administration. In these terms the revolution might be said to have occurred under Eisenhower, because the 1953 and 1958 changes sharply shifted the balance of power in the Defense Department toward the Secretary and the corporate J.C.S. The 1958 reorganization legislation—the last such for more than a decade following—was particularly significant because it put the Secretary squarely in the chain of command just below the President while reducing the Army, Navy, and Air Force to administrative, training, and logistical functions.

The conclusion in this essay, however, is that the Eisenhower Administration primarily provided the invaluable groundwork for a revolution which McNamara at least firmly consolidated if not entirely initiated. It was an aberrational Administration because the President was regarded by nearly everybody as the nation's foremost military expert. He was therefore almost compelled to act as his own Defense Secretary while those who served him in this position largely confined themselves to the third of the Secretary's three roles—D.O.D. "general manager." But knowledgeable individuals have reported that Eisenhower was clearly aware of his own exceptional situation, and that he acutely perceived any subsequent President's fundamental need for a vigorous and assertive Defense Secretary to impose strong control over the enormous defense establishment. He accordingly devoted more time and energy during his second Administration to securing the enactment of the 1958 defense reorganization than any other piece of legislation, and some commentators have said that only a president with Eisenhower's stature as a military authority could have succeeded in this effort to persuade the Congress against its strong traditional beliefs to create an extremely powerful Defense Secretary while substantially reducing the authority and responsibilities of the separate military services. The legislation still fell short of what he wanted but his last Secretary of Defense, Thomas S. Gates, was the first to operate under the provisions of the 1958 reorganization, and Gates' vigorous implementation provided a running start for the dramatic changes in the management of D.O.D. during the Kennedy-Johnson years.

President Kennedy's position was in many respects the reverse of Eisenhower's. Some knowledgeable individuals have suggested that Kennedy perhaps intended from the outset to be his own Secretary of State, in view of his strong interest in and studies of the diplomatic and economic dimensions of foreign affairs. But with respect to the military dimensions Kennedy was quick to see what Eisenhower had foreseen: the new President's need for a vigorous Defense Secretary. Kennedy found his man in Robert McNamara.

McNamara moved boldly and decisively from the moment he took office. He conceived of his new job somewhat along the lines of the industrial-executive model—a model that he had earlier taught (on the Harvard faculty) and had personally exemplified (at the Ford Motor Company). He was determined to be an activist leader, a boss-initiator, and not merely a passive judge of competing alternatives nor a negotiator among competing interests.[8] Among a variety of initial frustrations and disillusionments, three events in particular early in 1961 soon persuaded him that the D.O.D. which he had inherited was in "chaotic" condition, and that he would need to be even more assertive than perhaps he himself had originally imagined.[9] First, the reports that he received on more than a hundred special topics assigned to various Pentagon offices during his first few weeks on the job tended to contain merely the verbalized conventional wisdom from the limited perspective of each reporting office. Second, the situation in Laos was reaching crisis proportions just as President Kennedy was inaugurated, and the five-man J.C.S. (including the Marine Corps Commandant) presented five divergent and vigorously defended views to Kennedy and McNamara. Third, the Bay of Pigs situation produced a further loss of confidence on the part of the President and his Defense Secretary toward the nation's senior professional military officers.

McNamara's response to these three circumstances underscored several features of his thought processes and style of operation that significantly influenced his Pentagon revolution. First, he tended to form strong first impressions that later evidence could seldom alter. For example, his poor initial impression of the J.C.S. in particular and professional officers in general never significantly changed thereafter. (For an example in the opposite direction, he formed a favorable first impression of the idea of a TFX-type aircraft that later evidence was unable to alter.[10]) Second, his style of operation rarely presented a second chance for a group that he concluded to be deficient, because he tended to create a new group to do its work without any serious effort to improve the disfavored group. For example, some critics of Defense organization suggested that many functions assigned by McNamara to new or reorganized civilian offices at the O.S.D. level would have been more appropriately left at the O.J.C.S. level if he had been willing to teach the Chiefs to operate by his standards. Third, he arrived at the Pentagon in 1961 just as computers were accelerating a revolution already underway in business and industrial management.

Always a man to move quickly toward managerial innovations, he revealed a decided preference for the kinds of quantified-data analysis for which computers were useful, in contrast to all other forms of research.[11] Some observers speculated that it was in part this McNamara predilection for quantified data which led American officials in Vietnam to come up with the questionable use of "body count" statistics as a basic measure of "progress" in the war, although this and other numerical indices had been used to some extent as performance indicators in earlier wars.

The "McNamara Revolution" occurred at least in part because of characteristics shared by President Kennedy and his Defense Secretary. Both were impatient for quick, but carefully researched solutions, often not recognizing that solutions could not always be both quick and carefully researched; both were more than willing to innovate with new organizational arrangements; and both generally preferred to replace rather than to reform deficient organizational components. The Secretary was a blessing to Kennedy because the new President needed the kind of dazzling evidence that McNamara's procedures appeared to provide before running the risk of overruling professional military judgment, whereas Eisenhower's status as the nation's foremost military expert gave him considerably more freedom in this area. Several knowledgeable individuals have suggested that Kennedy originally based his military policy views on advice solicited from many and various officials of the separate armed services but, as he developed more and more confidence and rapport with his Defense Secretary while sharing the Secretary's dwindling confidence in professional military judgment, the President was increasingly willing to let McNamara run the Defense Department. McNamara, of course, prudently continued to keep the President well informed. The relationship between the President and Secretary was, if anything, even stronger in the early Johnson Administration than in the Kennedy Administration, with the only notable difference being a tendency on Johnson's part to hold longer and more frequent meetings with his Secretary and other defense advisers than Kennedy did (in part because of the growing preoccupation with the Vietnam War during the Johnson period).

The two most important organizational procedures and components of the "McNamara Revolution" were "PPBS" ("Planning, Programming and Budgeting System") and "SA" ("Systems Analysis").[12] PPBS is fundamentally a management tool in the area of cost accounting, assisting decision-makers to know what various ways of doing the same thing will cost in money ("cost-effectiveness"). It is a way of rationalizing the stages between sets of ends and means, and choosing among the sets. PPBS was a function lodged in the O.S.D. Office of the Comptroller, and was closely associated with McNamara's introduction of the "program package" concept and the "FYFP" ("Five-Year Force Plan," originally known as the "FYFSFP," or "Five-Year Force Structure and Financial Plan"). SA as it was used in the McNamara Pentagon was a management tool in many respects similar to PPBS and always involved within PPBS, except that it utilized a variety of kinds of quantified data (and occasionally nonquantified data) and it was applied to many kinds of problems beyond basic issues of monetary costs and budgets. The SA function was originally also lodged in the Office of the Comptroller, but was later split off into the separate O.S.D. Office of Systems Analysis under its own new Assistant Secretary of Defense.

McNamara's use of PPBS and SA afforded him several critically important advantages in his determination to be the boss-initiator in the Pentagon. First, and foremost, they gave him the means for generating and evaluating proposals on a basis independent from the categories and traditional terms of reference of the separate armed services and other lower-level D.O.D. components. He was able to require that all discussions and deliberations take place on his grounds and in his terms from a D.O.D.-wide perspective, and in this way he could and did involve himself in fundamental substantive issues long before they could crystallize into budget requests or verbalized conventional wisdom. Robert J. Art perceptively wrote:

Intuition and hunches—the major methods of his predecessors—were still necessary for making decisions; but these two could now be based upon a more complete, detailed knowledge both of what the military requirements were and of the options available to meet them. . . .
The revolutionary manner in which McNamara made his decisions . . . transformed the "expert" career bureaucrat into the "novice" and the "inexperienced" political appointee into the "professional." . . . McNamara freed himself from the secretary's usual dependence on the experience and knowledge of the military officer and the career civil servant. By demanding something that only he and his small personal staff possessed the experience and competence to do, McNamara declared insufficient or invalid, or both, the customary criteria for making decisions and the traditional grounds for justifying them.
. . . decisions were centrally imposed from the top down rather than "bubbling-up" from below. They were *McNamara's* decisions.[13]

Second, PPBS and SA procedures provided the Secretary with devices for improved financial management—especially long-range planning—and a better means for ascertaining exactly what kinds of military forces the U.S. was buying for any particular purpose or function. The implications of various policy options, and the interrelationships between the parts and the whole, were more clearly revealed. Major plans and programs were integrated in a more rational way, and what emerged was hopefully a coherent whole rather than a grab-bag of disconnected bits and pieces.

All coins have two sides, however, and the valuable uses and advantages of PPBS and SA decisionmaking procedures were accompanied by limitations, disadvantages and sometimes outright dangers. President Kennedy told the Joint Chiefs in a meeting sometime following the Bay of

Pigs episode that, when he asked for their views on national issues, he wanted their counsel in wide-ranging terms as "experienced men of the world" and not merely in narrow technical military terms. Kennedy obviously felt that the Chiefs' lifelong identification with formal military institutions had narrowed their vision. But a commitment to a particular tool or technique can restrict one's vision as much as a commitment to an organization or an institution. By emphasizing a single tool or technique, one is also emphasizing a single set of mental skills and intellectual perspectives tending to exclude other skills and perspectives. The dominant civilian officials in McNamara's Pentagon did not seem to realize that PPBS and SA procedures were primarily useful to the Secretary in his role as boss and general manager of D.O.D.—and even for this role there were important limitations—rather than in his role as over-all military adviser to the President or in his role as deputy commander in chief of the armed forces. The intellectual orientations and skills associated with PPBS and SA were of little use, for example, in the broadly philosophical enterprise of relating national power to national purpose or, at a somewhat lower level, in the task of understanding the place and nature of a war such as the one in Vietnam within the context of the rapidly evolving international political system of the 1960s or, at a lower level yet, in deciding which American general was best suited to command American forces in a war with such complex requirements as the one in Vietnam. But the intellectual perspectives and skills that might have been useful in dealing with issues of these kinds were accorded no institutionalized place and very little status in the 1961–1968 Pentagon.[14]

Some knowledgeable individuals have asserted several other miscellaneous disadvantages and limitations associated with decision-making procedures and organizational modes in D.O.D. during that period. One of these derived from the growing tendency to use the Office of Systems Analysis as the Secretary's personal support agency, with authority to dip in and out anywhere in D.O.D. gathering evidence to support a Secretarial decision. If, as Professor Art reported with respect to McNamara's early decision on the TFX aircraft contract, "He [McNamara] 'rigged' the decisionmaking procedures in order to prevent them [a board of military officers] from blocking the outcomes he wanted," then Systems Analysis apparently became the O.S.D. agency in charge of subsequent rigged decisions on the Secretary's behalf.[15] It was of course quite legitimate for the Secretary to think that he needed a small personal staff agency responsible directly to him which would "make the Secretary's case," i.e., to be *his* prosecuting attorney to make *his* will prevail within the Department or elsewhere, or, if he were himself being prosecuted in the Congress or elsewhere, then to be *his* defense attorney. The only problem with all of this was the fact that SA was consistently advertised as a group performing neutral objective studies "to let the facts speak for themselves." Therefore, because SA occasionally performed studies to demonstrate that there was hard quantified evidence for conclusions already reached earlier on other grounds, a "credibility gap" was bound to occur concerning SA's work in *all* cases. Two roles that do not mix are that of the partisan advocate and that of the neutral objective analyst.

Second, and in view of the above, some have suggested that D.O.D. needed a professional group of institutionalized "nay sayers" with the specific responsibility for finding fault with every conceivable policy and program in which faults could be found—including the Secretary's preferred policies and programs. The late Attorney General Robert F. Kennedy is said to have remarked during the early days of the Kennedy Administration that there always ought to be people in the Government charged with looking at everything "with a cold and fishy eye," but this function was apparently performed in the Pentagon of the 1961–1968 period only with respect to those things running contrary to the Secretary's preferences.

Third, some have said that SA and PPBS procedures were primarily useful for set-piece or isolated smaller-scale projects for which there was a finite concrete goal (such as, for a hypothetical example, redeploying a given number of forces from three places to five other places within six months). But these procedures, it was said, were incapable of providing a steering mechanism or a general sense of direction for overall defense policy. This would not have been important were it not for the fact that there was a consistent effort to use especially SA in this way, particularly in connection with SA's role in helping to prepare the Secretary's critically important "Draft Presidential Memoranda" (DPM's) for the White House. The DPM's were the most significant of the basic guiding documents of American national security policy during the 1961–1968 period.

Fourth, and somewhat related to the criticism noted immediately above, some have said that the "institutional memory" function was never a formal organized staff activity either in the Pentagon of the 1961–1968 period or in any earlier period. There was an Office of the Historian at the O.S.D. level, but this tiny group primarily provided archival reference services for other O.S.D. components on a request basis. There was no staff agency charged with saying, for example, "We tried that ten years ago, and it worked [or did not work]." Hence, it was said that a considerable amount of time, energy and money was repeatedly consumed in "reinventing the wheel," although this is doubtless a characteristic of most governmental agencies.

Finally, some knowledgeable individuals have said that the FYFP device within the PPBS procedures, instead of liberating policymakers by giving them a clearer picture of the future that they were deciding, tended to lock them into mental sets whereby they concluded that the future was largely foreclosed, or that attempting to alter the future through innovation was too costly. An incremental change today may be tolerable enough but, if compelled to dwell on its long-range costs and implications, a man might never take the first step that could lead to a journey of a thousand miles.

For this and other reasons, it was said that FYFP procedures tended to create a profoundly conservative antichange mentality and psychological climate among D.O.D. decision-makers at the O.S.D. level during the 1961–1968 period after their own initial innovations had been introduced.

The Secretary and the Professional Military

The most dramatic and salient features of the "McNamara Revolution" as it has been described here were key organizational and procedural arrangements introduced by the Secretary in the top *civilian* layers of the Department of Defense. These changes primarily resulted in the exercise of vast new decisionmaking powers within the circle of O.S.D. "shops" immediately surrounding and including the Secretary, and the introduction of systematic new (new, that is, for D.O.D.) quantified-data techniques of analysis which facilitated this relocation of decisionmaking powers. The preceding pages have reviewed some of the main advantages and main problems associated with these developments, as noted by knowledgeable individuals almost all of whom were key participants.

Another critically important aspect of these overall developments was the evolving role of the professional military officers and the traditional armed services. While an entire book would be required to cover this story in the detail that it merits, it will suffice here to touch briefly on some generalized conclusions. This account, again, will include some comments on both the favorable and the troublesome elements of these developments as viewed and reported by knowledgeable individuals.

The first thing to note is that, because the 1958 reorganization legislation and McNamara's implementation of it so greatly enhanced the powers of the Defense Secretary while comparably reducing the traditional separate services to repositories of trained men and equipment, the Secretaries of the Army, Navy, and Air Force and all of their attendant Assistant Secretaries and other civilian staff were reduced to line extensions of the Office of the Secretary of Defense. This trend was quietly underscored by the headline for an article in the *New York Times* of March 27, 1968, concerning the President's appointment of four new Assistant Secretaries for the three services. The headline read, "Four Aides to Clifford Chosen by Johnson." Even as recently as a year or two earlier it would have been politically untenable to suggest, for example, that an Assistant Secretary of the Army was in actuality an "aide" to the Defense Secretary, but by the spring of 1968 this inference raised no eyebrows in any significant quarter. The trend was even more emphatically underscored on January 6, 1969, when Defense Secretary-designate Melvin Laird rather than President-elect Nixon announced the new Secretaries of the Army, Navy, and Air Force. By 1969 it was therefore clear that *all* civilians in D.O.D. worked for the Defense Secretary, and the old term "armed services" or "military services" referred almost exclusively to the uniformed personnel of those organizations.

The foremost uniformed officer of the armed services is the Chairman of the Joint Chiefs of Staff (C.J.C.S.), although very little of his authority derives from statutes and directives. In terms of formal charters written down on pieces of paper, he is merely one among equals within the J.C.S. but, in terms of precedent and practice, he had come to enjoy a substantial range of not inconsiderable powers by the end of the 1960s. The precedents included the ways in which several Chairmen—especially Admiral Radford under President Eisenhower, General Taylor under President Kennedy, and General Wheeler under President Johnson—were able to make themselves highly useful and valuable to the Commanders in Chief under whom they served. The practices included the ways in which these recent Presidents and their Secretaries of Defense responded to the contributions of notable Chairmen by informally "institutionalizing" important functions for the C.J.C.S. The practices also included the ways in which the other Chiefs in important respects gradually came to defer to the Chairman and on occasion even explicitly delegated some of their collective authority to him. As a result, the Chairman became connected to a greater number of important decisionmaking clusters and networks in the foreign policy and defense policy fields than any other official including the President and the Defense Secretary. He was certainly the key link and sometimes the only effective link between the O.S.D civilian hierarchy and the uniformed services as a whole. Most knowledgeable observers felt that this trend in the roles of the C.J.C.S. was "a good thing," although he operated with an extremely small staff in view of his authority and responsibilities, and although some felt that the J.C.S. as a whole rather than the Chairman as an individual ought to have been more effectively in contact with the O.S.D. hierarchy and other decisionmaking clusters.

Of the three major centralized components within D.O.D.—O.S.D., C.J.C.S., and the J.C.S. as a corporate entity—the J.C.S. was the one which grew least in size, authority and responsibility after World War II and especially after 1958, notwithstanding that the 1958 reorganization legislation directed and implied a substantially enhanced J.C.S. role at the expense of the separate services.[16] There were several reasons for the retarded J.C.S. development. First, the Congress—although directing a larger J.C.S. role—placed a low statutory limit on the size and composition of the Joint Staff of the J.C.S. The J.S. was the only significant D.O.D. component that continued to consist almost exclusively of uniformed personnel on relatively short-term assignments without a permanent cadre of civil service executives. The Congress clearly retained a considerable degree of affection for the old separate services, with encouragement from the services. Second, inasmuch as the J.C.S. remained a confederation-like committee of sovereign representatives from co-equal organizations, it lacked the clearcut decisiveness of a straight executive line with one man in charge at the top. Third, and this most important reason relates to the first two, the separate services did not really want the J.C.S. to grow into an effective body. The leading officers of each service tended to feel that any growth in J.C.S. powers would result in a J.C.S. dominated by and/or allied with O.S.D., whereas in actuality an enhanced J.C.S. was probably the only vehicle for maximizing an effective voice for professional military judgment when confronted with an increasingly powerful O.S.D. Secretary McNamara was not much interested in implementing those parts of the 1958 legislation calling for more centralization of military authority within the J.C.S. mechanism precisely because he was concerned that centralized authority in uniform would compete with centralized civilian authority in O.S.D. In any event, glib generalizations about an over-all centralization of authority in D.O.D. after 1960 failed to note that the centralization was almost entirely on the civilian side, while decentralization and fragmentation along traditional service lines remained the actual pattern prevailing on the uniformed side.

Numerous anomalies persisted between what the 1958 legislation suggested and what actually happened. Insofar as the services supported the J.C.S. and its Joint Staff, the J.C.S. and J.S. initially responded to the McNamara challenge by becoming isolated and withdrawn. The basic annual document of the J.C.S./J.S., the "Joint Strategic Objectives Plan" (JSOP), was jealously guarded against outside civilian influences because this was to be their undiluted and "purely military" product containing the quintessence of the nation's professional military judgment. The officers were willing to strive for this at the sacrifice of relevancy, and they seemed generally unconcerned that the JSOP accordingly had little impact on national policy as expressed in the Secretary's authoritative Draft Presidential Memoranda. Some knowledgeable observers felt that the JSOP gradually became a better product, less burdened with conventional verbalized wisdom and more reflective of the newer analytical techniques introduced by McNamara's civilian entourage. They also felt that the J.C.S. had become less a "closed shop," that is, more often open to cooperative staff-type contacts and relationships with the O.S.D. civilian components and with Department of State offices. But no one suggested that J.C.S. progress in this direction had gone nearly as far by 1969 as it could and should go if the J.C.S. was to become a staff arm in which the Secretary could have great confidence—assuming that some future Secretary would be willing to notice whatever progress might have been achieved.

Another factor contributing to the schism between the civilian O.S.D. hierarchy and the professional military was what some have referred to as the "politicization" of the Chiefs. The Truman Administration almost unavoidably utilized the most prominent military heroes of World War II as J.C.S. members but, beginning with President Eisenhower and becoming more pronounced in subsequent Administrations, each new Commander in Chief tended to appoint a new J.C.S. membership much in the manner of picking Cabinet members and other civilian officials, i.e., military officers known to be receptive to the new President's thinking and not notably the creatures of a previous Administration. New regulations prescribing four-year terms for J.C.S. members not coinciding with a President's term could conceivably solve this problem, although not even most military critics thought that a President ought to be denied the privilege of naming his own top military team within the J.C.S. mechanism. Yet, a feeling persisted that the long-term credibility of the professional military corps depended in no small measure on a posture of political neutrality, with its professional value and authority resting on a discernible independence from any incumbent Administration. The problem was clearly heightened when a Secretary remained in office for as long as seven years, as in the case of McNamara, because under those circumstances there would be few senior officers who could not be described as creatures of that Administration.[17]

The separate services (in contrast to the J.C.S.) retained a far larger role after 1958 than the legislation indicated, because most officers retained a primary identification with and loyalty to their services, and this in turn was largely because most of the rituals and symbolism of the armed forces remained service-oriented. The basic patterns of career education and socialization were within the services, and few officers received assignments to the "joint arena" before having spent at least ten to fifteen years wholly within their own services.[18] A "joint mentality" was thus difficult for many to achieve relatively late in their careers. Most officers resisted assignments to joint duties as bad medicine to be swallowed as quickly as possible if unavoidable. The services controlled rank promotions up through the two-star level, and considerable circumstantial evidence suggested that a number of able officers who had spent "too much time away from their service flagpoles" (i.e., on assignments within O.S.D., O.J.C.S., the State Department, the White House, and elsewhere) were discriminated against in rank promotions higher than the colonel-captain level. For one example of the way in which a service orientation tended to dominate a joint orientation, each member Chief of the J.C.S. received most of his information and briefings from the staff of his own service—rather than from the Joint Staff—whenever major issues were up for decision within the J.C.S. The J.C.S. thus remained primarily an arena for reaching negotiated agreements among separate constituencies rather than a truly collective decisionmaking agency.

D.O.D. and the Department of State

Interesting and significant patterns emerged during the 1950s and 1960s in the external relationships of O.S.D. in particular, and D.O.D. more generally, vis-à-vis the White House, the Congress, and other Executive Branch agencies. Each of these sets of relationships is worthy of detailed study, but space limitations here dictate focusing on only the D.O.D.-State relationships during the 1961–1968 period.

The role of the Department of State in providing over-all foreign policy guidance for the military establishment has seldom been clear and unambiguous in American history, but the ambiguity was increased in the 1960s after the National Security Council (NSC) system of the 1950s was abandoned. The D.O.D.-State relationship between 1961 and 1968 was largely a function of the personalities and working characteristics of Defense Secretary McNamara and State Secretary Rusk, with McNamara quickly emerging as the dominant figure who enjoyed preferential status under Presidents Kennedy and Johnson. According to this interpretation, Mc-Namara on his own initiative largely generated the foreign policy perspectives used by D.O.D. in making defense policy, and these O.S.D. perspectives then dominated the over-all foreign policy of the United States. One noted columnist who subscribed to this interpretation was Joseph C. Harsch:

> One official who served in a high place under Secretary of State Dean Rusk remarked of him that "he never seemed to consider himself the equal of others around him."
> Several who worked around former President John F. Kennedy have remarked that Mr. Rusk seldom proposed policies, or made strong recommendations about policy.
> Foreign policy during the Johnson administration has been generated largely by the two strong men who in succession have been Secretaries of Defense, Robert Mc-Namara and Clark Clifford, and by the two brilliant men who have held the White House advisory post in foreign affairs, McGeorge Bundy and Walt Rostow.
> It is almost as though Mr. Rusk had occupied the position of chief of staff to a group of policymakers. He loyally carried out their policies. But the impression exists throughout Washington that he seldom actually shared in the building of the policies.[19]

McNamara's preferred interpretation was that a close friendly personal relationship developed early between himself and Secretary Rusk, and that the foreign policy guidance developed for D.O.D. through the device of McNamara's Draft Presidential Memoranda (DPM's) was consistently derived from informal consultations with Rusk and the President—often from frequent White House meetings including the noted "Tuesday Lunch" sessions.[20]

Whatever the nature of the McNamara–Rusk relationship at the top of D.O.D. and State and within the White House context, and whatever the source of foreign policy guidance prescribed by McNamara for use within D.O.D., other kinds of relationships between D.O.D. and State grew in number and strength in the 1960s. Some of these involved interchanges of personnel on duty assignments, and attendance at each other's schools (for example, foreign service officers at the National War College, and military officers at the Foreign Service Institute). Many informal personal contacts and a variety of rather more formal "coordinating committees" existed between O.S.D., O.J.C.S. and military service offices on the one hand, and State Department offices on the other hand.

Although the NSC system was abandoned by the Kennedy Administration, it and the successor Johnson Administration experimented with various arrangements for inter-agency coordination at one or two levels below the Secretarial level at the top. Some of these were *ad hoc* responses to particular problems or crises, while others were designed to treat a broader variety of considerations on a more or less continuing basis. For an example of the former, the "Special Group (CI)"—with CI standing for counterinsurgency—was created in 1962 in response to the crises in Laos, Vietnam, Cuba, and the Congo of 1961. Initially chaired by the President's Military Adviser, its members included the Attorney General, the Under Secretaries of State, the Deputy Secretary of Defense, and the Directors of C.I.A., U.S.I.A., and A.I.D. Although this group had largely gone out of existence by the mid-1960s, it was potent while it lasted—in large part because it had President Kennedy's urgent personal attention and because the President's brother personally assured that it made decisions and that those decisions were implemented. For an example of the latter kind of more continuing arrangement, the Contingency Coordinating Committee (C.C.C.) was created in 1964 as a result of President Johnson's concern whether the Government was prepared to deal with "brush fire" wars and similar disturbances in addition to the one then underway in Vietnam. The C.C.C. was chaired by the Deputy Under Secretary of State for Political-Military Affairs, and included representatives from O.S.D., O.J.C.S., and C.I.A. (The dual D.O.D. representation was a noteworthy precedent for the "SIG/IRG system," to be discussed below). C.C.C.'s mission was to maintain a systematic review of potential trouble spots around the world and to recommend to the C.C.C. chairman that he create an interdepartmental "task force" to prepare a contingency plan for any situation that seemed to warrant it. A total of eighteen full-fledged studies was thus initiated by the C.C.C., including ones that focused on a potential Arab-Israeli war, Indo-Pakistani hostilities, and potential civil war in Nigeria. The C.C.C. therefore demonstrated its foresight, but it lacked the rank and authority to make decisions or initiate action beyond recommending contingency planning.

The most important and potentially far-reaching innovation involving D.O.D. and State in the coordination of national policy was the establishment in 1966 of the "SIG/IRG system." SIG is the abbreviation for the Senior Interdepartmental Group (of which there was only one), and IRG is the abbreviation for Interdepartmental Regional Groups (of which there were supposed to be five). National Security Action Memorandum 341 (NSAM 341), conceived and drafted by General Maxwell Taylor, was the document that created SIG/IRG. Signed by the President himself rather than his Special Assistant for National Security Affairs, NSAM 341 specified that the Under Secretary of State would chair the SIG whereas other State officials would chair the IRG's and that the SIG and IRG's would have the power of executive decision. The intent, therefore, was to make them far more authoritative and powerful than mere communications-type coordinative mechanisms. Taylor wanted the SIG/IRG system to provide the Secretary of State *as an individual* with an opportunity to acquire considerable "delegated" authority from the President, although others saw it as a so-called "State-prime system" in which the Department of State *as an organizational entity* would acquire prime and ultimate authority in *all* decisions pertaining to over-all foreign policy including all military aspects and dimensions. These and other ambiguities not resolved in NSAM 341, such as whether the SIG and the IRG's were to report directly to the President or via the Secretaries of Defense and State, remained the subject of some differing interpretations among key individuals at high levels.

One of the most interesting features of the SIG/IRG system was that it provided for separate representation from O.S.D. and O.J.C.S., thus affording the first opportunity for the J.C.S. and J.S. to deal legally and directly with State and other key agencies outside of O.S.D. Some expressed concern that this opportunity for the professional military men to speak clearly and directly at the top of the Government on the widest range of important policy issues could undermine the ultimate authority of the Defense Secretary over the professional military, and perhaps open the door to crosscutting *ad hoc* alliances between lower D.O.D. and State levels which could also erode the Secretary of State's authority. But neither McNamara nor Rusk shared this concern, and both of their Departments generally gave strong support to the SIG/IRG system—including enthusiastic endorsement from the military services. In short, all concerned parties were apparently much in favor of this new mechanism, seeing it as a hopeful remedy for the confusion in interdepartmental deliberations that followed the abandonment of the Eisenhower Administration's use of the NSC system and the subsequent resort to a variety of improvised coordinative techniques during most of the 1961–1968 period.

As of the end of 1968 it was too early to say how the SIG/IRG would ultimately work. Implementation did not really begin until 1967, and the picture was mixed and uneven by the end of 1968. The future depended almost wholly on the way in which President Nixon organized his new Administration, the individuals appointed by him to key positions, and the system that he preferred to use (including a possible return to the NSC system of the Eisenhower Administration) for making and implementing over-all American foreign policy and defense policy. All indications pointed to the conclusion, however, that Nixon strongly agreed with the opinion of almost everyone who served in the Kennedy-Johnson Administrations as to the need for some sort of system that would be at least somewhat more orderly than the *ad hoc* improvisations of the 1961–1968 period.

A Few Remarks on D.O.D. and the Vietnam War

Any commentary on the organizational modes and policymaking processes of the Office of the Secretary of Defense in particular, and the Department of Defense more generally, during the 1960s, would be seriously deficient if it failed to include at least some discussion of the one overriding foreign policy issue of that decade: the Vietnam War. Although this essay is concerned with the process of making policy rather than its substance, process is not an end in itself for its own sake but must ultimately be related to policy outputs. Later historians—and people in general—seldom worry about process if it produces happy results, whereas even the most internally efficient and aesthetically appealing process will not redeem policymakers whose policies are disliked.

Students of governmental processes have not always recognized these considerations, and the professional literature on the linkages between any given process and the kind of policy which that process may be expected to produce is almost nonexistent.[21] Americans typically tinker around with organizational structures and processes whenever substantive policy outputs fall into disfavor, on the assumption that reorganized policy machinery will thereafter produce "better policy," but behavioral scientists who specialize in governmental processes can say very little as to whether this basic assumption is ever warranted beyond the obvious suggestion that organizational processes are seldom the only apparent variable. Nevertheless, the same unsubstantiated basic assumption will be used here to suggest that American policy in Southeast Asia in the 1960s—whether or not that policy had involved armed intervention—would have been better conceived, better implemented and better supported by the public if certain processes and styles of operation in O.S.D. and D.O.D. had been different. If these conclusions should be viewed as correct, they may indicate needed changes in O.S.D./D.O.D. processes and styles.

The first thing to be noted was the "closed" nature of the policymaking apparatus in O.S.D., and in D.O.D. more generally, in the 1960s. The self-imposed withdrawal and isolation of the Joint Staff of the J.C.S. was noted earlier. This—along with McNamara's continuing low regard for the J.C.S. and for professional military judgment in general—prevented an easy flow of ideas into and out of the J.C.S. arena. But O.S.D. itself was even more tightly closed. New ideas occasionally seeped into the J.C.S. arena through the separate services, each of which remained relatively open in part because each felt itself to be in competition with the other services. But O.S.D. was under McNamara's firm control and did not regard itself to be in competition for new ideas with any other group anywhere. Innovative ideas were generally interpreted as criticisms of set policy directions, and dissent in any form from any quarter was highly unwelcome. This closed condition when it originated in the early 1960s was perhaps in part a consequence of President Kennedy's strong desire to believe that U.S. policy in Vietnam was achieving desired results, which in turn produced a refusal to tolerate bad news. But the closed condition also resulted in part from the enormous sense of self-confidence pervading the entire top civilian hierarchy in the Pentagon.

Examples of the foreclosure of criticism and dissent are plentiful. The White House put pressure on both the *New York Times* and *Time* magazine to dismiss certain reporters in 1963 (including one Pulitzer prizewinner) who were not reporting the bright side of the Vietnam picture as Washington wanted to believe it.[22] In that same year the Chairman of the J.C.S. broke a firm precedent according to which any individual Chief could automatically obtain the Chairman's permission for an officer from that Chief's service to brief the entire J.C.S. In this case the officer was known to speak for a group in his service (some of whom were generals) who had serious reservations about many of the tactics of military escalation then being implemented, and the Chairman refused to allow this officer (who had just returned from a highly responsible position in Vietnam) to brief the Chiefs collectively or otherwise.[23] O.S.D. exhibited continuing resistance to the repeated suggestion that one noted specialist in counterinsurgency, retired General Edward Lansdale, be sent to Vietnam, in large part because it was felt that some of Lansdale's unusual approaches were in actuality implicit criticisms of existing policy—although Lansdale and some others who had earlier received a similar cold shoulder were ultimately sent over in 1965 when Washington became sufficiently desperate for additional help from people able and willing to go. Meanwhile, some scholars who were highly knowledgeable about Vietnam but who were known to have reservations about U.S. policy—for example, the late Professor Bernard B. Fall—were never invited to serve as consultants while other scholars who supported the policy were regularly flown in from as far away as Europe. At the same time, one of the most prominent of the defense policy research organizations was hired by O.S.D. to conduct a project showing that strategic bombing was having the desired results. Although any graduate student in the behavioral sciences could have seen that the methodology of the project was contrived to produce the preferred results, the project author was lionized in O.S.D. and at other high levels in Washington when he reported back with his findings in strong support of the bombing.

If the closed nature of O.S.D. in the 1960's—the stifling of criticism and the punishment of internal dissenters—was one aspect of the O.S.D style of policymaking and implementaion which was sharply revealed in the Vietnam experience, and if a greater receptivity to alternative ideas might have changed the course of events into more favorable directions, then a second major problem given the fact of the war was the failure to manage and lead it effectively and efficiently. A civilian official at one of the very highest levels in O.S.D. throughout the 1960s has suggested that the decision-making system proved wholly inadequate in the effort to move from planning and programming to the actual use of military power as an instrument of national policy in Vietnam. He noted that the decisionmaking process completely failed to make U.S. actions compatible with what senior American officials repeatedly asserted to be the primary and overriding American goal, i.e., to convert the Saigon leadership into a strong and popularly responsive government capable of meeting social and economic needs and capable of providing for its own military needs. He stated that no one in the U.S. Government short of the President himself had been put in charge of managing the total Vietnam effort.

This sobering account leaves one somewhat puzzled as to why it was necessary for someone to have "been put in charge of managing the total Vietnam effort," in view of the extraordinary authority granted to and generally utilized by the Secretary of Defense after 1958. In short, one wonders why a Secretary who was determined from the outset to be the "big boss" in the Pentagon was thus unable or unwilling to assume and exercise the full panoply of his powers in one of his three major roles—that of deputy commander in chief of the armed forces. The chain of command is clear, and it would appear that a straightforward comprehensive command post arrangement could have been worked out leading from the President to the Secretary to the J.C.S. to the theater commander. But if the alleged failure to have provided such a comprehensive system for directing the Vietnam effort was in fact the case, it surely points to the overriding lesson that any President and Secretary of Defense should learn from the Vietnam experience in the case of future shooting wars. Once a shooting war is underway, no President can be an effective President, and no Secretary of Defense can be effective in *any* of his roles, unless the Secretary is first of all effective in his role as deputy commander in chief of the armed forces. This is the way in which both contemporaries and later historians will ultimately judge any wartime President and his Defense Secretary, and every other accomplishment in foreign affairs will be treated as an alibi or an irrelevant item of information.

Conclusions and Extrapolations

Not even the harshest critics of O.S.D. and D.O.D. policymaking processes—whether those critics were civilians or in uniform—have suggested that the innovations in managerial techniques after 1960 should be eliminated and that the calendar should be turned back to the procedures and practices of an earlier period. On balance, the "McNamara Revolution" received generally favorable marks, notwithstanding the gross shortcomings emphasized even by some of the key revolutionaries themselves.

Some of the shortcomings, especially as they related to personal style, could be rather easily corrected, and it seems reasonable to assume that future Defense Secretaries will draw the appropriate conclusions. For example, a posture of appearing absolutely certain about one's facts and conclusions can have powerful short-range political advantages but severe longer-range penalties if the certitude and rectitude prove to have been not wholly warranted. For a second example, no manual on the psychology of leadership suggests that the day-to-day management of an organization of professional men can succeed if the leader consistently treats those men with icy and aloof disdain[24] as if he regarded them as hopelessly dull and incompetent—even if by his standards they are in fact dull and incompetent.

This emphasizes again the importance of maintaining morale especially in a military organization, and suggests that yet another role which a Secretary of Defense could usefully assume is that of "teacher"—patiently teaching the organization his practices and procedures and standards.

Some extrapolations from recent and earlier history point toward developments in the Department of Defense in the early 1970s. One very short-range prospect, given the generally favorable evaluation on all sides of those managerial practices imported by Secretary McNamara into the Pentagon from modern industrial management (such as PPBS and SA), is that these practices will be retained, although the organizational locus of these activities and therefore the effective locus of power could be somewhat shifted. But no future President is likely to disagree with Presidents Eisenhower, Kennedy and Johnson that an institutionally strong Secretary of Defense is an absolute requirement, and certainly no Secretary is likely to seek reduced powers to head and direct his enormous Department. The short-range prospect therefore more generally includes a further building on the foundations of the "McNamara Revolution" by correcting its shortcomings, especially its shortcomings in the over-all leadership of a shooting war, rather than any fundamental reversal of the basic directions of the "revolution."

On the other hand, every war in American history has been followed within a few years by a significant reorganization of the American military establishment. If one assumes that the Vietnam War will be concluded or at least greatly reduced in scope by about 1972 and that the U.S. has not by then become substantially involved in any other military action, an extrapolation from history would suggest some kind of reorganization within D.O.D. by about 1972. One logical possiblity would be an effort to carry out the centralization on the military side of the Pentagon within the O.J.C.S. mechanism called for by the 1958 legislation, to parallel McNamara's centralization on the civilian side within O.S.D. Any such effort would run up against almost two centuries of established practices and rituals associated with the separate services, as noted earlier herein, and the equally well established Congressional sentiment supporting these traditions, but an upcoming younger generation of military officers (and perhaps younger Congressmen) appear more receptive to centralizing measures within the O.J.C.S. framework.[25] Another possibility would be a reorganization of force units to accompany a withdrawal of forces from overseas along with a plan for rapid redeployment overseas in emergencies—thus allowing the nation to seem "to have its cake and eat it too" by stationing most American units on home soil although being theoretically capable of going rapidly into action elsewhere. Yet another possibility would be a reorganization of force units to emphasize so-called "civic action" programs such as economic, social and political community-strengthening efforts in underdeveloped nations where wars may occur.

The history of the aftermath of American wars also suggests Congressional investigations of certain wartime events. Reports on profiteering from the Vietnam War, notwithstanding McNamara's reputation for imposing tight controls on costs, were in circulation by 1968 in respectable publications, and this has always been a tempting field for Congressional investigators. [26] In any event, a number of circumstances surrounding the war pointed toward much more deference to the Congress in the future on the part of the Department of Defense in particular, and on the part of the entire foreign affairs policymaking community within the Executive Branch in general. Congressional activities could dictate other kinds of reorganizational measures in D.O.D.

Looking farther ahead into the middle and late 1970s, another extrapolation from history would suggest centralization tendencies moving ahead to the point where a merger of the Defense and State Departments would be proposed. The arguments in support would include the same ones used when "unification of the armed forces" was a major issue during and immediately after World War II, such as the elimination of "waste and duplication" but also an appeal for greater coordination and efficiency in America's overall foreign affairs enterprises at a time when the dividing line between what is military and what is diplomacy is much less clear than it once appeared. [27] The arguments against would include all of those used by the opponents of "unification of the armed forces," primarily appeals to a variety of traditions. If any such merger of Defense and State ever actually occurred, it would doubtless begin with centralization at the top while leaving the appearance of decentralization among relatively autonomous components at the bottom. But given the gradual and yet apparently inexorable centralization trends in contemporary organizations, it would be bolder to predict that such a merger would never be seriously proposed and perhaps attempted than to predict that it would be. But, even if Defense and State were ultimately merged by the late 1970s along with perhaps additional mergers involving other Cabinet agencies, a combined Defense-State Department by 1980 would probably be less significant in actually making policy than either agency had been in—let us say—1950. This conjecture rests on the gradual emergence in the late 1950s and 1960s of a formidable White House staff on foreign and defense policy that by 1970–71 was inexorably reducing Defense and State to roles more associated with implementing than with making policy.

Whatever may happen, however, one thing is clear enough. After the invention of the airplane around 1900 had erased the centuries-old utility of the coastline as a device for organizing armed forces into either armies or navies, depending on whether the forces were to fight on the landside or the seaside of the coastline, no easy and widely accepted principle for organizing armed forces has appeared. Subsequent rapidly accelerating changes in science and technology, and thus in mankind's life and society, have made the problem progressively more complicated. The future will therefore surely reveal a great many more improvisations, false starts, and halting efforts to move toward an ideal system for the organization, management and leadership of whatever armed forces that the United States may feel it must maintain.

Notes and References

[1] Harold and Margaret Sprout, *The Rise of American Naval Power, 1776–1918*, and *Toward a New Order of Sea Power: American Naval Policy and the World Scene, 1918–1922* (Princeton: Princeton University Press, 1939 and 1940, respectively).

[2] One of the best studies of this overall development from about 1900 to 1950 is Laurence J. Legere, "Unification of the Armed Forces" (Ph.D. dissertation, Harvard University, 1950). A perceptive study focusing on the 1944–1947 period is Demetrios Caraley, *The Politics of Military Unification: A Study of Conflict and the Policy Process* (New York: Columbia University Press, 1966). A thorough work covering the entire development but with special emphasis on the post-1945 to 1960 period is Paul Y. Hammond, *Organizing for Defense: The American Military Establishment in the Twentieth Century* (Princeton: Princeton University Press, 1961).

[3] Other books offering perceptive commentaries on overall developments in American military organization and policy following World War II include: Walter Millis with Harvey C. Mansfield and Harold Stein, *Arms and the State: Civil-Military Elements in National Policy* (New York: Twentieth Century Fund, 1958); Samuel P. Huntington, *The Soldier and the State: The Theory and Politics of Civil-Military Relations* (Cambridge: Harvard University Press, 1959); and Huntington, *The Common Defense: Strategic Programs in National Politics* (New York: Columbia University Press, 1961).

[4] In addition to the other works already cited, the earlier research serving as part of the base for this essay includes the following works by the author: Vincent Davis, *Postwar Defense Policy and the U.S. Navy, 1943–1946*, and *The Admirals Lobby* (Chapel Hill: University of North Carolina Press, 1966 and 1967, respectively); *The Politics of Innovation: Patterns in Navy Cases* (Denver: University of Denver Social Science Foundation and Graduate School of International Studies Monograph Series in World Affairs, 1967).

Much of the remainder of this essay (exclusive of the section on Vietnam) is based on the author's participation in a 1968 study by the Institute for Defense Analyses. This project was encouraged by the White House, was largely financed by the Ford Foundation, and resulted in a book entitled *The President and the Management of National Security*, edited by Keith C. Clark and Laurence J. Legere (New York: Frederick A. Praeger, 1969). The project's purpose was a thorough evaluative review of post-1945 organizational processes for making U.S. foreign and defense policies, with a special emphasis of the 1960–1968 period. Project teams conducted and prepared detailed records of long interviews with well over a hundred prominent officials and former officials. A group of external consultants, almost all of whom were distinguished scholars specializing in foreign and defense policy studies, was utilized. The over-all six-chapter project report was submitted to President-elect Nixon in December of 1968 for whatever use he wished to make of it in organizing his Administration. Because of assurances of non-attribution provided to persons interviewed, the author (who wrote the report's Chapter VI on the Department of Defense, a 105-page document in its original unedited form) will be unable to cite specific sources for most of what follows in this essay. It is possible and highly appropriate to express the author's deep appreciation to Laurence J. Legere and Delbert Arnold for their invaluable assistance in this research, but neither the Institute for Defense Analyses nor any group or individual associated with this project in any way is responsible for any of the views expressed here. The author alone bears the complete responsiblity.

[5] Variations of these three roles as well as additional roles are also evident in the responsiblities of the Chairman of the Joint Chiefs (C.J.C.S.), the Joint Chiefs (J.C.S.) considered as a corporate entity, and the individual Chiefs considered as the uniformed heads of their respective services. Space limitations here prevent further commentary on these lower-level role variations.

[6] The number-two official in only two Cabinet-level departments is designated Deputy rather than Under Secretary. This terminology was quite deliberate in the legislation providing for the organizational structure of D.O.D.

[7] One can take issue with the process or the substance of any particular managerial decision by the Secretary—for example, the TFX decision—but one can scarcely argue that the Secretary was not the final and appropriate locus of authority. Yet, some Congressmen and military officers have not always understood this, as is ably documented in a book by Robert

J. Art, *The TFX Decision: McNamara and the Military* (Boston: Little, Brown and Company, 1968).

[8] For McNamara's conception of his job in his own words, see the quotations from Hitch and Zuckert in Art, *op. cit.*, p. 166.

[9] See the excerpts from a McNamara speech to the American Society of Newspaper Editors as quoted in a dispatch by United Press International and printed in the *Denver Post*, April 21, 1963, p. 10A.

[10] One notable exception was McNamara's rather dramatic conversion in the fall of 1966 to the point of view that the Vietnam War at least in its original dimensions was a genuine social revolution. He blamed his earlier failure to see this on bad advice from the J.C.S., although he had allowed his distrust of the Chiefs to cut him off from important dissenting elements of professional military opinion that had argued the social revolution thesis all along.

[11] I am indebted to John S. Gilmore, Research Economist at the University of Denver's Denver Research Institute, for the following elaboration: "This was a time when ten years of corporate development, of new managerial thinking on budgeting, and control (in the accounting sense) was reaching its culmination. These methods of controlling decentralized and diffused operations had really started with the General Motors experiments under Sloan and hit their peak with the early development of conglomerates like Litton and Avco. I think the defense establishment experience was similar to that which developed in all but the very best run corporations, which was that this trend toward remote control of distant operations by rapid or real time reports led to the proliferation of reports and of alleged measures of effectiveness, and in both cases the measures of effectiveness were too often designed by people who were more interested in the bookkeeping side than knowledgeable in the operations side. However, the computer was a tool here, and a [late] contributor to a considerable revolution in management processes."

[12] I am greatly indebted to Paul R. Schratz, Director of International Studies, Uni-

versity of Missouri, for many useful and constructive suggestions to improve the accuracy and style of this paper not only at this point but at many other points herein.

[13]Art, *op. cit.*; excerpted from pp. 158, 162–164.

[14]For example, McNamara was known to have complained late in the Vietnam War that very few people surrounding him seemed to have known about the research on the effectiveness of strategic bombing in earlier wars—or, in any event, none of his staff people had told him about this research. But almost any military historian could have helped on this point, thus suggesting merely one other possible category of civilian specialists which might have been useful if incorporated into the O.S.D. entourage of substantive staff advisers and researchers.

[15]Art, *op. cit.*, pp. 164–165.

[16]Some basic statistics may be relevant. In 1961 the O.S.D. "shops" were staffed by 1,344 civilians and 407 uniformed personnel while the over-all O.J.C.S. agencies consisted primarily of 317 uniformed individuals. The comparable figures for 1967 were 2,273 civilians and 769 military in O.S.D., 517 military in O.J.C.S. These figures were provided by an authoritative O.S.D. official in the fall of 1868.

[17]The Secretary of Defense was vested with the authority to review and approve all promotions to three-star and four-star levels.

[18]Of the more than twenty major educational programs (service academies, undergraduate ROTC programs, staff colleges, war colleges, etc.) of the armed forces, all but three continued to be "owned and operated" by one or another of the three separate services.

[19]From Harsch's regular column in the *Christian Science Monitor* as reprinted in the *Littleton* (Colorado) *Independent* issue of December 26, 1968, p. 2a.

[20]The "Tuesday Lunch" came to be regarded as the highest-level policy forum in the field of foreign policy and defense policy during the Johnson Administration. Regular members originally included only the President, the Secretary of State, the Secretary of Defense, and the President's Special Assistant for National Security Affairs. The members added somewhat later were the Chairman of the Joint Chiefs of Staff, the Director of Central Intelligence, and the White House Press Secretary.

[21]For a further discussion of related considerations, see Ranney's introductory chapter in Austin Ranney (ed.), *Political Science and Public Policy* (Chicago: Markham Publishing Company, 1968).

[22]Reported in an article by the Pulitzer prizewinner, David Halberstam, in *Commentary* magazine, January 1965, pp. 30–34; the article was later reprinted in Halberstam's book, *The Making of a Quagmire* (New York: Random House, 1965).

[23]This officer, who enjoyed a highly distinguished record, was then promptly forced into premature retirement—not unusual in such cases.

[24]Unlike all of his predecessors, Secretary McNamara never accepted an invitation to address the student body and faculty at any of the service academies or war colleges—a traditional way for a Secretary to express his "concern for the troops."

[25]Among other things, the younger generation of officers is better educated than its predecessors. A reliable report on the promotion of a group of Army officers to the rank of lieutenant colonel during the winter of 1968–1969 indicated that a doctoral degree was almost an absolute requirement, and many senior Army officers also hold the same degree.

[26]For one such report on war profiteering, see James Reston's column, the *New York Times*, May 3, 1968, p. 46.

[27]One of the most significant but little-reported developments in the Vietnam War was the straight-line integration of all field force commands in 1967, with military officers and foreign service (civilian) officers merged into a single command line in each field force. This meant that civilian officials of the State Department and AID were actually in the chain of command over U.S. troop units.

CYRIL E. BLACK

Russian Interpretations of World History*

I

*A*ll countries in the modern era
face a problem of identity. This is particularly true of those countries that
were not among the first to achieve a modern way of life and that do not have
a glorious past on which to build their self-confidence. Under modern
conditions the state demands so much of its citizens in terms of taxes, military service, and other forms of loyalty—and is under such pressure from
the competition of other countries—that its leaders are profoundly aware
of the need to justify this loyalty and to demonstrate the correctness of
current policies and the ultimate hope for a better way of life.

Efforts to establish the identity of a nation must inevitably be made
primarily in terms of similarities and differences between it and other nations and groups of nations. In discussing the cognitive aspects of man–
milieu relationships, Harold and Margaret Sprout have noted that one must
study the ways in which peoples perceive of their environment in order to
understand their purposive responses to it.[1] In the case of the peoples of
Russia, their central problem in developing a sense of who they are and
where they are going has been to define their relationship to the states of
western and central Europe that throughout modern times have been seen
both as models to be imitated and as rivals to be overtaken and surpassed.
The essential element of this challenge has been whether Russia should
adopt European institutions to the exclusion of its own traditional heritage,
or alternatively should create its own unique modern culture in which
those elements of European culture that were of universal significance

---

* An earlier version of this paper was presented as the Henry Wells Lawrence Lecture in
History at Conneticut College.

Notes and References for this selection will be found on pages 388–390.

would be creatively adapted to Russia's needs and values. Many books and essays have been written in Russia on the subject of "Russia and Europe," and numerous works of scholarship have been produced by authors from the West European and English-speaking countries devoted to interpreting and reinterpreting the Russian interpretations.[2]

One form of this debate that has grown in importance through the years is that which has been concerned with finding Russia's correct place in the stream of world history. These efforts are devoted to identifying the main trends in world history, to describing the rise and fall of empires, civilizations, and cultures, and to assessing the relationship of Russia to these developments.

World histories can be many things. They can be, as is too often the case, simply histories of all the countries of the world laid end to end. They can be comparative histories, seeking to discover what is universal and what is unique in the evolution of countries and civilizations. They can be histories that seek in the past a pattern that will have predictive value for the future. They can also be academic histories, usually the most useful and the least exciting of these efforts—that seek in a cautious and balanced fashion to put all that is known about the past into an organized narrative without reaching any conclusion at all.

The three Russian interpretations of world history that will be discussed here share in some measure all of these characteristics. The first, by a nationalist, had as its purpose to elaborate a program for Russia's future greatness. The second, by a Marxist, was primarily concerned with exploring the past in terms of Marx's interpretation of history. The third, by a team of Marxist-Leninists, is a propaganda vehicle for the Communist Party of the Soviet Union in the form of an academic history.

II

Nikolai Iakovlevich Danilevsky was born in 1822 in the province of Orlov. His father was an army officer who had fought in the Napoleonic wars, and during his childhood the family was constantly on the move from one army post to another. Danilevsky was an unusually gifted child, and as a student of natural sciences at the University of St. Petersburg he was an outstanding success. His early concern with problems of social change was reflected in his interest in Fourier, and he was associated briefly with the socialist discussion group led by Petrashevsky. He was in fact held in prison for a few months in 1849 in connection with the investigation of the Petrashevsky group, of the members of which Dostoevsky was destined to become the most noted.

Upon his release in the following year, Danilevsky was sent in administrative exile for three years to Vologda and later to Samara, where he served as a clerk and translator. Having completed his advanced education before his arrest, Danilevsky now entered government service as a natural scientist.

He had a distinguished career as a specialist in fisheries, heading numerous scientific expeditions, and at the time of his death in 1885 he was a high official in the Ministry of State Domains. In the course of his career Danilevsky published 46 articles and books. Most of these were reports of his expeditions, but they also included a two-volume critique of Darwinism and a number of polemical articles on political subjects. He is remembered, however, not for his professional work but for his political hobby which resulted in the publication of *Russia and Europe*.[3]

The view of world history set forth by Danilevsky in his *Russia and Europe*, first published serially in 1869 and later issued in book form, was both an interpretation of the past and a program for the future.[4] The driving force of Danilevsky's interpretation was his reaction against the view, generally held in Europe in the mid-nineteenth century and widely accepted in Russia, that European culture and institutions were of universal validity, and that the principal problem of other societies was to become as much like Europe as possible. The science and technology of Europe were in Danilevsky's lifetime gaining universal acceptance, and it seemed to many that the absorption of Russia into European civilization was only a matter of time. Danilevsky believed this view to be fundamentally mistaken, and in support of his opinions he pointed to the widespread antagonism of the European states toward Russia, which had reach its climax in the Crimean War. We know that the juxtaposition of "Europe" and Russia was in fact by no means as clear-cut as Danilevsky believed it to be, and that on this issue as on so many others the European states were deeply divided. Danilevsky nevertheless took this supposed antagonism of Russia and Europe as a point of departure for his theory of world history.

The central feature of Danilevsky's theory was his analysis of the historical record in terms of "cultural-historical types," of which he distinguished ten: (1) Egyptian, (2) Chinese, (3) Assyrian-Babylonian, (4) Indian, (5) Iranian, (6) Hebrew, (7) Greek, (8) Roman, (9) Arabic, and (10) Germano-Roman, or European. History, in his view, did not move in a unilinear fashion but rather through this succession of cultural-historical types.[5] These types developed in accordance with five laws: (1) they had to have common linguistic bonds, and (2) political independence as a state or federation of states: (3) their cultures as a whole were not transmissable, although individual aspects might influence other civilizations; (4) they flourished best if they encompassed a diversity of peoples; and (5) after many centuries of development each cultural-historical type achieved a relatively brief period of four to six centuries in which all of its creative resources were put to full use, and thereafter it became sterile or was dissolved into other cultural-historical types.[6]

While maintaining that his cultural-historical types were self-contained and essentially incompatible, Danilevsky nevertheless recognized that scientific knowledge developed without regard to such artificial compartments. In a lengthy discussion of the history of science, he stressed the evolutionary process by which the various branches of science had developed from the initial collection of data to the eventual formulation of general laws, and the contributions made in each case by scientists from a variety of cultural-historical types. He concluded from this analysis that scientific knowledge was not necessarily a monopoly of the Germano-Romans, i.e., the Europeans, but could continue to evolve under Slavic auspices.[7] In Danilevsky's view, the essential qualities that determined the success of a cultural-historical type were not its productivity in the realm of scientific knowledge, but its ability to perform creatively in four spheres of activity: religious, cultural, political, and social-economic. He maintained that in the original primary civilizations—Egypt, China, Assyria-Babylonia, India, and Iran—these spheres of activity were not clearly differentiated. Religion, politics, and science were at such an elementary level that they formed part of a single value system. Other cultural-historical types were one-sided in their creativity—thus, the Hebrew was primarily religious; the Greek primarily cultural and aesthetic; and the Roman primarily political.[8]

This whole argument served as a background for Danilevsky's critique of the European cultural-historical type, which he considered to be nearing the end of its creativity. He recognized the unprecedented achievements of Europe in the spheres of politics, of art and science, and of industry, but he found many faults in the quality of its civilization. These he summarized in terms of a threefold anarchy: religious anarchy resulting from the efforts of Protestantism to establish religious truth on the basis of personal authority; philosophical anarchy, arising from a negativistic materialism that was beginning to preempt the role of religious convictions; and political-social anarchy, based on the contradiction between political democracy and economic feudalism. Thus the European cultural-historical type must, according to Danilevsky, be regarded as a failure in religious, philosophical, and social-economic terms despite its success in other respects.[9]

In contrast to this crippled and declining European cultural-historical type, Danilevsky wrote a glamorous account of the Slavic cultural-historical type which in his view was destined to take the place of the European—if the Slavic peoples understood their destiny and adapted their policies accordingly. It is perhaps not surprising, in view of his general outlook, that Danilevsky found the Slavic peoples to be capable of outstanding contributions in all four of the essential spheres of activity, and he discussed these at some length. Two quotations will serve to illustrate the tone of his argument. As regards religious qualities, he asserted that "From an objective, factual point of view, the Russians and most of the other Slavic peoples were destined by history to be, along with the Greeks, the principal guardians of the living tradition of religious truth—orthodoxy, and by virtue of this to be the continuers of the great work stemming from Israel and Byzantium—to be peoples chosen by God."[10]

So much for the past. As to the future, Danilevsky predicted that "Russia is virtually the only government that has never had (and in all probability will never have) a political revolution, that is to say a revolution having as its goal the limitation of the extent of power, the acquisition of all power or a portion thereof by any social stratum or by the whole mass of citizens— the expulsion of the legal ruling dynasty and the substitution of another."[11]

Danilevsky thus believed that the Slavic peoples were endowed with special virtues and predicted that their cultural-historical type, which was only at the start of its creative phase, was destined to supersede the Germano-Roman- or European-type. "The mainstream of universal history," he declared in his concluding paragraph, "originates in two sources on the banks of the ancient Nile. One, celestial, divine, flows through Jerusalem and Constantinople and reaches Kiev and Moscow in undisturbed purity; the other, earthly, human, divides its course into two main political and cultural channels—and flows past Athens, Alexandria, Rome—to the countries of Europe, temporarily drying up, but again being replenished by new, ever more abundant waters. On Russian soil a new spring breaks through, guaranteeing to the popular masses a just social-economic order. On the broad plains of Slavdom all these streams must flow together into one vast reservoir."[12] He then concluded his volume with a verse entitled "The Spring," published in 1835 by the Slavophil A. S. Khomiakov, which sings the praises of the spring in the bosom of Russia that is destined to allay the spiritual thirst of foreign peoples.[13] Khomiakov also left incomplete but voluminous notes on universal history to the middle ages, in which he sought to counteract European-centered historiography by exploring the religious and literary antiquity of the Slavic and Near Eastern peoples. A fragment of these notes was published in 1860 but a full edition was not issued until 1872, and it does not appear that Danilevsky was influenced by this work.[14]

The mixed metaphors and unnatural hydrography that characterize the tortured course of this bifurcated mainstream flowing from the banks of the Nile, reflect in an extreme form the logical confusion that characterizes some of Danilevsky's thinking. His *Russia and Europe* also includes so much emotional misinformation both about general history and about European politics that one is inclined to dismiss it as the irrational ramblings of a rabid nationalist or at least as a dire warning to natural scientists that they should stick to their last. Yet interest in Danilevsky's ideas has grown because he touched on certain themes that have been of continuing concern to later thinkers.

In the realm of historical theory, Danilevsky's conception of cultural-historical types, or of "civilizations" as we would call them now, has become one of the important structural features of recent efforts to interpret world history. There is an unresolved controversy as to the origin of this concept, but it appears to have been original with him to a considerable degree. Heinrich Rückert used the terms "cultural-historical" and "type," separately in this *Lehrbuch der Weltgeschichte in organischer Darstellung* (2 vols.; Leipzig 1857), and his typology of civilizations was somewhat similar to Danilevsky's. It is possible that Danilevsky adopted Rückert's terminology, but there is no definite evidence that he had ever read the German's work. There is also considerable doubt whether Spengler knew of Danilevsky's work, despite certain striking similarities in their conceptions of the structure of historical development and the destiny of European civilization.[15]

The significance of Danilevsky's work in this respect thus lies not as a predecessor of the twentieth-century historians who have based their work on the comparative study of civilizations. It lies rather in the fact that, in all likelihood independently of earlier students of civilization and without direct influence on later historians, he formulated a conception of civilizations that has proven to be useful as a means of organizing the complex materials of history. Not only Spengler, but more recently Arnold J. Toynbee, Alfred L. Kroeber, Pitirim A. Sorokin, Walter Schubart, and Rushton Coulborn, have all based their interpretations on "cultures" and "civilizations"—although none have employed these terms in the same way or reached the same conclusions as Danilevsky.[16]

Another of Danilevsky's themes that has come to fruition in the twentieth century, although again not as a direct result of his influence, is his advocacy of the formation of a Russian sphere of influence in Eastern Europe. He devoted two chapters of *Russia and Europe* to elaborating his conception of an all-Slav union comprising the Slavic and Orthodox peoples of Eastern Europe, with Constantinople as a kind of federal capital. Russia was to be the dominant member of this union, with its capital transferred to Moscow. It was this union of Slavic (and non-Slavic) peoples that was to constitute the cultural-historical type that would inherit from the Germano-Roman the role of dominant world culture.[17]

It is easy to ridicule this all-Slav union as a goal of Russian foreign policy, for none of Russia's intended partners were interested either then or later in entering into such a relationship and all looked to Western Europe—as indeed did Russia itself—for the basic models in their effort to achieve a modern way of life. Moreover the Poles, Czechs, Slovaks, Croats, and Slovenes, although Slavs, were Catholic or Protestant; the Rumanians and Greeks were Orthodox but not Slavs; and the Hungarians and Albanians, along with numerous other minorities, were neither. Yet as the early course of the First World War revealed the full danger to Russia of the coalition of Germany and Austria-Hungary, and as the vast costs of the war came to demand war aims of a commensurate order of magnitude, the Allies acceded to Russia's request for a territorial settlement that was not very different from what Danilevsky had in mind. In 1915 Constantinople and adjacent territories were assigned to Russia in a secret treaty, and on the very eve of the March revolution in 1917 the Allies acceded to Russia's request for a dominant role in the postwar frontier settlements in Eastern Europe. No one can say how a victorious Tsarist government might have sought to reorganize Eastern Europe after a defeat of Germany and Austria-Hungary, but the predominant view among Tsarist policy-makers was that the peoples of this region should be given their independence or autonomy under some form of Russian hegemony.[18]

At the end of the Second World War, Russia came much closer to achieving this goal. As a result of its occupation of Eastern Europe, and in a large measure with the agreement of its allies, the U.S.S.R. gained effective influence over all of this region and made a strong claim for the right to establish military bases in the Turkish Straits in the vicinity of Constantinople, now Istanbul. This latter claim was firmly rejected, but the underlying goal of denying access to this region to any other military power or alliance system has been effectively maintained since 1945.[19] What in Danilevsky's day were the dreams of an extreme nationalist, have thus become realities of European politics.

Danilevsky's conception of a future world order likewise seems less visionary in the light of the subsequent evolution of international relations. His theory of history was cast in universal terms, but his central concern—reflected in the title of his work—was the danger that Russia would be engulfed by a worldwide European civilization. It is interesting to note in this connection that Danilevsky regarded the United States as occupying a unique status. It was a country that possessed great natural resources and it had never been burdened by the need to defend itself against powerful enemies. It could therefore devote its resources to technological progress and did not require a highly structured political system. This freedom to concentrate on technology at the expense of political and military needs, which was not possible under European conditions, let alone under Russian, was nevertheless bought at a price, according to Danilevsky, for if the United States had possessed a powerful standing army it would have been able to solve promptly and in an orderly manner the political differences that led to a costly civil war.[20]

Although the United States—and the other English-speaking outposts in the new world—should logically have been incorporated in some form into the Germano-Roman historical type, Danilevsky did not discuss the question in these terms. The importance of the United States in his scheme of things was as a third center of power, collaborating with Slavdom to keep Europe in its place. The world order that he envisaged was thus one in which Europe, the United States, and Slavdom would be the three centers of power, and to these he assigned spheres of influence that encompassed the world: to Europe—Africa, Australia, and the southern peninsulas of Asia; to the United States—The Americas; to Slavdom—western, central and eastern Asia.[21]

Many things have changed since Danilevsky's day, and a United Nations now provides a common forum for all peoples. Yet the idea of a regional organization of the world has not been without responsible advocates, and it continues as one of the realities of international relations. Churchill's original conception of a postwar world order envisaged a number of regional units—the United States, United Europe, the British Commonwealth and

Empire, the Soviet Union, South America, and several others undefined in Asia and Africa—that would in turn send representatives to a Supreme Body.

The United Nations itself recognizes the principle of regionalism in its provision for permanent and nonpermanent membership in the Security Council. Moreover the United States, the United Kingdom, and Russia did in fact cooperate to contain an Axis Europe during the Second World War; the European Union movement seeks to create a continental organization that would in a significant degree counterbalance the United States and the Soviet Union; and China is evolving its own sphere of influence.

To note these various ways in which some of Danilevsky's conceptions have evolved is not to trace these developments to his influence or to attribute to his theories a predictive value that they did not possess The list of his views that were totally erroneous is much longer, and arose from his fundamental misunderstanding of European politics and especially his identification of Germany with "Europe."

III

Nikolai Aleksandrovich Rozhkov, unlike Danilevsky, was a professional historian. He was born in 1860 in the province of Perm, his father was a schoolteacher who eventually rose to be inspector of schools in Ekaterinburg (now Sverdlovsk), and he studied history at the University of Moscow. As a typical student of the 1880's he participated in political demonstrations, and in his student years he became acquainted with Marxism. While completing his professional training he taught classical languages, and from 1898 to 1906 he was a lecturer in history at the University of Moscow. He taught at a number of other institutions in the course of his career.

In the course of the revolution of 1905 Rozhkov became actively involved in politics, joining the Social Democratic party and associating himself with its Bolshevik wing. For a while he was close to Lenin, seeing him frequently and participating with him in political activities, although they were never in complete agreement as to policy. During these turbulent years Rozhkov devoted himself largely to journalism and organizational work, and in 1907 he attended the second congress of the Bolshevik party in London and was elected to its central committee. In the following year he was arrested, however, and after two years in jail he was exiled to Siberia.[22]

In Siberia Rozhkov continued to engage in journalism, but he gradually moved away from the extremist point of view represented by Lenin. He now contributed articles to the Menshevik press that emphasized the profound changes that Russia was undergoing and advocated evolutionary reforms rather than violent revolution. This infuriated Lenin, who now regarded him as a renegade, and in a public address in Paris in November 1911 he singled out Rozhkov for attack as a "liberal" and a "liquidator."[23] These were two of the harshest epithets in Lenin's vocabulary, the latter term referring to those who wished to "liquidate" revolutionary violence and substitute in its place evolutionary reforms.

Rozhkov returned to the capital as a Menshevik immediately after the fall of the Romanov dynasty, and served for a few months as assistant minister of posts and telegraph in the Provisional Government. His differences with Lenin were intensified during this period, and he was jailed twice in the early 1920's. Lenin never forgave him his defection, and in 1922 insisted that his Politburo reverse a decision to permit Rozhkov to reside in Moscow.[24] Only after Lenin's death was Rozhkov permitted to resume a more or less normal career.

Rozhkov must have been a man of enormous energy, for despite his political activity his bibliography lists no less than four hundred titles. Many of these were short articles and reviews, but they included a number of substantial works of scholarship. His principal works of conventional history were *The Peasant Economy of Muscovite Russia in the Sixteenth Century* (1899), and *The Origins of Autocracy in Russia* (1906). Many of his briefer writings reflect an interest in sociology, and his *Survey of Russian History from a Sociological Point of View* (1905), to the middle of the seventeenth century, anticipates some of the characteristic views of his later work.[25] Not until he withdrew from politics after 1917 did Rozhkov produce another major work. He left the Menshevik party in 1924, and during the remaining three years until his death in 1927 he was politically inactive. For four years after the revolution he was rector of the Second Pedagogical Institute in Leningrad, and he continued to be active in historical circles. The twelve volumes of his principal work, *Russian History from a Comparative-Historical Viewpoint (Fundamentals of Social Dynamics)*, appeared in Moscow between 1919 and 1926.[26]

In the period between Danilevsky and Rozhkov, the only Russian historian who devoted serious attention to the problem of mankind as a subject of history was N. I. Kareev. Kareev was the leading Russian historian of modern Europe, and is best known for his seven-volume *History of Western Europe in Modern Times* (1892–1916). He was also interested in the theoretical aspects of history, and his doctoral dissertation was concerned with *Fundamental Problems of the Philosophy of History* (1883; 3rd ed., 1897). In this early work he was concerned with mankind and with the idea of progress, which he interpreted in the conventional liberal sense of his day. His later theoretical works developed these themes further.[27] Although he did not write a world history, he published two short handbooks which set forth a scheme of world history.[28]

Kareev saw history as evolving from a diversity of national histories to a worldwide unity under European hegemony resulting from Western technical progress. He believed that Russia was rapidly being Europeanized, especially as a result of the reforms of Peter the Great and the emancipation of the serfs, and that it was destined to attain a European level of development and to participate as one of the great European powers in the establishment of a worldwide European civilization. He was therefore sharply critical of the Slavophils, and especially of Danilevsky, for maintaining that Russia was developing along non-European or anti-European lines and was evolving a civilization distinct from and superior to that of Europe.[29]

Rozhkov was a contemporary of Kareev's, and came under many of the same influences, but from early in his career he leaned more toward a sociological, and particularly a Marxist, approach. What is nevertheless striking about Rozhkov's historical work, and his political career as well, was his independence of mind. His changes from academic life to politics, and in politics from Bolshevism to Menshevism and later to a nonparty status, appear to have been the result not of indecision but of significant developments in his conception of history and politics. His final work on comparative world history represented the culmination of this process.

In this work Rozhkov referred to himself as a Marxist, and he was widely respected by professional historians in the Soviet Union in the 1920's. He has the further distinction, moreover, of being the only professional historian, Russian or otherwise, to have elaborated a general interpretation of world history along Marxist lines between the two world wars. It is important to recognize, in this connection, that in Rozhkov's lifetime Marxism did not represent a fixed or rigid set of categories, but rather a general point of view which individual scholars were free to develop as they saw fit. In other words, it was not the practice in his lifetime to draw a sharp line between orthdox Marxists and "deviationists." From the point of view of the ruling party in the Soviet Union in the 1930's, Rozhkov was a deviationist by virtue of having left the Bolshevik party before the First World War. From the point of view of European Marxism, there is no reason not to accept Rozhkov's self-evaluation as a Marxist.

Rozhkov's interpretation differed from Danilevsky's in two significant respects: it was structured in terms of traditional politically organized societies, or countries, rather than in terms of "cultural-historical types"; and the course of development of these societies was one involving a number of specific stages rather than a more general life-cycle. Indeed it was Rozhkov's scheme of stages that is the most characteristic feature of his interpretation. He believed that all countries passed through nine stages before reaching socialism: (1) primitve society, (2) savage society, (3) prefeudal, or barbaric society, (4) the feudal revolution, (5) feudalism, (6) the gentry revolution, (7) gentry rule (the old regime), (8) the bourgeois revolution, and (9) capitalism.[30]

In his work Rozhkov placed special emphasis on what he called social statics and social dynamics, terms borrowed from physics that reflected the scientism that was popular in his day. By social statics Rozhkov meant the interrelationship of social phenomena considered in a state of equilibrium. Social dynamics, by contrast, was concerned with the process of change. Rozhkov's social statics was derived from the necessities of economic life that affect social relations and in particular class structure. Political structure and culture in turn reflect the interests of the dominant class. He also believed that each class had a psychological character—what behavioral scientists today would call a "style" or "value system"—that was reflected in their policies. His view of social dynamics was not as well formulated, and indeed at one point he remarked that it was too early to describe the nature of social change. At the end of his work, however, he hinted that change in history is like change in nature, which is to say that it is evolutionary in character.

Rozhkov's periodization did in fact represent an alternation between static and dynamic periods. Thus his feudal period—the tenth to fourteenth centuries in England, and the thirteenth to mid-sixteenth centuries in Russia—was preceded by a feudal revolution against barbaric society and followed by a gentry revolution. The succeeding static period of gentry rule—James I and Charles I in England and 1725 to 1861 in Russia—was followed by a bourgeois revolution and another static period of capitalism.[31]

Rozhkov's theory of world history met with a good many criticisms on the part of his colleagues, despite their respect for his scholarship. Their principal objection was that it was not Marxist, it did not relate historical events closely enough to the class struggle, and in this sense was not dialectical. They pointed out, for example, that his period of the gentry revolution from the beginning of the reign of Ivan IV to the end of the reign of Peter I lasted 192 years, whereas the stable period of gentry rule lasted only 136 (1725–1861). For the later Soviet Marxists, revolution was supposed to be a short period of the violent transfer of power from one class to another, between long periods in which there was gradual development. They also objected to the fact that he regarded the state as inherently above parties, and concerned with the general welfare, whereas conventional Soviet Marxism regarded the state as an instrument of the dominant class.[32]

In considering these criticisms there is of course no reason to regard the later Soviet Marxists as exclusive authorities on the Marxist interpretation of history. Marx himself, and his contemporaries and imitators in England, France, and Germany, were much more broadminded and flexible in their view of history. They did not take Marx's writings as a narrowly defined dogma, but regarded them rather as a general guide which each historian could elaborate as he saw fit within the general spirit of economic determinism. What is significant about Rozhkov's interpretation for our purposes is that he saw changes evolving as a result of economic processes acting on society and ultimately on politics, on political institutions. He believed that this was an inevitable development that required no particular initiative on the part of political leaders. Although he himself had been active in politics, he did not advocate a political program. He simply wrote as an historian, developing the situation as he saw it from where he sat.

Yet he sat in a Russia that had just undergone a revolution marking the transition from the ninth stage—capitalism—to the tenth and presumably final stage of socialism. In this sense he was not immune to the events of his time and he regarded Russia as being in the forefront of historical development. "In this manner the Russian revolution of 1917 and the succeeding years," he wrote in his concluding volume, "represent an endeavor that was completely unavoidable and necessary for the victory of the socialist, proletarian revolution over the old order in Russia. Obliged by virtue of its origins in the combination of Russian economic and social forces united with ideological and practical scientific socialism, the Russian revolution and the state created by it constituted factors of highest importance in the task of achieving the victory of socialism throughout the world. To the question posed to the Russians by Vladimir Solovyov, what kind of an East do you wish to be—the East of Xerxes or the East of Christ—we can now reply that there is a third solution—history has made Russia the East of Marx, Engels, Plekhanov, and Lenin, a model of the confluence of the traditions of the West and of the East for the solution of the most important question of the contemporary era."[33]

IV

The third original history of the world written in Russia is the *Universal History* in ten volumes, prepared by an editorial committee under the chairmanship of Evgenii Mikhailovich Zhukov.[34] This is thus a collaborative work, written by some 400 authors, editors, consultants, and assistants. To this extent the biography of its editor-in-chief is not as significant for an understanding of this work as are those of his predecessors. Zhukov's life is nevertheless of interest since he is a typical Soviet "organization man" and is today the principal organizer of historical work in the Soviet Union. Born in 1907, he was trained as a diplomatic historian and his principal work is a collaborative history of international relations in the Far East from 1870 to 1945 which he edited. He joined the Communist Party in 1941 and since 1957 he has occupied the critical position of Scientific Secretary of the Department of History of the Academy of Sciences of the U.S.S.R.—a position that makes him the principal administrative officer and party guide for historical research in the Soviet Union. In addition to being chairman of the editorial committee of the *Universal History*, he is the leading historian of the Academy of Social Sciences of the Central Committee of the Communist Party of the Soviet Union, a member of the editorial board of the *Large Soviet Encyclopedia,* and a member of the boards of directors of the All-Union Society for the Dissemination of Political and Scientific Knowledge, the Soviet Committee for the Defense of Peace, and the Soviet Committee for the Solidarity of Afro-Asian Countries.[35]

It is interesting to note that the introduction of modern organizational methods into the writing of history has also added to the length of the product. Danilevsky's book was 557 pages in length, or about 200,000 words by rough count; Rozhkov's 12 volumes add up to 4,195 pages and about 1,260,000 words; and Zhukov and his colleagues wrote ten much larger volumes of about 2,400,000 words.

The organization of the *Universal History* reflects the interpretation of Marxism-Leninism that has been elaborated in recent years by Soviet ideologists. As compared with Rozhkov's version of Marxism, that of Zhukov not only provides a more rigid and clear cut periodization of historical developments but also relates history more c.osely to contemporary international affairs and to a program of future action.

In organizing his world history, Zhukov rejects the concept of "cultural-historical complexes," or civilizations, on the ground that they tend to emphasize the achievements of the more civilized peoples at the expense of others who are treated as nonhistorical peoples outside the range of history. "World history," he has written, "is the history of all nations."[36] The terminology that Zhukov and his colleagues use to describe the development of human society will be familiar to those acquainted with Marxism. The basis of change in history is the production of material goods, the development of productive forces, and the productive relations of peoples. Thus change takes place not through the automatic influence of economic laws but through individuals, classes, and the popular masses. The superstructure of institutions is altered as a result of changes in the economic base, but the superstructure may also influence the development of society.

"Universal history is a progressive process. Its movement forward is determined primarily by the productive forces of society, the development and perfection of the implements and means of production."[37] Historical development is presented in terms of five main progressive periods—the primitive communal system, slavery, feudalism, capitalism, and socialism. These periods are of long duration and they are separated by shorter periods of revolutionary transition. The main periods are defined in terms of the relatively more advanced countries of each epoch—and in effect slavery, feudalism, and capitalism correspond roughly to the traditional periods of ancient, medieval, and modern history. It is nevertheless recognized that no two peoples make these various transitions at the same time, and indeed some have never advanced beyond the primitive or slave-owning stage. Thus the modern era in general starts with the "bourgeois revolution" in England in the mid-seventeenth century, and in France in 1789, and these two countries are still capitalist. In Russia the transition from feudalism to capitalism was not made until 1861, but there capitalism lasted only until 1917 when Russia made the transition to socialism.[38]

The new Soviet *Universal History* represents a rather incongruous combination of features. It is in many respects a scholarly and thorough account, with many illustrations and excellent maps. Much of the narrative concerning specific issues is conventional by Western standards, and the traditional periodization of ancient, medieval, and modern history is not only retained but extended from Europe to the entire world. Superimposed on this framework, however, is a Marxist-Leninist interpretation that sees all of history as moving inevitably toward communism. This higher interpretation rests on propositions that are assumed, and no effort is made to demonstrate them or argue the Marxist-Leninist case in comparison with other interpretations.

This version of world history appears to have the propaganda mission of arguing the inevitability of the victory of communism throughout the world. The general tendency of this propaganda line is reflected in a major doctrinal article written by Zhukov in 1963. In this article he argues that, as a result of the Second World War, the basis of socialism has grown from an isolated U.S.S.R. to a "world socialist system" consisting of fourteen states under communist governments and their allies in other countries. "The character and content of the world revolutionary process in the contemporary epoch," Zhukov maintains, "consists of the merging of the struggle against imperialism of peoples building socialism and communism, of the revolutionary movement of the working class in capitalist countries, and of the national-liberation struggle of oppressed peoples, into the single stream of the movement toward general democracy."[39] He illustrates the inevitability of the world socialist system by asserting that, whereas in 1917, 77 per cent of the territory and 69 per cent of the peoples of the world were colonial, today only 7.6. per cent of the territory and 1.5 per cent of the peoples are under colonialism. This, Zhukov asserts, "is a result of the 45-year support by the U.S.S.R., and more recently of other socialist countries, of the national liberation movements."[40]

Zhukov sees as the main problem in the years immediately ahead the growth of the world socalist system until it encompasses all the peoples of the world. This he envisages as taking place primarily by peaceful means, the precise nature of which will differ from country to country. In the more advanced countries, including the United States, it is a question of the working class gradually taking power from the bourgeoisie. In the case of the less developed societies, it will take the form of a conflict between "capitalism" and "socialism," with domestic revolutions being a frequent occurrence. He also envisages the possibility that in some instances revolutionary wars may be started by peoples seeking to liberate themselves from colonialism. He maintains that when this occurs the Soviet Union is prepared to support such wars in a comprehensive fashion since these are just wars. In general, however, the current Soviet view asserts that the spread of socialism will take place not by war, and certainly not by international nuclear war, but by the steady pressure exerted at all levels on the part of those favoring the Soviet form of socialism. It is significant that in presenting his case, Zhukov is particularly concerned with the argument of the Chinese Communists that force should be used more often. It is his view that "the international Communist movement on the basis of a profound analysis of the relationship of the class strength in the countries being liberated and of the international arena, has reached the conclusion that the further development of these countries is possible in a noncapitalist manner, specifically by means of the creation of national democratic governments. Advancement in this manner will safeguard the struggle of the working class, the peasantry, and all democratic forces for bringing to a conclusion the anti-imperialist democratic revolution and as an end result can lead to socialism."[41]

The ten-volume history concludes on a similar note of confidence. It sees victory for "socialism"—in the Marxist-Leninist sense—as being achieved by revolutions of national liberation with the active participation of all progressive forces. The course of contemporary international affairs is described in terms of a duel between the democratic and progressive peoples under the leadership of the Communist and workers' parties, and the rightwing bourgeois forces supported by England and the United States. "The conflict between these two tendencies has taken on the character of a struggle for political leadership, for the hegemony of the national-liberation movements."[42]

A postscript is devoted to a review of the materialistic interpretation of history. It sees the fundamental course of historical development as the transition from lower to higher social and economic formations. Only the materialistic interpretation of history understands the nature of the laws governing this development, and appreciates that it is a development that can be carried out only through revolutionary action. To this extent the fate of peoples is in their own hands. In this effort, the more advanced peoples can help the less advanced. "In the end, the main result of universal history is mankind itself and the contemporary world in all the complexity and contradictions of its development which, in spite of exceptional diversity of forms and variations, nevertheless distinctly reveals its dominant and definite tendency—the movement toward communism."[43]

V

The most striking feature of these interpretations of world history is that they all reach the same conclusion: Russian institutions and values as they are evolving and are likely to evolve in generation or two after the writers' lifetimes represent the culmination of world history. If changes continue to occur after the culmination is achieved, they would have to take place within the framework of the Russian-led civilization, for there is nothing to indicate that some further or better civilization will succeed that of Russia at some future time.

Danilevsky was the least deterministic of the three, for he foresaw that his eleventh "cultural-historical type" would emerge only if the Russian government succeeded in carrying out the policies that he advocated. Rozhkov was a scholar who believed in the inevitability of socialism and in the primacy of Russia in achieving socialism first in 1917, but his eyes were turned toward the past rather than toward the future. Zhukov and his colleagues for their part, are fighters on the frontiers of a world socialist movement which they see as already having turned the corner toward worldwide acceptance.

There is much of value in all three accounts, for they represent the work of vigorous and active minds seeking to understand the past and the role of their country in that past. Yet their efforts must also be recognized as distortions of world history and of the age-old effort of man to understand his destiny. They are distortions because of their parochial ethnocentricity and their insistence that one chosen people is destined to lead the world for all future time. A good world history seeks to overcome parochialism rather than to sustain it, to base its interpretation on the entire experience of mankind rather than on just one part of it, and to formulate hypotheses about this experience rather than to present conclusions that claim the authority of immutable laws.

The interest in these three world histories lies less in their contribution to scholarship than in their reflection of certain main trends in the perception of their international environment on the part of Russia's leaders. Danilevsky was an isolated individual, and his ideas were more idiosyncratic then representative of the main trends of Russian thought in the latter half of the nineteenth century. He nevertheless expressed views which won wide support in the 1870's and 1880's, especially among leading elements of the Russian political elite. Similarly Rozhkov, although he broke with Lenin in the course of the revolution, and was out of tune with the later Stalinist historiography, was the first and for 30 years the only historian to offer an interpretation of world history that gave a key position to the Russian revolution from a Marxist standpoint. The *Universal History* edited by Zhukov, for its part, provides an official interpretation in the formal sense and reflects the views of the Central Committee of the Communist Party of the Soviet Union.

What the interpretations conveyed by these accounts suggest is that the sacrifices required by a society engaged in the effort to modernize can be sustained more easily if accompanied by a belief that this effort will achieve an honored place in "world history." Just as countries in the throes of a great war come to believe that right is on their side, and have no difficulty in attracting scholars to the task of writing history in support of this view, so in the heat of rapid political, economic, and social change it is not uncommon for expressions of confidence in the future to take the form of new interpretations of history. World histories represent the ultimate form taken by such interpretations, since they serve to relate individual peoples to their total environment in time and space.

World histories are most likely to be written in countries which combine a pride in their history and a traditional sense of destiny with a somewhat retarded position by comparison with societies most advanced in the process of modernization. Turkey, China, and Japan, among others, share these characteristics with Russia. They started the process of rapid political, economic, and social change somewhat later than the West European and English-speaking countries, so they must work all the harder to overtake and surpass. This phenomenon is not limited to countries such as these.

however, for what is Toynbee's message if it is not that Western Christendom must learn from the mistakes of the past if it is to fulfill its destiny? A milder and less distorted form of such interpretations is represented by the course in "Western Civilization" commonly offered to college students to convey the message that the "West" is in the forefront of mankind and that the destiny of the "non-West" is to become as much like the West as possible if it wishes to be "in." The related doctrine of "Westernization" is similarly biased.

To say that such views expressed in the form of world history are closely related to the psychological needs of the readers for whom they are intended, is not to suggest that the authors are not sincere or scholarly. The problems to which historians apply their scholarship are normally those to which they are led by their own life experience. As is the case with political and religious leaders, it is only the exceptional scholar who can lift himself above immediate concerns and seek to formulate generalizations that depart from the conventional wisdom of his contemporaries. We may not have a high regard for the theoretical qualities of the historical interpretations developed by Danilevsky, Rozhkov, or Zhukov and his colleagues, but they are of great interest for the study of the perceptions of Russian leaders.

Notes and References

[1]Harold and Margaret Sprout, *The Eco-logical Perspective in Human Affairs* (Princeton 1965), pp. 117–123.

[2]Good recent interpretations of the dia-logue between Russian and Europe are available in Alexander von Schelting, *Russland und Europa im russischen Ge-schichtsdenken* (Bern 1948) and V. V. Zenkovsky, *Russian Thinkers and Europe* (Ann Arbor 1953), and more generally in Thomas G. Masaryk, *The Spirit of Russia* (2nd ed., 2 vols.; London: 1955); Dmitrij Tschizewskij and Dieter Groh, in their *Europa und Russland: Texte zum Problem des westeuropäischen und russi-schen Selbstverständnisses* (Darmstadt 1959), have brought together thirty-six statements of the problem of Russia and Europe ranging in time from G. W. Leibniz to B. H. Sumner.

[3]The fullest accounts of Danilevsky's ca-reer and ideas, apart from that of N. N. Strakhov (see footnote 4), are J. J. Skupiew-ski, *La doctrine panslaviste d'après N. J. Danilevsky* (Bucarest: 1890); Konrad Pfalzgraf, "Die Politisierung und Radi-kalisierung des Problems Russland und Europa bei N. J. Danilevskij," *Forschun-gen zur osteuropäischen Geschichte*, Vol. I (1954), pp. 55–204; and Robert E. Mac-Master, *Danilevsky: A Russian Totali-tarian Philosopher* (Cambridge: 1967).

Briefer accounts are available in Frank Fadner, *Seventy Years of Pan-Slavism in Russia: Karazin to Danilevskii, 1800–1870* (Washington, D.C. 1962), pp. 314–338; Boris Mouravief, "L'histoire a-t-elle un sens? La doctrine de Danilevski et son developpement possible," *Schweizerische Zeitschrift für Geschichte*, Vol. IV (1954), pp. 449–477; Pitirim A. Sorokin, *Modern Historical and Social Philosophies* (rev. ed., New York 1963), pp. 49–71, 205–243; and Edward C. Thaden, *Conservative Na-tionalism in Nineteenth-Century Russia* (Seattle 1964), pp. 102–115.

[4]*Rossia i Evropa* [Russia and Europe] was first published serially in 1869 in the jour-nal *Zaria*, and in the book form in 1871. Four further editions were published be-tween 1888 and 1895. The book carried the subtitle *Vzgliad na kulturnyia i politiches-kiia otnosheniia Slavianskago mira k Ger-mano-Romanskomu* [An inquiry into the cultural and political relations between the Slavic world and the Germano-Roman]. The version cited here is the third edition (St. Petersburg 1888), with an extended biographical forward by N. N. Strakhov, v-xxxii.

[5]Danilevsky, pp. 38–94.

[6]*Ibid.*, 95–118.

[7]*Ibid.*, 119–171.

[8]*Ibid.*, 516–522.

[9]*Ibid.*, 523–525.

[10]*Ibid.*, 525.

[11]*Ibid.*, 534.

[12]*Ibid.*, 556–557.

[13]"Kliuch," *Polnoe sobranie sochinenii Alekseia Stepanovicha Khomiakova*, Vol. IV (8 vols.; Moscow 1900), pp. 216–217.

[14]"Zapiski o vsemirnoi istorii" [Notes on universal history], *Ibid.*, Vols. V–VII; the view of history reflected in these notes is discussed in A. Gratieux, *A. S. Khomiakov et le mouvement slavophile* (2 vols., Paris 1939), Vol. II, pp. 50–101; Orest Miller has treated the relationship of Khomiakov and Danilevsky in "Evropa i Rossia v vostochnom voprose" [Europe and Russia in the Eastern Question], *Slavianstvo i Evropa* (St. Petersburg 1877), pp. 264–315.

[15]This is discussed in Robert E. MacMaster, "The question of Heinrich Rückert's influence on Danilevskij," *American Slavic and East European Review*, Vol. XIV (1955), pp. 59–66; and also in Pfalzgraf, pp. 194–202; N. Strakhov, "Istoricheskie vzgliady G. Riukherta i N. Ia. Danilevskago" [The historical views of H. Rückert and N. Ia. Danilevsky], *Russkii Vestnik*, Vol. CCXXXIV (October 1894), pp. 154–183; and A. L. Kroeber and Clyde Kluckhohn, *Culture: A Review of Concepts and Definitions* (New York 1963), 53–54, 286–288.

[16]On this question, see Hans Joachim Schoeps, *Vorläufer Spenglers: Studien zum Geschichtspessimismus im 19. Jahrhundert* (Leiden 1953), 50 n.31; Robert E. MacMaster, "Danilevsky and Spengler: A new interpretation," *Journal of Modern History*, Vol. XXVI (June 1954), pp. 154–161; Hans Meyer, "Oswald Spengler und Seine Vorläufer," *Stimmen der Zeit*, Vol. CLXIX (October 1961), pp. 33–45; and Klaus von Beyme, *Politische Soziologie im zaristischen Russland* Vol. 52 (Wiesbaden 1965), pp. 52, 100–101. Useful earlier interpretations are Arthur Luther, "Ein russischer Vorläufer Oswald Spenglers," *Alere Flammam* (Leipzig 1921), 51–59; and M. Shvarts, "Shpengler i Danilevskii (Dva tipa kulturnoi morfologii)" [Spengler and Danilevsky (Two types of cultural morphology)], *Sovremennyia Zapiski*, Vol. XXVIII (1926), pp. 436–456.

[17]Danilevsky, pp. 398–473.

[18]On Russian war aims in Eastern Europe, see especially Alexander Dallin, and others, *Russian Diplomacy and Eastern Europe, 1914–1917* (New York 1963).

[19]John A. Lukacs, *The Great Powers and Eastern Europe* (New York 1953), pp. 569–677, summarizes these developments.

[20]Danilevsky, pp. 543–545.

[21]*Ibid.*, p. 463.

[22]The principal accounts of Rozhkov's career are in two series of articles, one in the journal *Katorga i Ssylka*, No. 32 (1927), including Rozhkov's brief autobiography (pp. 161–165), and sketches by L. S. Fedorchenko (pp. 165–172), N. Chuzhak (pp. 172–183), N. Teterin (pp. 183–189), and V. Bogoiavlensky (pp. 189–191); and a second series in the *Uchenye Zapiski Instituta Istorii RANION*, Vol. V (1928), including E. A. Morokhavets, "Kratkie biograficheskie svedeniia o N. A. Rozhkova" [A brief biographical account of N. A. Rozhkov] (pp. 7–14), N. Stepanov, "Politicheskaia deiatelnost N. A. Rozhkova" [The political activity of N. A. Rozhkov] (69–128), M. M. Bogoslovsky, "Iz vospominanii o N. A. Rozhkova" [From recollections of N. A. Rozhkov] (pp. 129–145), V. I. Nevsky, "N. A. Rozhkov—Revoliutsioner" [N. A. Rozhkov as a revolutionary] (pp. 146–156), and A. A. Gaisinovich, "Rozhkov—Uchitel" [Rozhkov as a teacher] (pp. 157–163).

[23]V. I. Lenin, "Manifest liberalnoi rabochei partii" [The manifesto of the liberal workers' party], *Polnoe Sobranie Sochinenii*, Vol. XX (5th ed.; Moscow 1961), pp. 396–410.

[24]Louis Fischer, *The Life of Lenin* (New York 1964), pp. 631, 634, 636.

[25]*Obzor russkoi istorii s sotsiologichskoi tochki zreniia* (2 vols.; Moscow 1905).

[26]*Russkaia istoriia v sravenitelno-istoriicheskom osveshchenii (Osnovy sotsialnoi diamiki)* (12 vols.; Moscow 1919–26).

[27]Kareev's principal theoretical works are *Osnovnye voprosy filosofii istorii* [Fundamental problems of the philosophy of history] (Moscow 1883; 3rd ed., 1897); and *Lektsii po obshchei teorii istorii* [Lectures on the general theory of history] (2 vols.; Moscow 1913–15), of which the first volume is on the theory of historical knowledge and the second on the theory

of historical process. Kareev's position in Russian historiography is discussed in M. N. Tikhomirov, M. V. Nechkina, and others, *Ocherki istorii istoricheskoi nauki v SSSR* [Essays on the history of historical studies in the USSR] (3 vols.; Moscow 1955–63), Vol. III, pp. 260–262, 474–487.

[28] *Glavnyia obobshcheniia vsemirnoi istorii* [The main themes of universal history], (Moscow 1903; 2nd ed., 1905); and *Obshchii khod vsemirnoi istorii* [The general course of universal history] (Moscow 1903).

[29] See especially the concluding chapter on Russia's position in universal history, in *Obshchii khod vsemirnoi istorii*, pp. 278–299; and Kareev's critique of Danilevsky in "Teoriia kulturno-istoricheskikh tipov" [The theory of cultural historical types], *Sobranie sochinennii* (3 vols.; St. Petersburg 1912–13), Vol. II, pp. 67–107.

[30] Rozhkov, *Russkaia istoriia*, Vol. I, pp. 21–22.

[31] *Ibid.*, Vol. VII, pp. 3–171; and Vol. X.

[32] The principal Soviet critiques of Rozhkov are R. A. Averbukh, "Evoliutsiia sotsiologicheskikh vozzrenii N. A. Rozhkova" [The evolution of the sociological views of N. A. Rozhkov], *Uchenye zapiski Instituta Istorii RANION*, Vol. V (1928), pp. 15–68; A. L. Sidorov, "Istoricheski vzgliady N. A. Rozhkova" [The historical views of N. A. Rozhkov], *Istorik-Marksist*, Vol XIII

[1929], pp. 184–220; and N. A. Rubinshtein, *Russkaia istoriografiia* [Russian historiography] (Moscow 1941), pp. 559–575.

[33] Rozhkov, *Russakaia istoriia*, Vol. XII, p. 347.

[34] E. M. Zhukov, editor-in-chief, and others, *Vsemirnaia Istoriia* [Universal History] (Moscow, 10 vols.; 1956–65): there is a German translation (Berlin, 10 vols.; 1961–68). A briefer world history, *Kratkaia Vsemirnaia Istoriia* [Short universal history] (Moscow. 2 vols.; 1966), written by a team headed by A. Z. Manfred, includes many of the same collaborators as the ten-volume work and reaches the same conclusions.

[35] *Prominent Personalities in the USSR* (Metuchen, N.J., 1968) p. 723.

[36] E. Joukov, "Des principes d'une 'Histoire Universelle,'" *Journal of World History*, Vol. III (1956), pp. 529.

[37] *Ibid.*, pp. 530–533.

[38] *Ibid.*, 533.

[39] E. Zhukov, "Natsionalno-osvoboditelnoe dvizhenie na novom etape" [The national-liberation movement at a new stage], *Kommunist*, Vol. XL (August 1963), p. 23.

[40] *Ibid.*, p. 24.

[41] *Ibid.*, p. 30.

[42] *Vsemirnaia Istoriia*, Vol. X, p. 608.

[43] *Ibid.*, X, p. 709.

Index